CANADIAN INTELLECTUALS, THE TORY TRADITION, AND THE CHALLENGE OF MODERNITY, 1939-1970

Canadian Intellectuals, the Tory Tradition, and the Challenge of Modernity, 1939–1970

PHILIP MASSOLIN

UNIVERSITY OF TORONTO PRESS
Toronto Buffalo London

© University of Toronto Press Incorporated 2001
Toronto Buffalo London
Printed in Canada

ISBN 0-8020-3509-4

Printed on acid-free paper

National Library of Canada Cataloguing in Publication Data

Massolin, Philip A. (Philip Alphonse), 1967–
Canadian intellectuals, the Tory tradition and the challenge of
modernity, 1939–1970

Includes bibliographical references and index.
ISBN 0-8020-3509-4

1. Canada – Intellectual life – 20th century.   2. Conservatism –
Canada – History – 20th century.   3. Canada – Civilizaiton – 1945– .
I. Title

FC95.4M37 2001   971.06   C2001-930512-5
F1021.2.M37 2001

This book has been published with the help of a grant from the Humanities
and Social Sciences Federation of Canada, using funds provided by the
Social Sciences and Humanities Research Council of Canada.

The University of Toronto Press acknowledges the financial assistance to its
publishing program of the Canada Council for the Arts and the Ontario
Arts Council.

University of Toronto Press acknowledges the financial support for its publishing activities of the Government of Canada through the Book Publishing
Industry Development Program (BPIDP).

For Karen. Love always.

Contents

Acknowledgments

My PhD supervisor, Doug Owram, deserves much credit for the innumerable suggestions and recommendations he made throughout the preparation of this study. His sage advice, patience, and kind words of encouragement helped me through the difficult times of the project. I owe a large debt of gratitude to Professor Owram; this work is much stronger because of his contributions.

I am grateful to the Department of History and Classics at the University of Alberta for financial assistance, and to the department's administrative staff for their invaluable help. I wish also to acknowledge department members Julian Martin, David Moss, and David Hall for their feedback and suggestions. Special thanks for their input go to Ken Munro, Allan Tupper, and Ramsay Cook. Robert Cole deserves special recognition for his substantial help and advice on certain important issues. Dr Cole and Christopher Hackett, along with my other friends and colleagues in the department, should also be recognized for their ongoing encouragement of my work.

The two anonymous readers of the manuscript must be singled out for their penetrating comments and apt recommendations. My thanks also extend to the Aid to Scholarly Publishing Programme for helping to fund this book.

I would also like to acknowledge the assistance of the many archivists and librarians who provided me with a great deal of help during the research phase of this project. Special thanks go to Dr Kathleen Garay of McMaster University Library archives and Nadine Small of the Saskatchewan Archives Board for their patience, knowledge, and help, and for their support of my project.

My friends and family also provided tremendous support and have shown much patience throughout the project and through the breadth of my academic career. My brother Leonard, two sisters, Antoinette and Roberta, and my dad, Lino, have been unwavering sources of strength and direction. My mom, Norma, has been a special inspiration and a guiding light.

Finally, I must acknowledge the special contributions of my wife, Karen Andersen. Karen helped in the final preparation of this study, when it was in thesis form. She has been extraordinarily patient throughout the preparation of my work. She has provided encouragement and inspiration and has always been a wonderful source of strength. This volume would have been much more difficult without her loving support. It is to her that I dedicate my book.

PM

CANADIAN INTELLECTUALS,
THE TORY TRADITION, AND THE
CHALLENGE OF MODERNITY, 1939–1970

1

Introduction

Like other western societies, Canada endured profound and irrevocable changes during its period of modernization. Starting in the late Victorian period, modernization was a slow and inexorable process that altered physical appearances and, more important, influenced the fundamental outlooks of Canadians. In its most general sense, modernity was the replacement of Victorian society – agrarian, religious, adhering to a rigid set of philosophical and moral codes – with the modern age: industrial, secular, and anti-philosophical. From an economic standpoint, it pertained to the arrival of an urban and industrial society that replaced a hoary agrarian-merchant system. Closely related to the process of urban-industrialization, modernization also involved the rise of a consumer, scientific-materialist, and technological society. As Canadian society became secularized and the agrarian way of life was eroded, educational systems also became modernized. In many ways, academic modernization is central to the genesis of the modern era. Finally, in the modern period, Canada's political relationships changed so as to replace colonial relationships and an Anglo-Canadian national identity with an autonomist-continentalist 'Canadianism.'

From a historical standpoint, the term 'modernization' is used in this work to understand some of the structural economic, social, and political changes that Canada has undergone over the past 150 years. However, 'modernity,' 'modernism,' and 'modernization,' are complex sociological concepts. They reflect more than historical social-economic developments. They also encompass philosophical and ideological changes. Philosophically, modernity implies the replacement of a Victorian value system with one more attuned to a secular and materialist society. It involves the subsuming of the moral and 'humane' values of former times and the emergence of new attitudes and values consistent with an industrial, technological, and consumer society. Perhaps most significant, it entails the sundering of Christian moralism, which informed the world-views of Victorian Canadians and suffused the intellectual life of the Victorian-Edwardian age. Modernism demanded the disintegration of a broad strain of cultural moralism that had underpinned Anglo-Canadian intellectual life throughout the Victorian period.[1] In the place of this intellectual approach, it offered a new system of values that stressed the secular, the material, the technological, and the scientific.

The process of modernization is definable as a set of historical events and ideological changes. We are concerned with discussing it as such. The preoccupation of this work, however, is with understanding modernity from the perspectives of social and moral critics. Harold Innis, Donald Creighton, Vincent Massey, Hilda Neatby, George P. Grant, W.L. Morton, and, with some qualifications, Northrop Frye and Marshall McLuhan, among other social commentators, are studied here for their appraisals of modernization.[2] These 'critics of modernity' presented strong views on the nature and implications of the modern age. They are bound together as a group because of their concerns over the dire effects of modernity and their desires to attune Canadians to the realities of the modern age.

The grouping of these critics according to their anti-modernist views is not always straightforward. Despite a rough coherence, the anti-modernists did not always speak with a unified voice. First, not each individual was concerned with every issue. For instance, W.L. Morton and Donald Creighton had little to say on the abuses of technology. Second, certain issues attracted critics who had a more ambivalent attitude towards toryism and modernization. Marshall McLuhan and Northrop Frye are examples. McLuhan's post-war work on advertising and technology showed that he was a moralist and a burgeoning anti-modernist. From the mid-1950s on, however, though maintaining his moralist point of view, McLuhan increasingly accepted modern technology and endeavoured to demonstrate how technology could enhance, rather than detract from, the modern experience. Although Frye criticized modern developments in the academic world, he, too, was more open to the sociocultural change brought on by modernization. What is more, both Frye and McLuhan were less articulate than the other critics in their consideration of Canada's 'tory' character. Clearly, they criticized Canada's relationship with the United States less frequently or systematically than did Creighton, Morton, and the other tory nationalists. Nor did they take pains to play up Canada's 'British nature.' While implicitly agreeing with many of the overarching values of Canadian conservatism – communitarianism, elitism, and an appreciation of organic, evolutionary change – they considered the advancement of a strident tory nationalism less relevant to the development of the nation.

The anti-modernists thus did not always echo each other's criticisms of modernity. The main reason is that the anti-modernists were not engaged chiefly as social or moral critics. With the exception of George Grant, they did not expend the majority of their intellectual energies in analysing modernization. Instead, they were academics, devoted to their individual intellectual specializations. As a result, they were eclectic and sometimes even haphazard in their considerations of the ramifications of modernity.

What is more, group coherence seemingly is undermined by outsiders to the group whose ideas intersect those of the anti-modernists. For instance, commentators such as Watson Kirkconnell and Claude Bissell appear, at first glance, to be just as concerned with the demise of certain educational values as were the main group of critics. In addition, other observers, such as A.S.P. Woodhouse and Roberston Davies, had something pithy to say on certain of the main issues, such as the demise of high culture and the advent of the mass society. Overall, however, these critics were peripheral to the main debate and hence failed to offer the breadth of understanding on the modernist question that the anti-modernists put forth. While they contributed an analysis of some of the various issues, they failed to ponder the greater implications of modernity. In effect, they were part of individual debates without fully comprehending how those issues formed part of the larger question of modernity. Further, their views lacked the broad moralistic orientation to modernization that was the hallmark of a strain of criticism dating back to the late Victorian period and that the anti-modernists themselves helped to carry forward into the late twentieth century. Ultimately, these commentators offered only a myopic perspective on the enduring aspects of modernity. As such, they cannot be considered mainstays of the anti-modernist coterie.

In spite of inconsistencies and a seeming lack of coherence, the anti-modernists did share characteristics that gave them a group identity. The first of these traits is an overarching conservatism that stems, for most of the critics,[3] from Canadian 'toryism.' The toryism of these anti-modernists is eclectic and borrows from different political traditions. What is more, it must be seen in the light of the Canadian tory tradition, which developed distinctly from British toryism and is therefore substantially different from its British namesake. Three notions are essential to the toryism of the group.

The first characteristic is a sense of community. Rooted in the loyalist tradition of the nineteenth century, the thought of the Canadian tories stressed the primacy of the community over selfish individualism. Conservatives conceived of society as an organism of functionally related parts. Such communitarianism enabled them to denounce American individualism, Jacksonian democracy, and the violence of America's political past, while lauding the merits of the dominion's peaceful, indeed evolutionary, development. It is because of this emphasis on the organic nature of the dominion that the tories adopted elements of Burkean conservatism. Unlike American political history, which represented an abrupt and violent break with the past, the Canadian tradition had, as a foundational element, Burke's 'partnership of the generations.' 'Society,' as Donald Creighton indicated, quoting Edmund Burke, is 'a "partnership in all science, a partnership in all art, a partnership in every virtue and in all perfection. As ... the ends of such a partnership cannot be obtained in many generations, it becomes a partnership not only between those who are living, but between those who are living, those who are dead, and those who are to be born."'[4] For the Canadian tories, society was organic, evolutionary, and anti-individualist, and therefore it had Burkean overtones.

Toryism also implies a sense of 'Britishness' as defined from a Canadian perspective. Tories explained that Canada was an advanced political entity – far superior to the republic – because of its British connection. The British nexus implied a set of moral virtues that placed the Anglo-Canadian world above other civilizations. This sense of Anglo-superiority is associated with and, in part, grew out of, the nineteenth-century Canadian imperialist movement.[5] The critics absorbed this ethic primarily through their family ties and loyalist surroundings. The case of George Parkin Grant is illustrative.

Both of Grant's grandfathers, George Munro Grant and George Parkin, were ardent imperialists who greatly influenced their grandson. George M. Grant advocated a strengthening of the British nexus, in the form of imperial federation, because he believed that the enduring association with Britain not only conferred on Canada considerable political status, but also gave Canadians a link to one of history's great civilizations. Through the British connection, furthermore, Canada could escape the crass materialism of North American society. Through imperial federation, Canadians could pursue righteousness at home and throughout the British Empire. For Grant, the Empire was as much moral and spiritual in its goals as it was political and material.[6]

George Parkin, like Grant, also stressed the civilizing and Christianizing virtues of British imperialism. For Parkin, as for his fellow imperialist Grant, there was a moral necessity associated with the Empire and Anglo-Saxon dominance. For both, Britain had been imbued with a moral superiority that not only justified its political expansion, but also made that expansion morally compelling. The ultimate message was clear: Britain was not only the most powerful nation on earth; it was also the most virtuous. As such, Canada, a British nation, must never let its ties to the great country lapse.

George P. Grant's father, W.L. Grant, was yet another imperialist, although of a slightly later period. W.L. Grant, like his father, George Munro Grant, and Parkin, emphasized the spiritual and idealist aspects of British imperialism and British civilization more generally. For Grant, imperialism implied social service as well as strength. Through imperialism, Canadian society could be greatly ameliorated; it could be transformed into a place 'in which every man, woman, and child had the chance to develop the best that is in them, and the strength that would protect that society in a world of imperfect, anger, and unreason.'[7] The dominion, Grant went on, should take its cue from Great Britain, whose history showed that a great people was made not simply through the exploitation of natural resources. Only continued association with the Empire could curb these materialist inclinations of the new world. The example of Britain, Grant concluded, presaging his son's later strictures, must be followed to foster a less mechanical and, indeed, more humane society.

The British nexus thus entailed for Canada participation in the advanced values and political traditions of the Empire. It also had nationalist overtones. As Carl Berger pointed out, the Canadian imperialists, those ardent supporters of the imperial nexus and Anglo-Canadian cooperation, were also Canadian nationalists.[8] The dominion, the tory nationalists instructed, was eminently better off tied to the advanced culture of Britain than it was exposed to the fallacies of republicanism. The Anglo-Canadian connection provided the means to defeat pressure from the Americans and enable Canada to develop as an autonomous community in North America. For the tory nationalists,

'Canada represented a declaration of independence from the United States, an attempt to build a second community in North America outside the American republic, one marked off from it, indeed, by the longer persistence of the imperial tie.'[9]

This group of conservative-nationalists contrasted starkly with a liberal-nationalist school that grew to prominence in the twentieth century and that argued that the imperial nexus was more a hindrance than a benefit to the emerging Canadian nationality. The anti-liberalism of the conservative-nationalists was a reaction against Can-adian liberals' view of the Canadian nation. What is more, tories' op-position to the Liberal party was a response to the perceived continentalism and pro-Americanism of the federal Liberals. By the early part of the twentieth century, in brief, two basic and dialectical strains of Canadian nationalism had been established. Despite the increased popularity of liberal nationalism, the tory approach – the 'Blood is Thicker than Water School'[10] of Canadian history – continued well into the twentieth century. The tory nationalism that existed in the late eighteenth century found its modern expression in the ideas of Innis, Creighton, and other tory critics.

The third element of toryism is eclecticism. Because Canadian toryism was in part anti-American and in part anti-individualistic, the conservatives at issue here did not trace their roots to pure British toryism. Certainly, there were commonalties between the two traditions. Maintaining law and order and the institutions of the British Crown, opposition to laissez-faire economics, and the staunchly conservative and anti-revolutionary aspects of British toryism[11] were present, at least in some vague form, in the Canadian variant. The key difference, however, was that Canadian tories were highly selective in adopting conservative ideas. In some cases they referred to the merits of Burkean conservatism, in others to Pittite and Peelite variants,[12] and in yet another instance, to Disraelite conservatism.[13] What is more, on many occasions the British political tradition as a whole (Tory, Whig, or other) is juxtaposed favourably against the evils of American republicanism. In a sense, then, the Canadian tories considered the entire British political orientation as 'conservative,' just as they denounced American political culture as 'liberal.' These monolithic understandings explain why they would cite Matthew Arnold so freely, discuss Edmund Burke so selectively, and chastise Jacksonian democracy so vehemently. In essence, the conservatives studied here were not political theorists or party ideologues; rather, they were myth-makers and social critics, who were influenced by current events and certain conceptions of history and the future. The perceived needs of the present and the future account for their selectivity and their imperfect understanding of theoretical antecedents.

In addition to conservatism, the anti-modernists cohere because of shared perceptions and critiques of Canadian society in the post-war period. Specifically, they railed against a society whose values they perceived to be in crisis. For the critics, modernization led to the emergence of certain values – technology, utility, and democracy in academia; cultural nationalism; and political democracy – that were inimical to Canada's historical value system and tory character. This crisis of values was manifested in historical trends and happenings, such as American-influenced mass culture, pronounced materialism and consumerism, and a culture of utility that developed within Canadian universities. Modern society, for the critics, was commodified, materialistic, and entailed a pecuniary culture concerned with 'having' and acquiring rather than with 'being' and the development of an awareness of a spiritual and philosophical existence. As shown in chapter five, for instance, consumer culture became, to the dismay of critics, coextensive with modern culture. Most perniciously, it succeeded in crowding out the cultural trappings on which western civilization was founded. As the commissioners of the Royal Commission on National Development in the Arts, Letters and Sciences (the Massey Commission) and like-minded observers demonstrated, consumerism was anathema to appropriate cultural development.

These common perceptions must be understood in the light of the history of the periods in which the critics wrote. Anti-materialism, for example, must be considered in the context of the post-war boom, an era of unprecedented material prosperity and consumerism. The Second World War was also extremely important to the critique of modernity. During the war, critics discovered just how much society valued the university. The entire defence of the so-called university tradition emerged from a period that seemed to undervalue, if not openly scoff at, the contributions of the arts and humanities. Conversely, the war showed that Canadians had become enamoured of the 'practical sciences' and the contributions of technicians to the war effort.

The war also furnished the shock that galvanized the critics of modernity. First, it laid bare the deplorable conditions and decadent value system of western society, which was especially apparent after the Holocaust. The war certainly exposed a crisis in values and beliefs and led intellectuals to question the principles for which the war was being waged. More important, it drove them to evaluate the liberal and democratic institutions upon which the west had been founded. Social scientists discovered that the war had resulted in the sundering of value and belief systems. They also understood that it had become their duty to articulate and defend these embattled principles. Historians, with their unique orientation to the past, were particularly active here, explaining the origins and longevity of western values and institutions. With other humanists, they took on the task of demonstrating the enduring relevance of these traditions by showing their significance to past societies.[14] For the critics of modernity, then, the war had given humanists a unexpected opportunity: it enabled them to become spokespersons for civilization and defenders of the embattled systems of values and beliefs.

The Massey Commission was the historical event around which cultural critics rallied. The commission raised awareness of the issue of cultural development in Canada. One of its main objectives was to underscore the cultural immaturity of the dominion. Increasing emphasis on material prosperity, commercialism, and American mass culture combined with indifferent attitudes towards higher learning and personal intellectual development. Post-war Canada, according to the Massey commissioners and other culture critics, was overrun with anti-intellectualism and a corrupted notion of culture. The critics articulated these views in the context of the Massey Commission; however, this cultural critique must be seen in the light of the broader penetration into Canada of American culture. Partly in an effort to give force to their commission recommendations, the culture critics characterized the post-war age as one unduly influenced by homogenizing, and indeed stultifying, mass cultural influences emanating from the United States.

What is more, the commission acted as a mouthpiece designed to articulate a particular vision of Canada's cultural development. The culture critics' idea of the good society was based on an Arnoldian view of the good life, one that was founded 'in the love of perfection' and that 'moves by the force, not merely or primarily of the scientific passion for pure knowledge, but also of the moral and social passion for doing good.'[15] As made clear in chapter five, the quest for perfection through personal intellectual development and critical awareness was indispensable to the good society. Matthew Arnold's humanism and the Arnoldian critical-moralist approach to cultural development permeated the outlooks of the critics. Following Arnold, anti-modernists stressed the pre-eminence of cultural over spiritual values. As Christians themselves, they considered the social good not as being rooted in a series of transcendental truths, but rather as part of functional values implanted in the history of western civilization.[16] Culture was for them what it had been for the late Victorian humanists: a beacon by which moderns could navigate through the darkness of the scientific-industrial society. The development of western culture seemed to be the only antidote to ineluctable modernization. The use of Arnold was thus an attempt to address the cultural 'anarchy' of the post-war period.

The intrusion of American mass culture into Canada during the 1940s and beyond was really a perception of the culture critics themselves.[17] However, there was tangible evidence in other fields – trade relations and foreign and defence policy – that Canada had come under the spell of the Americans. The critics' denunciation of American cultural imperialism and their anti-Americanism more generally must be seen in the context of Canada's increasing trade and foreign affairs ties to the United States. From the Second World War on, Canada began trading increasing quantities of its goods with the United States at the expense of trade relations with other nations, including Great Britain. Canadian exports to Great Britain and the United States were relatively equal throughout the 1930s. As an example, Canada traded 40.3 and 35.5 per cent of its total commodities to Britain for the years 1937 and 1939, while it exported 36.1 and 41.1 per cent of its total trade items to the United States for the same years. This tendency changed after the war, however, when the United States became Canada's single most important trading partner: for instance, Canada shipped 56 per cent of its total exports to the United States in 1960.[18] What is more, American investment in Canadian industries intensified throughout the post-war age. The Trans-Canada Pipeline project, which contributed to the downfall of the St Laurent Liberals, was an example of seemingly omnipresent American investment. Concern over American investment remained an issue throughout the 1960s and reached a crescendo in the latter part of the decade with the appearance of the Watkins *Report*, which reflected discontent among the intelligentsia and Canadians at large with large-scale American intervention into the Canadian economy.

Canadian ties with the United States were not limited to trade and economics. From the 1940s on, Canada became entangled in arrangements with the Americans that firmly placed the dominion within the

American defensive sphere. Beginning with the Ogdensburg Agreement (1940) and continuing through the post-war period with a string of defence and foreign policy initiatives – the North American Treaty Organization (NATO), Canada's involvement in the Korean War, the North American Air Defense plan (NORAD), and the Distant Early Warning (DEW) Line – Canadian governments presided over the Americanization of Canadian defence policy. The Liberal administrations of Mackenzie King, St Laurent, and Pearson, the critics claimed, were especially responsible for Canada's pro-American positions. Indeed, Liberal foreign policy established a Canadian dependence on American defensive planning and on an American outlook on the Cold War world. In this set of circumstances, Canada was stripped of its autonomy in foreign policy matters and moved, in Harold Innis's phrase, from 'colony-to-nation-to-colony.'

The advent of an American-controlled foreign policy and increased economic ties with the United States provides the background for much of the anti-Americanism of the critics of modernity. Yet something more insidious, and indeed 'American' – a homogeneous, mass culture – provided the backdrop for the intellectuals' social critique. The post-war era was marked by mass culture developments, including, as mentioned, a boom in consumer activity. It was also the time of the 'baby boom,' a period during which young, middle-class families were having babies in unprecedented numbers, buying houses, and moving to the suburbs. This generation of Canadians put enormous emotional and financial resources into raising their children. It was perhaps the most child-focused generation in Canadian history. Domesticity and child-centredness seemed the dominant mindset of most younger Canadians. In this environment, the critics suggested, the 'higher values' of Arnoldian culture, intellectualism, and a true understanding of democracy were set aside.

Developments in the history of education provide a final historical context that influenced the anti-modernist critique. As mentioned, the war proved to the critics the low esteem in which Canadians held the arts and the humanities. Also during the post-war period, higher learning and intellectual and educational standards more generally were in decline. An influx of veterans, many of whom, once demobilized, enrolled in Canadian colleges and universities was the first manifestation. Once the preserve of the social and intellectual elite, higher learning was now accessible to those who did not have outstanding intellectual credentials.

'Educational democracy' was also practised in Canadian grade schools. When baby boomers reached school age, they were met with a changed educational philosophy: 'democratic' or 'Deweyite' education. Stressing the personal development of students rather than the development of critical and other intellectual faculties, democratic education was denounced by Hilda Neatby and other traditionalists. For Neatby and others, progressivist pedagogy and the sheer numbers of the baby boom lowered educational standards and reflected the anti-intellectualism of the age.

Democratic education also appeared in Canadian universities. When the baby boomers reached university age, they enrolled in huge numbers. The resources of existing colleges and universities were stretched to the limit; by the mid-1960s several new institutions had to be built to keep up with the clamour for post-secondary education. Higher education was considered a right, not a privilege. By the late 1960s, the democratic university – a stark contrast to the privileged, elitist institutions in which the critics themselves had been schooled – had arrived.

Last, the utilitarian focus of Canadian universities that grew considerably during the war reached its logical conclusion with the advent of the so-called 'multiversity.' Unlike the university of the past, which had focused on the liberal arts, the multiversity was so variegated as to have no single, unifying vision. Further, it was influenced to an unprecedented degree by the needs of the community and by public funding requirements. Boards of governors and presidents attuned to the interests and desires of the public, not out-of-touch scholars, were the main ambit of power in the modern university. By the late 1960s the private liberal arts colleges of Canada's past had been transformed into massive public institutions with million-dollar budgets and enrolments into the tens of thousands. In this environment, the critics of the modern university lost all hope for the resurrection of academic traditions and the reinstatement of the liberal arts that they considered the lifeblood of higher learning.

The critics of modernity thus reacted against certain social, political, and educational trends that they believed adversely influenced Canada's societal development. These common, historically based concerns give coherence to the group. Clearly, they are core elements of modernity. However, there are other, more marginal aspects that are not dealt with in depth here. This work is less articulate on criticisms of issues such as immigration, ethnicity, and family. The reason is not that these issues are unimportant to the modernity question, but rather that the critics themselves tended to be less concerned with them, especially in the light of the more pressing questions. Indeed, the anti-modernists tended to be at best haphazard or at worst inarticulate about these subjects. For some, immigration and the changing ethnic composition of the country did not even qualify as significant aspects of modernity.

Religion is more complex. The process of secularization is without question integral to modernity. It was an important concern for the anti-modernists. All of the critics, except perhaps Harold Innis, were active adherents to their respective faiths. Nevertheless, they were willing to accept many of the most significant ramifications of secularization, such as the separation of church and state. What concerned them, however, was not so much flagging church attendances or the diminishing social role of the churches as the fact that post-war Canada had become a secular society, preoccupied with material attainment and neglectful of spiritual values, many of which flowed from Christianity. Indeed, their main concern was with the greater spiritual and philosophical degradation of Canada and the modern west, that is, the crisis of Christian and humane values that seemed inextricably tied to modernism.

In response to this crisis of spiritualism, the anti-modernists did not advocate a nineteenth-century-style Christian revival. Nor did they advance theocratic solutions or even encourage Christian churches to become more involved in social causes. Instead, the anti-modernists expressed their concerns about materialism and secularization in broader terms. Their pleas for an awareness of the humane and philosophical traditions of western culture were really efforts to redress secularization. Their vociferous critique of modernity was a effort to demonstrate the crisis of spirituality to an indifferent population. Thus, they attacked modernity not simply from the perspective of Christian dogma or values but rather by employing an overarching cultural-spiritual critique of modern society. Clearly, the critics of modernity were cultural moralists. In this work the critics' responses to secularization are dealt with in terms of this cultural moralism.

Thus, the cultural moralism of the anti-modernists implied much more than a critique of secularization. Nevertheless, it still had close ties to, and in a sense grew out of, the Christian moralism of the Victorian and Edwardian periods. As an example of the interconnectivity of the two streams of thought, two anti-modernists, Donald Creighton and George P. Grant, had direct links to the social reform movement of the pre-1914 era. Creighton's father, W.B. Creighton, a Methodist preacher and editor of the *Christian Guardian*, was at the forefront of the reform effort. Specifically, he was part of the Social Gospel movement,[19] which was composed of those who wished to make Protestant Christianity socially relevant. George Munro Grant, the philosopher's prominent ancestor, was likewise an advocate of liberal Protestantism and of de-emphasizing theology in favour of a practical, reform-minded Christian imperative. George P. Grant later rejected his grandfather's approach to religion. He denounced the progressivist tone of the Social Gospellers and social reformers in general (see chapter two). Nevertheless, the younger Grant, like his anti-modernist colleagues, continued to preach the good news of social improvement. Without using its religiosity, the critics nonetheless employed the rhetoric of advancement and social amelioration of the Protestant reform movement. Their ultimate purpose was the same as that of earlier social reformers: social betterment. Thus, they reflect the meliorative, moralist outlooks, if not the substantive recommendations, of the turn-of-the-century reformers.

Cultural moralism and social meliorism were two imperatives that underpinned the critique of modernity. There are other common characteristics of the group worth noting. The first and most obvious of these is the critics' staunchly Anglo-Canadian upbringing. Save for Hilda Neatby (born in Britain), the anti-modernists were all at least second-generation Canadians. Nevertheless, they had strong familial connections to their British heritage. Even Vincent Massey, who could trace his lineage back to several generations in New England, was fiercely proud of his ultimate ties to the old country.[20] Furthermore, the anti-modernists spent their formative years in areas where loyalty to things British was particularly strong. Innis, Creighton, Grant, and Massey were from 'British' Ontario. W.L. Morton, who was from Manitoba, also shared a sense of Anglo-Canadian pride. Morton himself later acknowledged the 'very British world' in which he matured. 'Everything in daily talk, much in daily use, the whole reinforced and exaggerated by the illusion called prestige,' he recollected, 'was British – the point of reference in politics and business, the seat of fashion, the school of manners, the centre of scandal. The table dishes were British made, both the cheap and the dear, the jackknives, the tea caddies, the aperients, the best boots, the heaviest coats, the finest hats. The yearly calendars tended to picture a heroic lion or an intimidating battleship. And over the little white schoolhouse ... the Union Jack staunchly flew – a provincial statute had a few years before said it must, as it's done until this year.'[21]

Besides this inherent 'Britishness' was a rural-agrarian bias. A common rural-agrarian experience bound critics together in much the same way as did shared British values. Harold Innis, Marshall McLuhan, and Hilda Neatby grew up on farms. W.L. Morton spent considerable time in his formative years working as a farmhand in rural Manitoba. Having no direct experience of the rural existence, the other critics nevertheless were attuned to the rigours and values of agrarian life. The Massey family business, of which Vincent Massey became president for a time, was involved in the production of farm implements. Although both were born in Toronto, Massey and Donald Creighton returned to their agrarian roots by spending much time in their later years in country homes east of the metropolis.[22]

This background was augmented by the rural biases of the Edwardian period, an age during which most of the critics matured. Specifically, it was closely associated with the British country ideal,[23] represented in *Howards End* (1910) and other works of E.M. Forster, as well as in John Macdougall's *Rural Life in Canada* (1913) and Stephen Leacock's *Sunshine Sketches of a Little Town* (1912), both of which were concerned with the debilitating problem of rural depopulation. In these works, the authors eulogized rural lifestyles and values while they criticized industrialization and urbanization as disruptive and menacing. Not only did these attitudes reflect the profound social transformation of the Edwardian age; ultimately, they provided context to the anti-industrial strictures of the next generation of critics.

The anti-modernists also derive group cohesion from 'elitist' attitudes and outlooks. However, their elitism was not born of socioeconomic or political privilege. In fact, all the critics, with the exception of Vincent Massey, were of humble origins.[24] The elitism of the critics was made manifest instead in their sense of intellectual superiority; more accurately, it was a notion that they had an immutable awareness of the course of human history. More than this, it was derived from the presumption that the critics themselves were the individuals most able to remedy the ills of modern society. In many ways, the critics believed they had an almost oracular insight into cultural development. This sense of superiority is apparent in the cavalier manner in which they dismissed mass culture and denounced consumerism, Americanization, and the arrival of the mass society.[25] It is most evident in their desire to establish a social hierarchy, not based on class, but rather in which social critics and moral philosophers gained heightened recognition. Critics vied for an increased social status, which other educated groups[26] were achieving, yet which was being denied to them. Ultimately, the elitism of the anti-modernists was founded both in an exaggerated reckoning of their social function and in a desire to increase, in the tradition of Plato's *Republic*, their station in the modern world.

The sources of this elitism are not easy to pinpoint. The confident, moralizing tone is probably a remnant of the critics' fundamentalist Christian heritage.[27] Bereft of its religious content, many of the anti-modernists' strictures were suffused with evangelical fervour and puritanical righteousness. Although dealing with secularized subject matter, the rhetoric of the anti-modernists betrayed its evangelical origins. The 'class' elitism of the critics, furthermore, was in part a reaction to the diminished social status of the academic in Canada. If salaries can be used to measure the worth of the professoriate, professors at Ontario universities after the Great War made considerably more than teachers or even engineers.[28] By the post-war period, however, professors' salaries reflected their relative decline in position. By 1945 the median salary of full-time instructors had increased by only about $500 over the post–First-World-War period. After enduring a decade and a half of virtually frozen salaries, professors did gain small increases throughout the late 1940s and 1950s.[29] Yet their earnings decreased relative to other professionals. The reality was that most professors led lives of genteel poverty, a condition that reflected their diminished status in Canadian society.[30] The anti-modernists wanted to redress society's iniquitous treatment of the intelligentsia. Banding together in a unified front against an uncaring, even ignorant, populace was one of the ways to achieve this end.

More fundamentally, the critics derived their sense of elitist identity from their membership in a very small group of humanists and social scientists. As J.B. Brebner argued in 1945, Canada was in desperate need of scholars because of the debilitating loss of so many of the educated elite.[31] The war, and before it the Depression, resulted in scores of scholars' leaving their academic posts and entering government and assuming private research projects. The exodus of many of Canada's brightest intellectuals to America and elsewhere further exacerbated this problem. Consequently, a relatively small group of intellectuals was left to defend against the eclipse of the humanities in Canada and the erosion of Canada's academic tradition. The experience of Harold Innis exemplified the embattled position of Canadian humanists. When the University of Chicago tried to woo Innis away from Toronto in 1944,[32] the political economist found it impossible to leave his university after preaching loyalty to young scholars. He believed he had much work to do in combating the problems of monopolies and oligopolies of knowledge and in promoting the venerable university tradition. The same forces that held Innis in Canada also instilled a sense of commitment in the small but loyal coterie of humanists and social scientists in Canadian universities.

The critics were also brought together because of personal and professional ties. Innis, Creighton, Frye, and McLuhan all taught at the University of Toronto. Massey was also affiliated with Canada's most eminent post-secondary institution: he served as chancellor of the university from 1947 to 1952. In addition, the anti-modernists were associated through personal connections and academic alliances. Massey and Grant were related through marriage: Massey was Grant's uncle. Massey also had a close working association with Hilda Neatby from the Massey Commission years on. Avid correspondents, intellectual collaborators, and eventually good friends, Massey and Neatby relied on each other for professional and personal advice and comradeship until Massey's death in 1967. Creighton and Innis also shared a close friendship and similar outlooks on academic and national problems.[33] Despite the occasional difference of opinion, Creighton and Morton often worked closely together.[34] Furthermore, although engaged in different academic disciplines, Grant and Neatby, both involved in the Massey Commission, were correspondents and, at one point, like-minded co-religionists. Finally, McLuhan's intellectual dependence on Innis needs no elaboration here. Not necessarily sharing similar disciplines,[35] research interests, or collaborating as an academic body, the critics nonetheless had common outlooks, predispositions, and shared insights, all of which were reinforced by a series of intertwining personal and professional bonds. As such, their status as a group of tacit intellectual collaborators can be firmly established.

Scholars have studied modernity, its proponents and critics, and the implications of modernization within the Canadian context.[36] That literature is augmented in this work by an examination of critics whose individual views are known and have been documented, but who have not yet been analysed as a coherent group. Looked at together, the views of the anti-modernists seem less isolated, less out of touch with the mainstream of Canadian thought. Indeed, in this analysis these critics are placed in the political and intellectual tradition of toryism and affiliated with a strain of social moral criticism, both of which stretch back well into the nineteenth century and forward into the latter part of the twentieth century. Clearly, the anti-modernists were part of a losing tradition, their voices muted by the clamour of modernity. Nevertheless, important aspects of the tory tradition still resonate and underpin Canada's current political culture. What's more, modernity is still with us. The critique of globalization, as an example, contains elements of economic and political sovereignty that were vital to the politics of the anti-modernists. The anti-Americanism that is an inveterate aspect of Canada's political culture and specifically the tory tradition likewise persists. Finally, the focus in this analysis on a conservative tradition is an effort, albeit small, to redress a body of literature that has stressed the liberal and the modernist traditions. Again, although the conservative tradition has languished and its efforts have ended in failure, the historiographic imbalance must be redressed. This study is an attempt to show that, even in a post-modern age, the vanquished in Canadian history must be given their due.

2

Science and Technique:
The Critique of the
Technological Consciousness

Canada in the late nineteenth century was in a period of transition. The traditionally rural and agricultural existence of many Canadians had begun to change rapidly, owing to the introduction of new technologies and industrial mass production. Despite an economic depression, production in the key sectors of the economy, especially that of Ontario, Canada's most populous and industrially advanced province, increased considerably from 1870 through to the early 1890s. In Ontario, for instance, coal consumption increased more than 2,000 times over the years 1869–1900. Toronto, one of Canada's leading industrial cities, rapidly developed in the 1880s. In that decade 'the total number of productive establishments in Toronto more than tripled, the number of workers doubled, capital invested increased roughly 265 percent.'[1] While economic and industrial growth slowed somewhat in Ontario and elsewhere by the mid-1890s, an economic boom hit Canada between the later 1890s, continued until 1912, and allowed a great deal of growth in machine technology and resource production and fostered considerable expansion of industrial plant. Between 1890 and 1910 the number of workers employed in manufacturing increased 350 per cent.[2] Certainly, Canada's was still an export economy until and after the Great War. Nevertheless, the Canadian intellectual and social experience of the late Victorian period reflected an emerging economic revolution.

To accompany economic and industrial expansion, Canada experienced advances in science and technology that were bound up in the Victorian view of progress and national advancement. A key component of the Victorian idea of progress was the notion that through understanding the physical world one could exert control over it. Perhaps the most significant intellectual development of the age was the extension of scientific assumptions that nature was knowable (and hence exploitable) through the use of empirical methodologies. The consciousness of Bacon had clearly come alive in the minds of Victorians. They saw history as an organic process with laws ready to be discovered; through the uncovering of historical laws, ran Victorian logic, society could be understood and reconstructed on a scientific basis. The progress of science and industrial production, in short, was the progress of civilization.[3]

Faith that science and technology would improve material conditions and secure a bright future had reached a high point by the 1890s. Canadians, for the most part, regarded scientific and technological advancement in this period as key to the industrial and therefore the economic well-being of their country. As a Queen's University scientist proclaimed in 1895, the nineteenth century 'may be described as a hundred years of human progress under the guidance of science.' The material well-being of western civilization had been achieved, he claimed, precisely because science and technology had wed and had engendered, in consequence, an unparalleled control over the physical environment.[4] In short, for Victorian Canadians, material progress had become tied to advances in technique and the applied sciences.

Faith in science and technology reflected Canadians' growing confidence in the applied sciences. This new appreciation seemed to be centred in Canadian educational institutions. As historian A.B. McKillop has shown, by the late Victorian period education in Canada was being transformed from a liberal arts orientation to a type of education that strove towards a 'healthy balance between culture and science.' Canadian industrialists and educators had led the campaign to lobby for the establishment of technical education at secondary schools in Ontario ever since John A. Macdonald's government had put forth the National Policy in 1879.[5] This campaign intensified after 1896 as local boards of trade, the Trades and Labour Congress of Canada, and the Canadian Manufacturers' Association badgered both the Laurier and later the Borden governments to fund and coordinate applied sciences programs.[6] Despite receiving a sympathetic ear from William Lyon Mackenzie King, however, who became the minister of labour in 1908, the cause of technical education would have to wait until the post-war Technical Education Act, which was designed to encourage the mechanical trades and increase the 'efficiency and productive power of those employed therein.'[7]

'Technical education' also reoriented the universities according to the technological ethic. The research ideal of nineteenth-century German universities had been foreign to Anglo-Canadian universities, and until the end of the nineteenth century, the main function of the latter institutions was to impart a general and liberal education. Instead of promoting 'research,' Anglo-Canadian universities encouraged pupils to partake in Arnold's 'best that has been thought' without necessarily requiring them to add to that learning. By the late Victorian period, however, the research ideal had begun to infiltrate Canadian higher education. No individual was more active in the promotion of the research ideal in Canada than University of Toronto mathematics and physics professor James Loudon.[8]

Loudon's 1877 presidential address to the Canadian Institute is the first clear statement of the value of the German research ideal to the Canadian university. In the address, Loudon extolled the value of the specialization within the sciences; as much as possible, he wanted to see universities encourage a specialized, professional research, based on the German model. He advocated the German system wherein the teacher would engage only in very narrow topics, so that his teaching would reinforce research. Furthermore, for the German plan to work, 'an enormous revenue must be available ... [with] a small standing army of professors, and a highly trained body of recruits.'[9] In Loudon's conception, scientific knowledge was not simply to be imported and then taught to so many students; rather, the expansion of scientific knowledge was to be the main objective. To that end, Loudon called for a fundamental reorientation of the way Canadian universities regarded scientific learning.

Loudon continued to lobby for the adoption of the German research ideal throughout the late Victorian period. With accelerating urban-industrialization, advances in industrial technology, the increase of commercial rivalries among industrialized nations, and a great rise in British imperial sentiment, Loudon identified an opportunity for the research ideal to gain greater currency among Canadians. In an 1899 Royal Society address, he showed the importance of research to the development of Anglo-Canadian society. Above all, he wanted to demonstrate how the adoption of the research ideal would mean industrial efficiency, material prosperity, and, ultimately, the continued moral and commercial leadership of British civilization. He declared to his attentive audience that the 'British nation [was] on the eve of an awakening'; the 'British mind' understood, he continued, that 'some vital connection really does exist between national progress and scientific discovery, and that the latter should be fostered in connection with the higher institutions of learning.' He contended that the 'spirit of research is lacking' within the Anglo-Canadian university, and, as a consequence, the British Empire's commercial supremacy vis-à-vis Germany and the United States was threatened. Through paying more attention to the advancement of knowledge, universities throughout the Empire could make a great contribution to maintaining British trade supremacy and, more important, to guaranteeing the material and moral advancement of British civilization. In concluding his speech, he commented on the 'effect of research upon the national life' of Canada. The institution of research would be integral to the progress of Canada; for Canada could no longer rely on knowledge from abroad. Instead, it had to develop a 'spirit of originality,' for which the universities would be primarily responsible. The time has come, he ended, 'when the research university must be regarded as the only university, and the task is incumbent on those in authority of elaborating a university system ... which shall have proper regard to the importance of this new factor as well as to the past and future of our country.'[10]

The significance of Loudon's speech was twofold. First, Loudon's desire to specialize and professionalize research reflected a change in the balance of Canadian scholarship away from the 'gentleman scholar towards the laboratory of the professional researcher.' Whereas scientific enquiry in Canada had been the province of the amateur outside the university, the research ideal had no tolerance for such a haphazard and unproductive approach to new knowledge. Universities that continued to employ such outmoded practices lost credence in the eyes of the newly scientifically minded populace and the advocates of the research ideal. Second, Loudon's piece showed how the universities, through fostering scientific knowledge, could be the instruments of the advancement of British civilization. Whereas in the past academics had regarded science as an adjunct of metaphysics, Loudon denied as invalid the role of the scientist 'to reconcile scientific theory with metaphysical or religious opinion.'[11] Instead, he insisted that scientific enquiry had a validity per se, and part of that validity was that it was a means to an end. Indeed, a great part of Loudon's contribution to Canadian science rested not only on his new approach to scientific knowledge, but also on his attempt to put into practice the Victorian idea that progress occurred through the use and advancement of science. This progressivist, utilitarian conception was to persist well beyond the late Victorian age.

Like Loudon, other Anglo-Canadian researchers assigned to science a vital role in the Great War. While science and technology had contributed to the horrific carnage of the First World War, there was still a sense that scientific research could be a positive, constructive force. The superiority of 'British' science and industry had been regained during the war, the argument ran, and again helped to advance British civilization. In a speech delivered to the Royal Society entitled 'The War and Science,' Dr A. Stanley Mackenzie, president of Dalhousie University, exemplified this view. Mackenzie indicated how the 'stresses of war' had forced England to realize 'the desperate situation in which she stood,' owing to the 'past neglect of scientific method.' The events of the war showed the negligence of English-speaking peoples in ignoring research. Yet for Mackenzie, the war also demonstrated how a free and democratic citizenry could recover and rediscover the centrality of science to the struggle for cultural supremacy. '[T]he scientific men of Britain,' he concluded, had made a significant contribution to the war effort.[12] Indeed, British science had been instrumental in victory.

For Mackenzie and others the Great War was a momentous period in the history of science, because it elevated scientific research to its rightful place. Mackenzie recommended that British peoples build on their triumphs and cultivate the pure and applied sciences. The 'interaction of the ideal and the ... utilitarian,' he wrote, 'spells progress.' He was particularly hopeful about the war's impact in Canada. 'The effect of the war upon Science,' he argued, 'should ... result in an industrial revolution,' which should be directed towards the proper utilization of natural resources and, hence, the 'stoppage of wastefulness.' Through the creation of a national science curriculum and through the promotion of scientific research by the Royal Society of Canada, he hoped that the research ideal could become firmly entrenched and that Canada's war experience would result in superior science education and facilities. Only then would the sacrifice not have been in vain.[13]

Mackenzie's remarks about science and the war certainly made for good speech-making. Yet the case was overstated. Clearly, by the Great War the research ideal already had become prominent in Canadian universities; the war merely galvanized existing public opinion and private resolve to develop the sciences at Canadian universities. As McKillop argues, the Royal Commission on the University of Toronto (1906) had been a watershed in that it marked the 'triumph of the notion that science, research, and professionalism should have a vital place in the modern university.'[14] Furthermore, during the war, the Ontario government had become financially committed to develop scientific and technical research. The provincial government allotted the University of Toronto $15,000 per year for research, a sum that was augmented substantially to $75,000 per annum in 1919. In organizational terms, the establishment of the School of Engineering Research in 1917 entrenched science and technical learning at Toronto. In response to the great demand for engineers and applied scientists, the Faculty of Applied Sciences (of which the school was a part) devised a plan to train its most accomplished graduates. The school, in short, was to serve both research and training capacities. Most of all, in cooperation with industry, it was to facilitate industrial and technical research.[15]

Advances in industrial research at Toronto notwithstanding, perhaps the most important and enduring example of the research ideal was the emergence of the National Research Council (NRC). The appearance in late autumn of 1916 of the Honorary Advisory Council (later to be named the NRC) created little fanfare. The nation was busy with other things, not the least of which was the prosecution of the war. The establishment of the council, nevertheless, had been a revolutionary achievement. Canada already had several scientific institutions that fit into corresponding government departments and that were responsible for the development of its vast staples and mineral resources, but Canadians lacked an institution devoted to developments in secondary industry and general science. They required an institution, in short, more compatible with university- than with government-sponsored research. The council was unique in that it enabled scientists themselves to devise and oversee research projects and advise government on their findings in a variety of fields. The types of projects the council dealt with in the early years – for example, production of motor fuel from alternative sources, better ways to use peat, extraction of sugar from sulphite liquor, and the use of agricultural wastes such as wheat straw and fish wastes for fertilizer – reflected both the needs of wartime Canada and the drive towards efficiency or the 'scientific' use of natural resources. However, the council's efforts to promote research and to tout the national importance of science endured well beyond wartime projects. Throughout its formative period, the NRC endeavoured 'to create a background of public opinion throughout the country which would appreciate and support the idea of research in general and especially the idea of industrial research.'[16] Scientists, such as Loudon and Mackenzie, had toiled many years to raise the profile of research in Canada. With the help of total war and the NRC they could show Canadians that the time was right to intensify the crusade for research.

The council's steady growth and in its contributions to scientific discovery demonstrate the institution's success as the chief propagator of the research ethic. Soon after its inception, the NRC began to address its shortcomings. The drive for the development of central laboratories, for instance, began in the summer of 1918 when the council recommended to the government the erection of a central scientific institute at Ottawa.[17] After a few failed attempts to pass a 'science' bill in Parliament that would establish a national scientific research institute, construction of the new 'temple of science' finally began in 1928 on the banks of the Ottawa River. But Canadian science required scientists and technicians to staff the laboratories. Early on, the council recognized the grave difficulties that would result from a lack of trained personnel. It set out to remedy the problem by allocating $10,000 to set up scholarships and fellowships. Within a decade it had granted 344 scholarships and fellowships to 199 students. Sixteen departments of science at twelve universities participated in the grant program. The NRC also encouraged research in progress or pending projects. By 1926 the council had assisted about 120 projects. Several of these undertakings, such as health studies on tuberculosis, vitamins, and insulin, as well as industrial fatigue and a study of ways to stimulate the economy, were of major significance. What is more, the NRC made important contributions not only to the advance of scientific knowledge, but also in measurable financial terms. Out of a half-a-million-dollar investment, for example, in a post-war project dealing with wheat rust, the council reckoned the long-term benefits in terms of increased yield of in excess than $25 million per annum more than compensated for the initial outlay. Similarly, it reported that a lobster discoloration remedy achieved at a cost of $2,000–$3,000 in grants and nominal laboratory fees generated an additional annual income of around $700,000 for the industry.[18] As always, the practical, utilitarian value of science was vital to the long-term promotion of the research ideal in Canada.

The emergence of the NRC culminated the efforts of scientific lobbyists to achieve public recognition of scientific research. In a symbolic sense, the council performed a utilitarian role in aiding industrial development and in rationalizing Canada's war production. Created largely in response to the material needs of war, it constituted a publicly supported institution, founded intellectually on the notion that, given enough resources, it could significantly contribute to Canada's material advancement. In short, it represented the triumph of the research ideal. In the minds of many Canadians and certainly those in the scientific community, research institutions like the NRC provided a means by which Canadians could survive in a world dominated by efficient, mechanized production. Indeed, the research institution was essential to the modernization of the nation. Through the establishment of the NRC, in the words of historian Frank Underhill, the Canadian government 'undertook a new national responsibility, the fostering of scientific research for the purpose of making us a more competent people in the modern world.'[19] A bastion of the research ideal, the council assisted the dominion's quest to count itself among the modernizing countries of the western world.

The NRC and other institutions of applied research certainly made manifest a new research ethos. The rise of the social sciences and the 'social service ideal,' however, also reflected the growing pervasiveness of scientific enquiry. As they did in other western countries, the social sciences emerged in Canada against the backdrop of a society that, although still largely rural and agricultural, was rapidly urbanizing and industrializing.[20] Their development must therefore be understood in the light of the changing social and demographic character of Canada in the late nineteenth and early twentieth centuries.

The long-term trend towards urban industrialization began during the so-called Laurier boom. In this period the population of the countryside declined relative to that of urban areas, and the cities, especially the largest centres, absorbed much of the overall national population increase. Between the years 1891 and 1911, for instance, Canada's urban population increased from 31.8 to 45.2 per cent of the whole. British Columbia and Ontario were more urban than rural by the start of the Great War. By 1921 Canada as a whole became a relatively urban society. Urbanization was also marked by a tendency towards concentration of population in a few large cities. Although in the Laurier period population increases in smaller cities were insignificant, larger cities experienced rapid growth. Montreal grew from around 200,000 in 1891 to over a half-million in 1911, Toronto increased from 180,000 to just under 400,000, and Winnipeg, recently a lonely outpost on the eastern prairies, expanded to 130,000 inhabitants.[21]

Not without reason, the study of the causes of social transformation became important in the 1896–1911 period. Church groups, individuals, and the federal government became concerned over the 'rural question' and sought answers to overcrowding, poverty, and crime, among other problems associated with urbanization. The poverty, prostitution, and crime that seemed to exist unchecked in the growing urban areas appalled J.S. Woodsworth and others involved in the urban reform movement. Canadian Social Gospellers also railed against deplorable social conditions in Canada's growing cities and focused on the immoralities of increased crime and prostitution, and the evils of drink. The new breed of professional social analysts who were emerging at Canadian universities provided detailed accounts of the impact of rapid social change. Sir Herbert Ames's *City below the Hill* (1897), William Lyon Mackenzie King's articles exposing the appalling conditions in sweated industries, along with Queen's University political economist Adam Shortt's ideas on the urban question were a few academic studies of urban problems.[22]

Like its counterparts in the Anglo-American world, nascent Canadian social science sought to understand the economic forces that underpinned the urban-industrial problem. Not only did social scientists observe the transformations associated with industrialization, but they also tried to understand the root causes and future effects of industrialism on Canadian society. They employed social scientific methods as tools to comprehend change. Political economist Adam Shortt, for instance, showed how by controlling and understanding economic activities it was possible to achieve progress without overthrowing the industrial-capitalist system. Shortt realized the abuses and inadequacies of the prevalent socio-economic system. He was certain, furthermore, that in exposing these deficiencies and suggesting alternatives, the current system could be reformed and become an instrument in the movement towards human progress. Only through rethinking industrial-capitalist development and redirecting humankind's purposes and politics, he argued, could conditions be altered and destinies changed. The formula for advancement was first to observe and understand the new material order of mankind and then to gain control over it. In addition, political economy, Shortt's own discipline, was best able to facilitate this twofold task. It enabled humankind's 'understanding of social reality' and prepared 'men and women to control their fate.' With other political economists, Shortt was convinced of the power of social science both to gain an accurate view of the material order and to help to perfect humanity's secular existence.

In the words of historian Barry Ferguson, Shortt's political economy 'encompassed nothing less than the analysis of "the material means of development of a civilization." In this way, political economy could set about devising a new understanding of the industrial-capitalist order that was now dominant in Europe and the United States and that was about to reshape Canada.'[23]

University of Toronto political economist James Mavor echoed Shortt's views on the modern uses of the social sciences. To Mavor, modern society had advanced from feudal times into the twentieth century because of scientific and technological developments. Along with material advances, however, came developments such as urban-industrialization, which, if left unchecked, could lead to revolution and the eventual overthrow of the industrial-capitalist system. By understanding material progress, Mavor averred, moderns could prevent social chaos and influence the direction of society. Political economy thus became important in Mavor's scheme precisely because it held the key to comprehending past and current socio-economic conditions. Through social scientific enquiry, solutions to societal problems became possible. The political economist was like a 'master mechanic tinkering with the machinery of society only to the degree required to maintain maximum stability and efficiency. Armed with an empirical knowledge of economic history ... the social scientist guided society to an orderly and rationalized technological future.'[24] To Mavor, the factual, social scientific understanding of the world was essential if society was to progress in a measured and materially prosperous manner.

In addition to social stability and material advancement, industrial efficiency was an objective of Canadian social science. Social scientists used it both to manage social development and, just as important, to enhance the credibility of the social sciences. Industrial efficiency implied the effective employment of resources in the productive process. Shortt was one of the first to recognize its central importance. Only through increased economic efficiency, he argued, could industrial society satisfy increasing human wants and needs. The benefits of efficient production and use of resources, moreover, were limited only by the finite nature of resources and productive capacity.[25] Shortt's Queen's colleague and fellow political economist Oscar Douglas Skelton went even further than Shortt in his advocacy of the efficiency ideal. Through ever-increasing efficiency, the industrial-capitalist system could overcome the limitations of resources and the exigencies of the productive process. Indeed, Skelton believed that the industrial system was remarkably dynamic, so much so, in fact, that it would continually expand to meet increasing human needs. All that was required was the proper management of resources and industrial processes to increase efficiency and ensure material advancement.[26] Most significant, for both Skelton and Shortt, political economists were those best able to suggest ways to increase production and make more effective use of finite resources. Comprehending the benefits of efficiency, they became responsible for discovering how the industrial system was to distribute wealth and goods over a wider body of people; their task was to solve the equation of increasing human needs and declining resources, the age-old problem of the dismal science. Far from isolating themselves in the cloistered surroundings of the ivory tower, Canadian social scientists thus began to understand the relationship between their work and the emerging social order.

Closely allied to the ideal of efficiency was the notion of expertise. The story of the development of the 'expert' within Canadian intellectual circles is very much the story of the decline of amateur reformers and the emergence within academia and government of the professional social analyst. Reform movements before the Great War were oriented towards solving the myriad problems of urban growth, rural depopulation, and industrial capitalism. Considered under the catch-all 'urban reform,' urban beautification projects, campaigns against gambling and prostitution, and the temperance movement all were the province of the amateur social worker. But the nature of the reform movement was beginning to change. The social science community was developing structures to deal with social problems and to gain a greater influence in the field of social welfare.[27] Social scientists worked within the universities and professional organizations to change the nature of the reform movement so that the views of experts (the social scientists themselves) became increasingly important. Through their growing participation in the urban and other reform movements, they asserted the predominance of expert analysis and affirmed at the same time their own social importance. Their message was clear: while the amateur had little place in the serious business of social analysis, the expert had become indispensable to the age of transformation.

The rise of expertise also involved changes within academic structures, but social scientists had to free themselves from the constraints of philosophy and theology before they could set about orchestrating reform. They had to professionalize the science of political economy.

Again, Adam Shortt and O.D. Skelton led the way in accomplishing this goal. In 1913 Shortt and Skelton proposed the foundation of the Canadian Political Science Association (CPSA). Providing a forum for political economists, the CPSA showed that the social scientist had a special part to play in modern society. The mandate of the new organization was to enable enlightened intellectuals from across the country to express their views and study social problems. The CPSA was an incubator for new social policy ideas that, it was hoped, would guide the social policies of governments. It was an instrument through which the new class of professionals could put forth their ideas and have their views integrated into social policy. Most of all, it was an example of the way expert opinion was made available to those in positions of power. Through their new organ, Shortt and Skelton demonstrated how political economy 'had an important and practical role to play, not only within the university, but also in the outside world.'[28] Far from being concerned with moral, philosophical, or strictly academic questions, the social sciences began to extend themselves well beyond the walls of the academy and the limitations of scholarly enquiry.

Bureaucratic appointments of experts also reflect the shift towards the professionalization of reform and the wider applicability of the social sciences. W.L. Mackenzie King was one of the first social scientists to make it into government. King brought to the labour portfolio a reforming impulse influenced by the latest social theories of Thorstein Veblen, Arnold Toynbee, and others of the new breed of international political economists. King's industrial peace policy, embodied in the Industrial Disputes Act of 1907, was an important reform initiative. His early political career, moreover, established a link between the state and the expert. Through the labour portfolio, King had found an outlet to implement his theories on social interaction in the field of labour relations. His work as labour minster mirrored the new political economy trend that looked away from positivism and 'deductivism' and emphasized instead 'ameliorative social activism.'[29] Through *Industry and Humanity* (1918), his main piece of scholarship, and through his work in settling labour disputes, King demonstrated the new penchant of political economists for countenancing, even prescribing, a positive role for the state in implementing social theories and policy recommendations. Although King's entry into government had more to do with politics than with his being an expert policy adviser, his appointment was nevertheless a significant step in the advancement of the professional social reformer.

Like King, Adam Shortt was active in establishing ties between the academic and governmental worlds. Also like King, Shortt endorsed the political economist's function to provide expert council to government. In 1905 he wrote that he thought the 'time was coming in Canada as in other countries ... when the Government should avail itself of the training and research of its university professors in various departments, thereby aiding their research and enabling them to bring back to their students some of the freshness and reality of concrete problems. In a sense this is what the Government has done in placing Mr King at the head of the Department of Labour.' King soon learned of Shortt's views, and it was not long before the Queen's political economist became a labour conciliator in King's department. In September 1908 Shortt left his academic post altogether and accepted an appointment as civil service commissioner. Shortt's appointment, like that of King a few years before, was significant because it allowed him to put into practice his ideas on labour in an industrial-capitalist society. It enabled him, above all, to fulfil the role of expert in government service. To underline the role of expertise in a changing society, Shortt, in a 1912 CPSA address, made clear the availability of a group of social scientists eminently capable of dealing with the exigencies of industrial development. He implored governments to take advantage of this pool of expertise. Governmental efficiency would not be served unless the official had access to expert information and judgment. The early twentieth century, Shortt concluded simply, was, after all, 'an age of experts.'[30]

Besides the professionalization and absorption into government of social experts, important assumptions and intellectual attitudes characterized the development of the social sciences. The most significant was the notion that society is knowable through the application of social scientific analysis. Through the social sciences and state interventionism, the social scientists contended, society became accessible to the individual and the group alike. In consequence, it could be altered, engineered so as to take advantage of the positive effects of industrial-capitalism and avoid the more unsavory by-products of the modern industrial order. Industrial efficiency, labour dispute boards, and other manifestations of expertise demonstrated the social scientist's ability to manage social change and control the exigencies of industrial production. Social scientists realized that an understanding of economic behaviours and social systems comprised the greatest contribution of the social sciences to the social order. Knowledge and, specifically, social scientific analysis were the means to deal with change, to shape circumstances, and to alter destinies.

Experts' involvement in government must be traced to the early efforts of King, Shortt, Skelton, and others to bring social scientific approaches out of the universities into the public realm. Problems associated with urban-industrialization and other difficulties tied to the modernization of the Canadian economy could not be dealt with by government alone. Only with expert assistance could the government come to terms with modern social problems and avoid a descent into social chaos. While the first generation of social scientific reformers must be considered in the light of the reform movement at large, it is nonetheless set off from other, amateur-oriented reformers in its consistent reliance on expertise as the foundation of reform. Subsequent generations of social scientists intensified the trend towards expertise. Shortt may have been premature in terming the period the 'age of the expert,' but it was becoming a more accurate description as Canadian society continued to modernize and Canadian social scientists struggled to keep up with changing times.

As it did elsewhere, in Canada the Great War of 1914–18 caused profound historical disruptions. Despite tremendous transformations, many Canadian social scientists agreed that post-war society, like the social order that had preceded it, was still accessible. Intellectuals such as Shortt and Skelton maintained the pre-war conviction that social scientists were those equipped to provide solutions and guide social development. Canadian society could deal with the economic problems and the social justice issues by heeding social scientific reform principles and advocating state interventionism.[31] Moreover, the war had done little to disrupt the idea of the social scientist as social engineer; in fact, by intensifying change it had reinforced the need for the social expert. It had served, further, to interconnect the university and society and to make society more reliant on university experts. After 1918 there was increased demand for those trained in finance and commerce and industry. The establishment at Queen's University of a new commerce department in 1919, for which Skelton and W.C. Clark had lobbied several years before, exemplified the recognition of the universities' role in solving post-war problems. Canadians looked more than ever before to the universities as important resources to deal with accelerating change. This increased attention, in turn, encouraged the academic expert, already inspired by the pre-war economic expansion, to step up his involvement in managing society's transformations. Many academics now sat on boards, became royal commissioners, took part in official surveys, and provided expert testimony for committees.[32] In addition, in the important field of economics, there was a tremendous increase in the body of scholarship. In the 1920s scholars produced more than forty books, and by the 1930s that number had tripled.[33] The post-war period was an age of ever-accelerating change, one ideally suited to the expansion of political economy and the extension more generally of the social sciences ideal.

Harold Adams Innis was one of the brightest of the interwar generation of social scientists in Canada. Innis's early scholarly career was very much a part of new social scientific trends towards an expanded role for social science in understanding social developments. Although he was to rail against what historian Doug Owram has called the 'government generation' later in his career, Innis comprehended the social scientist's role in mapping out economic development and how his own work in economic history helped to clarify socio-economic problems. His study of overhead costs, for example, and his concern for Canada's marginal economic development placed Innis alongside Shortt, Skelton, and others in the new political economy tradition. Innis agreed with the need to comprehend the nature of industrial society and to suggest alternatives for economic development. As a result, perhaps unknowingly he made considerable contributions to the Canadian social sciences and to the tradition of expertise.

Although unremarkable in many ways, Innis's *A History of the Canadian Pacific Railway* (1923) is notable; in this book he demonstrated for the first time three basic concerns that were to characterize his later work: the way western civilization was spread to the new world; the importance of geography to early economic activity; and the significance of staples to regional economic development. It was also important because Innis examined the building and operation of the CPR in terms of contracts, freight and passenger traffic, and capitalization and profits from 'an evolutionary and scientific point of view.' Most significant, however, in his earliest work Innis emphasized the triumph of human ingenuity, most notably in terms of machine technology, over the forces of nature. The main conclusion in *A History of the Canadian Pacific Railway* was that the construction of the CPR 'was the direction of energy to the conquest of geographical barriers.'[34] Innis regarded machine technology, in this case in the form of the railway, as the factor most responsible for economic change.

While at the University of Chicago, where he wrote *A History of the Canadian Pacific Railway*, Innis came into contact with the thought of political economist Thorstein Veblen. Veblen, according to Innis, was the first political economist to do a 'general stocktaking' of a society that had come under the influence of 'machine industry,' a major contribution to the history of political economy. He accepted into his own thought Veblen's concern with 'laws of the growth and decay' of socio-economic institutions and the impact of technology as key factors in institutional development.[35] Perhaps most important to Innis's understanding of the historical impact of technique were Veblen's theories on the introduction of advanced economic structures to marginal, non-industrialized structures, such as those of Canada's pre-industrial economy.

Innis's early scholarly work also was an attempt to avoid well-tried European models of economic development. Innis wanted to construct instead a paradigm that suited Canada's unique conditions. His 'staples history' involved the interplay of economic, technological, and geographical factors. It focused on the study of how the price system and technique of economically advanced countries adjusted themselves to their geographical surroundings and determined the economic growth of the new country. Most significant, Innis's view of economic development was predicated on the advancement of technology. Echoing Veblen, he argued that, as technology advances, there is a larger base of tools and know-how to build upon, increasing the effectiveness and general quality of the innovative process. Technical advance thus builds upon itself and uses the past as a basis for greater potential advance in the future at a quicker and more advanced rate.[36]

The development of the staples economy, furthermore, was dependent on the application of this ever-advancing technology to virgin natural resources. Indeed, in Innis's scheme the limiting factor of geography could be only lessened, and in some instances overcome completely, through the emergence and the subsequent employment of advanced technique.[37] Technology allowed embryonic economies, such as the fur trade, to develop; in eliminating barriers to economic progression, it provided the means by which new wealth could be created and accumulated. Along with advances in the price system (which occurred fundamentally in the same way as technical advancement), technique became for Innis the basis of economic change in marginal economies.[38]

Innis, like Veblen before him, was a 'technological determinist.' In addition to other contributory factors of economic development, such as geography and the availability of staples, by the early 1930s he was focusing increasingly on the primacy of technology to the development of Canadian economy.[39] Against the backdrop of the ruinous Depression, Innis emphasized more than ever before how industrial-age technology was responsible for Canada's current economic plight. In the books he wrote in the 1930s he dealt with the fragility of marginal economies that relied on technological advancement for economic expansion. Innis explained that as technology became more sophisticated, it became more costly. As overhead costs associated with advanced technique increased, he warned that there was also a greater danger that entrepreneurs or governments might cease investment in further technological development. Depression occurred when technological advance was considered to be too risky.[40] It was the most devastating result, he argued, of the interruption of the price system. Cycles of boom and bust, growth and decay, predicated on the investment and evolution of technique, characterized Canadian economic development.[41] To Innis, the economic retraction of the 1930s was a 'bust' period, a manifestation of the stranglehold of technique on economic development.

Innis's work through the early 1930s thus was an effort to address some of Canada's most pressing problems. As Adam Shortt had done before him, Innis used economic history as a platform on which to build a conception of current economic development. He worked hard to address problems that were rooted in the earliest phases of economic development but that impinged upon present economic circumstances. Like many of his fellow political economists, he devoted himself to the comprehension of Canada's material development; this knowledge, after all, was crucial to understanding the current economic malaise. Hence, Innis must be placed alongside his colleagues at Toronto and other Canadian universities, to whom the public and governments alike turned for answers. Like those of his colleagues, his scholarly efforts were directed in part towards addressing social problems and suggesting ways to liberate Canada from the exigencies of marginal economic development. Innis, in this early phase of his academic career, thus numbered among the new breed of Canadian social scientists.

Although his work in the 1930s must be regarded as part of the larger body of social scientific research of the period, Innis himself denied complicity in advancing the social sciences. By the late 1930s he had become disillusioned with political economy, a field of study beguiled by new trends in the social sciences: specialization, bureau-cratization, and the use of abstruse econometric models designed to explain economic advancement. He rejected the new direction of political economy and found himself, in consequence, on the margins of his own field of enquiry.[42] His turn away from the mainstream of social scientific development owed much to his reaction against the methods and goals of late-1930s political economy in Canada. It owed perhaps still more to his questioning of science and technique as influences in Canada's development.

The 1930s was a period of great transformation in the social sciences. Increased specialization was characteristic of this change. Political economy, for example, in Canadian universities of the 1920s and early 1930s still was a catch-all, which included sociology, political science, history, law, and, of course, economics. By the late 1930s, however, political economy had been transformed into the 'science of economics.' Other facets of the department developed into independent disciplines, largely divorced from their former associations. The fragmentation of political economy and other social sciences was due largely to current historical developments: the disastrous Depression and the pressing constitutional and foreign policy questions of the 1930s. Historians and political scientists studied proposed amendments to the federal constitution, discussed dominion-provincial relations, and debated the rights to neutrality in war. Economists, including Innis, felt themselves responsible for addressing economic problems, while debating commercial policies and public finance issues. Each segment of the social sciences thus had its own area of specialty. The time when university academics in the liberal arts dedicated themselves to philosophical absolutes was long past. Gone also was the initial wave of intellectual reformers who, through their scholarly work, had attempted morally to uplift society.[43] A new era of specialized scholarship, closely tied to the needs of government, was in existence by the late 1930s, revolutionizing the humanities and the social sciences.

As a senior scholar at the University of Toronto, in the most respected political economy department in the country, Innis was well placed to assess the transformation of the social sciences. He distrusted the specialization of knowledge in the liberal arts and was unimpressed with the new-found prestige of the social scientist. He warned that any social scientist who purported to know the truth about the Depression or any other of the economic or social difficulties of the time was intellectually dishonest and 'certainly wrong.'[44] Instead, he stressed that the economist must be aware of his limitations, especially in an era in which governments and the public relied heavily on his counsel. The social sciences had not yet developed to a stage where its practitioners could advise with assurance proper courses of action or governmental planning. Innis urged caution and restraint. He implored the social scientist not to become too taken with his new celebrity and influence in government and bureaucratic circles. He did not want scholars to relinquish their pursuit of the ideals of truth and objectivity. Instead, he recommended that social scientists continue their work until they were asked to participate in public debate. The social scientist should 'render the best advice of which he is capable that [he] might not do more harm than good to the economic structure.'[45] He should concentrate only 'on courses of disturbance and prepare himself for the occasion in which the politician may dare to consult him.'[46]

Innis formalized his views on the transforming social sciences in a 1935 article written for the *Canadian Journal of Economics and Political Science* entitled 'The Role of Intelligence: Some Further Notes.'[47] The paper was a response to studies by E.J. Urwick and by F.H. Knight, which dealt with the role of the intellectual in the social and political process.[48] It was an early statement of his opposition to specialization, the bureaucratization of academia, and other irksome developments in the social sciences. In essence, it was a diatribe questioning the function of the social sciences in the greater development of the Canadian state.

In 'The Role of Intelligence,' Innis highlighted the pitfalls faced by the modern social scientist. He warned that participation in government or business seriously impaired the social scientist's judgment and ability to achieve truth and objectivity. In pursuing vested interests in outside projects, Innis argued that social scientists developed a bias because external endeavours limited the range of their thought and understanding to the short-term interests of government policy or business planning. Social scientists' intellectual capacity became rigid because they no longer concentrated their energies on larger issues, such as the social effects of industrialization and technology. Rather, they insisted solely on resolving narrowly focused problems, such as distribution and overcapacity difficulties, achieving the foreign policy goals of the political party in power, or increasing the profitability of a particular business venture. Innis was convinced, for instance, that the penchant for acting as business consultants invariably clouded social scientists' judgment; for such academics had a vested interest in the projects they undertook. They became concerned with 'increasing profits and the increasing sales of products irrespective of the wants of the community, and [acted] largely in a predatory capacity.'[49] Those involved in governmental activities also allowed vested interests, in the form of partisan politics, to taint their judgment. Government officials employed social scientists chiefly for political gain. In consequence, government experts became nothing more than handmaidens of partisan politics. For Innis, the basic problem of the modern social sciences and their adherents was that they were too tied to the social circumstances they attempted to evaluate to make their analyses effective or scientific. They lacked, in short, the requisite objectivity to make clear-headed assessments of social problems and community needs.

Innis thus deplored contemporary trends in the social sciences precisely because they detracted from an objective assessment of society. For Innis, the greatest irony of the modern social sciences was the implicit claim that through specialized methods and closer associations with business and governmental institutions, social science could at once understand and attend to social needs. He argued, to the contrary, that only once the social scientist had realized that narrow approaches and vested interests impaired his ability to address social problems could the social sciences begin to contribute to the welfare of society. '[P]aradoxically,' he wrote, the innumerable difficulties of the social scientist,' once understood, also provided the starting point for 'his salvation.'[50] Tendencies towards specialization and vested interests would show the limitations of social scientists, namely, that the social sciences could not achieve absolute truth or objectivity but instead that they were restricted by wrongheaded methodologies and biased by governmental and business interests. The quest for the truth could begin only once the search for limitations was in process and biases became exposed. Innis concluded that the 'habits or biases of individuals which permit prediction are re-enforced in the cumulative bias of institutions and constitute the chief interest of the social scientist.'[51]

Through disinterested scholarly enquiry, social scientists, according to Innis, had the ability to observe regularities of behaviour. Through their observations they could begin to understand the social process and, over time, discover bias and approach objectivity. The experience and diligence of the social scientist thus were, for Innis, essential to the achievement of an objective, scientific analysis of society. 'The never-ending shell of life,' he wrote, 'suggested in the persistent character of bias[,] provides the possibilities of intensive study of the limits of life and its probable direction.'[52] The constant awareness of the existence of bias and its effects on scholarship was thus the most effective way not only to avoid it but also to attempt to overcome it. In understanding the function of bias social scientists could overcome deception and fallacy and discover the true nature of the social process.

Innis's view of the social sciences thus centred on the identification and elimination of bias. The scientific aspect of social analysis was premised on the scholar's ability to understand the limitations of his field of enquiry and to use that information as a means to comprehend social realities. Knowledge of those elements that seemed to impede an objective point of view was key to overcoming bias. While Innis did not deny the role of the expert in the social process, he was not prepared to accept the conventional view of the social sciences as a facile means to address problems and suggest social and economic policy alternatives. Rather, Innisian social science diverged from that of his contemporaries in its emphasis on the limitations and effects of bias on the social scientist and on the social process. It taught that awareness of the social scientist's deficiencies was the crucial first step in comprehending social needs and contributing to social development.

Innis's approach to social scientific enquiry was made manifest in his political economy of the 1930s. In the context of his work, Innis's efforts to acknowledge and accept the immutable conditions of Canadian economic development was a crucial starting point. In assessing limitations, political economists understood what could be done to alter economic realities and influence material growth. Comprehending the impact of technology and other uncontrollable factors enabled social scientists, by default, to gain insight into those elements in the historical process that could be changed. Grasping the nature of economic development, for example, Innis showed how there was a tendency to fall into the 'staples trap': that is, a movement towards economic expansion – increased exploration and exploitation of resources; growth of foreign capital investment in transportation technology – at a time when the growth of the staples economy simply could not be supported. He urged an adjustment of the tariff to alleviate regional economic disparities and, most important, a reassessment of the debt problem that had plagued Canadian economic development from the days of the fur trade.[53] Debts and the tariff were fundamental problems during the 1930s. They were problems with which the political economist could deal without being called upon to do the impossible:

that is, change the fundamental structures of Canada's marginal economy.

Innis's concern for constraints was not limited to his political economy. Rather, his later scholarship continued to be characterized by an attempt to identify and study those immutable features of historical process that determined change. He remained committed to the study of technology and industrialization as being fundamental to social development, and he continued to suggest methods of societal advancement. By the early 1940s Innis was awakened to the greater role of technology in society. He realized that, far from merely affecting material growth and decline, technology, in the form of media of communications, had became the most pervasive force affecting social development. Unlike transportation technologies, media of communications not only influenced material advancement, but also altered understandings and changed perceptions about the social-historical process. Above all, they distorted perspectives about society. Hence, they led social scientists astray in the pursuit of truth and in their efforts to comprehend social development. Communications technologies were, for Innis, a most dangerous source of cultural bias.

Innis's discovery of the media bias was highly significant. With this concept, he discovered the quintessential limitation that affected his own work and that of his colleagues. To understand media theory was to identify the source of bias and therefore to fulfil the basic purpose of the social scientist. Ultimately, the social scientist's role was to attempt to deal with communications by understanding their pernicious qualities. The study of media, in other words, enabled one to gain far-reaching insight into the social process; it therefore became the focus of Innis's later work.

Evidence of Innis's shift away from the neutral, static analysis of technology of his earlier career appears in his work of the late 1930s and early 1940s. In an important paper entitled 'The Penetrative Powers of the Price System,' Innis illustrated the impact of the price system in the emergence of 'neotechnic' industrialism and the cultural developments spawned by the 'new industrialism,' the most important of which were media of communications.[54] He saw a reflexive relationship between communications technology and the new industrialism in which communications technologies tended both to reflect and to facilitate the modern industrial capitalist state. The newspaper, for instance, had been co-opted in the new industrial order to foster the conditions (such as mass consumption) amenable to the growth of neotechnic society. Print media, in general, created 'patterns of public opinion or stereotypes' that fostered the conditions that 'appealed to the business mind.'[55]

In his work tracing the early development of the newspaper, furthermore, Innis expounded upon the pernicious effects of the printed word. Early in this century, the print industry, according to Innis, had achieved unprecedented control over the flow of information because of its unequalled power to disseminate information. Owing to technological advances, the newspaper became extraordinarily effective at 'informing' populations about social environments.[56] It succeeded in 'educating' humanity as to what was or was not valuable information. 'In a literal sense,' Innis asserted, 'wars are created as crime waves are created, by the newspaper';[57] journalists and their editors printed stories because of the story's marketability, not because of its accuracy or objective representation of reality. The proliferation of advertising, sensationalized and other forms of 'soft' news, and increases in subscriptions,[58] were additional manifestations of the print media's hold on the popular imagination. The print industry, along with newer, electronic communications media, imposed on an unsuspecting population a rigid understanding of the world by making available limited information. Science and technology, Innis added, not only improved the speed with which information was disseminated, but also selected the type of information distributed. 'Mechanized knowledge,' in the Innisian lexicon, referred to standardized world-views and the inability to escape a media-induced distortion of reality. It meant, in essence, an absence of liberty to develop independent assessments of one's environment. For Innis, then, the media curtailed understandings, outside and even within the academic world,[59] and entrapped populations into narrow assessments of reality. They represented the ultimate restriction on individual liberty to know and understand. Modern communications thus constituted the pre-eminent bias.

Innisian concepts of mechanized knowledge and the media bias originated in his early examinations of the printed word. The world that print media created and that Innis described – a world in which the media interfered with the perception of reality – is reminiscent of American journalist and social critic Walter Lippmann's theories on the 'pseudo-environment.' In *Public Opinion*, Lippmann created a dichotomy between truth and the popular view of reality. The latter, for Lippmann, was one in which the 'world outside' rarely conformed to the 'pictures inside our head' or 'pseudo-reality.' Focusing on the world of perceived realities, Lippmann argued that the half-truths of journalistic statement, designed more to sell papers than to inform or educate, characterized these pseudo-realities. Newspaper journalism had the power to create perceptions and understandings. In effect, it mediated reality through the creation of false environments. Most important, it established these pseudo-environments by shaping public opinion, itself a means to clarify a complex world and to provide ideas and viewpoints without which people would likely have no conception at all about surrounding events and social conditions. Public opinion, for Lippmann, was representative of a common or 'mass' world-view, 'simply ... an important part of the machinery of human communication.' As they did in the mechanization of knowledge, through public opinion the media created fictions to help to flesh out the mental images and interpreted events of those who had not experienced them. Thus, as they did in Innisian theory, they inserted 'between man and his environment' a pseudo-environment.[60] For both Lippmann and Innis, then, the basic cultural problem of the modern world was one of communication: instead of enhancing one's understanding of an increasingly complex world, media interceded in social relations in such a way as not only to interfere with the correct assessment of one's true environment, but also to dupe individuals into accepting mediated information as reality. Pseudo-environments fostered a false image of society. Because of their pervasiveness, modern media threatened to institutionalize pseudo-reality as a chief component of humanity's world-view.

If Lippmann's notion of public opinion anticipated Innis's concept of the monopoly of knowledge, then it also provided a foundation for the fundamental aspect of Innisian social science: the identification and elimination of bias. In both *Public Opinion* and *The Phantom Public* (1925) Lippmann proposed that the most informed members of society, social scientists, had a duty to expose false perceptions of realities. Their responsibility, in effect, was to reveal pseudo-environments. As Innis did a decade later, Lippmann demonstrated how the comprehension of false reality was the starting point in the discovery of truth. '[T]he study of error,' Lippmann asserted, was the 'introduction to the study of truth.' 'As our minds become more deeply aware of their own subjectivism,' he wrote, 'we find a zest in objective method that is not otherwise there. We see vividly, as normally we should not, the enormous mischief and casual cruelty of our prejudices ... There follows an emotional incentive to hearty appreciation of the scientific method, which otherwise is not easy to arouse and is impossible to sustain.'[61] As it was in Innis's conception, eliminating individual subjectivism was central to the achievement of objectivity and therefore the scientific understanding of social conditions. Like Innis, too, Lippmann saw as the ultimate purpose of the social scientist the breaking down of the prejudices that sustain a limited world-view, thereby addressing the problems inherent to modern culture, such as the press, propaganda, and ultimately public opinion. Both Innis and Lippmann were bent on establishing an approach that would ascertain the root causes of pseudo-environments. The quest for objectivity was the first important step in this mission.

For Innis, then, Lippmann's writings provided insight on the way entire cultures had been deceived and how social science played an important part in identifying and subsequently dealing with false perceptions of reality. The Innisian critique of modern media took from Lippmann's work its fundamental premise: the mediated existence resulted in the inability to see the world as it truly was, and only by recognizing this fact could humanity escape the effects of the media bias. Indeed, Innis's later work in communications theory owed much to the insights he gained from Lippmann on how 'media environments' became the means of mediating and indeed distorting the truth.[62]

Armed with Lippmann's insights, Innis undertook in earnest his critique of media of communications. True to his credo of avoiding limitations, he focused on the impact of media on historic societies instead of concentrating merely on the effects of modern communications. The only way to understand the modern bias, and thus to avoid falling under its spell, was to analyse eras that the modern media did not influence. Assessing the historical function of the communications bias, he argued, 'we [social scientists] are compelled to recognize the bias of the period in which we work ... The bias of modern civilization incidental to the newspaper and the radio presume a perspective in consideration of civilizations dominated by other media. We can do little more than urge that we must be continually alert to the implications of this bias and perhaps hope that consideration of the implications of other media to other civilizations may enable us to see more clearly the bias of our own.'[63] For this reason, Innis became concerned with the history of communications. He devoted the remainder of his academic career to examining the impact of communications on cultures.

To simplify, Innis's basic premise was that the means of communicating information rather than the information conveyed was essential to determining the nature of western civilizations. For Innis, communications technologies became important to study precisely because they intervened more than any other form of technology in the structuring of political and economic relationships. Each civilization throughout the history of the west was organized in accordance with the qualities and values associated with the notions of space or time. These spatial and temporal orientations constituted the 'media bias.' If a civilization's chief means of communication were spatially biased, such as paper or the printing press, then that society's social and political organization would also be concerned with spatial orientations: for example, the maintenance of imperial control over vast reaches of geographical space. Similarly, if the dominant form of communication were a durable medium, such as stone tablets or even the spoken word, the social organization of the culture would reflect a temporal bias, as is the case in a religiously oriented culture with time-biased institutions (churches). The dominant form of communication, in short, strongly influenced the social organizations, institutions, and cultural attributes of a society.[64]

Another fundamental premise of Innis's communication theory held that advances in technology of communication were the main determinants of change. Since media of communications shaped social and political organizations, a change in the means of communication entailed a change in the very make-up of civilizations. Innis showed how, throughout the history of the west, time-based cultures, such as Hellenic Greece, eventually gave way to spatially oriented civilizations, such as the Roman Empire, which, in turn, were superseded by the medieval world, all in accordance with the dictates of changing forms of communication technology. Similarly, the emergence of spatially biased modern society from medieval civilization was due to the advent of the printing press. Innis demonstrated, in brief, how the historical process was characterized by the replacement of one set of media-influenced conditions with another, usually of the opposite nature. This shift in bias was cyclical in nature in that spatial or temporal 'empires' rose and fell repeatedly, rarely existing in a relationship in which spatial and temporal forces balanced each other.

Whereas civilizations invariably decayed when new media were introduced, mid-twentieth century society proved anomalous: new media actually strengthened the existing monopoly of knowledge. To Innis, the most troublesome effect of modern communications media –

newspaper, film, and radio, among others – was that they oriented cultural and political institutions solely in terms of spatial qualities. This overemphasis on 'space' meant that 'temporal' values – the moral, the sacred, and the appreciation of the past – were beginning to disappear. The result was that humans, who had historically apprehended their social surroundings in relation to the interplay between spatial and temporal forces, could view their world only with reference to spatial concerns. Hence, they were preoccupied with the present, the future, the technological, and the secular. Recent technological innovations in the field of communications effectively destroyed temporal cultural values and replaced them with spatial values. 'The Western community,' Innis declared, referring to the printing press's impact on the technical-social relationships of the twentieth century, 'was atomized by the pulverizing effects of the application of the machine industry to communication.'[65] 'The overwhelming pressure of mechanization evident in the newspaper and the magazine,' he later wrote, 'led to the creation of vast monopolies of communication. Their entrenched positions involve a continuous, systematic, [and] ruthless destruction of elements of permanence [i.e., the values associated with time] essential to cultural activity. The emphasis on change is [now, with the advent of modern communications technology,] the only permanent character.'[66] Innis lamented that technology, in the form of communications media, reduced humanity's appreciation of time and tradition. The emergence of the new spatial monopoly created a paradox. Change, which pervaded modern industrial society, became the core value of the modern age. For Innis, thus, modern communications were at the root of the moderns' 'present-mindedness.'

Nowhere was the impact of modern technology more evident than in the academic's understanding of modern social conditions. Innis thought that print technology influenced civilization to such an extent that an appraisal of the functioning of media bias throughout the centuries became extremely difficult. 'The significance of a basic medium to its civilization,' he asserted, 'is difficult to appraise since the means of appraisal are influenced by the media, and indeed the fact of appraisal appears to be peculiar to certain types of media. A change in the type of medium,' he continued, 'implies a change in the type of appraisal and hence makes it difficult for one civilization to understand another.'[67] In other words, Innis argued that the impact of communications on each historical period distorted analysts' perceptions of the world. Because scholars fell prey to their socio-technical circumstances, it became difficult for them to understand the true nature of the media bias. Academics were inextricably bound to the intellectual and cultural environment that the prevailing media bias fostered. 'Media relativism' marred the efforts of intellectuals to comprehend past societies. It directed scholars to superimpose the values of their own culture on the civilizations under study. '[I]n using other cultures as mirrors in which we may see our own culture,' Innis claimed, 'we are affected by the astigma of our own eyesight and the defects of the mirror, with the result that we are apt to see nothing in other cultures but the virtues of our own.' Modern scholars thus suffered from the acute deficiency of being unable to appraise their own culture for what it was: a civilization with its own biases, its own distinct means of socio-political organization, and its own patterns of information transfer. Intellectuals, Innis concluded, were 'perhaps too much a part of the civilization which followed the spread of the printing industry to be able to detect its characteristics.'[68]

The space-biased monopoly of knowledge, which distorted perceptions and influenced institutions and values, was clearly reflected in the turmoil of the 1940s. The modern knowledge monopoly was manifested for Innis in the creation of an illiberal and undemocratic atmosphere in Canada and the west. Innis reviled governments' usurpation of additional 'wartime' powers. He considered these acts egregious infringements of liberty. Special controls in Canada, such as the War Measures Act, limited individual liberties while increasing the centralized authority of the state. For Innis and a few of his colleagues, the talk of war aims and of a new order after the war, sensitive to the needs of democracy, was nothing more than a smokescreen that obscured the realities of increased governmental controls and a manipulated democracy concerned with government by the few for the few and privileged.[69] With the resort to force and militarism during the war, Innis argued, society was unable to uphold the principles of freedom and democracy. 'We have resorted to force rather than persuasion,' he wrote in 1944, 'and to bullets rather than ballots.'[70]

Even worse than the increasingly illiberal atmosphere of wartime were governmental efforts to deceive populations into thinking that they contributed to the preservation of free and democratic societies. Through the vehicle of public opinion, Innis asserted (echoing Lippmann), government officials attempted to appeal to 'slogans in the interest of mass support.'[71] In this rabble-rousing climate, toleration and respect disappeared and the 'demagoguery of politicians' took over. With the aid of the press, nationalist rhetoric intensified and destroyed internationalism and the capacity for toleration and restraint. Ironically, to Innis, the rhetoric of politicians and propaganda machines 'educating' against the evils of Hitlerism contributed to the development of an illiberal, even Fascistic state at home. Innis, to be sure, loathed the emergence of a state in which power and control were pervasive features, allowing no room for counterbalancing forces to offset an increasing intolerant, undemocratic polity. He was an individualist who abhorred both the intervention of the state into the lives of individuals and a state in which bias and monopoly reigned supreme.

Innis principally objected to the rise of a cultural environment, in which state instruments, such as propaganda and public opinion, irrevocably influenced perceptions of reality. Falling prey to the propagandist, individuals lost the ability correctly to perceive their environment and to comprehend the debilitating effects of the war. Governments, in effect, controlled not merely the distribution of information but also directed the citizenry's understanding of the wartime world. Innis was profoundly concerned that propaganda and misinformed public opinion promoted and institutionalized biased understandings of current events. Above all, he feared that governments and press agencies, the institutions that put forth partial truths and proffered tainted information, monopolized the distribution of information so that there could be no balanced understanding of societal conditions.

The Second World War spurred Innis to action. It clearly showed the way that modern technology promoted biased understandings of current circumstances. It constituted for Innis far more than the loss of life or even the rise of unethical conduct;[72] it was associated with the rise of a monopoly of knowledge so pervasive that it interfered with moderns' freedom of thought and action. Innis comprehended that the mass media facilitated this anti-liberal wartime environment. He also knew that they made possible the widespread control over populations, whether through economic and political policies or through more direct measures, such as restrictions of personal liberties. Most significant, however, the war represented for Innis a period in which the media were so profoundly influential that moderns lost all reckoning of what had happened to society. In this media-induced haze they had become completely entrapped in their environment. That they accepted without question the validity of catch-phrases like 'making the world safe for democracy' exemplified this state of dissociation. Even the universities, the historic centres of creative thought, failed to understand the all-pervasiveness of limitations imposed on intellectual freedom. Academies, Innis declared, fell away even further from their old beliefs and yielded to the 'evils of monopolies in commerce and industry.'[73] All members of society had thus lost objectivity and the ability to comprehend what was happening around them. Summarizing the plight of the university and society at large, Innis wrote: 'The mechanization of modern society compels increasing interest in science and the machine, and attracts the best minds from the most difficult problems of western civilization. The machine is devoted to the simplification of these problems. The technological advances in communication shown in the newspaper, the cinema, and the radio demand the thinning out of knowledge to the point where it interests the lowest intellectual levels and brings them under the control of totalitarian propaganda.'[74] In the discourse on the impact of modern technology, the work of Harold Innis represents a departure. Concerned from the start with the role of technology in economic development, Innis soon realized the limitations of his earlier work, namely, the focus on material developments. He expanded the analysis of technique to discover the ways in which communications influenced historical cultural developments. Reacting against earlier materialist approaches, he began studying media as keys to the historical process. He endeavoured to comprehend how communications shaped societies, and hence he abandoned his value-neutral assessments of his staples period. From a historical point of view, he demonstrated the paradoxical nature of communications technology. He showed that communications technique inhibited the growth of free institutions and democratic societies, the hallmarks of high civilization. Most important, he displayed how it stifled free thought and, in turn, an understanding of the way modern media function. Historically diverse and pluralistic, knowledge had now become limited, circumscribed by the dictates of a centralizing, spatially oriented bias. Akin to a commodity, it was accessible only through tightly limited channels. For Innis, the modern media were thus ultimate instruments of control and centralization. As such, they constituted the bane of the modern age.

In its most advanced phase, Innis's technological critique centred on the pervasive and deceptive powers of communications technology. It involved a moral condemnation of both the type of society and the quality of thought that were produced in the modern, media-dominated civilization. It is significant that Innis's work diverged from the common assumptions of technology on which western society had developed. It indicted the 'will to technique,' a central ideology of the west, which exalted material advancement and equated technological advancement with cultural progress. Innis railed against the notion that human knowledge and technical achievement necessarily implied the democratization of culture and the enlargement of freedom. Indeed, he vigorously opposed the prevailing view of communications technologies;[75] instead, technology as it stood enslaved humanity and stifled human creativity. It wrested control of knowledge away from the individual and created a new dynamic inimical to human independence. It interfered in a most profound way with the individual and community consciousness and became, therefore, the most destructive cultural agent in modern times. Innis saw little good in the 'will to technique.' For this reason he devoted much of his later scholarship to the study of media of communications.[76]

Although Harold Innis may have overstated the case about the 'deliberalization' of western societies and the sweeping effects of the modern media, similar concerns engaged other Canadian intellectuals. Among these critics there was a sense that the war was an end-point from which arose a new control-oriented age. In a 1941 article historian Arthur Lower wrote about this new period. To Lower, the war had resulted in a 'vast increase in the edifice of control' over all aspects of life; 'at present,' he indicated, 'we have a very complete degree of political control: control of opinion, of personal freedom, assembly, organization, movement, and residence, and no great reverence for due process of law.' Lower continued, 'The innumerable boards and commissions thrown up by the war' were responsible for 'establishing mechanisms' to increase state control over the individual. The War Measures Act, moreover, 'a law which bestows complete and absolute power upon the dominion government,' was the main tool by which the state gained power over its citizens. Wartime restrictions on personal liberties signalled the emergence of a 'new kind of state' 'based upon control.' The 'unresolved problem,' he concluded, was whether that type of state would 'permit a free enquiry.'[77]

Fellow historian Donald Creighton shared Lower's concerns over the control-oriented state and the danger it posed to free thought. Writing in 1944, Creighton asserted that 'the war appear[ed] to have revealed certain unexpected weaknesses in the foundation of free speculation in Western society; and the present intensification of political power, as well as the vast extension of planning, may suggest other impending difficulties for the future.'[78] Like Innis and Lower, Creighton thought that wartime controls had gone too far, so much so, in fact, that 'the permanent values' were 'somewhat distorted, minimized, or overlooked in wartime.'[79]

Philosopher George Grant took an even more moralistic and fatalistic point of view. In a letter to his mother on the eve of the war he explained that 'War is becoming more supreme. Evil is completely predominant if you look anywhere. Force is being used on every side and everyone is hopelessly lost. Perhaps (although this is impossible for any government) force should be given up.'[80] Thus, to several observers the war seemed a turning point, one in which control-oriented democracies rivalled Fascist regimes abroad.

Musings about the advent of the control-oriented state were not simply empty rhetoric or the barbs of disaffected scholars against wartime educational policies.[81] Canada indeed had become extraordinarily centralized as a result of the war. In addition to overt measures such as the War Measures Act,[82] rationing, the regulation of wartime materials, and price controls, the government regulated businesses and labour, increased taxes, imposed controls on foreign exchange transactions, and gained control from the provinces over corporate and income taxes (under Wartime Tax Agreements, 1941), among a raft of other control measures. The dominion government, moreover, employed an army of civil servants to administrate the new powers. Numbering 46,000 in 1939, the bureaucracy in Ottawa had swelled to 116,000 by 1945. Crown corporations were established to acquire war materiel such as silk, uranium, and fuels, while they also ran diverse enterprises, such as airplane factories and telephone companies.[83]

The infrastructure of wartime controls did not disappear, moreover, at the cessation of hostilities. Most noticeably, clothing and food items, such as butter, meat, and preserves, continued to be rationed, and it was some time before the federal government restored taxation and other powers to the provinces. 'Reconstruction' and 'planning,' furthermore, watchwords in government and bureaucratic circles in an era of Keynesian post-war socio-economic development, protracted state control after 1945. Beginning in late 1943, it became clear that the central government would remain involved in key areas of social and economic planning. Fearing the resumption of the Depression and realizing the need to provide comprehensive social programs the King government endeavoured to translate wartime powers into the reconstruction period. These efforts culminated in the Dominion-Provincial

Conference on Reconstruction, where King's Liberals presented a plan to endow the central government with the financial power and legislative authority to guide Canada through the social and economic perils of the post-war period. Dissenting provinces charged that the dominion proposals were akin to the work of Hitler or Mussolini. Nevertheless, by 1947 the federal government had gained the power to continue to collect income taxes, in addition to succession and corporation taxes.[84] The federal government also enacted legislation in 1944 and 1945 to administrate demobilization grants to war veterans in sundry fields, such as education, business development, and agriculture, and it also enacted housing legislation, previously an area of provincial jurisdiction. While many in government circles lamented that reconstruction measures had not gone far enough, especially in social policies, it was clear that the government had succeeded in extending wartime controls past 1945.

Perhaps most important to the critics were governmental policies on higher education. Total war stimulated massive materiel requirements in terms of industrial and natural resources. There was a great need, therefore, for engineers and industrial technicians of all kinds to direct the war effort on the home front. The clamour for trained scientists, engineers, and health-care professionals by governments and the military meant that disciplines of practical value, that is, those disciplines deemed necessary to fight the war, rose in size and stature within university communities. Governments facilitated the growth of these so-called 'practical disciplines.' Premier George Drew, for instance, tried to alleviate the debt of Ontario universities so that they could better serve the needs of industry. Grants to Toronto ($816,000), Queen's, and Western ($250,000 each) were made, along with the important message that these gifts would become annual grants. To government and university officials, the materiel requirements of the Second World War indicated without a doubt the crucial importance of the applied and natural sciences to an industrial society. To emphasize the rise of the sciences, Principal Wallace of Queen's, declared in 1942 that 'The trend today is to science, applied science and medicine, and our best students follow that path.' 'The humanities,' he noted bluntly, 'are in eclipse in university life.'[85]

Receiving great impetus from the war, a 'culture of utility' had grown up around the modern university. Eager to show their usefulness in a time of crisis, the universities themselves were wont to emphasize the indispensable contributions they were making to the nation. Moreover, the war resulted in unprecedented publicity for the nation's universities. In 1945 the news magazine *Saturday Night* concluded that 'Learning as an end in itself [was] no longer valid in a nation which needs the minds of its youth for leadership in the rough new world to come.'[86] The news media pressured universities to foster the training of technicians and business leaders. Most of all, they reflected the prevailing popular opinion that universities ought to focus on training personnel for industry, government, and the professions and thus aid Canada's development in both war and peace.

This utilitarian view of higher learning was not universally appreciated. Shortly after 1939 concern had surfaced that university and governmental encouragement of the practical disciplines would erode the humanistic focus of Canadian universities. In late 1942 the Canadian Social Science Research Council (CSSRC) submitted to J.W. Pickersgill of the prime minister's office a brief, likely penned by Innis, outlining the effect of the war on higher education. In this brief particular attention was focused on the rise of sciences at the expense of the humanities. Most directly, it was a response to governmental policy of protecting university students, especially science students, from military service. Using classic rhetorical overstatement, Innis, in the brief,[87] condemned a government that seemed to be solely concerned with the practical components of higher learning:

> The Council strongly deprecates the tendency evident even in university circles to neglect the Humanities and to overemphasize the Natural Sciences. Recognizing the strong drift in that direction it appreciates its relation to the demands of the war effort, but wishes to point out the dangers of weakening the Arts tradition, the place of Humanities in modern democracy, and the possibility of losing on the home front as well as the war front in the struggle against authoritarian powers. Deterioration becomes rapid after the danger point has been reached and involves increasing problems with the continued length of the war. The neglect of the cultural standards of a generation of men in the war and in the postwar period is unfair to those who have participated and to the generation immediately following and has ominous implications for the whole future of civilization.

The CSSRC brief highlighted much more than the rivalry between university faculties for government funds and public recognition; it showed how the rise of technical education reflected the tendency to value material and technological advancement over equally important 'humanistic' social values. The triumph of the applied sciences over the arts reflected a society that had begun to turn its back on the seemingly less relevant liberal arts. Most of all, the struggle for prominence between the two main approaches to knowledge indicated a greater crisis of values in the western world. Diplomat and quasi-intellectual Vincent Massey explained that this malaise reflected a 'crisis in education.' At the root of both crises, he reasoned, was the imbalance of the values of technological society, a predisposition to favour technical over humanistic learning. Massey wanted the balance redressed. The universities, he wrote,[88] had a 'very ancient and very vital function to perform in the field of the humanities. Technological and scientific progress had not made this function obsolete: it has made it more necessary ... It is obvious that technology is of tremendous importance in modern life, but while it is a good and necessary servant it must not be allowed to become our master. No one passing through a university should fail to come under the influence of the humanities, because it is in this field – that of liberal education – that the student is enabled to acquire a true sense of values, to understand something about the relation of man to society, to distinguish between the real things in life and the fakes, to put first things first, and to sharpen his mental curiosity.'

Philosopher Grant also entered the debate, asking in 1950: 'Can it be doubted that Canadian universities today exist essentially as technical schools for the training of specialists?' Even humanistic disciplines such as history, the classics, and European literature were treated as technical subjects with no regard for 'the sweep of our spiritual tradition.'[89] Institutions of higher learning could scarcely be called 'universities,' in Grant's opinion, given the preponderance of technical disciplines and the highly specialized nature of modern scholarship. In a paper tellingly subtitled 'What Can the Humanities do for Government?' Creighton, referring specifically to the role of the historian, added his voice to those of Massey and Grant. 'Obviously,' he began, 'in an age characterized by the enormous prestige of the physical and social sciences ... and what is reverently described as "know-how," the claims made for the humanities can hardly be exclusive and monopolistic. But they are nevertheless very considerable, and it is perhaps not inappropriate that an historian should try to restate them.' Creighton speculated, commenting on the importance of the humanities to the art of government, 'whether the humanities would have lent themselves to such monstrous perversions' as the Second World War. 'One some-

times wonders,' he added caustically, 'whether if the old liberal education had continued its old sway, the modern world would have had so
many illiterate megalomaniacs as leaders, and whether such a cowed
and intellectually humiliated civil service would have been tolerated,
so often and in so many countries.'[90] As was true for Massey, Grant,
and the members of the CSSRC, Creighton comprehended the inestimable benefits of a 'liberal education.' He understood the impact of a
system of 'technical' learning and a society that championed the virtues of industrial-technological society over those associated with the
liberal arts tradition. For these critics, in short, the culture of utility was
further evidence of the predominance of the will to technique.

The debate over the validity of technical education was certainly not
confined to Canada; it was very much alive south of the border. Robert
Maynard Hutchins, president (1929–45) and chancellor (1945–51) of the
University of Chicago, was perhaps the most ardent critic of technical
specialization in American universities. Hutchins, like the Canadian
critics, maintained that education was incomplete if it did not refer to
the humanities' literary and humanistic inheritance.[91] He argued, furthermore, that specialized learning filled students with an ever-
expanding body of facts while it discouraged contemplation and wisdom. Specialization monopolized one's intellectual outlook and hence
made difficult, even impossible, open-mindedness, objectivity, and, in
its turn, a will to search for truth.[92] Scientific training was insufficient
to an understanding of social conditions; for it directed students and
scholars away from wider issues and emphasized instead technical
knowledge and other narrow forms of enquiry. To escape the deleterious effects of specialization, he concluded, the educational system
must be changed to promote 'cultural courses' with the effect of counterbalancing scientific education. Like his Canadian counterparts, in
sum, Hutchins was interested in a return to the values of the traditional liberal arts curriculum and ultimately in a reversal of direction
for higher learning.[93]

Hutchins's views on technical education were influential in the
1940s and the 1950s. They resulted in the greater awareness of the
plight of the humanities at Chicago and other American universities.
They also had considerable currency among Canadian intellectuals.[94]
Hutchins had a special impact on literary critic Herbert Marshall
McLuhan. McLuhan, a humanist himself, appreciated Hutchins's
humanism. To McLuhan, Hutchins stood for the Ciceronian ideal: education was designed to produce citizens with a wide learning, alert to

social problems. He accepted Hutchins's critique of specialization and his view that the individual had become nothing more than 'a technological functional unit in the state.'[95] McLuhan's affinity with Hutchins's position reflected his own humanist and moralist leanings of the 1940s and early 1950s.

Although Hutchins's humanism was more than palatable, McLuhan found the Chicago academic's educational approach unsatisfactory. In fact, he despised Hutchins's and Mortimer Adler's Great Books program, because this approach overemphasized the study of literary classics while ignoring the 'unofficial program of education,' 'carried on by commerce through the press, radio, and movies; only through a study and critique of unofficial education could the scholar comprehend the 'native and spontaneous culture in our industrial world' and, moreover, 'effect contact with past cultures.'[96] The study of the greats was only 'part of the solution';[97] it had to be supplemented with a study of modern culture replete with the analysis of contemporary cultural forces. Only by gaining insight into one's own culture could one become conversant with cultures of the past.[98] True to his own credo, McLuhan set about understanding the unofficial education of contemporary culture.[99]

By the mid-1940s McLuhan had turned away from literary studies and focused instead on a critique of the cultural role of technology.[100] Like Harold Innis, he presented a highly moralistic appraisal of technology and warned that the will to technique was at the core of the corruption of western values. Writing at the end of the war, McLuhan demonstrated the influence of technology to standardize human outlooks. Technology's most profound effect on modern society, he claimed, was the creation of 'the common man,' the unification of all humans as basic consumers. Modern advertising, a salient factor in the emergence of the common man, established witticisms, symbols, and behaviour patterns, as well as a common language of discourse. It provided, in other words, a shared experience. Advertising also altered existing perceptions of reality to accord with advertising strategies. 'The ad-man's rhetoric,' McLuhan declared, 'has knocked the public into a kind of groggy, slap-happy condition' in which 'are cushioned' the 'brutal shocks' of social realities. As evidence of this confused condition McLuhan showed how freedom for North Americans did not necessarily mean free and just government. Rather, according to the advertising ethos, liberty consisted largely of 'ignoring politics and worrying about defeating underarm odour, scaly scalps, hairy legs ...

[and] saggy breasts.' Through educating humans as to what to eat, how to look, and what to do, print media advertising fostered a homogenized, 'commercial culture.' Above all, it facilitated totalitarian control; for it allowed advertising executives and others to engineer society and, in a more insidious fashion, to alter perceptions and divert attention from pressing problems.[101] Echoing Lippmann and Innis and alluding to the idea of pseudo-environments, McLuhan thus expounded upon the pervasiveness of power and control in the industrial age.

For McLuhan, commercial culture concealed the cerebral needs of humankind. Reducing humanity to its 'lowest common denominator as consuming animal,' technology thwarted rightful human pursuits, such as the cultivation of speech and culture and, most broadly, the acquisition of the 'heritage of our entire civilization.' Nevertheless, McLuhan implored moderns to contemplate the humanistic virtues of literature and other artistic endeavours so as to establish a 'sense of communion, and wisdom for the common race,' and to regain the sense of true humanity.[102] Indeed, books such as *The Mechanical Bride: Folklore of Industrial Man* represented efforts to understand the processes by which 'the very considerable currents and pressures set up around us today by the mechanical agencies of the press, radio, movies and advertising.'[103] Only in accepting social forces, he reasoned, could intellectuals comprehend new realities with a view to overcoming them. In this way, moderns could realize the standardizing impact of the machine and begin to come to terms with '*Time*, *Life*, and *Fortune*' and other 'sinister portents' in the 'Century of the Common Man.'[104]

In *The Mechanical Bride*, McLuhan further developed his notion of the cultural role of technology. Technology redefined humans' relations not only with one another but also to industrial society. Through mass media, it created a new, servo-mechanistic relationship in which man became servant, and, in effect, it dictated the nature and pace of modern life. Technology was both invasive and enslaving. While it affected virtually every aspect of life, moderns neither understood nor cared about the effects of machine culture. Humankind simply unwittingly acquiesced to it. Commenting on the apathy directed towards modern technology and the insidious and illiberal characteristics of the mechanized age, McLuhan declared: 'A huge passivity has settled on industrial society. For people carried about in mechanical vehicles, earning their living by waiting on machines, listening much of the waking day to canned music, watching packaged movie entertainment and capsulated news, for such people it would require an exceptional degree of awareness and an especial heroism of effort to be anything but supine consumers of processed goods.' Through consumer conformity, technology, in its many guises, robbed humans of their individuality and freedom to understand the world. It was an 'abstract tyrant' that carried its 'ravages into deeper recesses of the psyche than did [for primitive humans] the saber-tooth tiger or the grizzly bear.'[105]

For McLuhan, technology was also responsible for profound social change. He argued that it implied 'constant social revolution.' In the recent past, for instance, the two world wars had 'led to an unimaginable acceleration of every phase of technology – especially advancing the universal social revolution which is the inevitable result of the impact of machines on human rhythms and social patterns.' Although McLuhan failed to explain the interplay between technological and social transition – his early studies were not much more than observations of the societal impact of technology – he was certain that technological advancement implied an acceleration of social change. Further, he contended that the advancement of technology was so pronounced in the recent past and humanity so profoundly altered by technological change that humans existed in a 'trance-like condition,' unable to appreciate the social effects of technology. Unlike times of prior 'social revolutions,' where humans could at least identify the nature and impetus of social change, the mid-twentieth century was so mired in the conformity of consumerism and other homogenizing effects of modern technology that social realities were extremely difficult to comprehend. Because the dynamic of the modern world had changed to make life 'increasingly a technological rather than social affair,' there were no more 'remote and easy perspectives.' Ultimately, there was no way to understand reality except through comprehending the role of technology. He concluded that humankind was embroiled in a 'technological nightmare' from which the only hope of escaping was to be aware of the pervasive effects of the machine.[106]

Although lacking the same sophistication, McLuhan's view of 'technology as tyrant' echoed the Innisian monopoly of knowledge and Innis's strictures on the stultifying nature of modern technology. It reflected an Orwellian world-view in which a technologically dominated society was embodied in the omnipresent 'Big Brother,' that is, in the triumph of technology, to create a totalitarian existence. Technology for McLuhan, as for George Orwell and Innis, was a facilitator that made possible the imposition of totalitarian controls on an unsuspecting populace. Ultimately, as Orwell had done in *Nineteen Eighty-Four*,

McLuhan expounded on the need to change the course of history lest humanity lose its human qualities and become a mass of soulless automatons, perpetually ignorant of its new plight. Like those of other like-minded critics, his was a dire warning indeed.

McLuhan's cynicism reflected a world in which the horrors of totalitarian regimes were still fresh. Even more, his critique mirrored a post-war society concerned more with consumerism and consumption than with issues of enduring relevance. The post-war period into the 1950s was one of great material prosperity for North America. Not only had Canada escaped the ravages of another economic downturn, it had emerged from the war with a vibrant economy characterized in part by a boom in consumer consumption. Owing much to a large increase in population (due to immigration and the so-called baby boom), consumers found a release for the pent-up demand of the previous era and bought houses, cars, and a plethora of other, smaller consumer items, such as radios, television sets, and products that reflected the shift in demographics to a younger population – Hula Hoops and Davy Crockett hats. Suburbanization was also a new phenomenon and it led to the construction of malls, schools, and roads. It meant a boom in new- and used-car sales; for suburban neighbourhoods were often located far from the workplace and off major routes of public transportation. Aided by intense and sophisticated ad campaigns, 'materialism,' in a word, 'became a deeply imbued social ethic' in post-war Canadian society.[107]

While many Canadians basked in the warm glow of material prosperity, there emerged by the late 1940s a strong reaction against the increasingly material and secular outlooks of Canadians. For Vincent Massey, the great transformation that Canada had undergone in the post-war era was due in large measure to material growth and an economic resurgence. 'We are no longer poor,' he announced at one of his several post-war addresses as governor-general. 'Canada in truth has been passing through a period of economic expansion unparalleled hitherto in extent, diversity and duration.' The dominion, he implied, verged on economic superpower status, which gave it international clout and helped to build the nation. Massey was quick to note, however, that material expansion was only one aspect of Canada's post-war development. Growth in 'matters of mind and of the spirit,' he commented, was the most significant aspect of national development. Indeed, Massey hoped that material advancement would be 'matched by knowledge and wisdom'; that Canada, in other words, would be characterized as much by intellectual and artistic accomplishments as by economic prowess.[108]

Massey did have misgivings. The balance between material and spiritual concerns had been gravely disrupted after the war, and materialism had been overemphasized at the expense of the intellect, free thought, and the other-worldly. For Massey, evidence of this decline of spiritual values existed in the 'humanities crisis.' The sundering of the humanities and of the philosophic tradition were the direct results of the rise of the applied and pure sciences. The demise of the humanities, according to Massey, reflected greater social realities. 'The neglect of the humanities [was] not a cause but a symptom of an age lured by science into the delights of materialism – for those who regard the pursuit of the humanities as a luxury, consider the automobile, the frigidaire and the TV set as necessities which no self-respecting family would be without.'[109] The demise of humane values in relation to material concerns demonstrated with disconcerting clarity the 'whole climate of opinion' of the consumer society.

In an unpublished paper written in late 1949 Innis also questioned the advent of post-war materialism. His primary intention was to study the reasons for which western society had come to have such a 'high regard for material things.' Tracing its historical origins, he argued that materialism, established as a 'universal value in the nineteenth century' in North America, had increased its scope through advertising and the media and because of the availability of resources. Like Massey, however, Innis was critical of the materialist ethic of modern society. Exacerbated by the media and commercialism, the ever-increasing concern with materialism presented moderns with a grave problem: the consumer orientation of society had developed to such an extent that it had become 'impossible [for moderns] to stop demanding new resources.'[110] Most important, materialism was such a part of the modern ethos that it threatened the existence of non-material values. Materialism, in other words, had become so ingrained in the psyche of western humanity that a concern for opposite values – tradition, beauty, and spirituality – were being lost. Indeed, Innis's admitted obsession with the values of 'time' spoke to an age increasingly characterized by the drive towards material acquisition and resource exploitation.[111]

Of the critiques of materialism, that of George Parkin Grant was one of the most detailed and profoundly thought out. Grant, Massey's nephew, had picked up his disdain for industrial life during his time in England, where he saw first hand the ravages of a long-lived industrial system. Furthermore, his grandfather, George Munro Grant, had greatly influenced his perception of industrial development. Writing around the turn of the century, G.M. Grant acknowledged the great strides Canada had made economically, but he questioned whether too great an emphasis had been placed on economic development and not enough on the cultivation of the minds and souls of men and women. Is Canada to be a 'city of pigs,' he wondered, or 'is it to be a land of high-souled men and women?' The elder Grant concluded that owing to a 'vulgar and insolent materialism of thought and life,' Canada had lost its moral focus and had been reduced to a consuming, unreflective mass of humanity.[112] So akin to G.P. Grant's social philosophy and so relevant to the ongoing struggle between matters of mind and the material world, the elder Grant's comments easily could have been uttered half a century later and been attributed to his grandson.

More than his grandfather, his uncle, or any other observer, G.P. Grant expressed his critique of the material world in terms of the process of secularization. For Grant, the almost obsessive concern with things material resulted in a rejection of the other-worldly. Ironically, this concern for materialism had its roots in religion itself, namely, Puritan Protestantism. Characteristic of Protestantism in North America, Grant's argument was that Calvinism had originally promoted piety and biblical truth, but over time, 'it destroyed its own spirit.' Intended to marry the secular and the other-worldly, the reformist spirit eventually lost a sense of the transcendent. As it did so, it began to 'take the world ever more as an end in itself.'[113] As the Protestant vision of the Kingdom of God on Earth declined, there remained only the idea that humanity can change the world for the better. Shorn of its religiosity and its focus on the afterlife, the reformed Protestant tradition was akin more to hedonism than to a combination of the secular and religious. Lamentably for Grant, the hedonism of mid-twentieth-century English Canada was in large part the product of reformed Christianity.

The most pernicious effect of reformed Protestantism was the promotion of a new concept of liberty. In 'The Uses of Freedom,' Grant explained that the basic conception of freedom of the reformed tradition – the introduction of the truth of Christ in the lives of humans – had been transformed: simply, 'the ability to change the world' without reference to Christian beliefs. Instead of gaining liberation through communion with God and religious mysticism, secular-oriented humans sought to gain control over earthly circumstances as a primary way to achieve liberty.[114] In mastering their physical conditions and therefore improving material circumstances, moderns, according to Grant, believed that they had freed themselves from the exigencies of the natural world and solved the puzzle of human survival. Freedom had become nothing more than liberation of humankind from the uncertainties of natural life and the imposition of order and control over material conditions.

Essential to this liberal-secularist conception of freedom, science and technology were instrumental in gaining mastery over nature. A critical epistemological change in modern history, scientific knowledge displaced religion as 'the only true knowledge'; 'it teaches one,' Grant claimed, 'how to change the world.'[115] To exploit natural resources and secure material growth, moreover, westerners had to alter their understanding of the uses of scientific knowledge, which was not, he explained, sought after for the pleasure of the mind; it was not an end in itself. Rather, this type of knowledge was a means of gaining practical benefits; above all, science was merely an instrument moderns used – first to understand nature and then to gain a measure of control over it.

Grant realized that the knowledge of technique had become integral to the modern world-view. Moderns, he argued, defined themselves in relation to technological and scientific advances. 'Technique comes forth and is sustained in our vision of ourselves as creative freedom,' Grant later wrote, 'making ourselves and conquering the chaos of an indifferent world.' Modern life was thus founded on the 'technological myth,' the idea that 'man has finally come of age in the evolutionary process,' since 'he has taken fate into his own hands and is freeing himself for happiness against the old necessities of hunger and disease and overwork.'[116] Society's ultimate 'good,' the moral conception upon which philosophy in the mass age was based, thus was founded in the freedom that science and technology engendered.

Not only did moderns define themselves in terms of 'technological freedom,' but they also propagated a technological world-view.[117] As Innis and others did, Grant attributed the rise of technical training to the perceived needs of government and industry. He realized that compared with the sciences, the humanities were neglected in funding and recognition. Above all, he criticized the penchant for preferring the study of the physical world over 'the study of the deeper questions of human existence.'[118] Grant lamented the decline of the philosophical and artistic traditions of the university, a trend that indicated the pervasiveness of new forces in industrial society that emphasized the current and the active and ignored the spiritual traits of humanity. Grant observed that the philosophic understanding of the good life 'simply for its own sake ... was neglected as archaic. To see the world in its wholeness was the equivalent to many of seeing the progress in our mechanical inventiveness. The more Canada has become part of the scientific society of the west, the more it has partaken of the ideas such as these, and the tragedy of its youth has been that the bond of tradition have been less strong with us than elsewhere.' 'Mass industrialism,' he went on to say, promoted certain ideas that had an 'almost incalculable spiritual change in the west.' Most irksome to Grant, moderns elevated materialist over contemplative values and hailed a life of action rather than one of thought and reflection. Like most pioneering countries, Canada had been predisposed towards material values and had little appreciation of philosophic enquiries.[119]

Despite efforts to understand this philosophic malaise, the 'mass world' ultimately had forsaken a 'philosophic approach.'[120] Even philosophers themselves, who had been entrusted to discover good and God's purpose in the world, fell prey to the new technological ethic. According to Grant, philosophers abrogated their responsibility as social critics and moral leaders of the community. Expounding on theories on positivism and pragmatism and separating philosophy and theology, Canadian philosophers, like their counterparts elsewhere, effectively made 'philosophy the servant rather than the judge of man's scientific abilities.'[121] Becoming a 'technical study,' philosophy forgot its historical origins and succumbed to the dictates of the mass society. Philosophy in Canada contributed to (instead of preventing) the development of universities as 'technical institutes.' As such, it reflected the all-pervasive character of the modern technological imperative.

As did several of his contemporaries, George Grant bemoaned the centrality of technology in the lives of moderns. In defining 'what we are,' technology, for Grant, alienated the individual from his true self because it reduced his higher, philosophical goals to the mere objective of obtaining technological freedom. People had thus became servants to the machine. Indeed, technology redefined the individual's outlooks and goals; most of all, it gave primacy to the singular objective of technological progress. People thus lacked liberty because the pursuit of technological advancement and scientific freedom became their 'dominant activity.' That dominance, Grant concluded, 'fashion[ed] both public and private realms' to the exclusion of the pursuit of other societal 'goods.'[122] Describing the illiberalities of the technological society, Grant proclaimed:[123] 'every instrument of mass culture [was] a pressure alienating the individual from himself as a free being ... The individual [became] ... an object to be administered by scientific efficiency experts ... Modern culture, through movies, newspapers and television, through commercialized recreation and popular advertising, force[d] the individual into the service of the capitalist system around him.' Philosophically, moderns understood nothing more than the pursuit of the specious truth of technological freedom. Ultimately, this false world-view trapped them into a monolithic, stultifying, and necessarily limited view of themselves and of their society.

Grant also objected to the sway of technology over modern value systems. His greatest indictment of modernity was that technological liberalism had become the sole 'truth' of modern philosophy. Uniquely modern, technological liberalism gained pre-eminence because it obscured other truths and philosophical traditions. It therefore stymied moderns' contemplation of different systems of thought. Ultimately, it circumscribed what they could think or believe; indeed, moderns comprehended their world only in the narrow terms that the technological ethos had established. Emphasizing these points, Grant claimed that 'the drive to the universal and homogeneous state remains the dominant ethical "ideal" to which our contemporary society appeals for meaning in its activity. In its terms society legitimizes itself to itself. Therefore any contemporary man must try to think the truth of this core of political liberalism, if he is to know what it is to live in this world.'[124]

As Innis and others believed, moderns, for Grant, had become metaphorically entrapped within their age. The technological imperative, to whose development they contributed, barred them from seeing beyond their own limited values and verities. Technological liberty had displaced the appreciation of timeless, transcendent truths. This philosophical transition had been so complete that society (including its scholars) mistook materialism and secularization for transcendent truth. Because of the technological credo, Grant and other critics reasoned, moderns were living a pseudo-reality replete with an illusory set of values that championed technical advancement and material prosperity. In its most pernicious form, the technological imperative was thus much more than a physical transformation. Instead, it implied a profound epistemological transition. It created a climate of ignorance, a consciousness that incorporated outlooks that had sundered transcendent values and redefined belief systems. Consumerism, the culture of consumption, and ever-increasing exploitation of natural resources were omnipresent reminders of the triumph of new values and false perceptions of reality. The technological consciousness, in a word, was indicative of the fall of western society.

At the turn of the century, a time of rapid economic and industrial expansion, most Canadians viewed science and technology as positive and progressive. The scientific-technological complex, modern Canadians thought, was integral to the betterment of civilization. Ideas of progress, expressed increasingly in the advancement of the human condition, were linked to material circumstances. Unfazed by total war, the nineteenth-century view of technology continued to define Canadians' attitudes towards science and technology. Reflected in growing consumerism and in a faith in expertise and social sciences, the technological imperative had come to characterize the modernization of Canadian society. Like other western industrial nations, Canada had gained all the ideological trappings of an urban-industrial society.

Reflecting on Canada's recent development, Malcolm Wallace, president of University College, characterized the modern era as one of change resulting from the 'role which science had come to play in our daily lives.' He claimed that changes in government and educational standards, changes in daily routines, and, indeed, changes in values and outlooks all were effects of science and technology. Science, he argued, had increased 'human productivity of goods to an incredible extent,' so that moderns could 'enjoy comforts and conveniences hitherto undreamed of.' He hastened to add, power and wealth, the products of scientific materialism, 'exercised a kind of intoxication over the imaginations of men.' While he understood the benefits of science, the 'scientific society' definitely had for Wallace a foreboding quality. After all, it had produced the Holocaust and the atom bomb and, as such, had guaranteed the ever-increasing and devastating scope of future war. Through providing more and better goods and, most dangerously, providing access to the levers of power, science, despite appearances to the contrary, had become 'the god of our idolatry.'[125]

Not everyone in Canadian society had come to accept without question Canadian cultural development. In their social critiques and theories intellectuals such as Innis, McLuhan, and Grant took pains to underscore the negative aspects of science and technology. Indeed, their works constitute strident rejections of the prevalent view of science and technology and objections to a modern condition that lauded technique as if it were a god. The technological critics acknowledged the role of science and technology to effect historical change and to facilitate a culture of utility that began to characterize Canadian society. Surely, technology had determined in large measure the nature of the modern world. Yet critics warned against the will to technique. They challenged materialism, secularism, consumerism, and other values associated with the scientific society. Most of all, they recognized that the insidious effects of science and technology created false impressions about the nature of 'the world outside.' Innis, McLuhan, and Grant questioned modern technology so vociferously not because they were technophobes, modern-age Luddites who wanted only to turn the clock back to simpler times. They did not oppose technology per se, rather, they preached against a force they believed was responsible for creating a false reality that drained from its adherents all recognition of truth and objectivity. They feared, above all, the consequences of technology-inspired false environments. They were afraid to exist in a world with no objective truth or means to circumvent technological environments. The technological society, in short, was a dismal 'pseudo-utopia' in which its inhabitants submitted unquestioningly to the dictates of the machine.

Veracity of theories and points of view aside, it is possible to understand how a highly critical view of science and technology could emerge in Canada alongside the more enduring 'liberal' conception. The views of the technological critics truly reflected the rise of Canada as a materialist, secularist nation. Canada had indeed undergone a tremendous socio-economic transformation in the first half of the twentieth century. Concerns over material development had characterized, in large measure, Canada's quest for nationhood in this period, and attitudes on the merits of economic advancement, carried over from previous times, began to intensify in a country increasingly engrossed in its material circumstances. These concerns were manifested in terms of a preoccupation with practicalities in Canadian universities, and in the predominance of political economy in Canadian social science. During the Second World War, because of the ever-increasing need for expertise to run a bloated bureaucracy and the materiel requirements of modern warfare, it had become easy to neglect long-standing issues of cultural development and to focus instead on production and efficiency. After 1945, with attention turned towards reconstruction and the application of Keynesian economic strategies, the time still did not seem right to address the larger issues of cultural development. Finally, in the context of an unprecedented and prolonged economic expansion and a growing and, for the first time, largely well-off population, it had seemed to many that Canada had finally arrived as a nation, if it had not achieved a quasi-utopian state. The focus on the materialism of a culture, by now totally enmeshed in material progress, seemed at last to have paid dividends. The post-war era was a period in which mate-ralist values became one of the most potent defining features of Can-ada's national character. This triumph of materialism was amplified in the views and thoughts of proponents, opponents, and the disinter-ested within Canada's burgeoning materialist culture.

3

The Modernization of Higher Learning in Canada I

During the years from 1890 to 1920 the university in English-speaking Canada underwent considerable change. Until the late nineteenth century, universities had been cultural outposts responsible for inculcating the values of British civilization in students living in North America. They were denominational institutions whose main duty was both to help to develop a 'dutiful, morally sound social order' and to allow a certain class of individuals within society 'access to the "higher" forms of learning.' Although applied and pure sciences had gained in importance by the end of the century, the liberal arts still dominated curricula. The study of the literary 'greats' and, more generally, the acquisition of a classical education were the main objectives of the vast majority of university students. The universities' reason for being was, after all, 'to provide a given generation access to the inherited wisdom of the ages and to the major branches of knowledge.'[1]

Universities had changed substantially by 1920. Canadian society, as we have seen in chapter 2, quickly evolved from an agrarian, resource-based economy to a relatively urban and industrial society, dependent on ever more important manufacturing and service industries. Institutional development reflected the socio-economic transition. The universities were no exception. Their development in the first two decades of the twentieth century mirrored the needs of an urban-industrializing nation. Commenting on the considerable change of the previous few decades, the University of Toronto chancellor, Sir Robert Falconer, noted in the summer of 1921 that 'the educational sky is thickly studded' with 'schools of agriculture, education, commerce, dentistry, pharmacy, journalism, [and] nursing.' Falconer argued, furthermore, that several newer pursuits, such as optometry and osteopathology, also were poised to be recognized as disciplines. While 'the old-established faculties' gave the 'University its character,' he concluded, extending the astronomical metaphor, '[n]ew stars being drawn into the orbit of older planets make an impressive constellation.'[2] Through the incorporation of new programs, the broadly based university whittled away at the liberal arts focus of Canadian universities. Like other larger Canadian universities, such as McGill and Queen's, Falconer's University of Toronto had to come to terms with the emergence of a multi-faculty university. With the growth of the scientific and professional schools, the introduction of commerce and extension programs, the building of new and elaborate research facilities, and a new-found focus on scientific research, Falconer accepted the fact that the Victorian university had vanished, replaced by new-style educational institutions that would meet the exigencies of a modernizing society. The age of the full-service institution had dawned.

No longer centres of moral guidance and classical learning, by 1914 universities, traditionally responsible for social issues, took on a new, strictly utilitarian alignment. Although greatly underdeveloped by British and American standards, the Canadian social sciences emerged as a means by which scholars and researchers could dispassionately assess socio-economic change and remedy industrial problems. University officials increasingly recognized the fact that social studies could contribute to Canadian social development. Research on socio-economic issues, for instance, took up much of the time of O.D. Skelton of Queen's University. James Mavor, head of Toronto's Department of Political Economy, attempted to convince students and fellow faculty members of the growing governmental reliance on social scientists for guidance in the policy-making of government officials. McGill principal, Sir Arthur Currie, proposed the establishment at his institution of a public administration program that the dominion and provincial governments could draw on for social service experts. At the University of Toronto, social scientists submitted a proposal to the senate to create a school of social service to 'investigate the problems of poverty and philanthropy, crime and its prevention, and government and its administration.' The members of the arts faculties were concerned about growing social problems and hoped to apply their training and expertise to 'alleviating social misfortune and remedying social maladjustment.'[3] At the Second Congress of the Universities of the Empire, Currie best summed up the new-found willingness of universities to develop programs to deal with social issues. He declared that 'times had changed' and that McGill's 'educational system must change with them if it is to serve a new environment.' Ancient knowledge must continue, he noted, but the new learning that had changed 'the face of the world' must be added to it. For Currie and others, it was through social studies that principles and theories could be best applied to meet the exigencies of modern life. They were the foundations on which society could be understood, and indeed transformed, so as to create new and progressive social environments.[4] Most significant, they entailed the scientific appraisal of society and an efficient means of reconstructing it. Thus, the social scientist could help to re-form society and give it the social stability it so desperately needed.

More important to the new utilitarian orientation of the universities was the advent of the applied sciences and scientific research. As we saw in the last chapter, the research ideal had become entrenched in Canadian universities by 1914. The Great War had provided added impetus to augment industrial research at the universities. To many advocates of the research ideal, the war had demonstrated beyond doubt the significance of scientific research. It also showed, however, that Canadian universities lacked the scientists and research facilities to provide for national security or to facilitate rapid industrialization. At McGill, for example, authorities concluded that science in all its branches must be taught to make up for the paucity of scientific specialists and research students killed in action.[5] The registrar and principal of Queen's argued, moreover, that the 'Universities of Canada should concern themselves with research in pure and applied science,' areas of enquiry that constituted 'the basis on which all industrial research must be laid.' 'The ideal duty of the Universities,' they contended, was to respond to the changing needs of industrial society by developing programs and facilities to contribute to new knowledge in the sciences. Lacking sufficient resources in the past, the 'Universities should be equipped and staffed to train the new army of researchers who are to assist in the application of science to Canadian industry.' To meet the challenges of the new age, they concluded, Canada must be prepared to emulate Germany's unwavering commitment to pure and applied science. Furthermore, it must expand and create a centralized control over industrial research in the universities, so as to be counted among the great industrialized nations.[6] For their champions, industrial research and development were not issues that impinged upon the evolution of the universities themselves; they were matters that affected the entire pace and direction of national development.

Outside the universities the general public also stressed the practical functioning of the university. By the end of the First World War, Canadians began to weigh traditional academic values against the notion of the university as a bastion of industrial knowledge and technical personnel. The *Canadian Annual Review* (CAR), for instance, noted that while the Canadian university still retained its British liberal arts traditions, a 'fabric of up-to-date, modern technical, commercial, industrial, agricultural and business instruction' had recently overlaid the older system of higher learning. Canadian universities, in the words of CAR editor Castell Hopkins, were attempting to 'keep up with developments around them' in a rapidly changing commercial and industrial world while maintaining Old World traditions and culture. Hopkins concluded that the universities were being 'influenced by public opinion' now more than ever, and the Canadian population was much more interested in activities such as the development of agriculture, the building of railways, the sinking of mines, and the 'transformation of the raw material into marketable, usable, products' than they were in 'the mission of Oxford or Cambridge.'[7] As was true for a growing number of university authorities, Hopkins understood not only the ever-closer relationship between higher learning and industrial society, but also the impact of public perceptions on the university's development.

Despite the progress of the technical schools, the humanities remained at the core of the university throughout the interwar era. Nevertheless, technical and professional instruction became increasingly central. As an observant Toronto *Mail* journalist indicated, Canadian universities after 1918 were torn between the British 'cultural' model and the newer, American model of higher education, which increasingly facilitated technical education and produced the knowledge, personnel, and equipment to meet the needs of an advanced industrial society.[8] Indeed, a struggle ensued between the two competing notions of higher learning, with individuals on both sides of the debate arguing the merits and demerits of 'technical education.' The history of the Canadian university in the interwar period was, as a result, marked by an uncertainty as to the basic purpose of the university. By the end of the 1930s, however, it had become clear that the public, governments, and university officials increasingly accepted the social utility of higher learning in Canada. The inexorable reorientation of higher learning towards 'operational utility'[9] in the interwar era did much to shape the nature of the modern university in Canada. By the 1940s the precarious equipoise between the competing visions had been destroyed and the balance was tipped in favour of scientific research and the professional ideal. The increasingly utilitarian orientation of higher education not only characterized the development between the wars, but also constituted a key facet of academic modernization of the Canadian university.

As A.B. McKillop has pointed out in his history of Ontario's higher education, developments in commerce, political economy, and the practical and medical sciences provided the best evidence of the emerging 'culture of utility.' In commerce or business administration there was a significant increase in the numbers of students throughout the interwar years. Enrolment in the finance and commerce section of the University of Toronto's Department of Political Economy rose almost sixfold, from 60 to 352 students in 1919 and 1932, respectively.[10] Student enrolments continued to increase at a rapid rate through the 1930s, in spite of the ruinous Great Depression. A 1946 estimate put numbers of commerce graduates for the years 1937 to 1941 at three times (1,065) the count of graduates for the 1922 to 1926 period (334).[11] By 1921, furthermore, there had already been a substantial number of Ontarians employed in white-collar employment linked to trade and commerce. The count continued to grow at a gradually accelerating pace through the Depression years into the 1940s. Most significant, the percentages of those occupied in this type of employment increasingly obtained their training in the province's colleges and universities. The 'age of the self-taught, self-made entrepreneur,' in McKillop's phrase, was drawing to a close.[12]

The reasons for the rise of commerce and trade were clear. Individuals within and outside university circles had begun to realize that an industrializing nation needed university-trained personnel who could cope with the growing complexities of banking, investments, and trade and finance, as well as business management. In the interwar economic climate, government and industrial officials were agreed that there was a great need for expertise in the fields of taxation, trade, and socio-economic reconstruction. They turned with growing frequency to the universities to address the problems of reconstruction and to meet the commercial and industrial exigencies of interwar Canada. Ever-increasing demands for experts in the areas of commerce, finance, and industry, furthermore, helped to legitimate commerce programs and aided in sustaining substantial student enrolments throughout the period.[13] Through participation in public hearings and enquiries and extensive work for provincial and federal governments, government officials and the public at large could see the practical uses of university training.[14] Tangible solutions to real socio-economic problems in royal commission reports and government white papers were eminently more useful than the seemingly irrelevant strictures of an out-of-touch professoriate. Advancing specialization, meanwhile, helped to gain for academics added notoriety within the universities themselves. As it had done in the United States and western Europe, the age of specialization and expertise had arrived in Canada. University commerce and trade programs (usually within the discipline of economics or political economy), in short, merged ever closer to Canadian business and industry and achieved a hitherto unrealized regard, all within a post-war world that wanted to forget the trauma of total war and move on to the more prosaic concerns of building a strong industrial economy and a prosperous nation.

The economic downturn of the 1930s did little to interrupt trends towards operational utility. In fact, the Depression actually amplified the significance of programs and personnel concerned with economic issues. It demonstrated how economic events could profoundly influence the lives of Canadians. Most important, it showed that theories on economic trends and cycles were not remote, academic, or irrelevant, but rather that they were critical to assessing and potentially overcoming the current malaise. Those equipped to broach the difficult questions of economic causation, in consequence, grew in prestige; they were the individuals, after all, entrusted with finding solutions to seemingly intractable problems. By the 1930s Canadian society had found a new and important place for political economists and others involved in addressing the causes of the enduring crisis. In a decade of despondency, economists and their social scientific brethren became the new shamans, the only hope to set aright a failing socio-economic system.[15]

Enhancing the prestige of economists and other social scientists, the Depression also accelerated the academic's role as governmental policy adviser. Most mainstream political economists agreed that the government ought to play a much larger part in directing the economy. Influenced to a considerable extent by Keynesian theory, they thought that academics should answer governments' calls for expert assistance. Political economists, they claimed, were those best qualified to advise on issues requiring special knowledge and insight. Aside from a few dissenters like Harold Innis, many scholars participated in public affairs in varying capacities. University scholars, for instance, prepared the vast majority of research reports written for the Royal Commission on Federal-Provincial Affairs, while a growing number of political economists participated in other governmental research projects or joined the civil service outright.[16] Continuing a trend begun in the 1920s, academics realized a growing opportunity to expand their social utility by rendering services to provincial and federal governments. The perhaps unnoticed consequence was the reinforcement of the utilitarian university.

As was true with developments in commerce and political economy, the evolution of the practical and medical sciences in the interwar years demonstrated the emergence of the ethic of utility. The rise of engineering is especially illustrative. Buoyed by the successes of the applied sciences during the first war, university representatives were confident that engineers could continue to provide for the material well-being of Canadians. Many within the applied-science community considered engineering to be a 'public utility,' responsible not only for the spread of acquired knowledge, but also for the enhancement of living standards and the amelioration of material conditions. Engineers considered themselves the 'primary agents of industrial society,' the 'shock troops of British civilization,' whose duty it was to propagate material progress stemming from the Industrial Revolution.[17] Civil engineers designed the bridges, planned the cities, and constructed the roads, factories, and office buildings, while mechanical, chemical, and electrical engineers discovered the processes, initiated the research, and compiled the knowledge on which current and future industrial development relied. Like political scientists or commerce students, the engineer, in the minds of the public and applied scientists alike, had a practical and very significant part to play in the material development of Canadian society.

Growth of engineering faculties and increases in enrolments reflected the engineer's new-found social status in Canadian society. Between 1920 and 1940 engineering enrolment at all Canadian universities increased almost threefold, from 1,500 to 4,381. Having established engineering schools only shortly before 1920, the four western provincial universities achieved the most pronounced increases. At the University of Saskatchewan, for instance, the numbers of engineering registrants grew from 36 to 503, while the increase at the University of Alberta was only slightly smaller, from 71 to 311.[18] All universities, except the University of New Brunswick (113), boasted enrolments of over 200 students. Even through the ruinous Depression years, engineering schools churned out students at a slow, but steadily increasing rate.[19] Canadian universities remained ready to provide the vital human resource for industrial expansion, even during a period of socio-economic crisis.

Like engineering, medical training became more and more oriented towards public service and the betterment of living conditions. From around the turn of the century, medical practitioners in Canada and elsewhere increasingly applied scientific methodology to treat illnesses. Through medical research, they achieved great successes in understanding the causes and natures of a variety of communicable diseases, such as cholera, diphtheria, dysentery, tetanus, and typhoid.[20] Many more advances, of course, lay in the future, as pneumonia, polio, and tuberculosis, among other diseases, claimed the lives of thousands. There were many more successes than failures, however, and people everywhere began to tout the amazing innovations of medical science. The reaction to Frederick Banting's discovery of insulin, for instance, provided ample evidence of the esteem in which the public held doctors and medical researchers. Canadians considered the discovery of insulin nothing short of heroic, and the story of Banting's 1922 triumph lived on well into the latter half of the century.[21] Perhaps most significant, the insulin discovery clearly demonstrated how the place of the physician had been transformed in the twentieth century to a status more akin to that of motion picture performers and other cultural icons than to that of other respected professionals such as lawyers, teachers, and clerics. The healing physician had captivated the public's imagination. Through the marvels of modern medical science, he was the one responsible for protecting Canadians from pestilence and for discovering the causes of, and providing the remedies for, the many diseases that plagued humankind.[22]

Like the engineer, the modern physician rose in prestige not only because of advances in medical science, but also because of the emergence of medical specialists. As those of other practical sciences did, the faculties of medicine at Canadian universities encouraged the growth of specialization and expertise. Medical experts began working in close association with university and other advanced research hospitals to take advantage of sophisticated equipment and large patient bases. In addition, advanced hospitals and medical faculties developed new fields of expertise, which they quickly subdivided into still narrower specialties.[23] Between 1913 and 1924, for example, the University of Western Ontario created eight specialized departments and hired many full-time staff. The University of Toronto reoriented its medical faculty away from the training of generalists, the emphasis on the teaching, and practice of medicine, and instead stressed research and full-time clinical instruction. By the 1920s the medical faculty was training students to become clinicians and medical specialists, as opposed to general practitioners.[24] The era of the medical generalist as academic and the unsophisticated medical researcher had ended. Indeed, the medical scientist shed the 'folksy image' and the outmoded equipment of the general practitioner of previous generations and rose quickly to become a 'symbol of supreme accomplishment' within the medical and university communities.[25]

The growth of commerce and economics, engineering, and the medical sciences illustrated the new direction of universities in English-speaking Canada during the interwar years. While retaining a focus on the liberal arts, higher learning in Canada increasingly emulated the structures and orientations of American and western European universities.[26] Through a growing concern for practical considerations like industrial and medical research and through providing expertise to deal with increasingly complex social issues, it became ever more responsive to the exigencies of the modern industrial society. The university became a focal point of practical research essential to the material development of the nation. Acknowledged by the public as storehouses of knowledge and expertise, institutions of higher education had begun their transformation from little-known cultural outposts to well-equipped research facilities, integral to the vitality of a modernizing nation. The utilitarian bent of the modern university owed much to a society that highly valued tangible applications of knowledge and that seemed indifferent to the spiritual and humane values of the traditional Victorian university. While maintaining strong links to the past, the values and ideals of Canadian higher education were being transformed to align with new social, industrial, and other developmental concerns. Both university officials and the public at large considered service to society one of the university's main functions. This new social service ethic was a major aspect of the university's development between the wars.

Along with these new perspectives on the functions of higher education, changing relationships with the modern state contributed to the modernization of universities. In an age of expansion, during which programs and facilities became ever more costly and increased student enrolments required larger staffs and additional plant, universities came to depend on government funding. Financial assistance did not come cheap, however. The financial nexus only amplified the social utility role of higher education; for governments and the public generally considered professors to be public employees, as opposed to independent intellectual agents. Universities, especially the larger ones, became accountable to provincial treasuries as university administrators became less concerned with academic matters and more interested in finances and maintaining positive relations with provincial governments. They also became answerable to the public, who wanted their taxes put to effective use and who, therefore, reacted adversely to academics who deviated from their rightful roles as social servants. Indeed, governmental and public involvement in university life characterized the interwar era. In this period, the major universities, which only recently had achieved autonomy from their religious overlords, began to relinquish that new-found independence to a new master, the modern state. As they became integrated in the expanding state, academic freedom, which was often more an ideal than an actuality, had once more come under siege. The modern state had replaced the church as the main instrument of control.

The 1920–1 Royal Commission on University Finances was evidence of the new relationship between the university and the state. It demonstrated, above all, the solidification of the connection between Ontario's non-denominational universities – Queen's, Western, and Toronto – and the provincial legislature. In a climate of growing postwar enrolments, the provincial minister of education, R.H. Grant, established a commission to address the question of financial aid to the universities. Sitting only a few short months, the Cody Commission (named after the commission's chairman, H.J. Cody) tabled a report that satisfied each of the universities. It recognized the advancing needs of higher education and the province's duty to provide funding for new facilities. The commissioners also noted that the annual grant of $500,000 to the University of Toronto was inadequate and ought to be augmented. They also recommended continued and perhaps additional funds for Queen's and Western. Of twelve recommendations, Queen's Park adopted eleven, as the Cody Commission became 'a vital blueprint for the renewal and expansion of higher education in Ontario for more than a quarter century.'[27]

Providing financial security when it was most needed, the Cody commissioners attached conditions to funding recommendations. Universities using provincial funds for campus construction had to gain provincial approval, and the commission suggested that universities ought to 'report on their work' during a regular 'University Day' in the provincial legislature. The commissioners suggested that the board of governors continue to control the provincial university, and that 'such a Board be truly representative of the whole Province.'[28] It is significant that this provision did much to eviscerate the spirit of the 1906 University Act, which was designed to avoid political intervention into university matters.[29] On the whole, the 1921 commission did much to take advantage of the financial vulnerability of the publicly funded universities. Financial entanglements with provincial legislatures, in short, entailed new controls and conditions to which universities had become bound to achieve financial viability.[30]

The accommodation between universities and governments also impinged upon issues of academic freedom, which figured prominently in the interwar decades. The principal of Queen's University, for instance, expressed concern over the problem of maintaining freedom of expression in a climate in which business-oriented boards of governors had an increasingly influential role. In a speech to the University of Manitoba's convocating class of 1919, R. Bruce Taylor echoed American academic and social critic Thorstein Veblen's view that university administrations had taken up a 'business-like expediency,' and had subordinated all former interests to 'pecuniary interests.'[31] It is doubtful whether Taylor accepted the Veblenian view that modern universities had become subject to the management and bureaucratic structures of American business culture. In Canada, higher education had not yet reached the same accommodation with business as it had in the United States. Nevertheless, Taylor pointed to the difficulty of maintaining age-old codes of free speech in a university climate dominated by business-oriented boards of governors. He feared, above all, that board members had become inordinately concerned with expansion and financial security and that they were therefore destroying an academic milieu conducive to scholarly activity.

Adding his voice to that of Taylor, E.E. Braithwaite, president of the University of Western Ontario, was concerned that some professors, especially political economists, might engage in self-censorship, so as to make their 'conclusions conform to the capitalists who might occupy a seat on the governing board.' The usefulness of such scholars and the institutions they represented, he concluded, would be 'seriously impaired' as a result. For Braithwaite, as for Taylor, the transformation of universities into corporations and the demotion of the academic to the status of factory employee was well under way, a tendency that was both disquieting and, indeed, potentially harmful to an institution reliant on liberty of thought and expression.[32]

Universities and their scholars also came under intense public scrutiny. The controversy surrounding Reuben Leonard, a successful businessman, philanthropist, and member of the board of the University of Toronto, was a case in point. Leonard became enraged upon reading *Labour in a Changing World*, a work that Toronto political economist R.M. MacIver had published in 1919. The book offended his sensibilities precisely because it advocated, according to Leonard, social chaos and anarchy. It had been written in the Bolshevist tradition and, as such, was repugnant to the existing political order. Most of all, Leonard thought that the University of Toronto ought to muzzle MacIver to ensure that additional subversive material be suppressed and that young minds would not be exposed to dangerous revolutionary philosophies.

In the protracted series of events that followed, Leonard expressed his views to Sir Robert Falconer, among many others within the university community.[33] Not satisfied, he continued his agitations against the MacIver book and other incidents of scholarly subversion until 1922, when Falconer convened a meeting of Toronto's academic community, designed to put the issue to rest. The first part of Falconer's address was a conventional retelling of the uses and purposes of academic freedom; it was essentially a placement of scholarly free speech within the larger context of toleration and the 'liberty of thought.' The principle of academic liberty, he claimed, could not be questioned if scholars refrained from participation in partisan politics. If professors were indiscreet, however, and chose to make 'political utterances' and to take part in party politics, then they exposed both themselves and the university they represented to public attack. Intemperate remarks, Falconer contended, might adversely affect relations between universities and the state; they might displease governments and induce them to cut financial and other support on which universities depended. Falconer's message was clear: academic freedom should not extend beyond the walls of the university, lest the individual professor endanger the liberty of his colleagues and the entire institution of higher learning. He recommended, therefore, that scholars desist from engaging in political activities and thus avoid imperiling the good names of their universities.[34]

From the perspective of achieving desired results, Falconer's address was astutely formulated. He played to the audience in reaffirming the significance of academic liberty, while at the same time he silenced Leonard and other critics of outspoken academics. More important, in making it clear that radical views impinged upon all within the university, Falconer induced academics to curtail seditious opinions and to engage, instead, in a type of self-censorship that encouraged compliance and conformity with current social standards. The ultimate result was to avoid inflaming public opinion or creating adverse government reactions against academics and institutions of higher learning. Falconer's words had the desired short-term effect at Toronto, since professors heeded their president's injunctions and refrained from uttering impolitic remarks.[35]

Falconer's talk was more than a stern warning to potentially wayward academics. Falconer spoke not only to the problems of academic freedom but also to the shifting relationship between the university and society. His implicit goal was to allay public concerns about the rise of Bolshevism and the possible emergence of revolutionary dogma. In directing scholars to remain neutral on political affairs and therefore requiring them to relinquish a wider conception of academic liberty,[36] he reassured government officials that the university had neither developed into a hotbed of radical thought nor evolved into a potentially destabilizing social establishment. In doing so, Falconer unwittingly showed how the state-run university had become a political entity that was responsible to the electorate and that therefore had to make concessions to popular opinion and influential members of the voting public. The Leonard-MacIver imbroglio, in brief, made manifest the willingness of state-affiliated universities to compromise fundamental principles in order to appease governments and powerful critics. The state's hold on the publicly funded university had never seemed stronger.

The Leonard-MacIver affair signalled the beginning of a trend towards further attacks on the idea of university autonomy. G. Howard Ferguson's rise to the Ontario premiership, for example, provided further controversy on the issue of academic liberty. Ferguson took a particular interest in university affairs, especially those at Toronto. He even went so far as to declare that he was 'the boss of the Toronto University.' Functioning as his own minister of education, he made sure that public complaints concerning matters of academic performance and discipline were passed to President Falconer for additional review.

While ultimately supportive of the president's decisions, Ferguson's actions not only annoyed Falconer, but also infringed on purely academic matters. Ferguson's meddling certainly mirrored the character of the man, his government, and his government's stable majority. It also reflected, however, the growing intrusions of government into academic affairs.[37]

Deeply suspicious of radicalism and foreigners and intolerant of political non-conformity, Ferguson posed even greater problems to Falconer and the Ontario professoriate. Informed of a case in which a student of political economist Gilbert Jackson had been assigned to read *The Communist Manifesto*, an outraged Ferguson immediately wrote to Falconer. He reminded the president that the work had been a prohibited publication and that it should not, therefore, find its way either into the hands of an impressionable young student or onto the reading list of a political economy course. '[T]hese works should be exterminated,' the premier fulminated, and should 'members of the staff either encourage or condone this kind of doctrine, they should be summarily dismissed.' The 'matter is too serious to be ignored,' he concluded.[38]

No sooner had the Jackson incident abated than Ferguson accused another Toronto political economist of inciting sedition. The premier charged C.R. Fay of teaching Marxist dogma. As proof, he referred Falconer to a 27 November 1924 article in the *Financial Post*. Because of these seditious views, Fay should not be 'the sort of man ... [we have] on the staff.' Ferguson continued, 'Surely, our Educational Institution should not be ... encouraging the activities of a Communist.'[39]

The outspoken and iconoclastic Frank Underhill was the next University of Toronto scholar to languish in the intolerant climate of the Ferguson regime. Somehow, Ferguson had been informed that the historian Underhill had taught, in one of his history courses, that Britain had shared with Germany responsibility for causing the Great War. For the ultra-patriotic Ferguson, this interpretation was nothing short of sedition. He questioned Underhill's use of his personal interpretation of events when so much documentation as to the true origins of the war was freely available. He threatened, furthermore, to force the dismissal of the young historian. In a letter to crony H.J. Cody, he stated that if the rumours were true and Underhill was indeed disloyal, he would be 'compelled ... to take the steps that might be thought drastic.'[40]

As happened in the Jackson and Fay incidents, this first Underhill fracas quickly subsided, as Falconer assured the bombastic Ferguson that the allegations against the historian were unfounded. Amid a political milieu that was increasingly inimical to errant professors and their dissenting views, however, it seemed only a matter of time before another episode of disloyalty or radicalism would spur Queen's Park to action. Indeed, only a few months after the first incident, a piece in *Canadian Forum* penned by Underhill raised the ire of the premier. The article, which exposed Underhill's aversion to the anti-Americanism of Canadian politicians, prompted Ferguson again to write to Cody. Ferguson warned that Underhill must exploit 'his talents on the job he is being paid for' lest the premier be 'tempted to tick off a number of salaries of some men who seem to take more interest in interfering in matters of public policy and public controversy than they do in the work for which they are paid.' In contrast to past episodes, on this occasion members of the governing board and others wholeheartedly supported Ferguson's position and agreed with the premier's views on the essential purposes of the university scholar.[41] Not even the temporizing of Falconer, should it have materialized, could have saved Underhill from the wrath of the premier and those responsible for a growing body of opinion directed against the Toronto historian and other insubordinate scholars.

Conflict over issues of free speech came to a head early in 1931. As usual, Frank Underhill was at the storm's centre. Trouble began when the Toronto Police Commission persuaded owners of halls and other meeting places not to rent out their facilities to the Fellowship of Reconciliation, an international and interdenominational association formed to facilitate international class and racial fellowship. Police officials claimed that the Fellowship was merely a front for communistic activities and played on the proprietors' sense of patriotism and anti-Communism to gain compliance. The incident outraged Underhill, who, with classicist Eric Havelock, drafted a letter that protested against the actions of the Toronto police. Underhill, Havelock, and the sixty-six other members of the university who had signed the note (including Harold Innis and Donald Creighton) argued that police actions threatened fundamental rights to free speech and assembly. Appearing in the four main Toronto dailies, the letters of the Toronto 'sixty-eight' claimed that the activities of the commission had nullified what 'has for generations been considered one of the proudest heritages of the British peoples.' Letters to the editor concluded, 'It is the plain duty of the citizen to protest publicly against such curtailment of his rights, and, in doing so, we wish to affirm our belief in the free public expression of opinions, however unpopular or erroneous.'[42]

The professors' declaration elicited a strong reaction. The public response was best represented in the press. Motivated in large measure by a prime opportunity to sell papers, the Toronto journalists and editorialists denounced the professors' stance. Taking advantage of the public aversion to the red menace, they characterized the Toronto 'sixty-eight' as a group of burgeoning Bolsheviks bent on allowing leftist radicalism to gain a foothold in Toronto during perilous times. Influential private citizens also echoed this view. Sir John Aird, president of the Canadian Bank of Commerce, advised that the professors should 'stick to their knitting,'[43] while Sir Edward Beatty, president of the CPR, denounced the penchant of scholars (especially young political economists) for teaching socialism.[44] The reaction of university officials was likewise unsympathetic to the sixty-eight. After publication of the letter, the governing board moved to dissociate the university from the professors' position. Board of Governors President Cody notified the newspapers that the professors did not speak for the university, while board member Sir Joseph Flavelle declared that 'every teacher is a trustee for the institution' and that no hasty or impulsive act 'shall jeopardize the progress and development of the University.'[45]

No dismissals or public censure of professors ensued. Yet the official university position concerning academic liberty was made clear. In failing to defend the professoriate, Toronto officials succumbed to popular sentiment and public pressure. Their unwillingness to anger the public or to draw the ire of an intolerant press showed just how much the university had become responsive to public perceptions. Indeed, they had become willing to undermine sacred university traditions so as not to jeopardize the public reputation of their institution and perhaps adversely affect its good standing at Queen's Park. By failing to defend academic freedom, university leaders showed how they had become concerned more with the university's public image and role as social servant than with the notion of academic free speech.

Underhill's clash with the Police Commission and subsequent incidents involving the issue of free speech illustrate the nature of the period. Even more than the 1920s, the 1930s were a repressive decade. In this climate of widespread economic malaise, many feared the emergence of left-wing movements that threatened the established order. The anti-Bolshevik campaigns that had ebbed and flowed since 1918 seemed to intensify after 1930, since the new economic climate seemed to many to be conducive to the rise of revolutionary movements and the undermining of the established order.

The decade was especially troublesome for those associated with the Co-operative Commonwealth Federation (CCF), and its intellectual offshoot, the League for Social Reconstruction (LSR). The Board of Governors at the University of Alberta, for instance, forbade the entire Arts Faculty to run for a seat in the House of Commons when it discovered that the head of the Department of Classics had been nominated to represent the CCF in a west Edmonton riding. The governing board at United Theological College, furthermore, disregarded recommendations and opted not to renew the appointment of King Gordon. It cited economic constraints for the decision. Many believed, however, that Gordon's affiliation with the CCF was the true reason for his ouster.[46] Many critics saw past the reformist bent of the CCF and the LSR and emphasized, instead, the revolutionary and radical Marxian orientations of the new left-wing movement. They opposed the CCF's mandate, as expressed in the Regina Manifesto, to establish 'a new social order' in Canada, one that would substitute planning for 'chaotic individualism.' They feared that subversive groups might capitalize on adverse economic conditions and foment social upheaval. Bolstered by the prevailing political mood, critics and several university officials approached the CCF with caution. Not only did they oppose the CCF's program, but they also baulked at the prospects of the insinuation of pernicious political dogmas into the universities. Ultimately, they abhorred the idea that the universities might be transformed into focal points of social revolution.

The CCF's isolationist, North-American-oriented foreign policy also angered opponents. The direction of Canadian foreign policy had become a rancorous issue as the likelihood of war increased. Outrage and calls for censure ensued after the University of Saskatchewan's Carlyle King made a 1938 speech urging that Canada not become embroiled in another war to defend British holdings.[47] Frank Underhill took a similar stand. When another critic of pro-British policy was not censured for his actions, Queen's Park went after Underhill.[48] Premier Mitch Hepburn denounced Underhill's strictures on the foreign policy connections of Canada and Great Britain. A founding member of both the LSR and the CCF, Underhill staunchly opposed foreign policy planning that closely linked Canada to British foreign policy. He advocated, instead, an isolationist stance. His isolationism meant, of course, that Canada should baulk at participation in future European wars. '[P]oppies blooming in Flanders Fields,' he wrote caustically, had no more attraction for Canadians.[49] Underhill's fractious statements infuriated Hepburn. George Drew (leader of the Opposition) characterized Underhill's utterings as seditious and demanded that Underhill be disciplined in a way 'befitting the crime he has committed.'[50]

Although favourably resolved, this latest Underhill imbroglio highlighted the ease with which academics could be made to answer for contentious statements amid the paranoia of the 1930s. It showed the intolerance for dissent expressed at the highest levels of provincial governments and university administrations. Most of all, it laid bare the apathy, if not the hostility, of government personnel, the news media,[51] and the population at large towards the issue of academic free speech. Speaking on the Underhill incident, B.K. Sandwell, editor of *Saturday Night*, expressed despair at the fact that no one had risen in Queen's Park to defend the fundamental issue of academic freedom. He chided the partisan members of the provincial Parliament who could not identify 'the embryo of totalitarianism' that was implied in the denial of free speech. Responding to the suggestion that university funding be curtailed as a warning to errant professors, he remarked that 'this is no time to be reducing grants to Provincial Universities'; instead, the 'doors of a liberal education must be thrown wide open in the hope that at least one or two who have enjoyed its benefits will find their way into a future Provincial Legislature.'[52] For Sandwell, the strengthening of academic freedom in all quarters had become the only way to cope with the erosion of the university traditions that seemed subject to attack with growing regularity. For the critics of the utilitarian university it had become vital.

Academic modernization, in all its forms, continued apace through the interwar period. Its effects did not go unnoticed: a small but vocal group of critics emerged. Like American opponents of the service-oriented academy, Canadian observers, usually university professors, questioned specialization, practical training, and the state's intrusion into academic life. Most of all, they criticized a concept of higher learning that deemphasized the traditional cultural role of the university and stressed, instead, the academy's emergence as service institution, sensitive to the exigencies of an industrializing nation. In exposing the deficiencies of the modern academy, they worked to reverse current trends and preserve the university's true social function: to ensure the vitality of the virtues of freedom, moral guidance, and the cultural traditions of western civilization.

Criticism of academic modernization emerged much earlier in the

United States than in Canada. Owing largely to advanced industrialization and a growing commitment to the principle of operational utility,[53] the modernization of American colleges and universities had been well advanced by the 1920s. Thorstein Veblen, as we have seen, presented a damning critique of higher learning that singled out as problematic the dominance of American business interests within university governing boards. In *The Higher Learning in America* (1918), however, he also highlighted the inadequacies of a system of higher education for which the 'pursuit of matter-of-fact knowledge' and scientific and technological specialization had become paramount. Veblen objected to a higher education that had been concerned more with providing students with mechanical and technical skills to deal with immediate concerns than with developing critical minds that could examine social and philosophical problems. Expedient interests, he averred, had come to 'the forefront of academic policy' as the academy turned away from philosophical values and towards 'transiently urgent matters of a more material and more ephemeral nature.' Integrated in the capitalist structure, the American university had been transformed from an institution responsible for the purveyance of intellectual and cultural values to a training school devoted to 'practical efficiency' and to the 'needs of earning and spending.' Most pernicious of all, it had begun a 'long-term drift' away from 'cultural interests' towards an agenda that was vocational and wholly utilitarian.[54] More than an indictment of the corporatization of the modern university, Veblen's work reacted against a nascent educational philosophy that, in adopting the notion of functional utility, had lost a sense of the academy's historic mission and had therefore abdicated its true social role.

Like Veblen, educational critic and reformer Alexander Meiklejohn of Brown University and later Amherst College had grave concerns about academic modernization. In an important article entitled 'The Aim of the Liberal College'(1921), Meiklejohn opposed the promotion in universities of 'specialized knowledge' as a way to address 'immediate practical aims.' He also railed against the inclusion of vocational training in university curricula. While he did not object to practical training per se, he was convinced that vocationalism had no place in liberal arts colleges. In addition, Meiklejohn urged academics and universities not to become involved in resolving social problems. Universities could best serve society by avoiding the vicissitudes of the world outside the academy and by performing their time-honoured function of providing the citizenry access to a liberal education.[55] Only in this way could liberal arts institutions contribute to the social order. Meiklejohn feared, however, that this basic objective had been ignored in favour of a new conception of the university in which vocationalism and involvement in extra-university affairs predominated. Echoing Veblen, he expressed concern that higher education increasingly reflected the secular and the materialistic bent of modern American society. Focusing more than ever on the material objectives of the modern world, it had ceased to function as an enclave of the liberal arts. It had abandoned, in consequence, its historical role of offering a philosophic understanding of the human condition. Universities and colleges had become bastions of specialized research and compartmentalized knowledge. As such, they had relinquished their fundamental purpose, the search for 'unified knowledge which is Insight.' They ultimately failed to serve as a beacon for a society that had lost its way.

An ardent critic of utilitarian higher learning, Irving Babbitt, like Meiklejohn, denounced the direction of the modern American university. A humanist scholar and Harvard University lecturer, Babbitt deplored the rise of the scientific approach and the advent of the free elective system at Harvard and other institutions. To serve an industrializing society, the universities had begun to neglect their central function, the discovery and inculcation of cultural values. Active in the New Humanism movement in the 1920s, Babbitt chided the technical orientation of American universities. He argued that the research ideal diverted academics from their rightful social duties, the search for a consensus of values. Universities and academics alike ought to resist contemporary trends, according to the Harvard scholar, and should not concern themselves with utilitarian disciplines such as engineering, medical research, or the other practical sciences. They had a much more important function: to set societal standards, which could be done only through the preservation of the best that has been thought and said in the western scholarly tradition.[56]

In stressing the secular and material conditions of human culture, moreover, technical education helped to erode the cultural role of the scholar. Indeed, the degradation of the university and the decline of scholarship meant disaster for future cultural development. Higher learning, for Babbitt, was in crisis precisely because scholars and others in society had begun to devalue its crucial contributions to civilization. Babbitt believed that the development of higher learning was of enormous importance to the evolution of American culture. With the university's transformation, cultural leadership would be lost and further growth of American civilization stunted. 'One is safe ... in affirming,' he wrote in the early 1920s, 'that the battle that is to determine the fate of American civilization will be fought out first of all in the field of education.'[57] Peering over the edge of the precipice into the future of higher education in America, Babbitt sensed that a fall was imminent.[58]

The issue of the social role of higher education continued to occupy the minds of educational critics into the 1930s. In a time of socio-economic decay, many gave renewed attention to the social purpose of the university. In November 1932, for instance, about 1,100 professors, university administrators, and other interested parties gathered at the Waldolf Astoria hotel to celebrate the 200th anniversary of Columbia University. Those attending the conference, tellingly dubbed 'The Obligation of Universities to the Social Order,' not only commemorated the anniversary, but also endeavoured to understand the university's contributions to modern social development. They tried to understand, in the words of Columbia's president, Nicolas Murray Butler, how the 'universities of the western world' had been 'in a measure directly responsible for the present chaos.' Butler specifically highlighted the function of the academy's practical disciplines in facilitating social progress. The natural sciences, he declared, which 'flourished and developed so rapidly under the direction and encouragement of the universities,' 'contributed immeasurably to the material content and variety' of humanity's existence. The modern university had thus fostered tremendous material growth and contributed greatly to the development of the modern industrial state. In so doing, however, it had 'released social impulsions for which no rational directions were indicated, and no adequate controls provided.'[59] Academics and administrators, Butler suggested, had failed to take account of the social effects of the new utilitarian university. The social responsibilities of the university seemed to have lapsed at a time of profound socio-economic malaise, a time when society most needed guidance and a steadying influence. For Butler and others, the obligations of scholars were clear: the balance between the social and practical functions of the academy had to be redressed.

The significance of Butler's recommendations had not been lost on the Canadian critics of higher learning. In a 1933 article appearing in *Queen's Quarterly*, P.E. Corbett (professor of law at McGill) identified 'expansion' as the chief evil in the development of the modern university. Specifically, he lamented the mindless replication in Canada of the drive towards functional utility of American institutions. Canadians took it for 'granted,' he asserted, 'that the fundamental problem with which they have had to deal was identical with the problem in the United States.' Canadian universities were, in consequence, subject to 'American methods' and, most dangerously, an overexpansion to meet the needs of an industrialized, materialistic nation. Corbett worried that they might thus fall prey to the forces of 'mechanical standardization' that had 'settled' upon peoples of the west 'like a plague' during the nineteenth century.[60]

Corbett most objected, however, to a system of higher education that was concerned with new educational trends such as adult learning, vocationalism, and an undue emphasis on the professions. He abhorred American educational progressivism, which legitimized these tendencies. In an attempt to reach the masses, progressivism undermined the fundamental purpose of the academy. Instead, 'teaching on the highest plane and the search for new knowledge were the highest functions for the university.' 'The university belies its essential purpose,' Corbett added, referring especially to adult education and technical disciplines, 'when it steps down to the masses of the unprepared.'[61] Thus, there was no room, in Corbett's conception of the university, for a 'democratic' approach to higher learning (see chapter 4).

Exposing the fallaciousness of democratic higher education, Corbett went on to formulate a 'test' designed to determine the value of new approaches to knowledge and to spell out the true function of the academy. The pursuit of new knowledge, he reasoned, could be furthered only if the work required 'a liberally educated and scientific mind for its efficient prosecution.' The scientific and scholarly pursuit of knowledge was valid only if it 'intensified' and 'deepened' the university's 'intellectual and scientific life.' New studies, for Corbett, had to enhance the existing 'academic riches' of the university; for the academy had to combine an 'ardent search' for new scholarly and scientific knowledge with the propagation of older learning. The search for new learning in the arts and science was doubtless important. Yet the academy was still entrusted with the task of expanding known knowledge. The maintenance of scholarly traditions and the transmission of older learning became the first great purpose of the academy, without which the acquisition of new knowledge could not be achieved. Higher education was, above all, a purveyor of knowledge and a custodian of societal customs and values. The academy must employ 'scientists and scholars of the first rank,' Corbett concluded, with a 'power and passion for original thought' and a penchant for preserving and passing on existing learning.[62]

Emphasizing a balance between the pursuit of new knowledge and the conservation of older learning, Corbett's musings took on a special importance during the interwar era. His comments reflected an early reaction against the development of an American-style, utilitarian educational system. They responded, above all, to the infiltration of American methods, focused more on the development of practical training and the emergence of specialized studies than on the advancement of existing learning and the promotion of the humanities and the pure sciences. As many of the American educational critics before him had done, Corbett highlighted the evils of the transformation of universities into training facilities and vocational schools. Essentially, Corbett's declarations constituted a warning: they were a reminder to all concerned that the modern academy must reconsider current policies and directions and instead refocus on its historic functions and traditional social roles. Through intellectual discovery and the production of 'cultural men and women,' Corbett hoped that Canadian academies would provide leadership for an imperiled industrial society.[63] Through the maintenance of older knowledge and wisdom, academics could assume their traditional roles as purveyors of social and intellectual values. Thus, the academy was for Corbett what it had been for Meiklejohn and the others: a central cultural institution within industrial society, responsible not only for the pursuit of truth and the discovery of new knowledge, but also for the maintenance of knowledge and the preservation of cultural standards.

Most academic leaders ignored Corbett's warnings, but a small coterie of scholars accepted the need to re-evaluate the direction of higher learning. Commenting on the function of modern social scientist, Harold Innis put forth a well-considered reckoning of the university and its role in modern society. Like several other critics of higher education, Innis focused on the modern academic's relationship to the state and society.[64] Responding to the prevailing intellectual climate of the 1930s, Innis argued that scholars had become enamoured of the intellectual's involvement in social and political affairs and that social scientists had succumbed to society's demands for answers to current social and economic difficulties. They were given, therefore, to making pronouncements about how to ameliorate socio-economic conditions. The public perceived the scholar as a central figure in the resolution of pressing social problems. Society had come to regard as panaceas social sciences like economics and to view economists as soothsayers, endowed with the capacity to address socio-economic problems through the application of advanced mathematics or the latest econometric models. To many, higher learning had never been more socially relevant, and the ties between social studies and the social order had never been so close.

In contrast to those who relished the growing social prominence of the university, Innis chided the recent working relationship between the social sciences and the outside world. The 'social sciences,' Innis proclaimed in 1935, had become 'the opiate of the people.'[65] Innis meant that undue faith had been invested in the ability of the academic to discover the truth and provide final answers. Indeed, the social scientific claim to objectivity and the unassailability of the scientific method were what rendered the social sciences incapable of discovering truth and solving deep-seated social problems. A product of the modern industrial world, the scientific approach was merely one of many limitations that hindered the scholarly pursuit of truth. In focusing academic enquiry on ever more specialized subjects, it led scholars away from a general understanding of their social environment. It provided increasingly detailed information on current social and economic issues – issues, according to Innis, of fragmentary importance in the light of widespread sociocultural development. Social scientists had become consumed with the minutiae of current economic and social problems and had lost a sense of Canada's place in the greater evolution of western culture. 'Intelligence in the social science,' Innis declared, 'tends to be absorbed in the abstruse and abstract tasks of adjustment and to be lost in specialization, with the result that it is unable to participate in the endless and complex and possibly fruitless search for trends.'[66] Society was ill advised, in short, to place its trust in academics who, in their unbridled haste to implement current scientific methods, had rendered themselves incapable of examining broad events and who failed, therefore, to fulfil their rightful social roles.

The 'contemporary-mindedness' and academic faddism that Innis spoke about afflicted the university at large. Seemingly bastions to which scholars could retreat to avoid narrow approaches to knowledge, the universities had also fallen prey to narrow interests. Like the social sciences, the modern university had lost a sense of its historic purpose to discover truth and seek wider meaning. As Innis noted, instead of the search for the truth, departmental routines and other peripheral concerns seemed to occupy the time of university personnel. University officials, furthermore, considered social scientists to be merely those capable of achieving scientific advancement and material progress. Hence, there was little acknowledgment of the critical role they could play in understanding and in placing into greater philosophical and historical contexts 'profound disturbances' such as the Great Depression.[67] Perhaps most important, Innis feared that free discussion in the university had become threatened. In 'Discussion in the Social Sciences,' a *Dalhousie Review* article first read to summer session faculty of the University of British Columbia in 1935, he argued that while 'mock battles have been fought in the defence of freedom of speech and freedom of the press,' no such rigorous defence of academic free speech had been mounted.[68] He meant that although advocates of the liberal society had championed free speech, they presented no like recognition of academic 'discussion.' On the contrary, modern democracies had become increasingly control oriented, creating a climate inimical to free academic discussion. The problem had especially acute in Canada, Innis explained, a country whose history had been marked by political and economic centralization. Canadian society was characterized by measures of control such as the establishment of a central bank, the growth of a vast federal bureaucracy, and the extension of federal controls over the provinces. In this environment, academics had abandoned their function as free thinkers and instead had succumbed to the dictates of governments, politicians, the public, and university authorities. Intellectuals, according to Innis, had become a 'tragi-comic group' used by political parties and governments for their own purposes. In trying to satisfy the demands of the public to understand their immediate environment, they spouted important-sounding statistics to try to impress their audiences. They had thus been reduced to the status of 'travelling comedians' 'masquerading as economists and prophets.'[69] In responding to the demands of governments and the public and trying to find a niche within the industrial world, intellectuals had become, for Innis, the playthings of an increasingly tyrannical social order. In this climate, the role of intelligence had been transformed. Once free to engage in the unremitting search for truth, it was now bound up in the immediacies of present circumstances. Discussion in the university faltered, in a society bent on limiting free thought and imposing strict controls.

In spite of appearances to the contrary, Innis's commentary on the state of Canadian intellectual life represented much more than nostalgic yearnings for the resurrection of the university tradition. Instead, in his writings he tried to make clear the social relevance of intellectual life. While appearing arcane and outmoded, the traditional academy could be a significant social force. Most of all, it could perform a vital role in counterbalancing the crass materialism that had beset Canadians. Like many American education critics, Innis understood the cultural role of scholarly activity. More than a cultural institution, the university was responsible for discovering the root causes of the contemporary problems; its duty was to expose the effects of control through engaging in the inexorable quest for truth. Through unending scholarly toil, academics could provide a point of reference from which moderns could comprehend social developments. In a striking paradox, intellectuals could do vital service by *not* participating in public life or becoming involved in 'vested interests,' both of which clouded their judgment and undermined their true purposes. Freed from biases of this kind, Innis averred, universities could provide vital service to a society that had lost all perspective. Despite the seeming contradiction, the traditional 'role of intelligence' had never been more socially relevant than at present. Aware of the futility of realizing this vital social role, Innis nevertheless had become devoted to illustrating for all to see the defects of the modern university and the academy's fundamental significance to the modern world.

Responding to academic modernization, Innis also referred to his personal academic circumstances. His disdain for the new developments in the social sciences and the university at large reflected his disapproval of changes to his own discipline. In the revealingly entitled 'The Passing of Political Economy' his distaste for the contemporary-mindedness of modern political economists generally was as much directed against narrow specialists as it was an indictment of his discipline as a whole. His discussion of how 'philosophy and theology' had been superseded by the 'new dogmas,' such as 'fascism, communism, [and] democracy' for the political scientist and 'occultism ... practical affairs,' banking, and others for the economists, was highlighted by his dismay at the demise of political economy at Toronto and elsewhere.[70] Above all, he lamented the passing of the social-philosophic function of political economy; that is, the traditional role of the political economist: to understand the nature of a social good, promote social unity, temper scientific analysis with an understanding of ethical and moral virtue, and, most of all, to comprehend great and subtle changes in civilization.[71] He was concerned about a discipline that held little regard for important scholars such as MacIver and Urwick, who maintained 'an interest in the fundamental problems of civilization,' and that instead hired and promoted men who buried themselves in their narrow specialties.[72] For an academic who considered himself within the older tradition of political economy and for whom the problems of civilization had taken on an urgent importance, developments in political economy had been disconcerting indeed. For a world mired in economic downturn and totalitarianism and poised on the brink of a second great war, the passing of the political economy and social philosophy traditions was truly disastrous.

That the interwar period was one of transformation for the university in Canada there can be no doubt. Despite the academy's evolution, however, there was little sense that the Canadian university was in crisis. Aside from the perspicacity of Corbett and Innis and the dissenting remarks of few others, who usually merely paid lip service to the virtues of academic free enquiry, most observers failed to address issues such as the advent of operational utility, vocationalism, or the university's social role. In contrast to the position of American critics of higher learning, it was only with the onset of the Second World War that Canadian critics fully realized both the changes that their universities had undergone and the vital importance of the academy to postwar developments. Indeed, the war did much to rouse Canadian academics from their complacency, and the period after 1939 was one of intense questioning of the function of the modern university. The war threw into question the purposes and objectives of key institutions, including the university. In a word, many observers perceived the war period as one of crisis for the Canadian academy.

Already by the late 1930s academics had begun to realize the impact that the war was to have on university life in Canada. Academic authorities seemed especially preoccupied with the potential contributions of scholars to a nation, and indeed a civilization at war. In an address given to students of Queen's University, for instance, Sir Edward Beatty explained that academics provided essential guidance for an emerging nation beset by socio-economic difficulties and threatened with political excesses from abroad. Anticipating the impending conflict, Beatty declared in his October 1937 speech that 'the destiny of our nation depends ... on our qualities of national courage and wisdom.' Moral and intellectual leadership provided by academics was central to the achievement of these attributes. Indeed, humanity at large, for Beatty, had become increasingly reliant on universities for guidance, leadership, and inspiration. 'There can no more important task to-day,' he ended, 'than that committed to the staffs of our universities.'[73]

Writing early in the war, historian Arthur Lower provided a much more detailed assessment than Beatty had of the wartime role of the scholar. He contended that the second war, like the Great War, did much to hasten the historical process. Not only had the economic and political uncertainty that marked the interwar period ceased, but the Second World War also marked the end of the 'old order'; western civilization was at the end of an era. Lower was concerned, moreover, about the character of the impending era, a period, he was convinced, in which the scholar and the university at large had a crucial role to play. In the 'The Social Sciences and the Post-War World' he argued that social scientists were responsible for 'divining the nature of the future, perhaps even essaying to act as midwives.' The new order was in the process of formation, and the academic, especially the social scientist, was responsible for both comprehending and moulding social transformations. 'We are at present at an exciting experiment,' he wrote, referring particularly to the evolution of Canadian society; Canadians were at the 'beginning of society,' and, realizing this fact, social scientists 'would be less than human if [they] did not do something about determining its shape.'[74]

Lower made clear, furthermore, that social scientists must be more than just observers and recorders of events; that is, they must be more than 'mere scientists.' Academics must also avoid infusing students and citizens with culture and therefore must renounce Victorian approaches to great social change. They must not be content 'to sit and watch society go by' and allow it to 'get so far past him that his observation' was of little value. Rather, they must 'create and affect society' and also describe it. They must become, according to Lower, active agents in society to help to shape and re-form it. For only in aiding in the direction of society could scholars explain the kind of world in which moderns lived. While maintaining the older function of promoting values and providing philosophic insights, social scientists now had to interpret and participate in the social process to make people 'feel at home in it and make adjustments with it.'[75]

Lower thus placed the onerous responsibility of comprehending the social order on the shoulders of academics. The current sociocultural crisis was an opportunity for academics to become involved in determining social directions. It was therefore an occasion to restore the social utility of scholars. Lower claimed that social scientists must become agents of society and actively participate in interpreting and changing the social order. They must do more than engage in scholarly activities; they must be 'men of deeds' as well as men of contemplation.[76] Hence scholarship must not be confined to the academy, but must be made accessible to all citizens. In this way, social scientists could fulfil their roles as scholars and citizens.

Writing during the first months of the war, James Thomson examined the more practical and immediate contributions of higher learning to the war effort. In the first part of 'The Universities and the War,' Thomson explained the immediate assistance that universities provided to help in the conflict. Applied scientists, especially engineers, whom Thomson considered to be as valuable as airmen, could provide essential service to the war effort. This 'special category' of university men brought special attributes, such as research skills and technical know-how, that ought to be exploited. 'Only a short-sighted policy,' he concluded, 'would deprive the men who have to do the actual fighting of the essential support the scientist can give.'[77]

Thomson was just one of several within and outside the university who were convinced of the fundamental importance of the technical expertise that universities provided. From the outset of the war, government and university authorities realized that the current conflict would be fought as much on the home front as on the front lines. The outcome of war was to depend not only on fighting skill or military acumen, but also on the mobilization of scientific and technical personnel.[78] Observers emphasized the highly technical nature of modern warfare and the need to develop a competent military-industrial complex, features absent from the Great War or any previous conflicts. The creation of a great reserve of technically trained men and women to build and run factories and to develop new and more potent weapons of war had thus become essential to the war effort. The Second World War was not to be merely a conflict of manpower and materiel but one in which scientific knowledge also figured prominently.

As chief production centres for technically trained personnel, universities were vital to Canada's war effort. Realizing the crucial importance of technical and scientific expertise, universities and governments made special efforts to ensure that the faculties of applied sciences continued to provide competent scientists and other technical personnel for the duration of the conflict. Fearing that the National Resources Mobilization Act of June 1940 might empty universities of male undergraduates, for example, the Department of War Services

exempted all university students from service.[79] Greeted most favourably by the National Conference of Canadian Universities (NCCU),
this move was designed to keep undergraduates, especially those
enrolled in the applied sciences, at their studies. Canada simply could
not withstand the loss of thousands of students, especially engineers,
medical professionals, and other practical scientists, to military
service.[80]

The commitment of university and federal government officials to
technical education continued throughout the war. Federal government leaders implored universities to maintain high levels of enrolment in the applied and medical sciences, especially after 1942, when
the shortage of manpower was most acute. During the First World War
universities had encouraged students to enlist, but after 1940 university officials maintained high registrations in the practical disciplines.
For instance, enrolments at the University of Toronto in the applied sciences, engineering, and medicine increased steadily to 1945 (with only
a slight decline in 1943). Arts and sciences registrations, in contrast,
had consistently declined from 1938 to reach a low in 1943–4.[81]

University leaders thus had succeeded in their mandate to provide
the human resources on which the prosecution of modern warfare
relied. They had managed to assemble, in A.B. McKillop's words, 'a
trained domestic army of engineers, scientists, dentists, and doctors.'[82]
In so doing, however, they not only fulfilled the wishes of civil servants and other government officials, but also contributed greatly to
the changing, increasingly utilitarian profile of the wartime university.
For many, the war had made clear the university's main societal
purpose: the academy was little more than a storehouse of technical
personnel ready to be called upon to meet the exigencies of modern,
industrial society. In making plain the university's wartime contributions, the war showed how universities and their men could render the
ultimate social service. It allowed all to see the tangible results of
technical education, how the seemingly esoteric academy had become
relevant to the development of a nation struggling through the vicissitudes of war.

Not all accepted this view of the academy, of course. Early in the war,
in fact, academics had warned of the possible deleterious effects of over-
emphasizing scientific and technical training. Indeed, in the majority of
his 1940 piece James Thomson warned against the transformation of
Canadian universities into schools of advanced technical training. As
we have seen, Thomson did not discount the technical role of universi-

ties. Yet he thought that higher education should offer much more than technical expertise. The insights of humanists and social scientists, he argued, had to supplement the studies of the applied scientist. For the work of the technical expert contained 'economic, political and psychological implications ... that can be grasped only by a mind that has moved through the kind of disciplines that are the fruits of historical, literary and philosophical training.'[83] Technical and scientific aspects of the war effort, in other words, formed only a small part of what the current conflict signified. Humanists and social scientists were responsible for discovering this wider meaning, that is, that the war constituted a great tear in the fabric of history. Academics' greatest responsibility was thus to place the current strife in philosophic and historical context in order to understand its greater cultural ramifications.

Thomson went on to explain exactly how enlightened intellectuals were to fulfil their obligations. The scholar must 'bring the old and intractable elements in human nature and its environment under the dominion of reason through understanding them and thus to become their master and not their slave.'[84] Thomson advised scholars to be aware of propaganda and other pernicious aspects of the wartime world that clouded human actions and cultural change. There was an urgent need, Watson Kirkconnell of McMaster wrote in 1941, adding his voice to that of Thomson, to clarify the 'realities of the situation' and the principles and ideals 'for which we fight.'[85] The best way to achieve these ends, Thomson claimed, was to bring 'the experiences of history and the humane ideals of emancipated minds' to the fore. Indeed, contextualizing current events was necessary if moderns were to comprehend change. Through such broad comprehension of the current malaise, Thomson added, 'the human scene is gathered into a wide vision, wherein results are assessed and conclusions reached by methods that lie beyond the heated excitements and prejudices of the moment.'[86] Such 'calm wisdom,' 'sure guidance,' and, most of all, 'enthusiasm for humanity,' were the critical gifts that academics brought to the problem. Without academic aptitudes and insights, he implied, modern civilization might fall into an abyss out of which it had little hope of extricating itself.

The war constituted a warning for academics. It was, in Thomson's words, 'a new summons to the universities' to compel them to do 'constructive thinking about the future.' It made clear, moreover, the function of the university not only to assess great historical change but also to provide a counterbalance to the dangerous forces that threatened western civilization. 'We must summon the teaching of history,' Thomson asserted, 'the variety of human life in literature, the patient processes of the sciences, and all the loveliness in art and music, blended with the wisdom of divine philosophy.'[87] For these academic inheritances liberated scholars from propaganda campaigns and allowed intellectuals to focus on wider problems and to address the needs of the modern order. They enabled the current generation to understand its connections to the thoughts and ideals of bygones eras. For Thomson, the 'great tradition' of the arts was thus central to the university's wartime role. It helped to liberate universities from the present and allowed them to assist in shaping the future.

Harold Innis expanded on much of what Thomson said. In the tradition of Thomson, Innis taught that only through advancing the scholarly approach could academics make a contribution to the current social order.[88] For the Innis of the 1930s, the scholar's main duty had been to avoid vested interests and maintain the commitment to objectivity and truth (see chapter 2). This axiom of academic obligation was even truer in the Second World War. Indeed, for Innis, the war represented far more than the loss of life or even the disruption of ethical conduct; it was at the root of the university crisis. The conflict helped to exacerbate the 1930s trend towards bureaucratization and precipitated what Innis saw as a mass exodus of intellectuals to the cause of 'winning the war.'[89] Governmental incursions into academia, Innis wrote, led 'to the withdrawal of social scientists from research work of a fundamental character' and lowered 'intellectual achievements in academic work.'[90] Academic pursuits suffered because scholars in the employ of governments abandoned the 'long run problems' that had once engaged the social scientist. Indeed, the government adviser or researcher was the exact antithesis to Innis's ideal scholar, who, unfettered by vested interests, involved himself in larger philosophical problems.[91] By the end of the war, furthermore, the 'academic mind' would become used to government needs, and academia would be transformed into 'a standing surplus reserve labour pool to meet the varying demands of government.'[92] University intellectuals would thus become merely a brain-trust of the party in power. Even more than he had in the 1930s, Innis showed how the heavy demands of the war on human resources meant the degradation of a noble profession and the diversion of academics from their rightful roles.

The war, Innis averred, also created a climate inimical to the arts, humanities, and the entire university tradition. Innis reacted as well to the attack on academic liberty, as had Thomson, who had warned the scholar against acting as the mouthpiece of Allied propaganda, and Lower, who held grave concerns about the future of free enquiry in the oppressive, illiberal atmosphere of the war.[93] Innis's views on this issue are especially evident in a wartime controversy involving none other than Frank Underhill.

In 1941 University of Toronto officials and the provincial legislature of Ontario threatened to dismiss historian Underhill for wartime statements that they believed to be offensive and contrary to the war effort.[94] Despite 'crossing swords' with Underhill on various occasions, Innis felt obliged to defend a colleague. He wrote an impassioned plea to the university's president (H.J. Cody), heavy with symbolic references to both his and Underhill's service in the Great War. He urged unity among university intellectuals to protect a 'fallen comrade' in what he perceived to be the 'war on the home-front,' that is, the fight to preserve the sacred medieval tradition of scholarly freedom. Innis objected strongly to the Ontario legislature's censure of Underhill and was willing to resign to defend his principles. 'If a man's position is endangered because of reckless fearlessness' to speak freely about the war, he proclaimed, 'I should be glad to run the risk of losing my own academic position to save him.'[95] What was more, Innis disagreed with an outside body's adjudicating on an issue over which it had no jurisdiction. Underhill's alleged wrongdoings were the concern of the university and the university alone.[96] Toronto had established an 'enviable reputation in the maintenance of academic freedom,' Innis concluded. If it damaged Underhill's reputation by not defending the Canadian historian, 'we lose the respect of other institutions' throughout Canada, Great Britain, and the United States.[97]

Innis's response to the Underhill affair was not merely an effort to support a censured colleague. Nor was it simply a defence of academic freedom. Rather, it called attention to a larger issue, an issue of 'vital importance' to the maintenance of freedom in a society at war.[98] The issue of academic freedom acted for Innis as a prism through which were refracted problems associated with liberal-democratic principles. As an example, the usurpation of additional powers by 'free' states was repugnant to liberal precepts. The rise of militarism and the increase of special controls like the War Measures Act limited individual liberties and greatly burdened the free-thinking individual's understanding of current philosophical difficulties. Like Arthur Lower (see chapter 2), Innis was profoundly concerned that the historic protection afforded scholars to express themselves freely had been eroded. To Innis, the war represented the twilight of liberty not only for the academy but also for western culture. In stifling free enquiry and directing scholarly attention away from academic obligations, academics had become part of the control apparatus of the modern state. In Innisian language, they were caught up in an intensifying monopoly of knowledge from which there seemed little hope of escape.

In 'A Plea for the University Tradition,' his most succinct statement of the university problem, Innis demonstrated how the university had come under attack from political and religious institutions and how it was able to avoid the adverse effects of knowledge monopolies. Innis reiterated that the university was an instrument that exposed bias and promoted truth. He showed, therefore, how it was the historical counterweight to bias. From the nineteenth century on, however, the western university had become less respectful of its central humanistic traditions and had thus succumbed to new scientific and empirical trends. In the mid-twentieth century, Innis added, the university fell away even further from its old beliefs and yielded to the tendencies of 'bureaucracy and dictatorship,' 'the intensification of nationalism,' and the 'evils of monopolies in commerce and industry.'[99] Indeed, by mid-century, the tradition of unbiased humanistic scholarship had clearly lapsed.

Innis went on, in 'A Plea for the University Tradition' and other writings of the 1940s, to detail the effects of monopolies of knowledge on the academy. For example, he bristled at his own university's efforts to streamline operations and eliminate courses deemed non-essential to the war. In a memorandum to President Cody, he complained that these activities were not only a breach of academic freedom, but also a blow to the 'prestige of the university' and a 'dismantling and weakening of the [course] structure' that the president and others had worked so hard to establish.[100] Innis also bemoaned the scant teaching resources available at the University as a result of the flight of scholars to government bureaucracies. In a letter to G.M. Weir of the Department of Pensions and Health, he explained that the lack of personnel meant that the fledgling graduate program at the University of Toronto was almost at a point where it had to cease work.[101] He also railed against the state's ever-increasing efforts to 'conserve knowledge.' When the state intervened in higher education, he argued, the university then became concerned with fact-finding to aid in the resolution of current problems and hence began to disregard longer-term cultural and philosophical difficulties. This tendency towards the conservation of facts, he wrote, was evident 'in the lack of interest in educational philosophy and in the tendency of educational institutions ... to avoid major philosophical problems of western civilization.' For Innis, the penetration of outside groups into university life was deep indeed. Summarizing his contempt for the politicization of the university, he complained that governments and political groups had been 'compelled to lend themselves to the systematic rape of scholarship ... Nothing has been more indicative of the decline in cultural life in Canada since the last war than the infiltration of politics in the Universities, and nothing has done more to hamper the development of intellectual maturity than the institutional framework of Canadian Universities which permits and encourages the exploitation of scholars, and plays the treasonable rôle of betraying the traditions for which we fought in the last war and for which we fight in this.'[102]

Innis's close friend J.B. Brebner agreed wholeheartedly with Innis's strictures on the state and scholarly life. In *Scholarship for Canada*, Brebner argued that swollen by the demands of the war, the modern state had participated in what amounted to an attack on academics. The state 'conflict[ed] sharply with intellectual and other personal freedoms,' he wrote. The current war produced political, economic, and philosophical pressures that necessitated a strengthened state with an enlarged bureaucracy. Requiring 'expertness and specialized knowledge as never before,' governments 'reached into the universities to obtain them, thereby often putting the blinders of specific political direction on eyes which serve wisdom better when they were able to look around freely.' Public opinion, he added, became 'less favourable to the scholar's spirit of free enquiry.'[103] Echoing Innis's sentiments in the aftermath of the Underhill affair, Brebner contended that the state persecuted scholars who presented ideas or opinions that conflicted with the rhetoric of the party in power. This devaluation of academic freedom and scholarly insight, he concluded, had plagued Canada throughout the course of the war.

Brebner, Innis, and others had recognized the illiberal effects of war on scholarship. They also had attempted to come to the aid of a system of scholarship under siege. In addition to matters of state intervention and the impact of war on academics, however, scholars had become gravely concerned about the academy's wartime reorientation. From early in the war it had become apparent that while the applied sciences had increased in status among government and the public alike, the arts and humanities had achieved no similar standing. On the contrary, as the conflict wore on, the relevance of the arts and humanities came into question. The situation came to a head in late 1942. By November academics across the country had heard of plans to curtail instruction in the arts for the duration of the war.[104] In response, Innis and other members of the Canadian Social Science Research Council (CSSRC) petitioned Prime Minister Mackenzie King to reconsider government plans. In its November memorandum, the CSSRC[105] stated its wish to 'encourage in every possible fashion a continuation of the Arts tradition in Canadian universities.' CSSRC members also pointed out that Canadian arts faculties were few, had small numbers of faculty and students, and hence were easy to maintain. What was most significant, the memorandum emphasized that 'the weakening of the Arts tradition' and the 'place of the Humanities' in favour of the natural sciences was not only unfair to those who fought to defend Canada in the war, but also held 'ominous implications for the whole future of civilization.'[106]

Innis and the others did not specify exactly what the 'ominous implications' would be, but the message was clear: the arts and humanities were of fundamental importance to the favourable outcome of the war. The war, the CSSRC implied, was as much a non-military struggle on the home-front as it was a struggle of men and materiel abroad. It was a conflict of 'cultural standards' and beliefs that had become besieged in the current climate. CSSRC members accordingly implored the prime minister to maintain the existing policy on universities, thereby 'ensuring the future health of our Canadian society.'[107] Despite assertions to the contrary, in short, Innis and the CSSRC membership insisted that the humanistic tradition was of vital importance, especially during a time of war.[108]

Despite failing health, Sir Robert Falconer, the former president of the University of Toronto, offered a clear statement on the significance of the humanities. In a 1943 piece, provocatively entitled 'The Humanities in the War-time University,' he responded to the recent issues involving the arts and humanities. Echoing Innis's earlier words, Falconer showed how scholars had relinquished their search for truth and objectivity and their role as 'neutral arbiters' and instead had been co-opted into the service of the state. The humanities, in consequence, had failed in this oppressive climate to fulfil their chief purpose of providing spiritual and personal freedom. Owing to the current focus on the conflicts of races, nationalities, and the preoccupation with the destinies of humankind, they had been unable to promote the intrinsic worth of the human character and to foster the conditions that historically had moulded the humanistic spirit. The war had resulted, in brief, in the blunting of the university's function of demonstrating the virtues of humanity and explaining the loss of the liberated human spirit.[109]

Like Falconer, Innis also expressed his views on the state of the humanities in the wartime world. Characteristically, he focused on the importance of the scholarly approach to knowledge and understanding. The humanities, he contended, were integral to the recognition of biased methods and to the adoption of a balanced approach. Humanistic scholarship effectively counterbalanced scientific approaches to knowledge and highlighted instead the non-quantifiable, non-scientific aspects of human behaviour. It was most useful in examining the philosophical and historical facets of human conduct, while it provided a counterweight to newer mathematical and scientific models of learning. Indeed, Innis advocated the resurrection of the 'Greek tradition of the humanities,' which had been marginalized in the modern university but had become integral to the 'the constant avoidance of extremes and extravagance.'[110] As always, Innis was wary of bias and argued that the reversion to the intellectual principles of balance and proportion of the ancient Greeks was vital to understanding the limitations of thought. Disdain for the Greek approach, moreover, was simply another indication that modern scholars failed to appreciate the vital philosophical problems of bias and monopoly. Innis was convinced that the decline of the humanistic-classical tradition meant the loss of understanding of the true nature of cultural change. What was perhaps most dangerous, it implied the loss of individual freedom to assess human conduct and to assert fundamental human qualities like the autonomous individual spirit. Stating the 'Greek problem,' Innis commented that '[w]e have been much concerned in academic circles with the decline of Greek, but I am afraid we do not realize that this is a symptom of an unwillingness to face the exacting demands implied in the study of Greek civilization. [As a result,] we have neglected the philosophical problems of the West.'[111]

Perhaps Innis's greatest lament on the university question, then, was the sundering of the balance and perspective of humanistic learning. However, concern over the decline of the 'Greek approach' was not peculiar to Innis's world-view. Indeed, it resonated throughout the Canadian humanistic community. In *The Humanities in Canada*, Watson Kirkconnell and A.S.P. Woodhouse published the results of a survey of humanities faculties across Canada. They found that humanists were in 'the midst of a movement that [was] reacting against excessive pre-occupation with techniques divorced from humanizing influences.' Kirkconnell and Woodhouse discovered that scholars like Innis disliked trends towards de-humanized scholarship and advocated instead a return to the humanist learning of the pre-modern university. They asserted that association with poets, orators, and historians detached the academic 'from the mere present, humanized his imagi-nation and elevated his sentiments.' As Innis did, they intimated that the humanities contained the eternal truths about the human condi-tion. The purpose of the humanities was to aid in the development of intellectual faculties to appreciate the 'full measure of humanity.'[112] In the tradition of the Greek humanists, Kirkconnell and Woodhouse championed the humanities as a balancing influence for moderns, enabling a complete understanding of cultural and human circum-stances. Indeed, the humanities' greatest role was to liberalize and to provide much needed perspective.

Kirkconnell and Woodhouse also argued that the humanities con-tributed to personal, intellectual development. They fostered 'inner cultivation.' The two scholars believed association with the beauty of art and the reason of philosophy would develop a 'greater esthetic sen-sitivity, a purification and refinement of emotions, and a keener, more creative experience of beauty.' In addition, the humanities promoted the ethical and moral awareness of the individual. Kirkconnell and Woodhouse contended that a liberal education was essential in mod-ern times rife with the perversity of war; for it embodied the moral val-ues of goodness and beauty and confronted 'the terror and cruelty of [the] contemporary world.'[113] Liberal learning was, in short, much more than mere instruction in the arts and letters; it was the means by which human virtues could be realized and the human condition, cor-rupted by the immoralities of the present age, could be set aright.

Kirkconnell and Woodhouse implied that the academy functioned to enhance the 'spiritual' elements of human existence. Indeed, for many scholars there was a strong sense that the university had become a cen-tre of spiritual uplift during an age of deteriorating moral standards. More than an institution to promote research or even to preserve old learning, it had become responsible for addressing spiritual problems such as totalitarianism and race hatred. Kirkconnell expounded on this fuller conception of higher education early in the war. Along with con-tributing to human knowledge and 'providing intellectual leadership,' the university and, specifically, the faculty of liberal arts functioned to heighten 'for each student the significance of life in its intellectual, aesthetic, and moral aspects.' The liberal arts, for Kirkconnell, operated to evoke the three basic 'powers of personality': the rational, aesthetic, and moral. Along with developing rational faculties and cultivating the appreciation of the beautiful, the liberal arts brought out a 'fundamentally religious principle in life,' an 'enduring foundation' for all human thinking and activity. They 'consecrate[d] one's will to the highest moral and spiritual principles.' Added to the purely rational-intellectual and cultural functions, humanistic scholarship enabled one to connect with the timeless and transcendent; it opened the individual to 'the realm of truth, beauty, and goodness.' Only through the realization of the artistic, moral, and religious heritages of the past, Kirkconnell concluded, could one achieve the full expression of humanity and, most important, free one's soul. The university had been central, in short, to the realization of the true nature of humanity and, as such, the liberation of the human spirit.[114]

While elaborating on no distinct spiritual nexus between the academy and the individual, Innis emphasized with Kirkconnell the significance of the university's duty to cultivate values. In addition to its 'major role' of recognizing the collapse of western civilization, the academy, Innis declared, must make possible a life of study to enable the students or teachers to understand cultural change.[115] Although profoundly influenced by the effects of the industrial and communications revolutions, the university was key to reestablishing a universal point of view and therefore to understanding the knowledge monopolies and control mechanisms inherent to the modern state.[116] Liberty to pursue truth, and hence the opportunity to gain universal insights, were most excellent qualities of the university tradition. Without true academic freedom, Innis explained, there could be no understanding of past or present, no insight into the future. The decay of scholarly free enquiry reflected a society in decline, a social order that shunned the enduring virtues bound up in the university tradition and stressed instead the values of power, force, and control. Only with the revival of university traditions during the dark days of the war could there be hope for the resurrection of cultural traditions intrinsic to the pursuit of truth. Scholars must, therefore 'dedicate themselves afresh,' Innis declared in May 1944, 'to the maintenance of a tradition without which western culture disappears.' Indeed, they had 'an obligation of maintaining traditions concerned with the search for truth for which men have laid down and have been asked to lay down their lives.'[117]

Lacking the grandeur of Innis's pleas for the university tradition, other humanists and social scientists nevertheless expounded on the role of the humanities and social sciences in promoting values and enhancing cultural traditions. For instance, responding to a letter from John Marshall (associate director of the humanities, Rockefeller Foundation) in May 1943, Donald Creighton discussed the historian's function in imparting cultural standards. Prompted by the recent collapse of the French, Creighton related, a small group of social scientists (including Creighton himself) met 'to discuss the subject of the social sciences in the postwar world.' The problem of values and the academy was especially important to Creighton's own discipline. Works such as 'The Failure of the Historian' (presented at the 1942 meeting of the CHA) and Queen's historian R.G. Trotter's piece on 'Aims in the Study and Teaching of History in Canadian Universities Today,' lent weight to Creighton's view 'that the whole problem of aims and values in the study of history in general, and of Canadian history in particular, has been lying almost oppressively upon us ever since the summer of 1940.'[118] Historians, he implied, were not merely responsible for chronicling, to the current generation, the minutiae of bygone ages. Their duty, on the contrary, was to preserve and teach cultural standards. Through learning about past cultures, individuals could both appreciate and assert timeless historical values and ultimately help moderns to cope with contemporary tragedies. Not simply a stuffy, esoteric study, history was, instead, of considerable contemporary importance.

Adding their voices to that of Donald Creighton, Innis, Tom Easterbrook, Carlo Ginsberg, and Marshall McLuhan, among others of the 'Values' Discussion Group, reflected on the question of values in the social sciences. They agreed that while the 'physical scientist can take a stand from which to view his data objectively, the social scientist is unable to avoid identifying himself with the data.' It was suggested during the March 1947 meeting that while the university should facilitate individual moral judgment and promote cultural values, these roles had languished during the war because of specialization, the rise of natural scientific methodology, and other manifestations of academic modernization.[119]

Contributing the main topic for discussion in a subsequent meeting of the 'Values' group, Marshall McLuhan contended that the arts were 'a storehouse of values.' The liberal arts, he argued, must be considered a balancing force to the emerging social sciences and natural sciences.

They were crucial, McLuhan and the others agreed, because they contained the grounding values, the traditions on which western society was built. The arts 'train perception and develop judgment,' it was concluded, and, ultimately, they armed individuals with a sense of timeless cultural standards.[120] Education in the liberal arts, in brief, provided the essential skills with which moderns could cope in a postwar world that continued to lack absolute standards and an understanding of cultural demise.

For scholars such as Kirkconnell, Innis, McLuhan, and other likeminded academic critics, the university tradition was as important to the mid-twentieth century as it had always been. The inculcation of virtues and the appreciation of the good life – the nineteenth-century conception of the university 'to make men' – seemed to several scholars to gain a new relevance in the 1940s. Amid the apparent 'decay of morals' and the 'breakdown of international codes,' a sense of 'personal responsibility' and perspective had been eroded.[121] For the advocates of the university tradition, a rekindling of the arts and humanities was central to the restoration of a stable social order. The academy's role of promoting a moral, socially responsible culture had become essential to a civilization that verged on collapse.

Critics of academic modernization thus were convinced of the need for a resurgence of the traditional academy. As we will discover in chapter 4, however, their view of the university was highly mythologized. Although based on historical fact, the 'university tradition' was more mythological in composition. The critics' motives in creating a historical fiction were twofold. First, as we have noted here, they wanted to bring into stark relief the current plight of the university. By contrasting modern institutions with the 'university tradition,' they could effectively demonstrate the dire conditions under which academics suffered. Commentators thus used rhetoric and sometimes even blatant hyperbole to further their causes. Second, and perhaps most significant, the university critics championed the plight of the scholar as a way to further their own ends. The 1940s were truly a period in which the prestige and utility of humanists had been called into question. Blandishments on the need for a rediscovery of 'humane' values and philosophic insights helped critics to gain a certain legitimacy and notoriety in a hostile age. The critics pronounced that, much more than the applied scientists, humanists were the defenders of western civilization. They protected moderns from the inhumanities of war and, most of all, culture from outright collapse.

This search for social pertinence and a 'restoration' of the scholar's traditional and, indeed, 'true' function was an effort to amplify the voices of humanists, which had recently been drowned out by the clamour of the war. Underpaid and clearly unappreciated, the critics perceived that the time was right to make their voices heard.

The Second World War was critical to the emergence of the modern Canadian university. Although the war had no part in initiating trends in academic modernization, it functioned to accelerate existing tendencies. Most noticeably, it showed to many the usefulness of universities as storehouses of technical personnel and as centres for industrial research. Universities gained a new-found notoriety and prestige among government officials and society at large, owing to their contributions to the war effort. As a result of the efforts of practical scientists, economists, and other social scientists, they achieved for perhaps the first time in their existence a widespread social relevance. As interest grew on the parts of governments and the general public and as enrolments and funding for the practical disciplines increased, Canadian academies shed their historical liberal arts orientation in favour of a technical and scientific direction that emphasized the social utilitarian function of higher learning. The siphoning-off of scholars to various extra-academic posts and the imperilling of arts programs that many considered irrelevant to the prosecution of war, furthermore, provided striking evidence that Canadian society had shunned older university traditions and was developing new ones. The long transition from the liberal arts and towards 'technical education' had received a tremendous surge during the early 1940s.

Along with revealing to many the value and operational utility of higher learning, the war provided the additional impetus for critics of the modern university. The conflict showed the extreme peril of modern society, and, most important, it laid bare the critical significance of the scholar and the university to the social order. Some academics considered the wartime as a transitory period, one in which a new society would emerge phoenix-like from the ashes of a razed culture. Other scholars contended that the imminence of cultural decay was manifested in the crisis of values and the decline of historic institutions like higher education. Whatever the causes and effects of the great historical disruption, university critics realized that academics played a central role in addressing the current cultural malaise. Far from being merely a centre for technical study, the university – and, in particular, humanists and social scientists – had a manifold part to play in contributing to the wartime world. Humanists and social scientists, in the minds of the critics of higher education, could see past the immediacies of war preparations, military strategies, and wartime politics to understand that the conflict had truly represented a disruption of western civilization. When the citizenry had been incapacitated by the propaganda and rhetoric of the war, for example, they perceived the withering away of liberties and the decline of democracy. Scholars had the insight, in other words, to recognize what others failed to see. Herein lay their ultimate worth to society. Indeed, the basic function of academics, according to the university critics, was to provide context and perspective and therefore allow a greater comprehension of cultural forces. Ultimately, the social role of intelligence had been clear to the critics of the modern academy: the uncovering of truth in the time of great peril.

More than understanding profound culture change, scholars also functioned to help the struggling social order in an extremely dangerous age. For some observers, such as Arthur Lower and Frank Underhill, university personnel ought to be able to access the levers of power in government and elsewhere and thereby operate as social agents, shaping the development of a young society. Other critics, most notably Harold Innis, Watson Kirkconnell, and A.S.P. Woodhouse, argued that scholars could provide an essential service to the social order by remaining at their posts. Innis contended that the search for truth through tireless scholarly activity was the only means through which academics could help to shape society. Kirkconnell and Woodhouse reasoned that humanistic learning was essential to understanding the realities of human interactions, since it enabled moderns to connect with their true natures. Moreover, Innis, Kirkconnell, Woodhouse, Falconer, and McLuhan, among other scholars, knew that the humanities were central to offsetting the modern trends towards practical, scientific education. The liberal arts tradition was the purveyor of the timeless values of western civilization. In preserving and conveying those virtues, humanists and social scientists could provide a vital service to society by offering an alternative to the materialist values characteristic of the modern world. Humanism could counterbalance a world obsessed with the scientific and the technological. Ultimately, it could help to restore stability and make a fundamental contribution to a nation at war.

In extolling the inestimable merits of a humanist education, the critics of academic modernization not only wished to address pressing social problems and lament the decline of the liberal arts; they also wanted to reach out to a society that had turned its back on the traditional university. Above all, their strictures were designed to show the social relevance of the liberal arts to university officials, government authorities, and the public more generally. The university, in mythological form, was an essential institution without which Canadian society could not properly develop. In a world in which the academic was marginalized and the value of scholarship was in dramatic decline, the university was much more than a social utility, a mere centre of research to be drawn upon for immediate developmental needs. Through the search for truth and the promotion spiritual values, the academy, to the advocates of the university tradition, remained a beacon, an institution that was to guide society to safety during perilous times. The social function of the university had been made obvious during a period of despair.

The arts and humanities thus had a social relevance that surpassed that of the natural sciences and other practical disciplines. The crisis of war had made that fact painfully obvious. The war provided the opportunity for humanists to demonstrate how the liberal arts could address that crisis. Ultimately, advocates of the liberal arts wished to gain for their work and the humanities generally the same notoriety that society had afforded to technical education. This was the main rationale for their inflated reckoning of the traditional academy. Lamentably, however, Canadian society had failed to understand the sociocultural pertinence of the traditional university. Indeed, the flurry of writing on the humanities signalled the relative demise of the arts tradition as much as it marked an effort to resurrect an institution undergoing profound change. The continuation of writings after 1945 on the demise of the humanist tradition indicated the ongoing march of academic modernization. The modernization of the academy, to be sure, did not end with the war. Rather, the 1939–45 period proved to be a mere starting point in the transformation of higher learning in Canada.

4

The Modernization of
Higher Learning in Canada II:
Academia after the War

Before 1939 the modernization of Canadian universities had been an evolution, beginning around the turn of the century and building momentum throughout the interwar period. The Second World War provided an additional impetus to changes that had already been well under way. The war accentuated existing trends away from the traditional liberal arts orientation of higher learning towards a greater pragmatism. The applied sciences and practical disciplines flourished, while the humanities and other studies deemed non-essential to the war effort seemed to languish. Once social critics and purveyors of cultural values, by war's end the universities had become renowned for their contributions to a technologically intensive war effort. They had responded to the unprecedented need for technical expertise and practical 'know-how,' and had achieved, in consequence, an unparalleled utilitarian focus.

For those preoccupied with the future of higher learning in Canada the crucial question was whether or not wartime developments in higher education were merely an aberration or a dangerous intensification of an existing trend. Even by the latter stages of the war, the answer to the query remained unclear. Discerning the aims of higher learning, however, again was critical to understanding the direction of the university. The National Conference of Canadian Universities (NCCU) report on 'postwar problems,' for instance, claimed that after the war 'universities will have an unprecedented opportunity to render an essential service to the nation.' Certain problems had to be solved, however, before Canadian universities could 'play their full part in the postwar world.'[1] Along with resolving immediate practical problems, such as finance, equipment, physical difficulties, and returning veterans, the report recommended that Canadian universities re-examine the role of the liberal arts within the university. In appendix five of the report, R.C. Wallace urged that universities make an effort to reintegrate humane studies within the modern university. They must move away from their tendency to emphasize practical over humanistic learning and instead integrate 'these two fields of knowledge into a unified whole.' The reassertion of humane learning, Wallace suggested, was key to the post-war development of Canadian universities. In his contribution to the report, Harold Innis agreed with Wallace that the war had contributed to the decline of the humanities and the social sciences.[2] As Wallace had done, he argued that the serious imbalance between the two main branches of knowledge weakened the university's service to society. In contrast to his fellow committee member, however, Innis urged that the primacy of the humanities and social sciences over the professions and the practical sciences be acknowledged. 'Reconstruction,' he concluded, would be futile without this critical first step.[3] Echoing Wallace and Innis, W.R. Taylor, principal of University College, summed up the post-war challenge of the Canadian university. 'The university of today,' he wrote in 1946, 'is in a state of confusion ... To effect some measure of reform there must be born in each university a resolve to examine itself and to order itself in its several faculties in accordance with the demands of a common purpose. Practically this would mean ... that all specialized, vocational, and professional training would be projected on a broad base of cultural subjects.'[4] Like that of Wallace and Innis, Taylor's message was clear: to fulfil its educative role and to provide service to post-war Canadians the university must curtail specialized training and place technical knowledge under the governance of humane studies.

Scholars' preoccupations about the post-war development of the Canadian university were justified. As it had been before and during the war, the ongoing development of the utilitarian university remained after 1945 a focal issue of higher education. Sharing the concern of scholars, the public and the media also queried the direction of the post-war university. In 1944, *Saturday Night* asked, 'Will Canada's Universities Meet [the] Needs of the Post-war?' and in the following year responded to its own query by stating: 'Learning as an end in itself [was] no longer valid in a nation which needs the minds of its youth for leadership in the rough new world to come.'[5] Two years later, a national Gallup poll revealed the degree to which Canadians believed universities ought to maintain their utilitarian emphasis. Of those canvassed, 60 per cent indicated that education should focus on 'practical subjects'; in addition, in newspaper editorials and magazine articles writers implored universities to focus on the training of financiers and business leaders.[6] Lamentably for the advocates of humanistic learning, they made no reference to the import of contemplation or humane values to post-war development.

Enrolment figures in the professional faculties also illustrate the increasing popularity of practical education. Of all professional programs only theology and agriculture did not experience growth in the 1940s and 1950s. Undergraduate enrolments in medicine in Canadian universities increased by 50 per cent (to 4,244), while dentistry (to 1,055), household science (to 1,598), and veterinary medicine (to 466) all doubled. Student registrations in nursing (to nearly 1,700), pharmacy (to nearly 1,500), and occupational and physical therapy (to 476) tripled, while engineering enrolments experienced the greatest overall increase: enrolments tripled to nearly 15,000 by 1960. Enrolments in other professional faculties, such as architecture, law, library science, education, and social work, also increased greatly. Graduate enrolments likewise experienced large growth. Full-time registration in graduate studies more than tripled to 6,518 by 1960.[7] Although overall enrolments in the arts and sciences also tended to grow, numbers of undergraduates in these fields declined, compared with student registrations in professional programs.[8] The dominant status of the arts and pure sciences continued to be eroded in the post-war era as the long-term professionalization of Canadian universities continued unabated into the 1950s and 1960s.

The creation of Carleton College also symbolized the rise of the 'professional' university. Responding to a perceived need for English-language college instruction, a group headed by Ottawa members of the YMCA, civil servant Hugh Kennleyside, and Henry Marshall Tory applied for and received charter status under the province of Ontario's Companies Act.[9] Not only was Carleton the first institution to be chartered under the Companies Act, which in itself symbolized new attitudes towards institutions of higher learning, it was also the first university not to have liberal arts departments at its centre. Carleton focused on journalism and public and business administration, rather than having English, philosophy, history, and the classics, along with the newer social sciences, as core disciplines. 'Adult' or 'continuing' education, which had been in existence for decades but which rose to prominence in Canada only after 1945,[10] was also important to the new college's educative mandate.[11] Departing from earlier models, then, Carleton College was a new type of educational institution, which provided an example for universities in the coming decades.

Other universities also struggled with the professionalization issue. In 1945 authorities at McMaster University stated that their institution would not succumb to current pressures and develop new schools of engineering, law, and medicine.[12] Only a year later, however, McMaster chancellor, G.P. Gilmour, indicated that the Baptist Convention (McMaster's governing body) wanted to incorporate secular Hamilton College into the Baptist institution under the Companies Act. The move bound the university to the business world. Indeed, the wider implications of McMaster's new structure were obvious: lured by large-scale corporate funding, the university had jeopardized its denominational identity and its historical orientation as solely a liberal arts institution in favour of a new accommodation with the secular world.[13]

In addition to the professionalization and secularization of higher learning, government funding of the post-war university became an important issue after 1945. First, very few Canadian universities stood outside the ambit of provincial government. The few universities that did not receive government funding by 1945 – mostly denominational institutions like McMaster – were secularized and therefore became eligible for state funding.[14] What is more, government funds became increasingly important to those universities already reliant on the public purse. Because of vastly increasing enrolments[15] in the demobilization period, Canadian universities required additional funds. Fortunately, provincial governments, assisted by buoyant revenues, recognized the dire need for money and made an effort to deal with the burgeoning funding malaise. The Ontario experience best illustrates how provincial governments participated in university finances. Acknowledging the importance of universities to winning the war and to achieving material prosperity in the post-war period, Premier George Drew's government vowed to free universities 'from the burden of their debts that is hampering their efforts,' thereby allowing them to cope with increased costs of research and the exigencies of a multitude of new registrants. Accordingly, Drew's government resolved in March 1944 to distribute grants totalling $1.316 million to the three eligible universities – $816,000 to Toronto and $460,000 each to Queen's and Western.[16] Other funding initiatives supplemented these grants (which were to become annual operational funding), including special grants providing for an Institute of Child Study at the University of Toronto and for Ontario medical schools. No longer strictly denominational, McMaster University was eligible for and received government financing, while the newly incorporated Carleton University (1952) now also received grants. Carrying out their earlier commitment to assist scientific research in agriculture, forestry, and mining throughout the province, the government also funded institutes of trade and vocational education, including the newly established Ryerson Institute of Technology (1948). Unlike his predecessor Mitchell Hepburn,[17] Drew understood the fundamental linkages between material development and adequately funded universities. Indeed, his efforts to increase public financing of Ontario's institutions reflected an age in which the merits of universities were adjudged according to their practical contributions to society.[18]

Increases in public funding notwithstanding, concern over university funding became even more important as the new decade approached. As it stood, government financing often only partially defrayed the rising costs associated with increased enrolments. Many universities had to finance increasingly costly capital expenditures in the absence of government aid. While some of them were able to gain private funding, the majority of institutions made economies in other areas like professors' salaries to try to compensate for the shortfall.[19] Such efforts were only partly successful, however, in freeing up the funds necessary to cope with post-war expansion. Much more money would have to be infused into the universities to deal with the post-war boom. Hence, more than ever before, university authorities made their way to provincial capitals with hands outstretched to secure additional grants. The ongoing quest for funds had reached a critical stage in the history of the Canadian university.

Amid the prolonged funding crisis, interested observers became concerned over how funds were distributed within and among post-secondary institutions. Provincial governments were predisposed to fund practical disciplines rather than the arts and humanities. Academic councils devoted to the applied sciences and practical studies also tended to be better funded. The development of the National Research Council (NRC) illustrated the funding bias. As happened during the Great War (see chapter 2), the 1939–45 war greatly stimulated the development of the NRC. The staff and budget of the council sharply increased only a few months after the declaration of war, a trend that was to continue throughout the conflict. By 1943, for instance, the council's budget was five times that of 1939. This wartime expansion continued in the post-war age. Because the post-war period was one of relative prosperity and, most important, because the war demonstrated to governments and the public at large the merits of funding applied sciences, the federal government was both able and willing to continue to provide the NRC with stable funding. Large-scale funding meant, in turn, that the NRC could go on contributing large sums to the universities, those institutions that continued in peacetime to train scientific personnel and undertake most of the country's fundamental and applied research. Indeed, the NRC granted almost $1 million to universities and colleges in 1947–8, compared with a relatively paltry $200,000 a decade earlier. It also had the financial wherewithal to introduce post-doctoral fellowships (1945) and to provide 'consolidated grants' to establish research groups and institutes. By the early 1950s budgets and NRC grants to universities continued their ascent. In 1960–1 grants-in-aid to Canadian universities increased almost tenfold to $9.5 million.[20] Under new president, E.W.R. Steacie (president of the NRC, 1952–1962), the bonds between the council and Canadian post-secondary institutions continued to strengthen.[21] Faculties of applied science and research had secured increasingly high levels of funding from government councils like the NRC and, by the late 1940s and early 1950s, from private agencies.[22] In a word, increases in post-war funding showed the esteem that Canadians held for the utilitarian university.

If funding is the measure by which the relative merits of departments and faculties were judged, then the humanities and social sciences stacked up poorly indeed compared with the practical disciplines. Whereas by the early 1950s the NRC had provided grants-in-aid in the millions of dollars annually, the Canadian Social Science Research Council (CSSRC) received only $718,850 from its inception (1940) until the creation of the Canada Council (1957). What is more, American philanthropic organizations, not Canadian governments or private corporations, provided the bulk of CSSRC grants. Like the CSSRC, the Humanities Research Council (HRC) fared poorly compared with the NRC. Its total revenues from its establishment in 1943 until 1957, the year before the inception of the Canada Council, was a meagre $356,423. Like the CSSRC, the HRC relied heavily on the Rockefeller and Carnegie organizations for contributions.[23] Canadians seemed to have little money indeed for the development of the liberal arts.

The consequences of inadequate funding were manifold. In practical terms, not only did Canadian universities lack sufficient money to aid all aspects of scholarly research (everything from travel to photostatic expenses), but they also harboured inadequate libraries and archival facilities. In 1947 Watson Kirkconnell lamented: 'Only ten academic libraries of 124 in Canada report [100,000] books,' a minimum standard established in 1922. Only four or five Canadian libraries today, he added, 'measure up to minimum American standards of twenty-five years ago.' To remedy the situation the federal government needed 'to take immediate practical steps towards the ultimate establishment of a National Library.' A national research facility and 'bibliographic centre' were essential, Kirkconnell concluded, to compensate for these deficiencies by making available extensive research resources to Canadian scholars.[24]

More important than even library resources were scholars' salaries. Scholarly remuneration at Canadian universities was well below that of academics at other western universities. J.B. Brebner, a Canadian who was working in the United States, complained that scholars' salaries at Canada's 'elite institutions' – McGill and Toronto – 'were at least 20 per cent below those of Boston, Chicago, New York,' and comparable British institutions. The salary issue, in consequence, impelled many of the brightest Canadian scholars to go south or to Britain. The leading universities had to take action, Brebner concluded in his 1945 report on the state of Canadian scholarship, to remedy this grave situation.[25] Watson Kirkconnell concurred with Brebner's assessment. He argued: 'One of the most crying needs is for the general upward revision of salaries.' Kirkconnell characterized the 'scale of academic salaries in Canada' as 'calamitous' and warned that if universities did not soon augment salaries, then many promising young scholars would be diverted to other professions or into the better-paid colleges of the United States.[26] Looking back on the immediate post-war period, B.S. Keirstead and S.D. Clark concluded: 'Because academic salaries were low, many of the best men have gone to the US or to government or business. Canadian universities as a result ... are tending to attract second-rate men with inadequate training.'[27]

Other problems, less readily visible but just as pressing, also flowed from the funding issue. For the critics of the modern university the most important of these was academic liberty. Just as the war had imperiled the free university, the post-war funding problem also threatened academic freedom. Critics pointed out that university administrators focused far too much effort and time on securing funds for their impoverished departments, faculties, or universities. As a result of this seemingly continuous search for funds, university officials of all stripes neglected their fundamental duties as scholars. University presidents, for example, in the past involved with academic issues, were now consumed with 'raising money and giving speeches.' J.B. Brebner, to cite one critic, advised that presidents ensure that their institutions stay focused on their main objective: scholarship. Instead of fund-raising, speechifying, and administrating, the president's role was to 'forward and to express the intrinsic function of the university.'[28] President G.E. Hall of Western offered an even broader admonition of university administrators: '[P]residents, deans and other officials in our universities,' he declared in 1949, 'have had to forsake education to become executive supersalesmen, leaders of delegations and beggars, so that universities [could] even remain in existence.'[29] Instead of being the chief spokespersons of the intellectual world, authorities were leading the modern academy astray. True to his pre-war and wartime positions, Innis also decried the 'business and political exploitation of universities.' Universities, he complained, appeared to be up for sale to the highest bidder. Ultimately, the infiltration of the pecuniary factor into academics would have dire results. 'To buy universities is to destroy them,' Innis concluded abruptly, 'and with them the civilization for which they stand.'[30]

The increasingly intense competition for government grants and private funding indeed threatened the character and integrity of scholarly activity. Brebner argued that, to flourish, scholarship must be free from outside influences. Talents, abilities, and the social usefulness of the scholars, he averred in a piece tellingly entitled 'Endowed and Free,' should not be wasted on 'applied scholarship' (scholarship commissioned by government or private industry). Above all, Brebner wanted to ensure that scholars did not submit themselves to the 'compromises, adjustments, and expediencies which are necessary in business, politics, and the professions.' For the association with these extra-academic groups would surely 'impair the very capacity for unprejudiced scholarship' that made scholars so valuable and so rare.[31] Keirstead and Clark also waded into the debate. With promises of large grants and ample salaries, research institutes seduced scholars away from their work to engage in 'factual research' that was of 'slight theoretical interest.' Much money and time were wasted as a result, resources that would be more usefully spent on 'creative scholarship.' 'Only a real passion for scholarship,' Keirstead and Clark concluded, could protect scholars from the corrupting forces of money and notoriety.[32] Only in focusing on unbiased academic enquiry, in other words, could scholarship remain pure and the university fulfil its fundamental purpose. In characteristically aphoristic style, Innis summarized the academy's struggle for scholarly autonomy: 'the university is essentially an ivory tower in which courage can be mustered to attack any concept which threatens to become a monopoly.'[33]

Certainly, the critics of higher learning considered freedom from outside influences critical to the ongoing viability of universities. The struggle for scholarly liberty, moreover, remained as intense after 1945 as it had been during the war. Yet tainted scholarship and the undue emphasis on the funding game were only part of critics' concerns. Indeed, a wider crisis of academic freedom became a growing preoccupation of critics. By the mid-1940s scholars had begun to realize the enduring quality of academic change. The wartime assault on the humanities was not an anomaly, the temporary consequence of the war; nor would universities necessarily revert to a prior stage of development once peace was restored. Rather, scholars recognized that the university had become an embattled institution and would continue to be held hostage by the society around it. As Innis claimed in 1944, higher education was 'besieged on all hands by villains,' a 'small and dwindling island surrounded by the flood of totalitarianism.'[34] The academy was indeed fighting for its very existence in the modern world. In the chaotic environment of the late 1940s and early 1950s the free existence of the academy in Canadian society seemed more than ever to be at stake.

The academic servility that Innis and others expounded upon was a complex phenomenon. More than merely the inexorable decline of the humanities and the rise to prominence of the utilitarian disciplines, the enslavement of the academy had wider implications. The most significant of these was the decline of the academy's 'true' historic function as the central spiritual and cultural institution of society. As suggested in the last chapter, the critics of academic modernization coalesced as a group first in their assessment of the mytho-historical role of the university. Second, they acknowledged the contemporary decay of academic traditions and attempted to find remedies for this grievous development. Indeed, the demise of university traditions, such as academic freedom, philosophic contemplation, and the growth of the utilitarian university, signalled more than an evolution of higher learning.

In the broadest sense, the decay of these traditions mirrored a profound change in Canadian society, the decline of its traditions of democracy and freedom, and an altered sense of cultural and moral values. Ultimately, the decay of the university implied, as Innis had suggested earlier, the decline of western civilization.

In an idealized conception of higher learning, critics claimed that the university's basic function had been to preserve knowledge and serve as a purveyor of the culture of the west. To use Arnold's phase, the university was to preserve the best that has been thought and said throughout the ages.[35] Its primary function, in the words of Vincent Massey, was to care for and preserve 'the entire inheritance of our civilization,' to maintain, in brief, 'the memory and evidence of ... accumulated cultural achievements, in the arts, and letters, in science, in philosophy and in religion.'[36] Universities, James S. Thomson claimed in 1945, 'belong to an international world of culture and knowledge. They are heirs of all ages, and claim the universal attainments of man's mind as their birthright.'[37] Higher learning, Donald Creighton agreed, had a conservative, Burkean function. One of its main purposes was to conserve the past, to record society's cultural inheritance, and to 'discuss' and 'interpret' those achievements 'in ways which are significant for new generations.' The emphasis of higher learning, he concluded, 'is necessarily in conservation rather than innovation; it is [the academy's] business to guard against the nihilism of rootless and disinherited marauders, [while preserving] the great traditions of a culture and the great traditions of a state.'[38]

More than serving simply as repositories for intellectual and cultural accomplishments, universities also had proactive functions. The first and perhaps most difficult to define of these functions was the academy's role as purveyor of moral virtue. Historically a humanistic institution imbued with Christian ideals, the academy was well placed to influence moral standards of the Canadian community. Perhaps most important, it was positioned to aid a population whose faith in humanity had wavered and a society in which confusion about spiritual values was rife. Indeed, critics of the modern university emphasized the role of academics to inculcate 'humane' and other quasi-religious and cultural values to bolster flagging faith in humanity. There was a need 'for the reacceptance of what may be described as an academic faith,' James Thomson declared in 1945, discussing the role of the academy in the post-war world. The last war had destroyed faith in the human spirit through perversities such as the mass destruction of humanity, the predominance of fascist ideologies, and, most devastating of all, systematic racial extermination. The university, Thomson argued, could restore faith in humanity. One of its greatest responsibilities was to teach students and Canadians at large that there was something to live for in a callous era.[39] In an age 'when mankind has ... been brought face to face with evil horror, ugliness and perversity,' Watson Kirkconnell and A.S.P. Woodhouse also looked to the academy for help. The 'ethical aspect' of a liberal education was essential in the 1940s, they averred, if Canadians hoped to attain maturity and 'apprehend moral values while confronting unflinchingly the terror and cruelty of [their] contemporary world.'[40] The 'will to good' that was inherent in a liberal education must be evoked to counteract the evils of the current age. 'The replacement of ignorance and brutality by knowledge, insight, taste and moral purpose' was indeed a crucial task for scholars. Just as Thomson had done two years previously, Kirkconnell and Woodhouse expounded upon the duty of scholars to the moral order. Simply put, they implored university men and women to recognize the moral dangers of the post-war era and to present humane alternatives.[41] Far from being irrelevant to the needs of a changing world, academics thus performed a critical moralizing function for a society that was in dire need of guidance.

Closely related to this moralizing role was the university's function as social critic. Academics had an obligation, critics of academic modernization contended, to assess social change and understand how society evolved. They were far from aloof scholars whose work had little meaning to the society around them. On the contrary, they were obliged to observe and make sense of their surroundings. Their work judged societal change and provided insight into correct courses of action for the future. More than social critics, university intellectuals had to act as social philosophers who became responsible for giving meaning to the social process and conveying that meaning to the public at large.

At no time was this role more important than in the mid-1940s. In an era not only of material but also cultural and indeed 'spiritual' reconstruction, the university critics put a heavy burden on the frail shoulders of academics. In a social climate increasingly inimical to 'humane knowledge' they looked to the university for remedies. Writing near the end of the war, Innis implored the university 'to play its major role in the rehabilitation of civilization,' which had 'collapsed.' The duty of scholars was, for Innis, to 'discuss the strategy for recovery.' Universities, he concluded, offered a 'platform on which [academics] may be able to discuss the problems of civilization.'[42] Richard M. Saunders, editor of a series of lectures on higher education, shared both Innis's sense of foreboding and his notion that educators were leaders in the effort to reconstruct society. 'The basic aim of education,' Saunders wrote in 1946, 'has always been to convey to each succeeding generation a clear conception of the meaning of life, and of its part in it.' In the current crisis, it was 'clearly incumbent' upon educational leaders, 'the guides and guardians of our youth,' to 'discover afresh the meaning and purpose of our life.' Modern society, he continued, had been set adrift in a 'sea of chaos.' Only with the aid of thoughtful scholars could it regain the 'intimate touch with sources of spiritual capital.'[43] In a 1947 convocation address, Chancellor Vincent Massey of the University of Toronto added his voice to those of Innis and Saunders. Massey warned: 'Our humane Christian tradition is now imperiled as it has not been for 1,500 years; imperiled not so much by physical forces ... as by opposing philosophies, pagan, materialistic, tyrannical, ruthless. Should [these forces] prevail, human freedom would be extinguished and what we know as Western civilization would disappear.' In the defence of western culture, he added hastily, the academy was key: 'Our universities stand both as the exponent and guardians of our ancient way of life. They bear the very seeds of freedom. We look to them for guidance in this confused and troubled age.'[44]

How, precisely, were scholars to aid in understanding and providing remedies for a society in tumultuous times? How, moreover, were they to make their fundamental contribution to society without leaving the cloistered surroundings of the academy? The response to these critical queries lay in the manner in which scholars approached scholarship; put in another way, it relied on whether or not they adhered to the 'philosophical approach' to scholarship.

In 1949 George P. Grant surveyed the development of philosophy in English-speaking universities for the Royal Commission on the Developments of Arts, Letters, and Sciences (the Massey Commission). In a 'special study' called 'Philosophy,' Grant highlighted, among other things, the importance of maintaining philosophy at the forefront of academic enquiry. As Innis and others had argued earlier, Grant showed how universities historically had allowed scholars to 'contemplate' and 'partake of the wisdom of the past' and 'to transmit this great tradition' to 'certain chosen members of the chosen generation.' The universities, he claimed, were society's 'centres of philosophy.' As such, they facilitated the rational and epistemological enquiry into human existence and provided all-important insight into society's traditions and future directions. An important duty of humanist scholars, Grant summed up, was to study philosophy, understand its messages, and pass them on to society: 'Such indeed must always be the role of significant philosophy – to affect the spirits of the intellectually gifted and through them to filter down into society as a whole.'[45]

Grant chose University of Toronto classicist C.N. Cochrane as an example of the type of 'gifted individual' to whom he referred. Cochrane was an academic for whom the philosophical approach was central. Perhaps even more important, his scholarly insights provided information on current cultural problems. To read Cochrane's *Christianity and Classical Culture* (1940), Grant wrote, 'is to understand that the history of the ancient world has been illustrated for him in the predicaments of his own society, and that he uses the example of the ancient world to throw his light towards the solution of modern predicaments. Clearly, what he says about Greece and Rome has been wrought in the furnace of what he has seen in his own civilization.'[46] Innis implicitly concurred with Grant's analysis. Indicating the value of Cochrane's study to modern social scientific research, he declared that 'the significance of the volume for social scientists is in its philosophical approach. In classical civilization reason asserted its supremacy and in doing so betrayed its insecure position with disastrous results ... The sweep of the Platonic state in the nineteenth and twentieth centuries and the spread of science has been followed by the horrors of the Platonic state. The social scientist is asked to check his course and to indicate his role in western civilization. His answer must stand the test of the philosophic approach of Cochrane.'[47] For both Grant and Innis, *Christianity and Classical Culture* was a model for modern scholars. Cochrane showed how the study of past cultures could provide insight into current philosophical difficulties. As such, the volume was an example of the correct application of scholarship. Above all, Cochrane displayed the central importance of the scholar as social philosopher in his role of enlightening and giving meaning to the social process. Of all the other merits of Cochrane's book, its socio-philosophical relevance was of primary significance to both Innis and Grant.

Like the approach of philosophers, the emphasis of academic critics was on the merits of historical enquiry as an aid to understanding the social order. For, as was true of the philosophical approach, historical enquiry further facilitated scholars' roles as social philosophers. It enabled them to see the present in the light of the past and therefore to gain a wider understanding of contemporary sociocultural tendencies. Historical perspective allowed scholars to escape 'presentist' biases, to emancipate academics, in other words, from the restrictions of contemporary viewpoints. Innis, himself an economic historian, extolled the virtues of the historical approach to scholarship. The study of historical 'empires' (sociocultural organizations), he argued, compelled scholars 'to recognize the bias of the period in which [they] write.'[48] Couching his thoughts in the terminology of his later scholarship, Innis urged that scholars be 'continually alert to the implications' of the media bias to contemporaneous and past societies. For through the examination of the impact of the media bias on past civilizations, academics might be enabled to see more clearly the effects of contemporary socio-cultural limitations.[49] Hilda Neatby, also a historian, implicitly agreed with Innis about the merits of historical perspective. History, Neatby suggested, enlightened us as to the nature of common, accepted moral and cultural standards of the west. Through the study of the past, historians were able to compare past realities with the current 'moral' conditions and convey their understanding to others outside the academy. Ultimately, they could provide the insight to enable modern humanity to overcome historical follies.[50] Vincent Massey also expounded upon the fundamental importance of history to understanding current sociocultural difficulties. Borrowing from Shakespeare's *The Tempest*, Massey declared, '"What's Past is Prologue." This I believe is true at any given moment in history.' Massey continued, 'It is most of all true in times of crisis. We are always moved by our own past. We act most surely and most effectively when we are not slavishly, but consciously and intelligently aware of this fundamental fact.'[51] History and historical scholarship acted thus as beacons for a civilization that had been led astray. Expounding upon the wider merits of historical enquiry, historian W.L. Morton contended that scholars used history not only to 'reinforce tradition' but also to open 'new paths of thought.' The historian's work, Morton argued, cannot but contribute to 'the development of the thought of its time, spring from it, pushing it forward, and turning it into new channels.'[52] Historical scholarship, for Morton and others, stimulated new and creative thought, while at the same time it provided perspective and (moral) guidance. Apart from all the relative merits of historical scholarship per se, historical enquiry, like the philosophical approach of Innis and Grant, had a very significant instrumentalist purpose: it had become a tool through which academics interpreted Canada's place in the modern world.

Not an academic tool in itself, humanistic learning contributed nonetheless to the critique of mid-century society. The humanities – philosophy, history, the classics, and literary studies – not so much provided a precise methodology by which scholars could recognize the deficiencies of the current age as they presented an ideal to which moderns could ascribe. Most significant of all, the humanities were, for many critics, an essential counterweight to the increasingly 'inhuman' modern world. Humanistic education could not only counteract the perversities of war, but also aid in neutralizing the more insidious yet pernicious tendencies towards materialism, consumerism, and a general preoccupation with the present and the secular. Allowed to flourish, the humanities, according to their chief advocates, would expose the inadequacies of mid-century culture in Canada, thereby facilitating the development of the good society. As happened during wartime, the humanities continued their critical service to Canada and western civilization throughout the post-war age.

In response to a perceived 'crisis of values' stemming as much from the decline of humanistic learning and the advent of technical instruction as from the shocking events of the war, critics turned to the humanities for guidance. Amid revelations about the Holocaust and other wartime atrocities and in the midst of academic confusion, especially in the arts and humanities, they turned to humanistic learning as a way to restore a sense of balance and stability. Again, the assertion of 'humane' values was all-important. In an article in the Queen's Quarterly, one critic declared that there had been a 'universal breakdown of values' and that it was incumbent upon humanists to 'rebuild these shattered values,' and most important to rediscover 'the values implicit in the humanities.'[53] Another scholar argued that humanities have a 'place answering the practical problems of life and living.' They provided humanity with 'standards of conduct' and increased the individual's 'powers of discrimination' so as to enable the achievement of 'a synthesis of desirable goals and objects.'[54] In other words, they could allow the individual to achieve a 'free personality' through the 'contemplation of beauty – beauty of conduct, beauty of form, beauty of sound and line and colour' and 'above all beauty of soul.'[55] Closely guided by the strictures of Matthew Arnold, humanists showed how the power of 'beauty' and 'conduct,' intrinsic to humane learning, were not only the hallmarks of the civilized personality but also a means by which to confront the terror and inhumanity of the modern world.[56] The rediscovery and reassertion of humane values, therefore, had become crucial; in building character and in civilizing the imagination, the humanities facilitated humankind's capacity to understand itself and the world outside.

There was an even more practical, quasi-utilitarian function for humane knowledge. In practical terms, the humanities provided moral and 'value' alternatives to the secular and materialist value system of the post-war age. Humane knowledge, in effect, functioned to counterbalance technical, scientific, and material values that had come to pervade modern society. In a piece entitled 'The Conflict of Values in Education,' James S. Thomson, president of the National Conference of Canadian Universities (NCCU), warned of the dangerous preeminence of scientific and technical values in the post-war world. Thomson criticized the prevailing intellectual milieu, not only one in which the modern mind had become divided between scientific and humane values, but also one wherein 'science and the scientific method' assumed a 'central place.' Like many others, he decried the fact that 'education should be concerned with things useful' and that humane knowledge was considered to be of no practical value.[57] The humanities, on the contrary, *were* pragmatic. Unlike the sciences, they could 'pronounce on values' and facilitate judgments on the human condition;[58] and because the analysis of social interactions was never more important than during an 'age of confusion' and since values were 'the very stuff of civilization,' their importance to society was difficult to dispute. 'Any society must give practical expression to its values in its system of education,' Thomson concluded; 'for education is nothing other than the self-perpetuation of any culture.'[59] In the 1947 NCCU presidential address, N.A.M. MacKenzie also assessed the pragmatic merits of humane and scientific knowledge. The humanities, like the sciences and the technical disciplines, had a tremendously significant contribution to make to post-war society. 'If man is to be a happy, balanced and fully developed individual living in peace and security with his fellow men,' MacKenzie declared, 'he must find an important place in his scheme of things for ... the humanities.' '[F]ood fuel, shelter, clothing, power, transportation,' and other material ends of life had been well taken care of, and considerable advances had been made in the areas of the physical and medical sciences. The humanities must be stressed, MacKenzie hastened to add, so as not to compromise the role of education to train the minds of young and old and 'so that they can understand and know themselves, and their society.'[60] Assessing 'The Present Status of the Humanities in Canada,' Malcolm Wallace also juxtaposed material advancement with the values inherent to humanistic learning. Material betterment, Wallace wrote in his special study to the Massey Commission, 'does not lead to the high satisfactions of the soul to which the arts and letters and speculation minister. It gives satisfaction, but it is an inferior kind of satisfaction, which excludes us from the society of good and great men ... whose achievements we might enter with a corresponding enlargement of our lives and characters.' He concluded, 'to cater to the growing capacity of these things' was 'the function of the humanities.'[61] In a 1948 address, University of Toronto chancellor, Vincent Massey, summarized the importance of the humanities in the scientific, materialistic age. Even in the modern age of utilitarian higher education, universities still had 'a very ancient and very vital function to perform in the field of the humanities.' Massey added, 'Technological and scientific progress' did not make 'this function obsolete: it ... made it more necessary.' 'No one passing through a university,' he averred, 'should fail to come under the influence of the humanities, because [through] liberal education ... the student is enabled to acquire a true sense of values, to understand something about the relation of man to society, to distinguish between the real things in life and the fakes, to put first things first, and to sharpen his mental curiosity.'[62] A life influenced solely by technological and material values, Massey implied, was truly an impoverished existence.

Finding its foundations in the humanizing function of the humanities, the ideal academy thus performed a broader, 'civilizing' role in Canadian society. Transmitters of humane learning and values, Canadian universities had become responsible for 'cultural activity' and for the spread of Canadian civilization. In a society that was preoccupied with material and technological advancement, they had become, in the words of the Massey Commission *Report*, 'nurseries of a truly Canadian civilization and culture.' Universities in Canada continued to be focal points of culture by mid-century because Canadians concentrated on material developments and hence ignored the cultural growth of their nation. Even by the early 1950s, as Vincent Massey, Hilda Neatby, and the other Massey commissioners noted, universities remained as they had always been: islets of civilization awash in a growing sea of materialism. In this atmosphere it was critical that they continue their historic role as cultural outposts. Higher education, the commissioners and other like-minded critics stressed, enabled Canadian society 'to strive for a common good, including not only material but intellectual and moral elements.' This overriding civilizing function had to be maintained; for if governments denied this purpose and with it the general cultural education of Canadians, 'the complete conception of the common good is lost, and Canada, as such, [would become] a materialistic society.'[63] Put in another way, if Canada was to grow up from a crass pioneer society into a mature, civilized nation, governments would have to guarantee the security of the universities as garrisons of Canadian culture.

In sum, while academic critics lamented the decline of university traditions, they also put forth an idealized conception of higher learning, which, they hoped, might replace the dying academy. Yet, more than simply the reassertion of historic traditions and attributes of the academy, critics assigned a detailed social function to this quasi-mythical entity. Whether enabling moral judgments, civilizing and 'acculturating' Canadians, or affording historical or philosophical insights on contemporary cultural problems, the university had a vital, ameliorating function. Whereas the modern university had become responsible for the material betterment of Canadian society, the humanistic academy served society in a much more important way: it enabled humanity to remain tied to its traditions while helping moderns to cope with contemporary societal malaise. Indeed, critics countered notions of the modern, utilitarian university with their own practical, socially relevant conception of higher learning. In emphasizing the practicalities of humane learning, in short, critics endowed the idealized, 'true' academy with a renewed sense of social purpose. In an age in which the civilizing and humanizing purposes of the university seemed to be in eclipse, they became vociferous proponents of vital academic traditions.

Critics of the modernizing university thus presented an idealized conception of the academy as a counterweight to the technical, utilitarian university that had developed rapidly during and after the war. They also attempted to answer the ever-pressing question, 'What is the use of an Arts education anyway?'[64] We have discussed in detail the modernization of higher education in the wartime and immediate post-war periods and how critics endeavoured to make the academy and its scholars socially relevant. We must now place the notion of the true academy into historical context to understand how critics' analyses evolved in relation to surrounding historical conditions. There were three main developments that influenced the post-war critique of academic modernization. The first of these was the perception of cultural crisis.

'Crisis,' 'chaos,' and 'upheaval,' to be sure, are overworked terms. They were frequently used, nevertheless, to describe and understand the sociocultural climate of the 1940s. In 1941, as we have noted, historian Arthur Lower announced that the old order was in its death throes and that a 'new order' was taking shape.[65] Lower was referring not only to the modernization process but also to the disappearance of an Anglo-Canadian civilization and its replacement with a new sociocultural order. This sense of impermanence and imminent change increased during the latter stages of the war and the immediate postwar era. Writing in late 1945, J.S. Thomson claimed that the war had promoted an 'international revolution' marked by ever-increasing change and violence. It was, in his words, 'a first-rate crisis in the development of civilization,' one, he warned, that did not disappear with armed victory.[66] Inspired in part by Oswald Spengler[67] and Arnold Toynbee, Harold Innis became consumed with understanding the rise and fall of civilizations. He argued that by the mid-twentieth century the culture of the west, which had developed over thousands of years, was in its final stages of decay. In Innisian parlance, cultural decline implied the emphasis of 'spatial' qualities – a preoccupation with the present, the technological, and the secular – rather than time-biased values – an appreciation of the moral, the cultural, and the historical. The entrenchment of spatial values involved 'a continuous, systematic, [and] ruthless destruction of the elements of permanence essential to cultural activity.' He added, 'The emphasis on change' was the 'only permanent character' of the decaying west.[68]

In some instances, cultural crisis was more fabrication than reality. Supporters of and participants in the Massey Commission and others in the so-called culture lobby, for example, highlighted the precarious status of culture so as to get governments involved in promoting cultural activities. As historian Paul Litt has argued, cultural pressure groups wanted to create an air of crisis 'to spur the government into action.' They wanted to show how after 1945 culture in Canada was at a 'critical turning point' and how the 'future of the arts in Canada hung in the balance: they could either flourish or collapse' depending on whether the federal government provided funding for the development of culture.[69] 'Lowbrow' culture, such as hockey and mass media entertainment, flourished in the post-war climate, while areas of high culture, such as Canadian publishing and, most important, the Canadian university faltered.

Historical realities, however, underlay the concern about cultural collapse. The Holocaust was perhaps the starkest manifestation of the brutality of warfare, the inhumanity of mid-century society, and general cultural decay. Only apparent after the war had ended, the extent of the campaign of racial extermination carried out by the Nazis shocked Canadians and others in the western world. Indeed, memories of the Holocaust were so powerful that they completely discredited theories of racial inequality as a subject of serious intellectual enquiry. Transmitted by educators and parents, the Holocaust would make racism abhorrent to future generations of Canadians.[70]

By the late 1940s 'thermonuclear holocaust' had also become a grim reality for post-war Canadians. First, the threat of nuclear warfare showed that the callous disregard for human life readily apparent in the war had not ended with the cessation of hostilities. For many observers humanity's inhumanity continued unabated after 1945. Perhaps most significant, the prospect of mass destruction made real the perilous state of western civilization. The sense of impending doom that the resort to weapons of mass destruction implied reflected profound social change and signalled great uncertainty for the future. As J.A. Corry later remarked, the concept of nuclear war represented 'the crumbling of old verities and certainties.'[71] It was, as Hilda Neatby claimed, an 'age without standards.'[72] Even more than the destruction of the traditional system of values, it also implied widespread hopelessness, a general sense that cultural rehabilitation had become impossible. Commenting on the plight of insightful, humanistic scholars – those responsible for cultural regeneration – and, indeed, the moral bankruptcy of a civilization that countenanced atomic weaponry, Innis verbalized this despondency. 'The middle ages,' he explained, had 'burned its heretics and the modern age threatens them with atom bombs.'[73] There was thus little hope for either the scholar or civilization at large. The problem of the university had truly become the problem of modern society.[74]

As powerful as nuclear destruction was both as a dehumanizing force and as a symbol of impending cultural decay, many Canadians nevertheless looked past the broader implications of civilization's decline. Though certainly aware of surrounding political, military, and social developments embodied most clearly in the rise of Soviet Communism, Canadians focused instead on more prosaic concerns. Young Canadians married, started new families, and procured the material goods necessary to the establishment of a stable home life, while government officials became increasingly focused on the material development of their country. The period after 1945 can be characterized as one in which Canadians sought the security that they had lacked throughout the war and the Depression years.[75] Whether at the individual or at the national level, material prosperity was key to the search for stability.

Since Confederation Canadians had been preoccupied with the material development of their nation. In times of peace, the tariff, free trade, and national policies that governed, among other things, the exploitation of resources usually were central political and economic issues. By the late nineteenth century, Canadians had decided to be no longer 'simply the drawers of water and hewers of wood';[76] rather, impatient with their country's slow economic advancement, they opted to take control of their material development through policies of industrialization and general economic modernization. After initial successes before 1914 the uneven growth of the 1920s and the economic malaise of the 1930s meant that the nation-building process was coming to a grinding halt. The questions economists, government officials, and concerned Canadians asked were: Would Canada be able to sustain the economic momentum established during the war, or would it revert to depression? Would Canada remain among the elite industrialized nations of the world, or would it lapse into second-rate status among the economic powers of the western world? The post-war era was potentially a critical turning point in the material progress of the nation.

Canada underwent a period of tremendous economic expansion after 1945. Rapid and sustained development quickly assuaged fears of economists and other governmental experts that Canada's economy would again slide into depression. Reductions in expenditures on military supplies were offset by mega-projects, such as the construction of the Trans-Canada Highway and later the development of the St Lawrence Seaway and the Trans-Canada Pipeline. By the late 1940s, furthermore, a resource boom was contributing to the strong economy. There was expanded production of pulp and paper, lumber, asbestos, gypsum, aluminum, and, most notably, oil and gas throughout the period. Stimulated especially by the Korean War, exports of Canadian resource goods reached new levels and greatly contributed to economic prosperity through the 1950s and 1960s.[77] Consumer spending also assisted the post-war boom. After 1945 there was considerable latent demand for consumer items because of government rationing and the general scarcity of consumer goods during the war. Owing to both full employment and forced savings programs like war bonds, moreover, Canadians had substantial savings available and used their extra money to buy automobiles, houses, refrigerators, and other consumer items that were not readily available before 1945. There was a 'powerful demand,' one writer declared in 1946, 'for everything one can eat, wear, read, repair, drink, ride, and rest in.'[78]

A shift in demographics, known popularly as the 'baby boom,' did much to reinforce existing consumer trends. As Doug Owram has shown, new families became preoccupied with the concept of home and the development of family life as a means of achieving the stability they had lacked throughout the war. To this end, not only did Canadians marry and have children at unprecedented rates, but vast numbers also bought houses. For their new houses, which usually were situated in sprawling suburbs, they purchased household items of all kinds. Municipalities constructed new roads, sewers, and other facilities, while private firms built malls and other amenities to serve the new subdivisions. Car ownership also increased among new suburbanites; for private transportation became more of a necessity than ever before in the isolated suburbs. The economic value of the suburban phenomenon is difficult to overestimate.[79]

More than preceding generations, the parents of the baby boom generation were preoccupied with the development of their children. Whatever the other implications of this 'filiocentrism,'[80] it can be asserted that parents of baby boomers provided as never before for the material welfare of their offspring. Manufacturers became rich on the success of fads such as Hula Hoops, Barbie Dolls, and Davy Crockett hats. Others profited through furnishing the more mundane needs of babies and small children, such as baby formula, clothing, and toys. Parents also provided for leisure activities by enrolling their children in Boy Scouts and Girl Guides, taking them to movies, and buying televisions sets. Filiocentrism, modern advertising and marketing, and a relative affluence, in short, combined to produce perhaps the best-clothed, best-nourished, and, indeed, best-leisured generation of young Canadians in history.

Whatever the relative benefits of material advancement, the critics of higher education uniformly rebuked the growing materialism of the post-war age. A common complaint was that Canadians were so preoccupied with material betterment that they ignored the spiritual and philosophical concerns of their nation. Discussing the post-war materialism of Canada, Hilda Neatby bluntly remarked: 'At no time in western history has any nation totally ignored the importance of national recognition of, and support for, non-material values.'[81] Less given to hyperbole, George Parkin Grant was nonetheless implicitly sympathetic to Neatby's main point. Chronicling the deficiencies of Canada as a contemplative, 'philosophical' country, Grant claimed that Canada remained as it always had been: a pioneer nation concerned with materialism and material ends. As such, this dynamic young country did not understand the 'tragedy and complexity of maturity' and was thus 'basically unphilosophical.' Ultimately, Grant wrote, Canada's preoccupation with the material implied a 'distrust of philosophy as taking men's minds away from the obvious practical things that need to be done.'[82] The neglect of the humanities and the humanistic traditions, Vincent Massey added, was 'a symptom of an age lured by science into the delights of materialism.' The pursuit of new houses, larger and more luxurious cars, and more hours in front of the television set was demonstrative of the wrong-headed priorities of the Canadian people.[83] Joining the voices of Grant, Massey, and others, Wallace railed against the obsession with the material. While material pursuits were necessary, he averred, the overemphasis of material betterment 'does not lead to the high satisfactions of the soul to which a love of the arts and letters and speculation minister. It gives satisfaction, but it is an inferior kind of satisfaction, which excludes us from the society of the good and great men of the race into whose achievements we might enter [through the aid of a humanistic education] with a corresponding enlargement of our own lives and characters.'[84] In stressing material gain, the critics concluded, Canadians promoted only one small aspect of the national identity. Canada was prospering in a material sense; spiritually, it was becoming increasingly impoverished.

An age in which material values were emphasized above all others, the post-war period was, in addition, a time during which Canadians, especially social observers, were concerned with political values and the socio-political development of western societies. For many Canadians (and, indeed, their American counterparts) 'democracy' became a watchword, a term that connoted fair and just government and differentiated the political cultures of the west from those of totalitarian states, especially the growing Soviet bloc. It was associated with the political values of freedom, the rule of law, justice, and good citizenship, as well as a plethora of non-political virtues, including Christian values and the ideals of western culture more generally. Yet democracy was not to be taken for granted. The Second World War certainly had proved the superiority and ultimate desirability of the democratic system. The emerging Cold War, however, showed that western democracy was still under attack. As External Affairs Minister Louis St Laurent noted in a 1947 speech, Canadians realized that 'a threat to the liberty of western Europe, where [their] own political ideas were nurtured, was a threat to [their] own way of life.'[85] Canadians reviled Communism not only because it was the post-war manifestation of twentieth-century totalitarianism, but most of all because it represented a profound menace to Canada's democratic existence.

Although Canadians, on the whole, were never as fervent cold warriors as were the Americans, they nevertheless denounced as evil the Communist system while lauding the merits of democracy. Even Canadian scholars became embroiled in the ideological debate. A spate of articles that pronounced on the democracy issue appeared in learned journals, books, and other academic writings. The work of Queen's political scientist J.A. Corry was perhaps the most significant of these compositions. The first edition of *Democratic Government and Politics* (1946) was designed to provide an introduction to Canadian college and university students to the subject of democratic government. Corry's work, declared one of the book's reviewers, met an urgent need of the times. In explaining democracy to both students and the population at large, Corry made it much easier for Canadians to appreciate and defend it. If the advocates of democracy had one or two more tracts like Corry's, he concluded, then it would be much easier to defend the democratic faith. Like Corry, Watson Kirkconnell wrote on the needs of Canadian democracy. In his *Seven Pillars of Freedom* (1944) he endeavoured to make prescriptions on how to maintain freedom and democracy. Notably subtitled *An Exposure of the Soviet World Conspiracy and Its Fifth Column in Canada*, the book represented an attempt both to expose the fallacies of Communist ideology while showing the importance of the western system of values – including, among others things, religion, cooperation, education, and justice – to support the 'edifice of Canadian and world liberty.'[86] The tenor of Kirkconnell's work was one of warning: world citizens, including Canadians, must be ever aware of the dangers of Communism and other threats to democratic liberty; they must remain dutiful, moreover, to fight for their own liberty through maintaining an environment in which values fundamental to that liberty may be freely expressed.[87] The Canadian democracy that emerged after 1945 was frail indeed and must be protected at all costs.

Democracy certainly was a term used as a synonym for good and just government and was juxtaposed to other ideologies, especially Soviet Communism, to display their defects.[88] It was a multi-faceted term, however, and it was not always used in a positive sense. Many mid-century social critics stressed democracy's negative connotations, equating it with mass movements of the post-war era such as consumerism, materialism, and, perhaps most significant, the emergence of a pervasive and uniform 'mass' culture. The Massey Commission, for instance, was highly critical of 'democratic' culture. In fact, members of the commission despised mass culture because they believed that crass commercialism rather a communal or critical spirit inspired and informed it. Democratic culture was to be scorned, moreover, not because of the fear of mass participation in sundry cultural activities but because it implied a degradation of standards. In appealing to the greatest quantity of people, it sacrificed the intellectual improvement fostered by high culture and, in consequence, broke Canadian society's links with its cultural heritage. 'Hockey Night in Canada,' 'Gunsmoke,' 'Leave It to Beaver,' and other manifestations of 'lowbrow' culture dulled one's sensibilities to the merits of high culture. Ultimately, democratic culture detached Canadians from their cultural inheritance by undermining the transference of the 'best that has been thought and said.' For the Massey commissioners, then, democratic culture was truly a pernicious influence in post-war society. It was, in the words of the biographer of the commission, 'monolithic and menacing; it stultified and then manipulated a gullible public.'[89]

Democracy also had important implications for post-war educational critics. Not only was democratic education, with mass culture, part of the general democratization of Canadian society, it also contributed to the educational crisis current in the post-war period. 'Democratic' or 'progressive' education, like mass culture, were pejorative descriptions used to indicate the decay of learning standards and educational systems. To educational critics it symbolized the renunciation of an elitist, principled education and the adoption of a system in which standards were brought to the level of the lowest common denominator of the masses.[90] Vincent Massey stated the issue in stark terms. Speaking about the post-war expansion in university enrolments, Massey claimed that there were many students who ought not to be there. These students lowered standards. 'It is surely inefficient and indeed undemocratic,' he noted acerbically and not without irony, 'to allow students not intellectually fitted for university work so to inflate our classes as to limit the opportunities enjoyed by those with a serious purpose, a desire to use their education, and real promise of giving some leadership in after-life.' Quoting educational critic H.A.L. Fisher, Massey summarized his position: the 'university stands for quality; to perform its "proper function it must safeguard itself against the admission of the unfit."' 'Mass education,' he concluded, was surely 'a contradiction in terms.'[91]

The critique of mass education put forward by Massey and others had a practical historical base. In the post-war period there was a tremendous strain on the Canadian educational system at large. This strain primarily took the form of growing enrolments for both primary and secondary schools and for the universities. Canadian universities were the first educational institutions to experience large-scale expansion after 1945. Assisted by the Department of Veterans Affairs (DVA), which provided students with tuition fees and a living allowance, veterans flooded into the universities. By the 1945–6 academic year, veterans comprised almost one-third of all university registrants, helping full-time enrolment jump to 61,861. In the following year they formed almost half the aggregate student body of nearly 80,000 students. Enrolment figures remained high until 1950–1, when only 6,126 DVA veterans enrolled.[92] It was not until the end of the decade that enrolment numbers recovered and surpassed those of the post-war boom.

Just as the 'crisis of numbers' in the Canadian universities subsided, primary and secondary schools experienced another difficulty. Largely because of the demographic impetus provided by the baby boom, enrolments across Canada vastly increased throughout the 1950s and early 1960s. Each year after 1952, in fact, established a new record for enrolments. Registrations in primary and secondary schools by 1961 had grown by an astounding 1.2 million over the 1950–1 academic year. The increases were so large that Ontario and Alberta, two of the fastest-growing provinces, opened a new school every day over a two-year period. Schools in southern Ontario used the innovative 'split shift' to cope with increasing numbers. While new schools were being constructed, some students attended classes from 8:00 a.m. until noon, while the second 'shift' of students attended from 1:00 to 6:00 p.m. Teachers also had to be found to educate the growing masses of students. Provinces set up recruitment committees to visit high schools and encourage students to consider teaching as a career.[93] Despite the successes of recruitment campaigns and the employment of increasing numbers of married women,[94] there was still a shortage of teachers. Only by facilitating a quick entry for teachers into the classroom could provinces obtain sufficient numbers of teachers. Educational standards dropped precipitously as a result. Boards of education required new teachers to study a reduced number of high school courses and then take a six-week summer-school course before they could teach courses of their own.[95] These less-than-qualified educators formed the core of the emerging educational system in Canada.

In this climate, Hilda Neatby, the foremost critic of educational democracy in Canada, pontificated on the detriments of democratic learning. Neatby's well-known tract, *So Little for the Mind* (1953), was, indeed, in part a diatribe against the 'democratic method of education.' Echoing Massey and other educational critics, Neatby argued that progressive education led to diminished standards by bringing the levels of overall instruction down to that of the poorest students. To serve the whole child, and indeed all children, as progressivists argued, encouraged mediocrity, laziness, and a lack of fulfilment. Yet the problem of democratic education was even more fundamental than the decay of educational standards. Neatby objected most to progressive education because it was bent on developing a system of education in which students would develop their interests in concert with the common, 'democratic' interests of society. She abhorred platitudes such as 'democracy in the classroom meant democracy for the nation' and, by extension, the defeat of totalitarianism, and the notion that progressive education made good (i.e., democratic) citizens. On the contrary, she argued that, in indoctrinating students with the 'values' of 'democracy,' progressivists prevented exactly what they hoped to gain: the search for liberty. In clouding young minds with the rhetoric of democracy, they blocked the quest for moral virtue, cultural beauty, and, most significant, the attainment of personal liberty, all of which flowed from the traditional liberal education. Far from being a liberator, then, democratic education was in fact a tyrant. 'Progressive education,' Neatby concluded, was not 'liberation'; it was, rather, 'indoctrination both intellectual and moral.'[96]

Discrediting the 'false democracy' embodied by progressive education, Neatby was now prepared to demonstrate how traditional education fostered the liberation of students and moderns more generally. In *A Temperate Dispute*, a follow-up to her highly controversial but best-selling book of the previous year, Neatby showed that matters of mind and the enduring principles of western civilization were crucial to the maintenance of a true and free democracy. The 'fervour of religious faith, the absolutism of moral principle, [and] the freedom of mind' were 'a few priceless things' essential to democracy's struggle for survival in a 'chaotic world.' Democracy, Neatby declared, was the 'fruit of these roots,' and hence these essential principles must be 'renewed with each generation or democracy will be destroyed.' Without them, 'mere happiness, interest, group integration, self realization' – the trappings of false democracy or, alternatively, 'democracy of the herd' – prevailed, and ultimately true democracy would be compromised. The traditional, liberal arts education was critical to Neatby's system because it offered to students the freedom 'to speak their minds on essential matters.' Most important, it enabled moderns to seek out timeless moral and intellectual virtues and hence allowed them to avoid the 'slavish conformity' that was so much a part of democratic education and indeed the entire post-war age. Where progressive education was a tyrant, an illiberal instrument in an increasingly unfree age, traditional education – along with its corollaries, contemplation and free and critical enquiry – was precisely the opposite: it was an agent of liberty to be employed to combat the illiberalities of the period. On the centrality of traditional education to democracy and the destructiveness of mass education to this educational principle and to democracy at large, Neatby concluded: '[We] possess [a] tradition of learning, deliberate, rational learning as one of the first values in life, as essential to our humanity and to our civilization. It has moulded the common life of the western world. Those who weaken the tradition, no matter how good their motives, are indeed committing a double sin against democratic principles. They are taking advantage of our ignorance and carelessness to deprive us of something that we truly value; and they are attacking the principle which has given life to democracy in the past and which can nourish it in the future.'[97]

The critique of 'mass' education was not simply a response to the question of the uses and abuses of democracy that were au courant after 1945. Rather, it was a subset of larger concerns regarding societal attitudes towards scholarship and intellectualism more generally. Hilda Neatby's educational critique again is illustrative. A chief theme of Neatby's educational analysis was that progressive education was both anti-intellectual and, most significant, representative of an age that increasingly ignored intellectual values. Ostensibly, the progressivist program was for the all-round development of students. In reality, as Neatby explained, the progressivists addressed students' physical and psychological needs but ignored their fundamental intellectual requirements. 'Intellectual training,' she asserted, was 'no longer the chief and special responsibility of the school.' Instead, progressivists assumed that 'critical thinking,' 'problem-solving,' and other intellectual attributes could be reduced to the level of technical instruction, and therefore had no value per se. These 'dangerous assumptions' were significant, Neatby hastened to add, because they 'emerged naturally from our modern way of life.'[98] They reflected, in other words, a society that favoured material and technical values. Indeed, Deweyite education, with its emphasis on practical applications and instrumental knowledge, both symbolized and was the product of the greater anti-intellectualism of modern civilization.[99] Thus, not unlike the university critics who likened the decline of the humanities to greater civilizational decay, Neatby and others believed that progressive education meant much more than the erosion of scholarly methods and standards; it signified the malaise implicit to a materialistic, anti-intellectual society.[100] To criticize the defects of Deweyite education was therefore to criticize the deficiencies of modern society itself.

Informed by debates over values and taking place in an age of 'academic democratization' and (perceived) civilizational decline, the postwar period was truly a tumultuous one for the modern university. The 'academy in crisis' notion that had come to characterize the modern university's wartime experience continued. Funding difficulties, increasing enrolments, and growing secular and governmental control, as well as the ongoing degradation of the university's humanizing and civilizing functions, characterized this conception. Amid the turmoil of the post-1945 world, educational critics like Neatby highlighted the inadequacies of modern higher learning while offering a notion of the ideal university, an alternative, they hoped, to academic modernization. In spite of their efforts, however, Canadian universities continued to modernize throughout the 1950s and 1960s. As Canadians moved farther away from the crisis atmosphere of the 1940s, their voices, although never fully muted, became increasingly difficult to hear amid the clamour of the modernizing and democratizing academies.

Unlike the period that preceded it, the mid-1950s were relatively quiet for the modern Canadian university and its critics. While there were still those who depicted apocalyptic scenarios for the university and modern society at large,[101] informed critics of higher learning generally turned their attention to more prosaic concerns.[102] The 1956 meeting of the NCCU exemplified the shift away from the 'crisis of values' and 'decline of civilization' analyses of earlier critics and instead

university problems were examined in terms of practical considerations of money, numbers, and government and private funding. Like
their predecessors, conference delegates were well aware of the
impacts of technical education and the anticipated increases in enrolments – issues that had preoccupied university critics now for some
time. They were much more willing than pre- and post-war critics,
however, to accept rather than overturn the process of academic modernization. The 1956 NCCU conference thus presented a new breed of
university critic, whose willingness to accept the modern university
showed just how far the process of academic modernization had progressed.

The 'crisis of numbers,' as it became known, was the main theme of
the 1956 meeting of the NCCU, which had been proclaimed 'Canada's
Crisis in Higher Education.'[103] The NCCU's executive committee
called the conference to examine the implications of an NCCU symposium held a year earlier on the topic of university expansion, at which
Edward Sheffield, dominion statistician, announced alarming enrolment figures to his audience. University enrolments, he claimed, were
likely to double by the mid-1960s; the 64,200 university students currently enrolled (1953–4) would likely increase to more than 130,000
registrants ten years later.[104] Outlining the anticipated increases in university enrolments, Claude Bissell, president of Carleton University,
concurred with Sheffield's admonitions and cited statistics comparable
to those presented by the federal bureaucrat.[105] In the paper read at the
1956 conference he did what he had set out to do: provide the statistics
to substantiate the common cry that there was a wave of students
ready to flood the universities. Yet neither Sheffield's nor Bissell's predictions proved accurate. They were, in fact, far too conservative.
Unprecedented numbers of young Canadians, rising educational
expectations, and economic prosperity combined to augment drastically the numbers of students who would enrol in Canadian universities in the coming decade and beyond. Sheffield had to revise his
enrolment estimates upward four times in the late 1950s and early
1960s. In 1964–5, 178,200 students were registered in Canadian universities, a nearly 10 per cent increase over the predictions of Sheffield,
Bissell, and others.[106] Enrolments increased so dramatically that the
numbers of universities in Ontario, Canada's most populous province,
increased threefold in the 1960s. Simon Fraser University, the universities of Calgary, Lethbridge, Regina, Winnipeg, and Brandon, added
their numbers to Trent, Brock, and York universities of the growing

system of higher learning in Ontario. Once reserved primarily for privileged members of Canadian society, the young Canadians who, by the 1960s, were filling lecture halls in the tens of thousands no longer considered higher learning a privilege but a birthright. Referred to by critics and others since the early 1940s, the day of the 'democratic university' in Canada had dawned at last.

While the chief underlying theme of 'Canada's Crisis in Higher Education' certainly was the issue of growing enrolments, the NCCU committee that established it did not want merely to expound on statistical and demographic problems. Rather, committee members viewed the enrolment issue as a 'vivid background for the analysis of fundamental educational issues.' Along with the prosaic concerns of staffing and student problems, they identified two main educational problems facing modern universities. First, and most broadly, they addressed the question of the 'future of the educational structure, and the extent to which [Canadians] might expect radical alterations in the traditional make-up of [their] universities.' They realized not only that higher education was becoming democratized but also that Canadian universities were in a final stage of transition from liberal arts centres into modern research institutions largely responsible for the material well being of the nation. It was the implicit mandate of the conference and delegates to expound upon this change and what it meant for the future of higher learning in Canada.[107]

In a paper entitled 'Educational Structure: The English-Canadian Universities,' Sydney Smith, president of the University of Toronto, endeavoured to elaborate on this transition and, perhaps most important, the adaptation of the traditional academy to the modern world. Commenting on the enduring structure of Canadian higher learning, Smith noted that even by the mid-1950s universities were remarkably similar in that they consisted of a central faculty for arts and sciences along with one or more professional divisions. They had therefore retained much of their historic character, in spite of the development of an industrial-technological society and the ravages of two world wars. Despite this continuity, however, Smith argued that change was imminent. The historic structures of the academy had been retained, but society had become inimical to the traditional university. Many tell us, Smith declared, that 'in the electronic age, when hundreds of traditional skills and attitudes are becoming obsolescent, the era of the expert has arrived and that of the scholar has gone; that a mechanized economy has no understanding of, or patience with, the ivory tower;

and that frustration and defeat are in store for us if we oppose or attempt to modify the trend of the times.' 'The ivory tower scholar,' he continued, quoting Claude Bissell, '"is concerned with an intensive detailed analysis of something that is often remote in time, theoretical in nature, and apparently unrelated to any of the pressing, immediate needs and questions of man. He is paraded as the ultimate in ineffectual, a quaint survivor into this industrious age of a leisured and discredited past."'[108] 'Perhaps his attitudes and skills are already obsolescent,' Smith concluded despondently; 'he should adjust to the pressures of contemporary society, abandoning the distant horizons for the immediate scene, the exactitude for the generalization, the individual insight for the Gallup poll, the silent study for the crowded round table or the wordy "workshop," the library for the television set.'[109]

Smith was indeed less than sanguine about the continued persistence of traditional scholarship. He believed, nevertheless, that an accommodation could be reached between the university and its modern environment. The university and its scholars did not have to succumb to the 'industrial and technological' motif. Rather, by asserting the intrinsic value of a liberal arts education, they could present an alternative viewpoint to modern instruction that was preoccupied with science and technology. They could help to resist the 'mechanization of universities' and society in general by curbing scholarly and societal penchants for technological, scientific, and instrumentalist knowledge. There was potential, Smith reasoned, for both instrumentalist and liberal arts learning alike. Whether or not the humane knowledge could continue its historical function was dependent upon scholars, university officials, and Canadians at large.[110]

E.W.R. Steacie[111] and others who discussed scientific and technological education, the second main theme of the conference, were even more willing than Smith to realize an accommodation between the two chief branches of learning. Unlike many university critics before him, President Steacie of the National Research Council did not value humanistic learning above other types of knowledge. Instead, he set out to show the inherent compatibility of the pure sciences as academic disciplines. To accomplish this end, he differentiated pure from applied sciences. Concerned with 'development for practical purposes and the use of scientific information,' he claimed, applied science was instrumentalist knowledge and therefore 'merely an adjunct to technology.' In contrast, pure science was akin to humane knowledge because it was concerned with the 'purpose of advancing knowledge

for its own sake' and therefore, like the liberal arts, with the advancement of the truth. There was nothing intrinsically flawed with scientific knowledge per se. Only when the 'interests of individuals or
bodies which furnish financial support, or society which furnishes
pressure' or other outside interests interfered with the pursuit of scientific learning were the pure sciences compromised. Apart from instrumentalist or utilitarian applications, the sciences therefore could be
included rightly among the pantheon of scholarly pursuits.[112]

Although innately inimical to the university ethos, technical education also could be 'humanized' and therefore become reconcilable with
the modern conception of the academy. In a paper on the interrelationships of the humanities and sciences, John Ely Burchard demonstrated
not only the compatibility of the two branches of knowledge, but also
how, when combined, they strengthened each other to develop insightful, well-rounded humanists and scientists. Referring to the crucial role
played by scientists in the Cold War arms race, Burchard expressed the
necessity of developing scientists and technologists with a humanist
conscience. When not accompanied by humane values, he claimed, scientists' concern for the welfare of the human state was in danger of
being lost. While scientists had been 'excellent Jeremiahs,' demonstrating the inadequacies of their science, they were 'less effective as
Moseses,' leaders of citizens. Only through the 'right education' and
absorbing 'the great truths of the humanities' was there 'hope in finding a Moses among scientists.' Humanistic learning, for Burchard,
trained scientists 'to be querulous about everything and not only about
scientific truths.' In so doing, it enabled them to become 'the leaders
and not followers of men.' Indeed, he felt that humane and scientific
knowledge existed in a complementary relationship. Neither the
humanities nor the sciences alone could protect humankind against
naïveté and wrongheaded thinking: 'Combined, they may sometimes
fail; but the man who has experienced both will have a better chance'
at approaching truth. Commenting on the ultimate necessity of a
'humanized science,' Burchard concluded, 'I had rather bet the security of the world on a substantial number of this kind of men than on a
horde of skilled and obedient technicians.'[113]

In spite of the efforts of Burchard and other critics to reconcile and
accommodate humane and technological knowledge, by the late 1950s
most Canadians preferred the 'obedient technician' to the well-
rounded intellectual. The modern university emerged fully fledged in
Canada not long after the 1956 NCCU conference. It was marked as

much by the rise of technical learning and the concomitant demise of the academic traditions of the academy as by the decline of all but a very few fervent critics of academic modernization (namely, Northrop Frye and George Grant; see below). Even those moderate critics who dominated the conference were largely muted by the time the NCCU convened its next major conference.[114] Their endeavours to conserve university traditions through the integration of humane values into modern academic structures failed as the new structures began to achieve the primacy once enjoyed by the liberal arts. Symbolic of the ultimate transition to the modern university, the appeal for a reaffirmation of university traditions and a sundering of the burgeoning 'multiversity' seemed more than ever to be empty rhetoric to university authorities and most Canadians. By the early 1960s, the words of the critics seemed irrelevant to a society that had little regard for the traditional function of the academy.

The technological impetus created by the Cold War and the attendant arms race figured prominently in the emergence of the modern Canadian university. By the late 1950s the second stage of the Cold War had begun, during which participants vied to become the world's most prosperous nation and to develop the world's most sophisticated weapons systems. Because engineers and technologists were critical to the achievement of both of these goals, higher education was again mobilized, as it had been in the 1940s, to win the new war. As it had been during the Second World War, education in the sciences and technical disciplines was vital to victory in the arms race. Governments in Canada and the United States feared that unless universities accelerated the timetable for the production of technologists, the Cold War would surely be lost. There was cause for concern, since many within and outside academic circles felt that North Americans had lost their intellectual and technological advantage over the Soviet Union. The Russian launch of Sputnik in October 1957 confirmed this concern. The Sputnik crisis amplified the inadequacies of North American educational systems, while showing, at the same time, the superiority of Russian technical education. It put tremendous pressure on university officials to revamp their educational structures to produce more engineers, scientists, and technologists in order to catch up. Ultimately, it stimulated a renewed sense of urgency to develop technologists to meet the immediate demands of the Cold War. Shortly after the Sputnik launch, for instance, the Ontario minister of education told the presidents of his province's universities 'to reassure those of the public who are anxious about present conditions that everything is being done and will be done to strengthen and support the service rendered by the Ontario Universities.'[115] In university reports issued throughout the late 1950s, furthermore, the desperate need for advanced research in science and technology invariably was discussed.[116] As the NCCUC president declared in 1961, no one denied the need for the very best professors and equipment in the pure and applied science laboratories of the country's universities.[117] Nor did governments deny the universities the support required to bolster the training of scientists and technologists. In the 1958 Royal Commission on Canada's Economic Prospects (the Gordon Commission) the Canadian government affirmed its commitment to establish a 'more elaborate provision for research' so that Canada might accelerate its 'rate of technical advance' and 'maintain [its] position in relation to other countries.'[118] Government support for fundamental scientific research was as logical as it was unequivocal. In the aftermath of Sputnik, the modern university had become responsible once again for the survival of the nation.

In addition to providing the crack front-line troops to be deployed in the Cold War, universities also proved essential in furnishing society with the highly educated workforce that was central to an advanced industrial economy. Scientific and technical training not only had military applications but also was highly significant to the economic well-being of the nation. As the Gordon Commission noted in 1958, 'the pace of growth and development depends largely on the ability to use the fruits of scientific reserve, technological improvements, and advanced mechanization.' In the advanced economic world of the late 1950s, 'the abilities of scientists, engineers, administrators, and skilled people of all kinds are being called increasingly into play.'[119] More than training the engineers and other technical personnel, however, economic theorists considered modern universities to be focal points of economic growth. Citing Peter Drucker's *Landmarks of Tomorrow* (1959), Claude Bissell showed how education was not an overhead cost (as considered by conventional economic argument), but rather was a capital investment. The development of educated people was, in Drucker's words, 'the most meaningful index of the wealth-producing capacity of a country.' In *The Affluent Society* (1958), J.K. Galbraith, as Bissell also indicated, had come to the same conclusions. Galbraith had argued that the universities were poised to produce a 'new class' that was to have the knowledge and technical resources to strive towards economic prosperity and 'peaceful survival itself.' Since education was the 'operative factor in expanding [this] class,' Galbraith concluded, 'investment in education, assessed qualitatively as well as quantitatively, becomes very close to being the basic index of social progress.'[120] In a more practical sense, furthermore, there was a tremendous expansion in administrative, financial, and public sector positions by the late 1950s and 1960s. Canadian society required teachers, lawyers, doctors, and bankers, along with engineers and other trained specialists. Because of the swift growth in the numbers of white-collar jobs, the university now was called upon more than ever to satisfy the demands.[121] Ontario's minister of education, William Davis, put into perspective society's reliance on the modern university. 'Today as never before in our history,' Davis declared in 1963, 'our very survival, our future development and prosperity as a nation depends on the proper education of our youth.'[122]

The birthplaces of a new, educated class, the universities were regarded increasingly as centres of social and economic advancement. In assisting Canada to become a 'noble and puissant nation,' as Claude Bissell described it in his keynote address to the NCCUC in 1961, society and the universities emphasized more than ever before the utilitarian aspect of higher education.[123] Indeed, the 'culture of utility,' which reached back to the interwar period, achieved renewed precedence by the 1960s. Not only did the universities convince communities of their importance to the nation, but an increasingly heavy reliance on provincial largesse helped to place the universities squarely within the public domain. Once primarily privately funded, increasing capital expenditures and the continuing explosion in enrolments meant that universities had to look to government for handouts. Indeed, by the mid-1960s governments (especially provincial governments) were covering the lion's share of university costs. Despite the protests of scholars about infringements on academic autonomy, moreover, provincial governments were reticent 'to sit passively on the sidelines and let each institution follow its own autonomously conceived fancies.'[124] Rather, they took an active interest in systems of higher learning that they funded, and, perhaps more important, that were increasingly considered by the voting public as integral to the well-being of their communities.

Aside from necessitating increased dependence on the public purse, the massive expansions of the early 1960s implied a change in the very nature of higher education. This concept of change is perhaps best encapsulated in the term 'multiversity.' President Clark Kerr of the

University of California, who coined the word, meant by the term that the modern university was so variegated that there was no 'single vision' to shape it. For Kerr, the 'intellectual world had been fractionalized.'[125] As the universities expanded and interests continued to diverge, moreover, academies found that their utilitarian roles took on added significance. Only through functioning as economic and technical storehouses and providing higher learning to the masses of young Canadians could the universities find any unifying purpose. Presidents and boards of governors had to weigh the often conflicting interests of funding goals with the educational ideals, and public demands for the accommodation of larger numbers of students with educational standards. Whereas smaller institutions could still claim that the 'liberal arts constitute the centre of their educational offerings,'[126] universities large or small nevertheless had to be 'guided by utilitarian considerations if they [were] to receive the understanding and support required from the community.'[127] Motivated by this new utilitarian purpose, the universities had become ensconced in the public ambit as the location of power, in Kerr's words, 'moved from inside to outside the original community of masters and scholars.'[128]

Academic critics were divided on the issue of the so-called multiversity. Critics such as George Grant and Northrop Frye continued to denounce the demise of the traditional university and criticized the monstrosity that Kerr expounded upon. A key participant in the struggle against academic modernization during the wartime and post-war periods, George Grant continued to speak out against the advent of the multiversity. A subtext of his 1960s analyses on the predominance of technological liberalism was the decline of religious and contemplative traditions. In becoming the handmaiden of the technological society, the modern university had not been true to its role as a spiritual and philosophical centre. Grant saw that the ultimate goal of North Americans was to build a 'noble technological society of highly skilled specialists who are at the same time people of great vision.' He did not dispute the magnificent results of the research orientation of the universities, especially in the natural sciences. In exchange for these great achievements, however, Grant realized that the universities had lost vital components: justice, knowledge of the beautiful, and a notion of where people stand in relation to the divine. In short, Grant continued to lament the loss of the universities' main purpose: the duty of its scholars to lead society in the pursuit of truth, justice, and beauty.[129]

Adding to Grant's imputations against the modernized university,

Northrop Frye also provided a renewed perspective on old problems. For Frye, the university was not a mere extension of society's social-technological aspirations (as it had become for many latter-day critics of the university) but instead stood outside society, analysing it and assessing social interaction. It was a kind of 'social laboratory' that provided 'insights into the structure of society, nature, or the human mind' and thereby facilitated an understanding of the modern world.[130] Higher learning's defining function, according to Frye, was to evaluate and challenge the accepted views of society. 'If one's view of society has been formed by great philosophers,' he reasoned, 'one cannot be satisfied with the view of it taken by luxury advertising.' In other words, by challenging accepted views, higher education could assist in discerning falsehood from reality. In a world dominated by the material and technological, it helped to 'awaken minds' and liberate students from prominent modern fallacies: thinking of education and life more generally merely in terms of the adjustment to a comfortable, material existence.[131]

In exposing falsehoods and thus in fulfilling their critical function, Frye argued further, universities enabled students to pursue truth and, ultimately, to gain freedom. By discrediting the utilitarian objectives of the modern world, they allowed students to focus on the study of great art and literature, absorb 'the discipline of the scientific method,' and understand 'the wisdom of the ages.' Academies were therefore society's 'powerhouses of freedom' because they exposed false thinking and directed their adherents to the truths inherent in the beauty of art, philosophy, and the good life. But Frye did not limit the emancipatory function strictly to university students and teachers. Rather, the 'free' university was symbolic of the achievement of a greater, societal emancipation. The university meant much more to society than its physical manifestation as a group of buildings, or as a main receptacle of knowledge. The university represented, Frye wrote, 'what humanity ... is free to do if it tries ... Wherever there is respect for the artist's vision, the scientist's detachment, the teacher's learning and patience, the child's questioning, there the university is at work in the world.'[132] For Frye, academic freedom thus meant much more than liberation from outside interference; rather, the pursuit of academic truth implied the achievement of a greater social truth and, ultimately, the emancipation of humanity.

Both academic liberty and the university's function as critic were central to Frye's conception of higher learning. What is more, like earlier academic critics, Frye postulated a social mission for the university. He considered the university to be central to the adaptation of modern humanity to changing social realities. Society was in 'a state of process,' a revolutionary state striving towards future ideals.[133] Through its function as social critic, the university was to make sense of the revolutionary process and therefore lead society through its perilous times. Against the backdrop of tremendous socio-economic change, expanding enrolments, the ongoing development of the multiversity, and student radicalism in the university, Frye singled out higher learning as a stabilizing force. In a society in a state of constant change and confusion, the university was a place of refuge. 'The university,' Frye pronounced, 'by virtue of its emphasis on the cultural environment, the supremacy of mental discipline over personality, and academic freedom, has the resources for forming a bridgehead of flexible and detached minds in a strategic place in society.' As it was for Innis and others, for Frye the academy was best able to perform its social function by serving as purveyor of cultural, moral, and humane truths. It is ironic that, in presenting historical perspectives on society, the university was able to provide insight on modern problems. It best fulfilled its function, Frye averred, 'by digging in its heels and doing its traditional job in its traditionally retrograde, obscurantist, and reactionary way. It must continue to confront society with the imaginations of great poets, the visions of great thinkers, the discipline of the scientific method, and the wisdom of the ages, until enough people ... realize that it is a way of life.'[134]

Problems arose, however, in that society in this revolutionary age was fraught with misconceptions and misunderstandings about what was happening to it and, perhaps most significant, to the academy. Modern humanity, according to Frye, simply did not understand the civilizing and humanizing mission of higher learning. The immense perspective engendered by experiencing imaginations of great artists and scientists, in consequence, was in danger of being lost. Society was likewise in peril of misapprehending the revolutionary process of contemporary times and, as a result, of regressing as a civilization. Present society, Frye asserted lugubriously, 'is not predestined to go onward and upward.' Reacting against the driving elements of mass culture, Frye claimed that society had been transformed into a mob culture; 'hucksters,' 'censors,' and 'hidden persuaders' had turned 'literature into slanted news, painting into billboard advertising, music into caterwauling transistor sets, architecture into mean streets.'[135] Most important, the academy itself – the last refuge of civilization – had become a reflection of this debased culture and therefore contributed to society's demise. Frye harshly criticized the modern university because it had become full of itself and excessively proud of the essential economic-technological role it performed in society. 'If the university,' Frye warned, 'like so much of the rest of our society, falls into the habit of rationalizing its prosperity as a kind of virtue, it will have been kid-napped by that society and will have betrayed its special function.' Alluding to lowered educational standards, the advance of technical instruction, and the triumph of Grantian technological freedom more generally, Frye made an even stronger statement on the deleterious effects of education in the age of mass democracy. The 'beliefs and aims' of a democratic society, Frye asserted, scuttled the 'attempt to give the university student a kind of perspective on what the whole of the learned human race' had achieved. Social pressures continued to endanger universities, he concluded, by forcing them 'to work out and teach some kind of democratic philosophy.'[136]

In denouncing modern education trends and providing a justifica-tion for the enduring relevance of the traditional academy, Northrop Frye reacted against his social and intellectual milieus. Although not hostile to material advancement per se, Frye chided a society that had become obsessed with the material and the technological and had fallen prey to the trappings of mass culture. Intellectually, he distin-guished himself from the growing numbers of academic observers who were willing to work within the limits of modernized and democ-ratized higher education. Against advancing tendencies in higher learning Frye stood firm, a strong and loyal advocate of the merits of the traditional academy. Furthermore, in advocating traditional educa-tion, he provided a link to the academic critics of former times. Through Frye we see a connection to the university critics of the 1940s and early 1950s. Even more notably than the roles played by George Grant and the dwindling numbers of other non-conformists, Frye's great success as university critic was to bring the tradition of dissent into a period that was increasingly inimical to the ideas and uses of the historical university.

Despite the efforts of Grant and Frye, however, academic observers were not receptive to a reversion to the principles of traditional higher learning. While always paying at least lip service to the enduring bene-fits of the liberal arts and a classical education, commentators like J.A. Corry were less willing than their colleagues to eschew the multiver-sity. In a group of addresses given throughout the 1960s and published in 1970 under the apt title *Farewell the Ivory Tower*, Principal Corry of Queen's University presented his opinions on the process of academic modernization. Although Corry was unwilling to concede that the universities were mere handmaidens of the state and therefore bereft of vision, the leitmotif of his addresses was that the universities found their focus through service to society. Corry explained that the relation between the university and the state had recently changed. Whereas in a political climate in which laissez-faire attitudes and individualism predominated, the 'medieval' university, aloof from society, could be justified; in a democratic society, it could not. The university, in other words, had to adapt to new circumstances and realities. While Corry was not averse to the traditional principles of the university – scholarly freedom, tenure, and the importance of humane values and contemplative traditions – he did object to ivory towerism and the aloofness of a system from the community that paid the bills. Universities must be kept free, he claimed in 1964, for theirs was 'essential work that can only be carried on in the flexible conditions of freedom. Governments in Canada affirm this just as strongly as anyone else. Equally, it will not be denied in any responsible quarter that governments which guard the public interest and provide increasingly heavy support for universities out of public funds need assurances. How can they claim the continued confidence of the taxpayer unless they can say with knowledge that his money is being wisely spent in the public interest?'[137]

Linked through increasing taxpayer funds, then, the universities had a responsibility to the communities they served. For Corry, this obligation to society would be fulfilled when the universities could 'interpret the felt needs of society,' which included the 'utilitarian interests' of the masses of new students. The universities ought to accommodate students harbouring these pragmatic inclinations as long as 'their numbers do not overwhelm us.' 'The world's work,' he continued, 'must be done.' 'Much of that work requires knowledge and disciplined minds of an order that universities are best equipped to provide. The universities need to keep in close touch with the workaday world. Common sense and practicality never come amiss, even in universities.'[138]

Far from reforming society, making it aware of its inherent flaws (as Harold Innis and like-minded critics advocated), Corry thus implored the university to adapt to society, to fit into its fundamental structures and to aid in the achievement of its ultimate goals. Corry was not alone in his denunciation of the ivory towerism of the Canadian university. Arthur Lower, who had frequently spoken out against cloistered scholarship, implicitly supported Corry's arguments. Society was now full of 'plain, work-a-day people,' he claimed, 'getting "equaler and equaler" as the days go by.' Scholars must not isolate themselves from these individuals but rather should endeavour to understand the 'people they are working with, their social and economic background.'[139] Canadian universities, Lower suggested in conclusion, must work diligently to eliminate the remnants of nineteenth century elitism and thereby enable themselves to relate to the new and changing world. Claude Bissell, president of the University of Toronto, also expounded upon the modern university's integration into society; he believed that society had accepted both scholars' 'assumptions about the importance of higher education and the necessity of meeting its enormous needs.' The role of the university, he continued, could be 'seen in different terms and [expressed in] a more elaborate and stimulating context. We can talk about universities not in terms of subsistence, but in terms of expansion; not as production lines for business and the state, but as a principal means whereby our economy, our political structure and our culture grow and change.'[140] Even Marshall McLuhan, in the context of his media studies, elaborated on the university's new societal function. In the 'electronic age,' McLuhan asserted, universities had relinquished their centuries-old function as 'the main processing plants for young minds.' Instead, they had become the means by which society could understand cultural change and social environments, which he felt had become dominated by electronic media of communication. As highly decentralized institutions, able to access and understand the nature of electronic information transfer, universities became 'the principal organs of perception for the entire society.'[141] Neither simply a training ground for the elite of a bygone culture nor the ivory tower, the university had developed into the hub of all society.

For McLuhan, Corry, and the other interested observers, then, the university had become integrated into its social environment. While still hoping for the persistence of humanist and other university traditions, they accepted that the modern academy had become a reflection of broader social change. The academy had developed into an agent of society, and most within and outside the academic world were willing to accept and accommodate this fait accompli. This willingness to accommodate the demands of the modern world and to abandon not only the ivory towerism but also the humanistic focus of past critics was a powerful manifestation of the sway of the modern university. As one critic declared in 1961, the days of supremacy for the humanist had passed. Humanist scholars can no longer 'defend their right to a place in the sun'; rather, 'science, technology, and the humanities must cooperate and live in mutual dependence.'[142] While remaining true to their purpose and traditions, added another commentator, the universities had to address the 'needs of government, of industry and of society over the long haul.' They must 'move with the times' and 'adjust to the changes in society.'[143] Once harshly opposed, there was sombre resignation among academic observers that the modern university had arrived at last.

By the 1960s Canadian universities were completing a process of academic modernization begun several decades earlier. Modern institutions scarcely resembled their late-nineteenth-century forebears, which had been cultural outposts responsible for inculcating the virtues of British culture and for helping to develop a 'dutiful, morally sound social order.' In an age of astonishing expansion, economic prosperity, and democratic ideals, they also shunned their former responsibility as access points for the sons of the elite to the higher forms of learning. Characterized by democratic education, a growing culture of utility, the advent of the multiversity, a more intimate relationship between universities and their government and private benefactors, by the late 1950s the modern university was firmly ensconced in the modern realities of mass enrolments and million-dollar budgets. Inherently conservative institutions, universities did indeed retain some of the educational structures that would meet the challenges of the new age. The arguments of George Grant, Northrop Frye, and others are testaments to the strain of conservatism that marked academic life even into the 1960s and 1970s. Because academics were faced with the immutable forces for social change after 1945, however, a newfound willingness to accommodate modern exigencies sundered their reactionary predilections. Critics such as Frye and Grant had been marginalized more than ever before in the advancing tide of 'academic modernists' because they refused to accept the university's current societal role. Whereas immediately after 1945 critics wondered whether recent trends towards academic modernization were mere aberrations, their counterparts a decade and a half later harboured no illusions about the fate of the traditional academy. The acceptance by scholars of academic modernization was, ultimately, the most telling manifestation that the end of the long evolution had been reached and that the modern university was born.

5

Battling the Philistines: The Quest for Culture in Post-War Canada

With academic modernization, social critics in Canada preoccupied themselves with the development of culture. Concern mounted among these intellectuals that culture – defined broadly as the social, political, and artistic activities of a society and in more narrow, Arnoldian terms as the pursuit of moral and social perfection, truth, and beauty – had reached a crossroads. After 1945 the nation achieved significant diplomatic recognition for its role in the war, and became one of the world's most prosperous countries. Yet despite its military-diplomatic and economic triumphs, social observers realized that Canadian culture had not developed along with the material and political aspects of the nation. For some critics, Canada as a cultural entity had stagnated; for others, it threatened to regress, reflecting the wider cultural decadence of the western world.

During the period 1945–70 there was a consistent critique of cultural developments. This critique ebbed and flowed. It sometimes took on an utter despondency, reflected in critics' perceptions of the post-war crisis of values and in the eventual triumph by the 1960s of mass society. In between, the critics were less pessimistic; they held out hope that cultural decline could be reversed and that Canada might become an islet of civilization among a sea of American culture. The twenty-five-year period after the war was indeed one of re-examination, of both the nature of Canadian culture and how that culture reflected a larger national identity. Centred about the Massey Commission, the cultural critique endeavoured not only to define and defend 'culture' in Canada, but also to promote a view that was unique to the dominion. Critics thus tried to define and mould the Canadian identity from a cultural perspective. Against the historical backdrops of growing consumerism, materialism, and cultural 'Americanization,' critics became embroiled in what they perceived to be a death struggle to preserve older cultural forms and orientations. Moreover, in a period in which Canada's self-perception seemed ever-changing, they saw themselves as providing an understanding, based sometimes in historical fictions, of a young nation. As such, they attributed to themselves a similar social significance to that of their intellectual compatriots, the critics of academic modernization. For both groups, in some cases the same individuals, the betterment of society was the pre-eminent objective. Cultural amelioration was, indeed, a broader manifestation of humane values and the traditional university more generally. Along with the technological and academic aspects of modernization, the critics of modernity felt that post-war Canada faced crises of culture and of national identity. It was the self-imposed responsibility of these cultural analysts to respond to the problems and suggest alternatives. They perceived themselves as an elite cadre of soldiers whose unwavering duty it was to repel the onslaught of the ignorant and uncivilized. For the critics of mass culture, the barbarians were at the gates.

The 'crisis of values' that characterized the 1940s was an important point of departure in the analysis of cultural decline. Reflecting more than the embattled arts tradition in the academy or the advent of a modern scientific and materialist society, the problem of values represented greater cultural decay. In a 1946 article entitled 'The End of an Age,' for instance, W.H. Alexander expressed concern about contemporary attitudes towards moral and cultural values. Moderns, he explained, were 'drawing towards an end of a period of about two thousand years' because, instead of allowing themselves to be guided and directed by ethical precepts, they showed little regard for 'moral principles of action.' Inspired by scientific and technological achievement, he added, they ascribed to a new, though false notion of morality. Alexander illustrated his point by discussing the impact of nuclear warfare and the horrors of Hiroshima. Outwardly, he wrote, the nuclear attack had destroyed the city of Hiroshima and tens of thousands of people. Inwardly, 'it [had] destroyed the whole basis of mankind's interrelations.' Leaders of nations and their peoples ignored the moral implications of mass destruction in favour of the higher 'goods' of national survival and loyalty to the state. The achievement of victory by whatever means necessary became, according to Alexander, the greatest moral purpose of all. This new 'moral' focus, however, subordinated older moral principles like the sanctity of human life. Indeed, the attainment of military and economic power through scientific and technological expertise had replaced Judeo-Christian values as the hallmarks of morality. For Alexander, the lamentable reality was that, although false, the scientific-technological ethic nevertheless character- ized modern outlooks. Ultimately, this false understanding implied dire consequences for all of western civilization. Bereft of concern for the ethical and the transcendent, he concluded, modern civilization was morally bankrupt and was decaying more quickly than any other culture in history.[1]

The connection between cultural decadence and the advent of a technological consciousness was also a theme on which other post- war observers commented.[2] In a paper entitled 'The Unbinding of Prometheus,' James Thomson also showed, among other things, the deleterious effects of the technological imperative. Thomson's piece presented a 'Promethean' theme: while humanity gained a measure of control over its environment through technological innovation (thereby achieving liberty and becoming 'civilized'), there were limits to technological freedom. The gifts of civilization, in Thomson's words, 'carry their own problems with them, from which as yet no way of escape has been found.' As did Alexander, Thomson believed that the quintessence of these concerns was the problem of nuclear destruction. Through nuclear science humanity had discovered the ultimate means of controlling the environment. Yet, through weapons of mass destruc- tion, atomic technology also implied a breakdown of morality and humanity. 'A fearful conflict,' Thomson wrote, discussing the current war and the prospects of nuclear annihilation, 'now engages the ener- gies of almost the entire human race.' He went on, 'The tragic spectacle is rendered more terrifying by the scientific skill employed in the vast holocaust of destruction.' Even the courageous and heroic activities of humans could not relieve moderns 'from a sense of foreboding in the contemporary impasse.' Modern humanity was 'haunted by a convic- tion that war is an Apocalypse of civilization's diseased state now cry- ing out for anxious thought and drastic remedy.' Underlying the tragedies of nuclear warfare, however, was the most tragic reality of all: humankind was unable to comprehend the need to re-evaluate its current state; it was incapable of rectifying its own folly by under- standing that it had become obsessed with science and technological advancement. Nuclear warfare was simply a manifestation of modern humanity's ultimate foolishness. It was the last in a chain of tragedies

that began when Prometheus stole fire from the gods. Modern humanity, Thomson concluded, had begun to pay the penalty for its Promethean folly.[3]

As it had for Alexander, the technological ethic had become for
Thomson a defining ethos of the modern west. It presented itself as the
only true course to freedom and cultural progression and, in so doing,
deflected attention away from alternative cultural values and thereby
distorted the modern view of cultural advancement. In 'The Influence
of Science on the Cultural Outlook,' S. Basterfield, as Alexander and
Thomson had done before him, elaborated on the interrelationships
between science and cultural development. Basterfield claimed that
while the advance of science made for a financially 'richer culture,' it
also narrowed the vision of moderns and catered to 'a largely adoles-
cent view of the world.' He asserted that the technological ethic (the
achievement of power and control, especially over nature), to which
both Alexander and Thomson had referred, negatively affected the
appreciation of cultural and moral values. 'The unprecedented success
of technology, the anticipated power over nature, and the vast wealth
from natural resources,' he wrote, 'have dimmed the vision of moral
and aesthetic values to such an extent that while we may pay lip service to the matter of custom and tradition, we regulate life essentially
by material values and those activities to which applied science so
obviously ministers.' North Americans exalted consumerism, technological gadgetry, and the 'magic of science' to provide 'know-how' and
to enhance material development at the expense of cultural and spiritual values. Religion, Basterfield argued, was 'no longer a matter of
sincere belief' nor a matter of 'personal experience and spiritual fellowship.' Rather, it had been transformed into 'mainly a social activity
and a community enterprise centred in a church.' In contributing to the
eclipse of the humanities, the sciences had also undermined traditional
values and ethics. They had come to embrace their role as initiators of
material and technological progress.[4] Once great philosophers, Basterfield asserted, scientists had estranged themselves from philosophy
and attendant moral questions and therefore shirked their responsibilities to the social order.

The decline of philosophical and other cultural values, however, had
grave consequences for modern society. While Basterfield hoped that
traditional values could be preserved by resurrecting the philosophi-
cal-humanistic approach, he was prepared to contemplate the worst.
If left unguided by moral and cultural virtues, Basterfield warned,

moderns might 'prostitute science to the most evil purposes' and allow it to lead to civilization's ultimate demise. Unless they recognize the implications of the assault on values for which 'prophets, poets and artists have striven through the centuries,' the world 'may decline into a technological barbarism.'[5] In simple terms, aesthetic and moral virtues were key to the enduring vitality of western civilization.

While commentators like Basterfield focused on the effects of science and technology, other critics used related, though slightly different explanations for the apparent decline of cultural values. In an article written for the *Dalhousie Review*, K. Rayski-Kietlitcz of Acadia University examined the impact of the North American 'utilitarianism' on cultural advancement. In Canada and the United States, Rayski-Kietlitcz claimed, the emphasis on practical fields of education was disproportionate to other branches of knowledge that offered no 'immediate and visible material gains.' This over-active pragmatism, moreover, directly influenced widespread indifference on the part of North Americans to cultural values. In focusing on material development and practical achievements, North Americans largely ignored cultural developments that were likely to have little practical use. Evidence of this lamentable reality, Rayski-Kietlitcz added, existed in the esteem in which most Canadians held the 'heroic business man' and, alternatively, the 'occasional contempt in which the intellectual professions [were] held.' Lacking a proper balance between practical and intellectual or cultural virtues, it was not surprising that North America had languished culturally compared with Europe and other 'older' civilizations.[6]

Discussing the true nature of liberty in modern civilizations, Peter Viereck also railed against Canadians' over-abundant concern with things practical and material. As well, Viereck claimed that morality, not a simplistic view of material progression, was the key to liberty and therefore the advancement of culture. In a piece entitled 'Two Aspects of Freedom,' he argued that 'freedom rests not solely on the material basis of merely economic prosperity and merely political constitutions. Freedom, including the most material economic and political freedom, rests ultimately on ethical values.' A standard of morality was a precondition for the establishment of social and economic advances. Society could achieve economic gains, Viereck explained, only 'by a credo that subordinates economic gains to individual freedom.' Depending solely on the idea of economic betterment, and therefore compromising freedom and justice 'for the sake of organizing total tyranny,' however, society lost not only freedom but economic advances as well. Viereck suggested that, without ethical and moral absolutes, both replaced with the transient 'goods' of material growth, society was neither free nor capable of ameliorating.[7]

Also discussing the significance of ethical standards, philosopher John A. Irving asserted that the 'problem of values' was the 'central philosophical issue of the twentieth century.' The basic purpose of Irving's article, aptly entitled 'Moral Standards in a Changing World,' was to comprehend why moderns had come to question eternal moral standards. Rapid technological and scientific development, growth in the medical sciences, and the 'bitter controversies between capitalists and communists,' Irving wrote, were among the important socio-historical factors that 'produced the moral restlessness of our times.' In such an environment, moderns had begun to question 'ultimate values.' 'Confronted with changing conventions in a changing world,' he explained, 'many people have come to feel that there are no universal moral standards at all.' The confusion of the modern age had led to moral relativism. Moderns had replaced universal values with moral standards that were firmly rooted in the world of science and the material. In shunning transcendent values, Irving hastened to add, they had brought themselves to the 'rim of the abyss.'[8] For, although deteriorating because of conditions of unprecedented change, universal moral standards were nevertheless essential to dealing with the current crisis of culture. In failing to realize this fundamental reality, Irving and the others implied, modern humanity was contributing to its own demise.

For Irving, as for Viereck, Rayski-Kietlitcz, and the others, the decline of values necessarily implied sociocultural deterioration. Harold Innis was another of the social observers who became preoccupied with the vitality of western culture. Like his many co-critics, Innis considered 'values' to be a key component in the disintegration of civilization. He cited the demise of the humanistic and arts traditions within Canadian universities as having 'ominous implications for the whole future of civilization,' as several critics of academic modernization had done.[9] He also wrote at length about the demise of spiritual values within the increasingly materialist culture of post-war Canada.[10] As we have seen, the analysis of the decay of 'philosophic' values was central to Innis's social criticism of the later 1940s and early 1950s. Consideration of the importance of moral and spiritual values was never far beneath the surface of any of Innis's later writings.

Innis, however, went further than his colleagues in his critique of modern society. Although important as a concept per se, the decline of

values was, for him, a way of broaching a subject of greater significance: the degeneration of modern western civilization. Whereas fellow critics preferred to expound upon the crisis of values rather than
elaborate on the connection between values and cultural decay, Innis
was intrigued by the intricacies of cultural development. An important
paper entitled 'Minerva's Owl' illustrated Innis's new-found preoccupation with cultural decadence. Reading before the 1947 meeting of the
Royal Society of Canada, he elaborated on the processes of cultural
transference and decline. Minerva, the Roman goddess of war, and her
attending owl, representative of wisdom and intellectualism, symbolized the relationship between force and the flight of culture through
time and over geographical space. Minerva's owl took flight once conditions had deteriorated and the protection of scholarship and cultural
activity had been undermined. It sought out 'new areas with possibilities of protection' so that cultural activity, reliant on organized force,
could continue to flourish. Once scholars and other cultural figures no
longer received the protection they required from political or ecclesiastical organizations (centres of power), the new civilization declined
and the symbolic bird of passage began its journey anew. Civilizations,
Innis claimed, collapsed because of the 'weakening of [the] protection
of organized force.'[11] They were re-established once the culture-force
relationship had been revived and the nexus between cultural and
political entities was renewed.

Originally, Innis continued, Minerva's owl took flight from classical
Greece, where political and cultural forces first had allied themselves.
It then continued its journey through the ages, tracing a path through
Europe, and finally reaching the New World and the modern industrial period. At this point, however, Innis became concerned about the
survival of things cultural and intellectual. Political organizations and
other societal manifestations of 'force' no longer concerned themselves
with the protection of intellectuals but instead were 'actively engaged
in schemes for [their] destruction.' Obsessed with consumerism and
technological advancement, Innis suggested, North American society
had become hostile to intellectual and cultural activities. Once patrons
of the arts and an intellectual life more generally, the holders of power
within modern society ignored as irrelevant long-standing cultural
and intellectual traditions. In so doing, they undermined the critically
important accommodation between force and wisdom.[12] Ultimately, in
Innis's scheme, they threatened the safety of Minerva's owl and with it
the survival of the ancient scholarly and cultural inheritance.

As discussed in chapter 2, Innis detailed the effects of technology, specifically of media of communication, on cultural change. We will not elaborate, therefore, on his notions of the emergence and decay of historic 'empires.' What is important here, however, is that Innis was not a lone voice on the topic of cultural degeneration. On the contrary, his ideas fall within a broader socio-intellectual context. Along with the critics of modern values, Innisian thought reflected a growing body of literature on cultural development. Innis himself admitted that his essay 'The Bias of Communication' relied heavily on the insights of A.L. Kroeber's *Configurations of Cultural Growth* (1946),[13] and elsewhere, he noted the influence on his writings of Oswald Spengler's theories of cyclical cultural development.[14] The theories of Arnold Toynbee also informed Innis's work,[15] as they did that of many of Innis's contemporaries. Indeed, Toynbee's 'metahistorical' approach to the past (employed in *A Study of History*, reappearing in an abridged edition in 1946) proved to be very popular among post-war historians. This approach appealed to intellectuals such as Innis and others who viewed the past not as a simple linear progression from primitive to advanced forms, but rather as a cultural process with vicissitudes, none more discouraging than those expressed in the contemporary period.[16] *Civilization on Trial* (1948) and *The Prospects of Civilization* (1948) reinforced Toynbee's chief message for the modern world that forces, such as democracy, technology, and material growth, interfered with the age-old struggle to develop an intellectual and spiritual life. Aphoristic, prophetic, and largely pessimistic, Toynbee's history captivated contemporary social observers who themselves were trying to make sense of the deepening crisis of civilization.

Even more influential than Toynbee's theories were the thought and social criticism of Matthew Arnold. Although Arnold wrote in the mid-nineteenth century, the critics of the post-war era found his ideas to be pertinent to current circumstances. Like Spengler and Toynbee, Arnold was a prophet of cultural decline. The 'anarchy' he referred to in his most famous tract, *Culture and Anarchy*, suggested two kinds of cultural malaise. First, mid-nineteenth-century British society was mired in spiritual anarchy. The burgeoning middle class had developed an untrammeled preoccupation with the socio-economics of laissez-faire and also had become increasingly disdainful of mainstream religious and intellectual activity. Arnold also connected spiritual anarchy with the inevitable advent of modern democracy in its various forms.[17] Indeed, Arnold deplored the materialistic outlook of his culture's 'philistines,' the nouveaux riches of the Industrial Revolution, and the vacuous self-indulgence of the 'barbarians,' the aristocracy. He dreaded the consequences of current socio-historical realities. Democratic initiatives, such as the widening of the franchise and the introduction of a system of universal elementary instruction, preoccupied Arnold because they implied the massive disruption of Britain's political and educational systems. Most of all, Arnold thought that the growing materialist orientation of society meant an increasing disregard for the preservation of things spiritual and cultural. Mid-Victorian times were 'anarchic' precisely because they failed to take account of the overarching significance of spirituality and, just as important, of 'sweetness' (beauty and artistic perfection) and 'light' (critical thought and intellectual pursuits). Thus, democratic and populist tendencies, an anti-intellectual bent, and a pronounced disdain for cultural traditions combined, for Arnold, to produce a morally and intellectually vacuous culture. It signified, in starkest terms, the advent of a civilization in peril.

The parallels between Arnold's observations and those of his mid-twentieth-century progeny are unmistakable. The sundering of traditional, timeless virtues and the expression of the newer, but transient, material values that J.S. Thomson and the others discussed, mirrored Arnold's trepidations about growing philistinism. One also notes the sharp criticism of anti-intellectualism common to both Arnold and his intellectual descendants. The failure to appreciate cultural and philosophical values signified to Arnold and later critics a profound disregard for intellectualism. Most striking, moreover, is the notion of the present as an age of enduring social change. For Arnold, the mid-Victorian period was one in which civilization languished amid the arrival of democratic education and a materialist, anti-intellectual culture. The modern, materialist, consumer age was also 'anarchic.' Indeed, both critiques put forth the idea that the present was besieged by moral relativism and cultural philistinism. Forces of history had intervened to disrupt the perilous equipoise between culture and anarchy and to undermine the civilized way of life.

The notion of cultural decline must also be historically contextualized. Although increasingly prosperous, Canada, to the culture critics, readily displayed a 'cultural poverty' after 1945. Despite considerable artistic achievement in the past – the accomplishments of the Group of Seven and the triumphs of authors such as Frederick Philip Grove, Stephen Leacock, Hugh MacLennan, and Frank Scott – Canada, in the eyes of the critics, had remained a cultural backwater. Culture (Arnoldian culture) was a matter of bookstores, a very few theatres, and literary salons. Canadian and American philanthropic organizations had constructed concert halls, libraries, and other cultural amenities and had provided aid to a few scholars through grants and scholarships. Yet in many respects, the complaints of the critics were justified; cultural accoutrements in Canada compared poorly with those of the United States and countries in Europe. Canadian governments also had little to boast of in terms of promoting culture. In spite of aiding the development of the National Gallery, the Canadian Broadcasting Corporation (CBC), and the National Film Board (NFB), they had largely stayed out of the field of culture. Unlike their counterparts elsewhere in the western world, they were niggardly about funding cultural organizations and focused instead on more concrete initiatives such as immigration policy and maintaining full employment. Indeed, cultural policy not only belied Canada's origins as a pioneer colony but also reflected Canadians' pragmatism and penchant for material success. Summing up Canada's cultural plight in 1951, historian Arthur Lower asked: '[C]an anyone deny that ... Canada is still not far from a cultural and spiritual desert? Can it be denied that its people in the mass are highly Philistine, despising the intellect, able to understand only action, opaque to thought and to imaginative creative emotion?'[18]

Editor, playwright, and humorist Robertson Davies did not contest the thrust of Lower's queries. Davies, in fact, was one of the growing number of Canadian intellectuals who criticized Canada's cultural achievement. Unlike many of his fellow academic critics, he chose to express his criticism through the fictional realm of the theatre. Written during the final stages of the Second World War, *Hope Deferred* (1945) is the first of Davies's plays that deal with the topic of cultural impoverishment.

Davies's play is based on a historical situation in which Count Frontenac, the governor of New France, attempts to bring to the New World some of the refinement of the French court by planning a production of Molière's *Tartuffe*. It develops when Laval and Sainte-Vallier, high-placed clergymen of New France, persuade Frontenac to abandon the production. They argue that the 'humble people of new France,' especially the Indians, would not understand that the piety Molière mocks is really false piety. They intensify their opposition by calling for the abandonment of all plays. It is at this point that Davies, through his fictional-historical characters, makes his most telling comments on the significance of culture to Canadians. The bishops want the inhabitants of New France to develop a religious piety first and foremost because this piety will make them a great people. They care little for artistic and cultural development; in their view, New France was to develop culture on its own over time. Frontenac and Chemène, the other main character of the play, vigorously oppose the bishops' position. Frontenac asks the bishops (without receiving a response), 'Are you asking me to reduce the intellectual tone of this whole country to what is fit for the Indians and the shopkeepers?' Chemène also queries the objectives and outlooks of the clergymen. 'Goodness without the arts,' Chemène claims, 'demands a simplicity bordering on the idiotic. A simple man without the arts is a clod, or a saint, or a bigot: saints are very rare [sic]: clods and bigots are many. Are you trying to put my country into their hands?'[19] Like Frontenac's question, Chemène's query also is left unanswered.

In *Hope Deferred*, Davies comments on the values and inclinations of the post-war period even though the play is set in the late seventeenth century. Frontenac's 'shopkeepers' are reminiscent of the modern-day middle class who were concerned much more with material prosperity than intellectual pursuits. The Indians, the most populous group living in New France, remind the reader of the indifferent masses of modern times. Further, the efforts of Frontenac and Chemène against Laval and Sainte-Vallier symbolize the struggle for cultural development in a society that is colonial and primitive. Their defeat signals the demise of cultural values and the enormous difficulty of establishing an appreciation of the arts in Canada. As Susan Stone-Blackburn has pointed out, Davies also makes direct references in the play to Canada's contemporary cultural malaise. 'Statements such as "we are always twenty years or so behind the old world in our thinking, and I dare say we always will be" and "it will be a thousand years before this country has such a quantity of brains that it can export them without causing a famine at home" point from the past to the present without seeming [to be] flagrantly anachronistic. This defeat for the forces of culture suffered early in Canada's history,' Stone-Blackburn concludes, 'appears to be an ill omen of things to come rather than a temporary loss on the way to victory.'[20]

Davies continued his criticism of the Canadian indifference to cultural values in *Overlaid*, the second of his one-act plays. Completed by the spring of 1946, *Overlaid* establishes a dramatic tension between two main sets of values: the pragmatism, Puritanism, and anti-intellectualism of Ethel (the daughter of an Ontario farmer) and George Bailey (an insurance salesman) versus the cultural vitality and joie de vivre of Pop, Ethel's father. In the play, Pop receives a $1,200 windfall, and he and Ethel discuss what to do with the money. A seventy-year-old farmer, Pop has worked hard to eke out a meagre living, yet he yearns for a greater existence than farm life could ever provide. Like his deceased wife, his entire community is 'emotionally undernourished'; its people, Pop claims, lack 'food for their immortal souls' and thus have 'little shrivelled-up, peanut size souls.' He wants to use the windfall to travel to New York City to flee the narrow pragmatism and antipathy to beauty of his community. Most of all, Pop wishes to partake of the richness of the cultural life that had been absent throughout most of his existence. Ethel, a 'hard-faced woman of forty,' is appalled by the blatant waste and frivolity of her father's plans. She cannot comprehend Pop's desire to expand his experiences. She feels strongly that the money should be put to a more practical use. She wants to use the windfall to purchase a large granite headstone to mark the grave of her mother. Above all, she wishes to be remembered as a respected member of the community and believes the headstone is the best way to accomplish this objective.[21] *Overlaid* ends when Pop, responding to Ethel's emotional pleas, relents and grants his daughter her wishes.

Ethel's triumph, and her persona more generally, have considerable symbolic significance. Representing more than simply the parochialism of a rural community, Ethel's character reflects Canadians at large. She represents the penchant of Canadians for subordinating things cultural and spiritual to a life dominated by the practical. Like the compatriots she personifies, Ethel does not seem to be aware of any other mode of living. As Davies comments elsewhere, 'Canada is a vast collection of Baileys and Ethels,' overly concerned with the significance of living earnest and morally responsible lives.[22] Ethel's ultimate victory also represents the conquest of pragmatism over a life of cultural fulfilment. *Overlaid*, like *Hope Deferred*, ends with the frustration of cultural aspirations. Although Davies endeavours to give voice to the merits of emotional and spiritual enlightenment, *Overlaid* ultimately reminds its readers of the intense difficulty of achieving a spiritually enriched life in Canada. Like its predecessor, Davies's play is ultimately concerned with the defeat of the forces of cultural edification.

Penned in 1949, *Fortune, My Foe* was Davies's most sophisticated treatment to date of the ongoing theme of cultural poverty. The play displayed an 'overt Canadianism' in that its characters included new immigrants, long-time residents, and native Canadians, all of whom are embroiled in a discussion of the merits of Canadian society.[23] Cultural destitution and artistic deprivation, again, are the themes of *Fortune, My Foe*. The play is set in a university town in the modern day and therefore speaks directly to the plight of culture in modern, urban Canada. If culture could flourish in any area of the dominion, then surely it would prosper in an urbane setting, presided over by numerous intellectuals. That it does not demonstrates, for Davies, the pervasive indifference of Canadians everywhere to cultural activity.

There are two plots in this full-length piece. The main storyline is set in Chilly Jim Steele's establishment. The key interplay is between Nicholas Hayward and Idris Rowlands. Hayward is a young and promising English professor, who is contemplating a move to the United States, where his talents would be better appreciated and rewarded. Rowlands is a middle-aged professor from Wales, whose failure to foster in his students the same love he feels for the arts has made him cynical and bitter about Canada. The play centres around Nicholas's decision to abandon Canada and take a job in the United States. Rowlands chastises his younger colleague for thinking about leaving a nation in grave need of scholars and cultural leaders so as to make more money and achieve greater acclaim. While Canada's 'raw, frost-bitten people have numbed [his] heart' and therefore left him a cynical and bitter man,[24] Rowlands nonetheless attempts to persuade Nicholas not to quit his country in search of greater recognition and better remuneration. Canada, Rowlands argues, desperately needs its scholars and artists even if it does not appreciate them. Without such intellectuals to teach other Canadians the value of art and scholarship, there would be no hope for a better Canada. Ultimately, Rowlands hopes to convince Nicholas to make the same sacrifice he made for the greater good of expanding the country's spiritual and cultural outlooks. While the central conflict in the play is Nicholas's internal struggle to decide what course of action to take, Rowlands nevertheless is important as a kind of alter ego through whom Davies expresses the plight of the intellectual and Canadian cultural activity more generally.[25]

The secondary plot revolves around Franz Szabo and his story. Szabo, a recent immigrant from Prague, is a puppeteer, who has recently fallen on hard times. Instead of prospering in his chosen field, he works at Chilly Jim's as a dishwasher. Szabo's storyline is much like that of the main plot. Common to both characters is the problem of finding in Canada an environment that will nurture artistic effort. Indeed, Szabo's wonderful marionettes are as unappreciated by the unschooled masses as is Nicholas's literature. Davies demonstrates the antipathy to Szabo's art in a scene in which Szabo presents a part of a puppet show to Mattie Philpott and Orville Tapscott. Philpott and Tapscott are a locally influential duo who could gain funds for Szabo's productions if they were favourably impressed, but they are semieducated and raise numerous infuriatingly mundane objections to the show. Rowlands, who is also present at the performance, can no longer bear Philpott's and Tapscott's insensitivity to Szabo's art. In a climactic moment, Rowlands, in a drunken rage, destroys the puppet show and drives the pair of 'donkeys' out of 'the temple of art.' While Rowlands, greatly embittered by the incident, warns Szabo that 'Canada will freeze your heart with folly and ignorance,' Szabo is less pessimistic than the old professor. Szabo argues that he is an artist and that artists 'are very very tough.' 'Canada is my country now,' he declares, 'and I am not afraid of it.' Although there may be 'bad times' and 'misunderstandings,' he resolves to be 'tough' and 'hopeful too.'[26]

The scene provides considerable insight into Davies's view of the cultural prospects of Canada. First, it reflects the low regard in which the Canadian middle class, represented by Philpott and Tapscott, held highbrow culture. It also shows the growing impatience and frustration of the intellectual with the unwashed masses. Ultimately, however, Davies's message is one of toleration and restraint. Through Szabo, he reaffirms his most important theme, brought out by Rowlands earlier in the play: Canadian scholars and artists must be committed to their country in spite of the inhospitality its citizens have shown them. Canada, Davies suggests, continues to be a land of cultural philistinism. Yet in *Fortune, My Foe*, he acknowledges an increasing need to counter philistinism with a determined attempt to foster cultural growth. Through Szabo, Davies teaches that Canadians should be resolved to thwart the Baileys, Ethels, Philpotts, and Tapscotts of the world and instead continue the struggle for spiritual fulfilment. He sums up this sentiment in a final soliloquy by Nicholas, who is heartened by Szabo's resolve to endure cultural philistinism and help to nurture Canadians' artistic sensibilities. 'Everybody says that Canada is a hard country to govern,' Nicholas pronounces, 'but nobody mentions that for some people it is also a hard country to live in. Still, if we all run away it will never be any better. So let the geniuses of easy virtue go southward; I know what they feel too well to blame them. But for some of us there is no choice; let Canada do what she will with us, we must stay.'[27]

At its base, then, *Fortune, My Foe* is a play that countenanced dogged persistence in the search for cultural enrichment. Hence, it is unlike *Overlaid* or *Hope Deferred*, which were much more pessimistic about the capacities of intellectuals and artists to overcome Canadian philistinism. Nevertheless, *Fortune, My Foe* advanced the same leitmotif that characterized Davies's earlier post-war plays: cultural deprivation. This theme was also readily apparent in the ideas emanating from the Royal Commission on the Development of Arts, Letters and Sciences, the Massey Commission.

Called in 1949,[28] the commission was to examine broadcasting, federal cultural institutions, governmental relations with voluntary cultural associations, and federal university scholarships. Yet it had a more general purpose. The mandate of the Massey Commission was to investigate the current state of Canadian culture. Consistent with the widely held notion that cultural values were in eclipse, it endeavoured to assess the reasons for cultural degeneration. The basic assumption of the commissioners[29] was that long-suffering cultural institutions, intellectuals, and advocates of culture more generally had to endure a period of heightened indifference to highbrow culture.[30] Like Innis, Davies, and others who commented on cultural decline, the propagation of the perception that Canada was embroiled in an acute struggle for culture was a main goal of the commissioners.[31]

.There is little doubt that cultural impoverishment was one of the central themes of the commission. After discussing the goals of the inquest, the Massey commissioners turned to a discussion of the impact of geography on Canadian cultural activity. The 'isolations of a vast country,' they claimed in the Commission *Report* (1951), 'exact their price.' Art was a form of communication through which artists came together, maintained contacts, and hence facilitated cultural attainment on a national scale. National gatherings of voluntary societies engaged in the fostering of cultural activities were indeed essential. Problems arose, however, because often modes of nation-wide communications were prohibitively expensive. 'Canada has bound herself together with expensive links of physical communication,' the commissioners argued, and 'these exact a tax which the artist can bear less easily than can trade and industry.' Geographical isolation, they added, also deleteriously affected national cultural institutions. The problem was most acutely experienced through the fact that nationwide institutions like the

National Museum were located in Ottawa, far from most of the dominion's regions. Again, the forces of geography conspired against the cultural development that other civilized nations of the western world
took for granted.[32]

Aside from the handicap of geography and a small and widely dispersed population, the commissioners and their associates examined
Canada's cultural pedigree to gain clues into Canada's cultural plight.
In a 'special study' on Canadian letters, Edward McCourt addressed
the problem of literary development. Canadian writers, he asserted
bluntly, had failed to 'create a national literature of much significance
to Canada or the rest of the world.'[33] Four factors, he went on to argue,
accounted for the paucity of literary works. The first of these was Canada's colonial spirit.

McCourt claimed that Canadian artists to the present 'slavishly imi-
tated' other greater works. 'Such an attitude,' he warned, worked
towards the 'discouragement of all creative writing; because creative
writing, in its very name, implied a process which can have no truck
with mere imitation.' The Canadian publishing industry, McCourt continued, was also responsible for arrested literary development. Almost
completely consumed by profitability, it was loath to 'take a chance'
on work that it deemed likely to be unprofitable. Next, McCourt
reproached the Canadian reading public. Canadian readers, he noted
acerbically, were 'ignorant'; they had 'no tastes or opinions of [their]
own' and were unable to 'discover genius.' Even in the mundane practice of purchasing books, Canadians fell far behind their counterparts
in Europe and the English-speaking world. Because of the 'small size
and wide dispersion' of Canadians, the reading public did not 'buy
enough books to make it even nearly possible for the Canadian writer
to live on the proceeds of his work, or the Canadian publisher to profit
much from the publication of Canadian books.' Hence, McCourt identified the 'impossibility,' 'under existing conditions, of creative writing
becoming a full-time profession in Canada.' Last, the critic bore
responsibility for the neglected state of Canadian letters. McCourt
argued that aside from university quarterlies and 'one or two newspapers and *avant-garde* publications,' 'most literary criticism in Canada is
beneath contempt.' Reviewers of prose and poetry alike gave attention
only to those works touted elsewhere, and their reviews were generally unsophisticated and formulaic. Yet the retarded development of
literary criticism did not surprise McCourt. The intelligent critique of
literary works, he claimed, was usually the 'concomitant of a mature

culture.' Since criticism 'grows on what it feeds on,' he concluded, it was inevitable that 'in Canada its growth should be somewhat stunted.'[34]

With McCourt, other contributors to the commission's special studies volume acknowledged the 'unripe state of national culture.'[35] Along with Canadian letters, Canada, according to the critics, lagged behind other civilized nations in a diversity of 'cultural' fields. In his special study for the commission, Robertson Davies commented on the status of Canadian theatre. Using theatrical dialogue to convey his ideas, he argued that development of theatre in Canada was in a perilous state. Serious theatre simply could not compete with newer entertainments like the movies, and the failure of many a travelling company provided grim evidence of this reality. While acknowledging that there was an audience for familiar, 'first-rate theatre,' Davies doubted the capacity of Canadians at large to appreciate 'unfamiliar' classics. Canadians were an 'illiterate people' in this regard; for they 'fear[ed] the unknown as only the ignorant and truly lazy ... fear it.' In this matter, he asserted, Canadian society 'desperately need[ed] reform.'[36] Malcolm Wallace added his voice to those of McCourt and Davies on the matter of cultural development. Echoing the sentiments of the critics of academic modernization, Wallace claimed that the humanities had lost their 'pride of place' in Canadian culture. The humanities were not yet moribund, but men of intellectual inclinations were increasingly losing interest in the study of humanity. 'The study of man, his origins and destiny, the values he should approve in life,' Wallace declared, 'leave most men cold. [These men] have no time or desire merely to stand and stare while they speculate on the meaning of the universe, its beauty and tragedy, its infinite complexity. Foolish thoughts of good and ill seem to have lost their appeal.'[37]

For philosopher George Parkin Grant, modern Canadian society had all but ignored the significance of contemplative and spiritual traditions. Grant, as we have discovered, believed that Canada was an 'unphilosophical' country because it was concerned chiefly with 'the practical business of a pioneering nation.'[38] In stressing the practicalities of nation-building, it had eschewed the contemplative and therefore compromised an appreciation of the beautiful, the cultural, and the transcendent.[39] Canada, in consequence, had failed to develop the philosophical maturity of older societies.

Hilda Neatby implicitly agreed with Grant's views on Canada's cultural immaturity. She believed that the basic problem was the absence of a national consciousness of the past. Canada was an inexperienced nation that had not yet 'contrived to explain itself to itself.' The reason for this lack of national self-appraisal, she continued, was that most Canadians were 'indifferent to any history' and were content rather to live in the present and the future. This ahistorical tendency was troublesome because, without a historical sense, Canadians would find it difficult to understand the fundamental character of their nationality. Under these circumstances, cultural development would be problematic indeed. No 'community,' Neatby concluded, 'can achieve maturity without a sane and intelligent awareness of its past.'[40]

The theme of cultural impoverishment having been firmly established in the minds of critics, the Massey commissioners proceeded to assess the reasons for Canada's spiritual immaturity. Three interrelated forces affected the development of culture in Canada: the mass media, the rise of mass culture, and the 'Americanization' of Canadian culture. In facilitating the rise of lowbrow culture, these factors, the commissioners argued, contributed greatly to the crowding out of serious culture; more fundamentally, they created an environment inimical to cultural activity. They so negatively affected cultural values that Canadians not only began to ignore and even revile high culture,[41] but also increasingly considered fare such as sporting events and radio soap operas as staples of their daily cultural diet. In accepting without criticism the trappings of mass culture, the commissioners suggested further, Canadians were becoming more and more 'American' in their cultural outlooks. In the face of the invasion of pervasive new communications media, they were losing a sense of who they were as a people at a time when the Canadian identity was only beginning to be fully expressed. Through the mass media, cultural Americanization caused Canada, as a cultural entity, to be in great peril.

In the introduction to the *Report*'s section on the 'mass media,' the Massey commissioners discussed the potentially harmful impact of modern communications. To illustrate their points, the commissioners juxtaposed the contemporary world with the world of Canadians 'born earlier than 1923.' One-half of Canadians, they wrote, had passed 'their formative years in a society where radio was unknown, where the moving picture was an exceptional curiosity rather than a national habit, and where as a consequence the cultural life of most of the communities centred about the church, the school, the local library and the local newspaper.' Aided by the church, there was a considerable musical tradition extant in the society of this period. In literary matters, schools, teachers, libraries, and librarians 'did much ... to create and to satisfy a taste for good books.'[42]

Contemporary society, however, provided a stark contrast to this bygone era. Dominated by the mass communications media, the commissioners suggested, the modern world had contributed to the demise of the cultural traditions of the older period. While radio, film, and the weekly periodical brought 'pleasure and instruction' to remote locations, and 'added greatly' to Canadians' enjoyment, there was 'some danger' that Canadians might forget that 'music and drama and letters call for more than passive pleasure.' Canadians, in other words, might forget that culture was not an idle or frivolous activity, a matter of mere entertainment. They might neglect the fact that traditional cultural activity was a serious business and that it ought to remain the lifeblood of the contemporary age, as it had in the past. It seemed to the commissioners that music, theatre, and other serious culture had little chance of influencing the present as they had in past eras. Currently, radio shows, movies, and other entertainments passed off as 'culture' precluded participation in true cultural activities. Nowadays, the commissioners complained, 'opera has a rival in "soap opera," and perhaps a "pin-up girl" grins from the exact place on the wall where used to hang a portrait of a shy young woman of twenty.' 'It will be unfortunate,' they concluded with a considerable sense of foreboding, if 'in this new world of television, of radio and of documentary films ... we hear no more our choir and our organist in valiant and diligent practice of the Messiah.'[43]

The new mass society thus had done much to challenge older cultural values and to replace those virtues with new ones of dubious merit. Yet precisely how did the mass media contribute to cultural decline? Unlike Harold Innis, who, writing while the commission sat, elaborated on how communications media influenced political and social structures, the commissioners were much less theoretically innovative. In contrast to Innis, moreover, they believed that the content of the mass media, as opposed to the technology itself, was all important. Indeed, Vincent Massey, Hilda Neatby, and the other commissioners did not object to the mass media per se. Rather, they deplored the fact that modern communications were being used improperly to further commercial and entertainment purposes and that, as a result, the dissemination of serious culture had been severely curtailed. The example of radio broadcasting is instructive.

Appraising the history of broadcasting in Canada, the Massey commissioners remarked that the Canadian Broadcasting Corporation (CBC, established in 1936) had had 'tolerable success in combating commercialization and excessive Americanization of Canadian programmes.' On the whole, the CBC had 'performed its duties satisfactorily' and had fulfilled its original tripartite function: 'an adequate coverage of the entire population, opportunities for Canadian talent and for Canadian self-expression generally, and successful resistance to the absorption of Canada into the cultural pattern of the United States.'[44]

There were, however, a few major criticisms of the CBC. Not opposed to broadcasting's entertainment function per se, the commissioners nonetheless countenanced a re-evaluation of commercial programming. In the opinion of the commissioners, the CBC had become too reliant on entertainment-oriented commercial broadcasting.[45] What was more, this overemphasis on diversional programming implied a diminution in air time for cultural and educational programs, the mainstays of public broadcasting. Commercialism tended 'to have an unfortunate effect on the content' of many programs; commercial radio stifled 'original creative writing' and imposed 'a dead level of mediocrity' on its broadcasts. The commissioners asserted, moreover, that very little 'Canadian expression' could occur through commercial radio. Indeed, they associated commercialism with 'Americanization' and argued that commercial broadcasts left little opportunity for the development of indigenous programming. The Massey commissioners considered American-style 'soap operas' to be particularly offensive forms of commercial programming. Referring to criticisms from 'authoritative sources,' they claimed that most of the serials reviewed were unsatisfactory, 'guilty of melodramatic exaggeration, unreality and an excessive use of commonplace and stereotyped forms.' Too many local stations, they indicated, referring to soap operas and other commercial shows, offered these types of unworthy broadcasts, 'programmes which must be described as regrettable.'[46]

The commissioners also were concerned that the new medium of television might inundate Canadians with commercial programming. Taking advantage of a break in commission proceedings in the spring of 1949, Hilda Neatby went to New York to study the merits of television. After watching several hours of broadcasts, she reported to Chairman Massey that television was an unrewarding occupation because it was dominated largely by commercial programs.[47] Reflecting Neatby's influence, the commissioners commented in the *Report*:

'Television in the United States is essentially a commercial enterprise, an advertising industry. The sponsors, endeavouring to "give the majority of people what they want,"' frequently choose programmes of inferior cultural standards, thinking to attract the greatest numbers of viewers. And as television greatly intensifies the impact of radio, so television commercials intensify the methods of appeal to material instincts of various kinds, methods which now disfigure many radio commercials.'[48]

Commercialism, then, was problematic, because it overemphasized broadcasting's entertainment aspect and therefore excluded the other, more meritorious informational and didactic functions. Along with commercialization, the Massey commissioners also criticized national broadcasters for not exploring 'more fully Canadian capacity and taste in purely intellectual matters.' According to the commissioners, the CBC gave inadequate attention to 'the serious intellectual needs of adults.' It had not expended enough money or effort on worthwhile music and other intellectual pursuits. They also chided the CBC's 'radio talks' policy, which often encouraged speakers to participate who had 'no special knowledge or reputation in their fields.' Indeed, CBC authorities often chose speakers 'because they [had] a natural facility for broadcasting' and 'because the popular approach of the amateur [was] thought to have special appeal to the average listener.' The commissioners objected to this policy because they thought that the Canadian listening public ought not to be sheltered from intellectual arguments and rarefied discussions. Canadians, on the contrary, ought to partake of the privileges of their French and British counterparts, who regularly had the opportunity of listening to 'talk shows' of 'scholarly quality.' It should be a set principle, they asserted in summary, that all CBC talks, 'even the most popular,' 'should ... be acceptable to the expert and enjoyed by the layman.'[49]

Repeatedly affirming their desire not to foist refinement on the masses,[50] the Massey commissioners nonetheless wanted to ensure that broadcasting became a tool for promoting serious culture. There was no reflex disdain for communication technologies, even for the newer media of radio and television. Instead, the commissioners considered the electronic mass media to be crucial to the betterment of Canadian culture. The mass media were, after all, the conduits through which cultural interests could reach the masses. They provided the means of disseminating information, while facilitating widespread education and cultural improvement.

The Aird Commission on broadcasting (1929) became for the commissioners a template for how to employ the electronic media. In radio, the Aird commissioners saw 'a great potential instrument of general education and national unity.' To achieve this laudable end, the commissioners recommended that a national company 'be founded to own and operate all radio stations' in Canada, that private commercial stations come under the control of this company or be eliminated, and that eventually, high-power stations be established to cover the whole country.[51] Making no direct connections between the objectives of the two inquests, the Massey commissioners nonetheless implied that the Aird Commission recommendations might be applicable to current circumstances. The broadcast media could become in the 1950s what the Aird commissioners of 1929 had hoped that they would be: instruments in the employ of the federal government to foster culture and the development of a national spirit. At a time when commercialism and lowbrow culture were flooding the airwaves, the commission recommended that government wrest control of broadcasting from commercial interests so as to safeguard the proper educational and cultural function of broadcasting. In terminating commercialism, the proliferation of inappropriate popular programming, and other pernicious manifestations of modern broadcasting, it would be able at last to harness the inestimable benefits of the modern media.[52] Broadcasting was, after all, a 'public service,' not a commercial industry.

Like the commercialized mass media, mass culture also threatened Canadian cultural development. While generally using the term *culture* in its positive, Arnoldian sense, essentially as an interchangeable term for 'high culture,' the Massey commissioners also recognized a new form, *mass culture*. Mass culture differed from popular culture, which the commissioners associated with pastimes, folklore, customs, and other cultural trappings, all of which they considered positive and non-threatening. While popular culture was a manifestation of indigenous, often local, cultural expressions, mass culture was mass produced, packaged, and carefully marketed. It was a form of widely dispersed and consumed popular entertainment. Disseminated by the mass media and inspired by ever-expanding commercial interests, it included popular entertainments such as movies, gossip columns, television shows, and the reviled soap operas, all made available in vast quantities to millions of people.

Whereas the commissioners tolerated popular culture as expressions of genuine cultural experiences, they reproached mass culture as a new and dangerous element in modern society. From a practical point of view, they thought that the majority of Canadians spent much more of their leisure time than ever before in listening to Charlie McCarthy, going to movies, or engaging in other fruitless pursuits. As a result, there was much less time for the opera, the theatre, 'serious music,' or other high-culture activities.

Mass culture caused even greater problems. In appealing to the greatest number of people it encouraged homogenized viewpoints and impaired critical thinking. Mass culture was repugnant to the sense of independent, individual exploration that characterized high culture because it repressed human tendencies towards intellectual growth. Most of all, it undermined the chief objective of high culture: to foster individual intellectual self-improvement. In presenting a new set of norms to which the 'common man' was compelled to subscribe, mass culture distorted and devalued the existing set of cultural and intellectual virtues. In Arnoldian parlance, it hindered the pursuit of sweetness and light. For a country like Canada, struggling to attain a cultural identity, mass culture presented a grave threat. As summarized in one commission brief, in pursuing 'escapist' entertainment, Canadians did nothing 'to satisfy creative instincts, stimulate the imagination, or cultivate the mind ... The result [was] mental and spiritual lethargy ... an empty life.'[53]

For the commissioners, mass culture was thus monolithic, manipulative, and enfeebling. It symbolized a society that valued mindless entertainment over intrinsically meritorious intellectual and cultural pursuits. As such, it acted like a prism through which were refracted the attitudes of the commissioners towards greater socio-historical issues. The first of these was the perception that the fundamental values of democratic civilization were in crisis.

By 1945 the Allies had finally defeated the Fascist powers. Yet almost immediately after the end of the war, a new form of totalitarianism, Communism, had emerged to endanger western democracy. Democracy seemed yet again to be under siege. This time, however, it became embroiled in a battle of ideas, a war of ideologies. To win this new conflagration, citizens of the west had to reassess their very way of life. For many intellectuals, as we have seen, this reassessment involved a reassertion of age-old cultural values. Only through the rediscovery of these traditional virtues could the 'scientific materialism' of post-war age be combated. As Anton C. Pegis asserted in a brief submitted on behalf of the Pontifical Institute for Mediaeval studies at the University of Toronto, modern civilization's greatest challenge was not merely to save itself from nuclear destruction. Rather, it was 'to discover its own spiritual character or to discover, in other words, what it is to be a civilization.' In a statement reminiscent of the strictures of the prophets of cultural decline, Pegis pronounced that 'the conditions of existence and the spirit which should animate [culture], and the meaning of law, and the meaning of government, and meaning of man ... are the questions which are ... in the balance today.'[54]

Expounding upon the relationship between the humanities and government and the role of humane values in the frightful age of power politics, historian Donald Creighton implicitly concurred with Pegis. At a time when 'international politics seem to have degenerated into a species of brutal and provocative gangsterism,' he wrote,[55]

> ... the real function of the humanities is the production of civilized men and trained and cultivated minds. Never before in the history of the world have there been such enormous accumulations of appallingly destructive power; never before have international politics been carried on in such direct, simple and uncompromising relationship with power. And yet, at the same time, never before have there been so many, and such emotional appeals to vague and grandiose collective faiths, to so-called ideologies which are invested with all the sanctity of a revealed religion and to which we are all expected to yield a blind and unquestioning adherence. The humanities may help save us both from these delusions of moral grandeur and these brutal appeals to physical force. They serve constantly to remind us that our culture is not a creed which we are divinely justified in imposing forcibly on other[s].

Intellectuals such as Pegis and Creighton stressed the spiritual and humane origins of western civilization. Ultimately, they urged, the west had to re-examine itself to have a chance at spiritual and cultural fulfilment.

The emergence of mass culture, however, according to the Massey commissioners, hindered the process of cultural self-examination. They believed that mass culture was repugnant to the achievement of spiritual edification. They reviled mass culture precisely because it interfered with the spiritual introspection that the western world so badly required. What was most dangerous, mass culture offered a set of 'false' values that crowded out essential cultural and humane virtues. As noted in chapter three, Massey and other intellectuals became concerned about the emergence in the post-war period of a consumer economy and an associated proliferation of materialist values. They worried that Canadians had become so preoccupied with material growth that they ignored transcendent spiritual and cultural values. Along with growing materialism, mass culture provided an added threat to this important objective of cultural self-examination. Through advertising and an emphasis on commercialism and consumerism, it accentuated the development of the materialist society. As Hilda Neatby explained, mass culture was the handmaiden of consumerism and commercialism. The mass cultural content of private broadcasts, she argued, tended to be 'a mere by-product of the advertising industry.' 'Radio,' she went on, 'is not a public service: the radio man is not, and does not profess to be the counterpart of the journalist or the editor. He is an advertiser, employed by commercial companies for advertising purposes. The final criterion for his programme must be "will they sell the product?"'[56]

In *The Mechanical Bride*, Marshall McLuhan also connected 'mass' and 'consumer' cultures. He showed how advertising, merely another of the myriad forms of mass culture, created a set of new and spurious consumer values. McLuhan pointed out, for instance, how magazine advertisements tried to show their audiences that consumerism was the sole definer of social status. Those who consumed certain products at the prompting of marketing executives were perceived as more 'cultured' than those who did not. Status was conferred on them not because of who they were as individuals or because of what they thought; instead, they gained status because of what they purchased and how their consumer appetites qualified them to fit into a larger culture of consumers. Along with millions of other people, advertising agencies taught them that 'culture and distinction' were matters of consumption alone.[57]

Similarly, the Hollywood film industry encouraged consumerism. Hollywood's 'Love-Goddess Assembly Line,' McLuhan suggested, 'educated' women on how to look and what to wear. Again, moderns achieved status by consuming a product, this time the ideal types depicted in Hollywood films. Like the marketing agencies, Hollywood influenced moderns to conform to 'universal' standards and to assert their identity not by being individuals but instead by harmonizing with the larger group. As such, it integrated women into a larger, increasingly homogenized culture.[58]

As McLuhan suggested, the rise of mass culture involved more than the acceleration of materialism or the establishment of a new set of consumer standards. It also impinged upon the debate on the intellectual values of modern civilization. As did the other critics of modernity, the Massey commissioners deplored the homogenizing effects of mass culture. Vincent Massey and Hilda Neatby especially disdained the conformity that 'mass society' produced. Like Marshall McLuhan's consumer, modern man, according to Vincent Massey, had 'lost all sense of individuality.' 'His personality,' Massey wrote, was 'allowed to express itself in customs, badges, metals or degrees ... but strong and disturbing characters [were] discouraged. Non-conformity [was] unwelcome; eccentricity [was] banned.' With the hallmarks of individuality destroyed, Massey ended, the common man, to his great detriment, had been 'gently absorbed [into] the mass.'[59]

Hilda Neatby, who had a close intellectual collaboration with Vincent Massey,[60] also commented on moderns' 'neglect of the individual' and their 'preoccupation with the mass.'[61] She agreed that moderns had been losing their identity and individuality in the mass age. In accepting common points of view and adopting increasingly uniform outlooks on the world, they had succumbed to 'group conformity.' Acceptance within the group, not 'freedom or independence' from the collective, Neatby explained, was 'now thought of almost as a positive good'; 'withdrawal from the group or rejection by it is a corresponding evil.' Oddly, according to Neatby, moderns had shunned self-discovery and instead had come to seek identity in conformity. They repudiated 'formally imposed rules or duties' and resisted sociocultural obligations and other manifestations of 'external conformity.' Yet at the same time they desired an 'essential unity' that was to be gained 'through the common life of the group.' In other words, they sought their 'individual' identity through group interaction. However, in so doing, Neatby warned, they had eschewed one form of conformity for another. Ultimately, moderns denied themselves their inherent nature as individuals. More important, they undermined the individualist values that had been so much a part of the western tradition.[62] Characteristic of the mass age, group conformity, in the critics' view, yet again had exacted a ruinous toll on modern humans.

Closely connected to 'group conformity' was the idea of intellectual homogeneity. Like individuality, critical free thought also seemed to the commissioners to be in eclipse. As Vincent Massey explained, moderns had little regard for the 'critical faculty' and had generally rejected 'the guidance of reason.' They instead developed 'irrational mental habits' consistent with what had been known as 'the rule of the tribe,' but what was now euphemistically called '"group integration" or respect for the consensus.'[63] Hilda Neatby also scorned intellectual homogeneity; for her, as for Massey, the affinity for the 'mass' had had a profound effect in diminishing humans' rational and critical faculties. Moderns valued neither the capacity to think and reason nor the distinction of the individual within the group, both of which Neatby claimed to be defining features of humanity. Rather, amid the growing tendencies towards mass culture, moderns had become increasingly 'driven by common instinct or mass emotion.'[64] Lacking a critical sense and rational capacity, Neatby concluded, humanity's fundamental nature had been undermined. 'Rejecting the guidance of reason,' as Massey put it, moderns had become 'automata, ready to give an instant and uniform mechanical response to the man who presses the right button.'[65] Harold Innis stated the matter in a slightly different way. 'Modern civilization,' he argued, 'characterized by an enormous increase in the output of mechanized knowledge with the newspaper, the book, the radio and the cinema, has produced a state of numbness ... and self-complacency perhaps only equaled by laughing gas.'[66] For Lewis G. Thomas, Canada and the western world had been 'overwhelmed by a homogenizing process that was reducing everybody to similarity and pushing down things of the mind rather than raising the ability of people to appreciate things of the mind.'[67] The individual in this modern, Orwellian age seemed to have become merely one of the herd.

Hindering individual thought and human expression, the so-called herd instinct also had deleterious social and political ramifications. Ideologically, the twentieth century had been characterized by the emergence of totalitarianism and by a commensurate rise in ideological threats to liberal democracy. Propaganda and the mass media had greatly contributed to the rise of Fascist governments and had continued after the war to strengthen worldwide Communist movements. The Holocaust and other barbarities of wartime further signified the masses' susceptibility to campaigns of mass persuasion. Moderns, it seemed, had been vulnerable more than ever before to participation in mass movements.

In a climate of 'group thinking' and homogenized viewpoints, the commissioners feared that they were prone to false ideas and pernicious political doctrines. The masses, in Neatby's phrase, had exposed themselves 'to manipulation and to misery.'[68] George Grant was particularly forthright on this point. 'The effects of this surge of propaganda over the world,' he argued, had 'devastated the human mind. Grant went on, 'Satiated with this cheapened drug, the appetite of the public becomes so deadened that it is unable to distinguish between the truth and lies concocted for political purposes. The process whereby the individual submerges himself into mass movements becomes accelerated.' Propagandists negated moderns' individuality and their 'finer sense,' 'so that their aims remain identical for long periods of time in those of their fellows' and so that 'they accept easily the political ideas of their leaders.' 'Propaganda, far more effective and far more insidious than physical force,' concluded Grant, became the 'means whereby civilization may lose its finer instincts and political freedom may become the despised product of a past age.'[69] In one submission to the commission, the contributor commented on the effects of the herd instinct on democracy: 'Few Canadians go to college ... [T]he majority of them do not attend high school ... They have fallen into the habit of accepting with too much credulity and too little critical evaluation the fare which the publishing houses, the press, the films and the radio send them ... Such an attitude of willing suspension of disbelief towards whatever appeals to their desires is dangerous to the success of the democratic state.' Without 'intelligent critical evaluation on the part of ... citizens,' the writer claimed in conclusion, liberal democracy would be in peril.[70]

Exposing the masses to ideological fallacies, group thinking thus had actually endangered democracy. To the culture critics, however, there was another, more insidious assault on democratic principles. The rise of mass culture was tantamount to the development of a 'false' sense of socio-political freedom. True democracy, the commissioners noted, did not imply, as was commonly held, unmitigated majoritarianism. Nor did it involve the sundering of individual or intellectual values. Instead, influenced by environmental conditions, moderns had misapprehended the meaning of liberal democracy. They had mistakenly identified group thinking, the participation in consumer and leisure activities, and mass culture generally, as expressions of liberty. Yet for critics, freedom clearly did not mean obeying the orders of consumer suggestion, nor the 'right to be and to do as everybody else.'[71] It could not be achieved by being one of the herd. Rather, as Hilda Neatby stated, the principles of true liberty could be gained only through 'the fervour of religious faith, the absolutism of moral principle, the freedom of the mind.' These principles were those on which

western democracy had been founded. Only through their preservation and the resistance of the spurious values of mass culture, she
ended, could civilization endure.[72]

People living in the mass age had been deceived, according to the
critics, into thinking that mass culture offered true liberty. This misap-
prehension had potentially perilous consequences. By adhering to a
false idea of liberty, modern humanity had put democracy in peril.
Group thinking and consensus generation entailed the abandonment
of intellectual achievement and cultural and spiritual fulfilment, the
true hallmarks of freedom. The triumph of the practical and present-
minded over the contemplative and moral meant the sundering of liberty. Accepting 'ignorance with complacency,' renouncing 'the contemplation of greatness for the worship of the common-place,' and finding
time 'for everything except solitary thought,' Massey declared, modern society had devolved into a 'democratic barbarism.'[73]

Furthermore, in a turnabout tinged with irony, mass democracy fostered the authoritarianism it so stridently opposed. Uniformity of
thinking and action were more than intellectually and culturally stultifying; they also implied, for the critics, a conformity reflecting modern
totalitarianism. 'If we content ourselves with mere happiness, interest,
group integration, self-realization,' Neatby explained, 'we are not
bringing up free men and women. We are conditioning units for mass
servitude.'[74] Commenting also on the pseudo-freedom intrinsic to
mass democracy, Donald Creighton wrote that democracy had become
'a vaporous, pervasive incense, floating in a supposedly edifying fashion over nearly everything, and yet, oddly enough, arousing its
devoted worshippers to truculence abroad and illiberality at home.'[75]
It had become, in Massey's mind, 'that most abused of all words.'[76]
Once denoting individual and social liberty, mass democracy had
become repressive and monolithic, the epitome of repression.[77]

Challenging democratic and other core values, mass culture thus
implied for the commissioners much more than simply the rise of popular forms of entertainment. What is more, it was joined by 'cultural
Americanization' as a leading factor imperiling Canadian culture. A
good philanthropist, helping Canadians to develop universities and
other institutions, the United States had also become a leading world
exporter of culture, inundating Canada with radio and television programs, films, music, and other mass offerings. The influx of material of
this sort, however, concerned commissioners and like-minded critics.
The culture critics thought that it hampered the growth of an indige-

nous and autonomous Canadian civilization. More important, 'cultural Americanization' meant the subsuming of cultural values and traditions. Since American culture was quickly becoming indistinguishable from mass culture, cultural Americanization implied a homogeneous, mass civilization devoid of distinctiveness and connections to the cultural past. American culture, therefore, hindered the critical effort to maintain traditions as a means of building a strong civilization. Along with mass culture and the mass media to which it had been inextricably bound, it presented serious threats to Canada's cultural future.

Early in their *Report* the Massey commissioners expounded upon the American fact. They highlighted Canada's presence in North America as a chief factor influencing its cultural growth. 'Canada,' it was noted, had a 'small and scattered population'; its people were 'clustered along the rim of another country many times more populous and of far greater economic strength.' The majority of Canadians spoke a language shared with the Americans, leading to particularly close ties. This series of conditions was significant because it made the dominion especially susceptible to cultural invasion from south of the border. B.K. Sandwell encapsulated the culture critics' position in his special study to the commission. Canadians, 'especially those of the English tongue,' Sandwell wrote, 'must inevitably be highly receptive to every kind of communication from the United States.' Owing to Canada's geographical proximity to the United States and the size and wealth of America, it was equally inevitable that 'such communications should be very numerous.' Canada, Sandwell declared, 'was the only country of any size in the world whose people read more foreign periodicals than they do periodicals published in their own land.'[78]

Particularly irksome to the commissioners were the effects of cultural Americanization. While some American exports were positive, much American cultural produce had 'no particular application to Canadian conditions.' The commissioners singled out 'children's programs of the "crime" and "horror" type,' as being 'positively harmful.' 'News commentaries' and 'live broadcasts' emanating from the United States, they argued, were 'designed for American ears' and almost certainly had 'an American slant and emphasis.' While stressing Canadians' right to enjoy American cultural offerings – '[c]ultural exchanges are excellent in themselves' – the commissioners held deep reservations about the long-term merits of the flood of American culture into Canada. The 'vast and disproportionate amount of material coming from a single alien source,' they announced, 'may stifle rather than stimulate our own creative effort.' Passively embraced 'without any standard of comparison,' they added, making oblique reference to the stultifying qualities of mass culture, this influx might 'weaken critical faculties.' Whereas the cultural connection had, on the whole, aided Canada, the commissioners concluded, Canadians 'must not be blind ... to the very present danger of permanent dependence.'[79]

Although most Canadians were oblivious to American influences, the culture critics were keenly interested in the origins and spread of American culture. They deliberately overlooked Canadians' participation in lowbrow culture and instead indicted the Americans for the growth of the mass society. Not only did the United States generate mass culture, but it also foisted lowbrow culture on unprepared citizens in Canada and elsewhere in the western world. B.K. Sandwell, to take one example, blamed Americanization for the demise of high culture.

Opera, serious music, theatre and other examples of high culture, Sandwell claimed, had declined because they were activities that appealed to only a segment of the populace. Amid pressures to gain the largest possible audience and therefore to generate the greatest amount of advertising revenue, broadcasters favoured lowbrow, popular entertainment over high-culture alternatives. The American-inspired 'tendency to cater almost exclusively to the mass,' Sandwell asserted, was 'hardly favourable to a high cultural level in entertainment.' Canadians, he argued further, lived in a period 'in which the number of [cultural] impressions received from a distance is vastly greater ... than was the case a generation ago.' These cultural incursions had dangerous implications. Owing to American mass cultural influences, Canadians had become practically indistinguishable from Americans in their cultural tastes. Through the homogenizing effects of mass communications, Sandwell concluded, their 'mental attitude' had become so close to that of Americans that they received 'American broadcasts and cinema productions with no sense that they [were] "foreign" products.' For Sandwell, the infiltration of American culture into Canada meant the alteration of Canadians' cultural sensibilities.[80]

In a brief to the commission, the Mainland Branch of the Canadian Authors Association put the matter even more bluntly. 'For years,' the branch argued, 'Canadians have been flooded with American moving pictures, American radio programs, American magazines, American books ... We have become unsure of anything Canadian in concept ... Something should done before the Canadian viewpoint is lost entirely.'[81]

Of all the commissioners, Vincent Massey, a former ambassador to the United States, was most passionate on the issue of Americanization. Although the Canada of the post-war period had a stronger sense of national identity than it had had in the past, Massey argued, external pressures, primarily from the United States, had also become stronger. At best, benevolent American influences – mainly the generous support of universities and other cultural institutions – stymied Canadian initiative and the potential for growth. At their worst, American cultural activities saturated Canada's popular culture and transformed it into a duplicate of the American variant.[82] In a BBC broadcast dealing with the contents of the Commission *Report*, Massey summed up Canada's 'external problem.' There was 'a danger,' Canada's former high commissioner to Great Britain announced to his British listeners, 'of arresting the development of the Canadian national character.' Only through the promotion of a 'national, Canadian consciousness' could the harmful effects of the American cultural connection be allayed.[83]

Philosopher George Grant used much more powerful rhetoric to denounce the cultural aggrandizement of the United States.[84] Canada, Grant declaimed, was 'being challenged to defend itself against a barbaric Empire that puts its faith in salvation by the machine.'[85] Canadians, Massey's nephew implored, must 'not simply accept their assumptions about human life from more important nations of the western world'; they must 'realize ... how much of that tradition has already been trodden under foot ... [because of their] concentration on ... the mass society.'[86] By threatening traditions, the cultural imperialism of the United States had transformed Canadian society. Canada's 'spiritual climate' was 'largely formed by ... partaking in the ideas' of American civilization, which, 'during the years of Canada's development, was being transformed by the new mass industrialism.' Grant continued, 'With that industrialism went certain dominant ideas that effected an almost incalculable spiritual change in the west.'[87] American culture thus had altered ideas and modes of living. Ultimately, it weakened 'bonds of tradition.' American-inspired mass society, in short, had fundamentally changed the cultural direction of the dominion.

The media, cultural Americanization, and mass culture all posed serious threats to Canadian cultural development for critics. While a main purpose of the Massey Commission was to expound upon these menaces, the commissioners also took it upon themselves to define culture and to aid the process of cultural maturation. High culture was especially important. Acting as a link to traditions, it operated, in the minds of critics, as a counterweight to American culture. Its preservation therefore became vital to a society increasingly enticed by mass culture. High culture also fostered the critical abilities that would help to expose mass movements as false. Most important, it enabled an appreciation of moral and aesthetic values and the capacity for individual cultural improvement. As such, it was a vital remedy for the modern crisis of values. The Massey commissioners and other critics, in short, endowed high culture with a new moral authority that rivalled the significance of Christianity to past societies.

High culture had become for critics a panacea with which to address the ills of modern life. It helped to shape tastes and inform opinions of 'cultured' individuals. Not only that, it was the lifeblood of a nation's cultural existence. As N.A.M. MacKenzie explained, 'the refining of the emotions, the intellect, and taste' was essential to the preservation of a country's 'cultivated life.' The best way to ensure that Canada's cultural life would grow in 'the worthiest tradition' was to encourage individuals to be 'cultivated people' – 'people in whom the habit of self-cultivation has created the capacity to respect and admire.' MacKenzie argued that society, being responsible for transferring creative traditions and fostering cultural activity, must allow the cultured person to flourish, especially at a time when cultural traditions were at risk.[88]

Unlike the culture of the masses, furthermore, high culture favoured quality and edification over sheer entertainment and universal appeal. 'Canadian achievement,' the Massey commissioners asserted, depended mainly on the 'quality of the Canadian mind and spirit.' This quality was determined 'by what Canadians think, and think about; by the books they read, the pictures they see and the programmes they hear. These things, whether we call them arts and letters or use other words to describe them, we believe to be at the root of our life as a nation.'[89]

High culture was, indeed, a foundation stone for the edifice of Canadian culture. In addition, advanced education, literature, the arts, and other forms of high culture performed, according to the critics, a didactic role in modern Canadian society. Through a variety of means they inculcated ideas, habits, attitudes, and sensibilities determined over the ages to be intrinsic to culture. In Arnoldian terms, they encouraged an appreciation of sweetness – beauty, goodness, and other transcendent virtues; and light – enlightenment, education, open-mindedness, the acquisition of knowledge, and insight. Partaking of high culture facilitated individual exploration, contemplation, and intellectual growth. The cultured individual, as Neatby indicated, was especially concerned about intellectual and contemplative matters. Self-realization, she argued, came not from group integration but from 'losing oneself for a time in contemplation of something greater than and beyond oneself.'[90] Agreeing implicitly, philosopher George Grant championed the benefits of the 'rational contemplation of the Good – simply for its own sake';[91] participating in the contemplative life enabled modern individuals to understand themselves more completely and to gain insight into the traditions and future directions of their society. Massey argued that the 'cultivation of the mind [was] to be valued for itself.' The 'respect of ideas; intellectual honesty; mental alertness; clarity of thought and precision of expression; critical sense to detect the real from the spurious; awakened imagination; and the ability to discern beauty,' all were hallmarks of the cultivated imagination.[92] Malcolm Wallace perhaps best captured the resounding significance of intellectual and spiritual edification. Humanity found 'ultimate satisfaction ... in the world of beauty and of thought,' Wallace told the commission in his special study. 'Not to enter this world is to remain forever a child. It is to neglect the rich inheritances of the ages, which must be claimed before it can be possessed, the possibility of putting away childish things and sharing in the larger life of the race. It is to be content with stagnation in place of growth, to lose the seat for new experience in absorption in material pleasures.'[93] Only through intellectual self-exploration, in other words, could modern humanity regain a sense of its past, its traditions, and its enduring identity. Cultural improvement thus led, in the words of Watson Kirkconnell and A.S.P. Woodhouse, to the 'full measure of humanity.'[94]

As Kirkconnell, Woodhouse, and others suggested, cultural development also implied the expression of 'humane' values. For these and other intellectuals, individual edification implied the realization of the pre-eminent human purpose to search for truth and spiritual fulfilment. Humanity had to rise above the instincts it shared with the animal world. Instead, it must assert spiritual, intellectual, and other traits that made it unique in creation. Hilda Neatby, for instance, spoke of the need to maintain a 'rational objective truth' and the 'reverence for human personality as such' through 'a continuing and increasing respect for matters of mind.' Fervent religious faith, the belief in absolute moral principles, and free intellectual enquiry were central components of the human character.[95] They transcended time and location and, as such, formed the core of the western system of values.

Christian humanism thus was emerging as a main feature in the cultural critique of Neatby and the other anti-modernists. In an age that seemed increasingly hostile to individuality and humanity's spiritual and cerebral objectives, the culture critics clung to humanism not only as a way to counteract materialism, consumerism, and other destructive forces, but, more important, as a means of self-realization. 'The Humanities,' Malcolm Wallace proclaimed in his special study, gratified 'some of the deepest human cravings – to see and hear beautiful things, to understand the complexities of personal relations, and to speculate on the baffling origin and meaning of men's lives.' They were concerned, he went on, 'with beauty in all its forms, and with speculations regarding human relations and meaning and values in human experience.'[96] The humanities stimulated the individual's sensitivity to the human values in art, morality, and religion.[97] They were the chief purveyors of the values intrinsic to the human condition.

Hilda Neatby agreed wholeheartedly. A liberal education had as its highest goal the 'gaining of a humble conception of the greatness of human nature and human society, and of vastness and complexity of the universe.'[98] It 'convey[ed] to all,' she continued, 'the intellectual, cultural and moral training which represents the best in a long and honourable tradition of Western civilization.'[99] Like that of the critics of the modern university, moreover, Neatby's educational ideal eschewed mere fact-finding and was concerned instead with developing well-rounded individuals. The preservation of ancient values and the development of the human character were central to Neatby's educative conception.[100]

Vincent Massey also championed humanistic education. Instead of being preoccupied with know-how, the liberals arts encouraged the cultivation of the individual's 'mental powers' and 'the development of certain habits of mind.' Facts and figures, he claimed, 'must not be crammed into young minds, to be only of temporary use.' Rather, the individual should never be 'taught more than he can think about.'[101] For Massey, contemplation and consideration thus were the most important aspects of a liberal education. In characteristically blunt fashion, Harold Innis encapsulated the basic purpose of liberal arts learning. Educational institutions, he wrote, should not consider students as 'sausages to be stuffed' with facts and information. Rather, they must place less emphasis on 'content and more on the character of instruction.'[102] Modern educators, Innis concluded, must be 'fundamentally concerned,' like the ancient Greeks, 'with the training of character.'[103]

Inextricably tied to human individuality and the expression of human nature more generally, high culture, and specifically the 'cultured individual,' contributed to the good society. High culture not only led to the development of good and moral individuals, but also produced, according to the critics, good citizens who would make positive contributions to the social order. Familiarity with high culture was necessary to produce an aware and truly democratic citizenry. As Neatby noted, civilization depended in large measure on the 'creative minority,' who made 'proper use of its leisure time.'[104] The responsibility for developing the good society, in other words, rested with the scholar, the artist, and other cultured individuals. In an age of 'democratic barbarism' and 'scientific materialism,' only the truly civilized, the culture critics argued, had the wherewithal to understand their ever-changing environment. Blessed with a liberal education and a civilized outlook, they were best able to comprehend the effects of an increasingly uncivilized age. As Neatby remarked, the 'inner meaning' of education was to 'create desirable social attitudes and intellectual appreciations' so as counteract the 'moral confusion and intellectual barbarism' of present times.[105] The cultured individual, she indicated, was the social figure who had 'vision and insight' and who was, by definition, 'a seer.' 'He convey[ed] the truth by which, literally, men and nations live. He shows what life is in all its aspects.' Lacking artists, philosophers, and scholars, western society risked 'premature decadence and a relapse into barbarism.'[106]

For Massey, as well, the liberally educated individual was well placed to lead. His education allowed him to comprehend and criticize the world in which he lived. Through it, Massey averred, he was enabled to 'acquire a true sense of values, to understand something about the relation of man to society, to distinguish between the real things in life and the fakes, to put first things first, and to sharpen [his] mental curiosity.' He was able to comprehend, therefore, the pernicious effects of mass society and form 'a bulwark against standardization.'[107] Cultured individuals, Massey asserted, employing military imagery, were the 'spiritual weapons' to be used as a defence against 'pagan, materialistic, [and] tyrannical' assault on western culture.[108]

Discussing the social contributions of intellectuals, the most important of society's cultured persons, the Massey commissioners wrote: 'The philosopher with his contemplative and critical tradition may serve as a useful brake on the rightly impetuous man of action, a brake often needed in the world of today. Moreover, the man of letters can help to produce the atmosphere in which he can do his best work ...' 'The study of the arts and letters,' they concluded, as if to stress Massey's own views, helped 'to form "the citizens with trained minds, liberal and informed opinions, good taste, and critical judgment without whom a national civilization is impossible."'[109] While the masses had become increasingly confounded by the exigencies of mass society, creative individuals not only had comprehended their modern milieu, but also had worked to create an environment in which cultural activity could flourish. As such, they had become, for the culture critics, the leaders of the modern world, indispensable agents in overcoming the pernicious effects of the mass age.

Taken out of context, the culture critics' blandishments on the cultivated mind and cultured individuals seem to be stark anachronisms. In an age dominated by materialist and pragmatic concerns and in which there was little use for intellectual values, they appear to be romantic yearnings for bygone eras and better times. There was, however, considerable affinity after 1945 for the 'socially relevant' intellectual. As the critics of modern academics did, the culture analysts took pains to underline the social relevance of the humanist, the enlightened social prophet. The question now is why they were so intent on advancing the cause of the 'civilized' intellectual. Indeed, what was it about their social-historical environment that impelled them to undertake such a measured, articulate, and often highly passionate defence of humanists and other high culturalists? And, most significant, what made them, as humanists themselves, feel so marginal or even so irrelevant?

The answers to these questions are manifold. Doubtless, critics were sincere in their ultimate objective to lead moderns to the good society. Their critique was nonetheless a response to prevailing social and historical circumstances. From a personal perspective, the culture critics themselves were the seers and artists that they described in their writings. Hence, in extolling the merits of academics and high culture, they were calling attention to themselves and, more important, their place within society's hierarchy. The increasingly vocal defence of high culture and humane values must be seen in the light of a social climate in which the humanist was sorely underpaid and lacked the status of scientists and technologists. A related issue was the effort to raise public awareness of the social utility of humane learning, which reflected a period of crisis for the humanities. As we saw in chapter 4, during the war and post-war periods the humanities in Canada experienced great distress. They were periods, most of all, during which government and university officials and society at large questioned the social merit of the liberal arts and, by implication, the creative intellectual. In extolling the virtues of high culture and defending humane values, the critics were reacting against this callous new world. Explaining the merits of high culture, they attempted to show that, like practical learning, high-culture values, too, had an irreplaceable social worth. Like technological know-how, humane learning was truly, in Massey's phrase, 'useful knowledge.'[110]

The culture critics thus reacted against a social order that they perceived to be anti-intellectual and anti-cultural. Along with the demise of the humanities and university 'traditions,' the advent of a democratic, 'mass' society reflected modern trends. Certainly, the emergence of the mass society was an evolution, a protracted process that took place over decades. The reaction against mass movements likewise went back before the war and beyond. North American social critics, especially Americans, responded to the 'Babbitry' of mass society from the late nineteenth century on. For Canadian high culturalists, however, the post–Second World War period was exceedingly important because of the rise of the mass society. Critics, especially the Massey commissioners, felt that the post-war age experienced the unprecedented growth of the materialism, consumerism, and anti-intellectualism that marked mass culture. Most irksome, a pervasive American cultural imperialism hung like a massive black cloud over an unsuspecting population. More than in any other period in the past, American culture reached into Canada to influence the lives of increasing numbers of Canadians. Facilitated by the electronic media and an enfeebled populace, the era after 1945 thus promised to be the culmination of a trend generations in the making. Notwithstanding Canada's colonialism and its penchant for borrowing and absorbing other forms, cultural Americanization was, for the critics, as uncompromising as it was inevitable. Only the supreme efforts of a few high culturalists, in their minds, could help to redress this monstrous development.

The reaction against mass society was grounded largely in the perceptions of critics. There are, however, a few tangible historical developments to substantiate the claim of a society that had become increasingly inimical to high culture. There was, as we have indicated, the advent of the utilitarian university and democratic education. Exacerbated by the 'veterans' boom' and the threat of exploding secondary and post-secondary enrolments, critics feared that the academy, the last bastion of cultural refinement and philosophic analysis, would succumb to the dictates of the mass world. Just as important, modern Canada was flooded with materialism and crass consumerism. Canada had achieved unprecedented economic development in the years after the war, and prosperity was spread over the vast majority of the population. Always a country that prioritized material development, Canada now seemed to the critics to be captivated by material progress and the growth ethic. As an economic world power, Canada had come of age.

Aside from historical conditions, the critique of culture must be grounded intellectually. The culture critics owe much to the thought of Matthew Arnold. In *Culture and Anarchy*, a gospel for many culture critics,[111] Arnold explained that the chief defects of mid-Victorian society could be remedied by redressing the balance between the material and commercial and cultural aspects of life. There were two ways to restore the equilibrium. First, one could try 'to give the masses ... an intellectual food prepared and adapted in the way they [thought] proper for the actual condition of the masses.' While laudable, this attempt to indoctrinate the populace in the ways of culture was nonetheless intrinsically flawed. Culture, Arnold claimed, did not attempt to 'teach down to the level of inferior classes'; nor did it 'try to win them for this or that sect of its own, with ready-made judgments and watchwords.' Rather, it sought to make all citizens, regardless of social distinction, 'live in an atmosphere of sweetness and light, and use ideas ... freely, to be nourished and not bound by them.' Society's cultivated persons, not representatives of specific classes or social-political interests, Arnold added, had the greatest role to play in promoting this 'social idea.' Society's cultured individuals were not merely those who possessed certain knowledge or those aware of the importance of culture pursuits. Instead, they were defined in part by their affinity for spreading sweetness and light. 'The great men of culture,' Arnold explained, were 'those who have a passion for diffusing, for making prevail, for carrying from one end of society to the other, the best knowledge of their time ... to humanize it, to make it efficient outside the clique of the cultivated and learned, yet still remaining the *best* knowledge and thought of the time, and a true source, therefore, of sweetness and light' (italics in original). The creative individual was, for Arnold, as he was for his intellectual descendants less than a century later, essential to social advancement. In establishing a milieu suitable for cultural flourishing, he facilitated humanity's march towards social perfection.

In fostering cultural activity, itself the chief bulwark against anarchy and tantamount to 'the pursuit of perfection,' the cultured individual performed his most vital social role: the pursuit of the good society. '[H]e who works for sweetness and light,' Arnold declared in conclusion, 'works to make reason and the will of God prevail.'[112]

For the culture critics, Arnoldian high culture was central to the achievement of the good society. As important as liberal humanist values were, however, they realized the unpopularity of high culture among the Canadian population at large.[113] Realists, they recognized the seductive qualities of science and materialism and the quasi-hypnotic effects of mass culture on the Canadian populace. They understood, consequently, the difficulty of creating a society in which the cultured individual figured prominently, one that was as preoccupied as they were with the attainment of 'sweetness and light.'

The critics suggested two remedies for the cultural quandary that faced them. First, they proposed the heretofore uncommon remedy of state intervention in cultural affairs. Knowing the ravages of a commercial, foreign-based mass culture, the commissioners made as their chief recommendation public support of culture. Indeed, the majority of part II of the Massey *Report* dealt with the commissioners' 'view on how the national government may appropriately advance [Canada's] cultural and intellectual life.' The dominion government, the commissioners stressed, must follow the example of European countries and even of Britain, which had recently allowed cultured individuals the financial freedom to pursue their work. Canada had to endure strains imposed upon it by demographic and geographical factors. Government provided aid in commercial, transportation, and other fields of endeavour to overcome these limitations. Similar assistance ought to be given to 'companies of players,' 'orchestras,' and 'concert artists,' 'whose regular and frequent appearances in the great and small communities of Canada [were] of importance to our well-being as a civilized community.' The commissioners urged, furthermore, federal aid for radio and television broadcasting. Essentially a public service and therefore in need of considerable increases in funding, the CBC ought also to receive public funds. That broadcasting would function as a powerful tool in the promotion of Canadian culture was adequate justification for the use of public revenues. Finally, along with museums, libraries, archives, and other national cultural organizations, the commissioners advocated public funding for the most important of cultural institutions: Canadian universities and a proposed council for the promotion of the arts, letters, humanities, and social sciences. Reflecting the common cry of the university 'funding crisis' of the later 1940s, they proposed that the federal government 'make annual contributions to support the work of the universities' on the basis of provincial populations.[114]

Equally important to the funding of universities was the creation of the so-called Canada Council. The commissioners emphasized that the council would need considerable federal support to finance its operation. Money grants were required to diffuse the arts, letters, and sciences at home and to promote Canada abroad. In their own words, the commissioners 'were under no illusion that the results that ... may be achieved from the creation of the Canada Council can be obtained cheaply.' The critics understood that the expansion of culture was an expensive proposition. It was nevertheless an activity crucial to the well-being of the Canadian nation. As such, its merits far exceeded the monetary values that the commissioners and others placed upon it. 'If we in Canada are to have a more plentiful and better cultural fare,' the Massey commissioners reasoned, 'we must pay for it. Good will alone can do little for a starving plant; if the cultural life of Canada is anemic, it must be nourished, and this will cost money.' The investment was 'modest,' they ended, 'in relation to the returns which ... [Canadians] could reasonably expect.'[115]

More subtle than government interventionism, the Massey commissioners' approach was to enlist the support of cultural nationalism to achieve their ends. The commissioners dovetailed the growing sense of 'Canadianism' of the post-1945 period with their own ideas on natural identity. Specifically, they integrated concerns for Canadian development with their own preoccupations about the dominion's cultural state. In consequence, they grafted onto Canadian nationalism issues of personal edification and cultural development. In the words of the Massey Commission's biographer, 'Liberal humanism and nationalism combined to form a high-minded and defensive strain of Canadian cultural nationalism.'[116]

The first notion basic to cultural nationalism was a sense of cultural uniqueness. In a climate wherein pernicious ideas and social influences easily crossed frontiers, especially undefended ones, culture critics found it necessary to articulate and thus bolster Canadian values and cultural characteristics. Canada's distinctiveness vis-à-vis the United States was among the most important of these attributes.

Vincent Massey, the most vociferous proponent of Canadianism, was the commission member who most eloquently expressed Canada's cultural distinctiveness. The effort to keep Canadianism intact, he wrote, 'could only be successful ... if [we Canadians were] aware of the differences which distinguish[ed] us from the United States and [gave] us our significance here in North America.' While there were similari-ties between the two cultures, he continued, there were 'certain principles' that contributed to Canada's uniqueness. Canadian society, for instance, did not share the intolerance of an American society that countenanced 'racial discrimination and third degree police methods.'[117] What was more fundamental, Canada also had patterns of ideas and culture of its own.[118] Owing much to the British connection, Canada was culturally distinct from the United States and other foreign states. Politically, Canada's tolerance, liberal-mindedness, and respect for the rule of law emanated from the political values of the Empire.[119] In 'cherish[ing] law and liberty,' Massey declared, Canada held the same basic political values as the United States. Its 'manner of cherishing,' its 'constitutional and symbolic expressions,' Massey hastened to note, were different. Rather than through republicanism, Canadians 'express[ed] the common good, the public welfare in parliamentary institutions' that had always derived their authority from the Crown. The interactions between the Crown and Parliament showed how 'liberty can be enjoyed without disorder, and that authority can be exercised without tyranny.'[120]

In addition to sharing British political values, Canada benefited intellectually and culturally from its historic nexus with Britain. For Massey, Britain was the conduit through which humane values were passed to Canadians. Cultured individuals in Canada had profited greatly from British academic and spiritual traditions. Unlike their American counterparts, Massey wrote, quoting Dr Dodds, the president of Princeton University, they appreciated 'the "power of ideas and spiritual values in history, literature, and philosophy."'[121] They have received 'from across the water the belief that education is primarily a spiritual matter; that it must be concerned with the individual; that the humanities must hold their old pride of place in its pattern; that the university is no place for the pedant, for it has always been the glory of learning in the British Isles that its virtues have been closely woven into the stuff of daily life.' He concluded, 'All this,' was 'part of a great inheritance.'[122]

Massey and his fellow commissioners also endeavoured to explain how, through cultivating the mind and spirit, Canada might develop as a united culture. They acknowledged Canada's cultural duality as a factor that ranked with mass culture as an obstacle to accomplishing this objective. There were two Canadian cultures, B.K. Sandwell declared in his special study for the commission. They were 'almost wholly separate one from the other.' '[O]nly after making very large allowances for this limitation,' he continued, echoing the 'two solitudes' thesis that was gaining currency after 1945,[123] was it 'possible to speak of a Canadian culture at all.'[124] Massey agreed that there were 'natural differences between Canadians of French and Anglo-Saxon origin.' He stressed, however, that Canada's dual culture was a strength, not a liability. The French and English languages had given 'the world its present civilization.' A Canadian with both languages, Massey continued, 'not only contribute[d] to the unity of his country, but he add[ed] to his equipment as a civilized person.'[125]

Despite differences, Canada's two cultural groups had much in common. Most significant, they shared a common system of values that was especially important to the modern age. English Canadians, Massey wrote, had 'come to respect more and more the standards and values' which they found among Quebeckers. 'In a world which seems given more and more to materialism,' he added, 'they hold to religion as the guiding force of life. As education appear[ed] to become increasingly mechanistic they still give culture and the humanities an honoured place in their schools and colleges ... [S]urely there is much that each of us can learn from the other.'[126]

Neatby concurred with her friend and mentor on the transcendence of cultural values across linguistic, religious, and cultural boundaries. She primarily focused, however, on religious virtues. In a letter dated 13 August 1953 she asked fellow commissioner, Reverend Georges-Henri Lévesque, to explicate the spiritual affinities of the two cultures. In a breathless barrage of questions, she queried how an accord between French- and English-speaking Canadians on spiritual values would be an invaluable tool for fighting the abuses of modernity:[127]

Would it be right and suitable to suggest that there is in Canada a most hopeful and heartening tendency for serious members of the Protestant and Roman Catholic communions to come together in the realization that the whole fate of society depends on the application of Christian principles and Christian dogma to current problems and that we may hope to suggest that a Protestant democracy which is degenerating into license can learn much from a Roman Catholic society which has never lost sight of the divine principle of authority and that, on the other hand, the Roman Catholic society may, in association with Protestants, gain a fresh recognition of one of your favorite maxims, that liberty as well as authority comes from God?

For Neatby and Massey, therefore, Canada's two cultures had many similarities and, most important, reinforced each other and the goals of liberal humanism. As such, they contributed to the emergence of a single civilization within the Canadian state. There truly could be 'unity in diversity,' as pointed out in one brief from Quebec.[128] Summarizing the idea of a common culture out of which an interest in a shared cultural life could develop, the commissioners declared: 'We thought it deeply significant to hear repeatedly from representatives of the two Canadian cultures expressions of hope and of confidence that in our common cultivation of the things of the mind, Canadians – French- and English-speaking – can find true "Canadianism." Through this shared confidence we can nurture what we have in common and resist those influences which could impair, and even destroy, our integrity. In our search we have thus been made aware of what can serve our country in a double sense: what can make it great, and what can make it one.'[129]

The optimism that underpinned the notion of cultural unity arose in the unique circumstances of the post-war age. During the period after 1945 Canadians had become more aware of their accomplishments as a nation. Canada had emerged victorious from a war in which it made a fundamental contribution to the Allied cause. The country was economically prosperous and had gained increased recognition among international powers for the critical role it had played in achieving peace. For the culture critics, in particular, Canada was in a state of becoming – almost a blank slate upon which recommendations for the achievement of cultural improvement could be inscribed. In its broadest sense, the Massey Commission wished not only to defend civilization, but to build up Canadian culture almost ex nihilo. It engaged ultimately in the intrinsically positive task of constructing a national good society. Despite fears of nuclear annihilation, burgeoning totalitarianism, and cultural imperialism, then, there was considerable optimism about the future of Canadian 'civilization.' For most Canadians, the critics of culture included, the dominion was coming of age.

The idea that, as a nation, Canada had reached a critical mass also was reflected in a larger intellectual context. Put simply, the post-war period was one in which Canadian intellectuals at large, especially historians, became preoccupied with defining and expounding upon the Canadian identity. For Harold Innis, the development of the country as a national cultural entity hinged on Canada's relationship with Great Britain and the United States. In 'Great Britain, Canada, and the United States' (1948), Innis argued that Canada had shunned its British affiliations and fallen into the American military, economic, and cultural spheres of influence. Parodying A.R.M. Lower's recent work, Innis wrote that Canada had 'moved from colony to nation to colony' during the prime ministership of W.L. Mackenzie King.[130] Nevertheless, Innis implored Canadians to overcome American imperialism in seeking out a 'third bloc,' separate from the American empire and Soviet Communism. Canada had the potential of acting as a marginal entity because it existed on the periphery of the United States. It could therefore produce, in Innisian terminology, a monopoly of knowledge to counter that of the two main power blocs. Canada, Innis added, further benefited from its ties to Europe and Great Britain, which were, like Canada, peripheral to the American empire yet under the increasing threat of American domination. Historical cultural-political connections could allay the effects of burgeoning cultural realities. 'The future of the West depends on the cultural tenacity of Europe,' Innis concluded, in characteristically dramatic terms. 'Canada must call in the Old World to redress the balance of the New, and hope that Great Britain will escape American imperialism as successfully as she herself has escaped British imperialism.'[131]

In censuring American imperialism, Innis advanced ideas on the dangers of cultural dependence that resembled those put forth by the Massey commissioners. In 'A Footnote to the Massey Report,' Innis showed how Canadians were in a death struggle to preserve their culture amid the 'pernicious influence of American advertising' and the 'omnipotence of American commercialism.' Cultural continentalism, he suggested, threatened Canada both with the destruction of British cultural ties and with the demise of cultural independence. Canadians were indeed 'fighting for [their] lives.' As the Massey commissioners did, Innis beseeched Canadians to respond to American imperial incursions. Specifically, he advocated an 'energetic programme' designed to offset 'dangers to [Canada's] national existence.' He applauded national cultural efforts like the establishment of the National Film Board 'to weaken the pressure of American films' and the efforts of universities and other educational and cultural organizations to advance Canadian culture.[132] He praised the 'appointment and report' of the Royal Commission on National Development in the Arts, Letters and Sciences. The Massey Commission was vital to the cultural life of Canada because it gave voice to cultural concerns and it strengthened the position of cultural institutions.[133] Above all, Innis lauded government broadcasting policies that were intended to mitigate the influences of American radio and television programming. One of the very few tools available to Canadians, he claimed, was a nationalized system of communication. 'By attempting constructive efforts to explore the cultural possibilities of various media of communication, and to develop them along the lines free from commercialism, Canadians might be able to make a contribution to the cultural life of the United States' and, perhaps, to that of the world at large.[134] To put the matter in Innis's theoretical parlance, to escape the pervasive influence of advertising, popular culture, and the electronic media not only implied the avoidance of the modern, 'American' monopoly of knowledge, but also implied an opportunity for cultural development. Only by deflecting American cultural imperialism could the Canadian identity survive and flourish. Thus, for Innis, as for the Massey commissioners, the struggle for cultural autonomy in North America was the sine qua non of Canadianism; it had become indispensable to the development of a distinct Canadian identity.

Innis's close friend and fellow historian Donald Creighton was also preoccupied with Canada's relations with the United States. By the late 1940s and early 1950s Creighton, like Innis, was worried that Canada was awash in an enlarging sea of American imperialism. In an age of close military and diplomatic ties with the United States, Canadian foreign policy was the focal point of his critique. Since the Ogdensburg Agreement of 1940 and the establishment of the Permanent Joint Board on Defense, Canada had increasingly succumbed to continentalist pressures and had evolved American-oriented defensive and foreign policies.[135] Its deference to American foreign policy decisions increased under the North Atlantic Treaty Organization (NATO) and during the Korean War. Canada, in consequence, was in danger of becoming a mere colony of the Americans, 'a kind of northern "banana republic."'[136] 'In the north,' Creighton wrote, to emphasize American defensive supremacy in Canada, 'Americans build and man our radar installations ... in the east ... they hold and occupy military bases. The foreigner sits firmly astride the eastern approaches to our country; and the base, a primitive form of military imperialism, grimly questions Canada's claim to control her own destiny.'[137]

As Innis did, Creighton implored Canadians to find an alternative to this acquiescent relationship. 'Good relations with the United States must continue to be an important objective of our foreign policy,' he stated in 1953, 'but good Canadian-American relations will not necessarily enable Canada to make its own contribution to the solution of the world's crisis, and may actually prevent it from doing so.' Canada, he added, had 'outgrown North American solidarity as an end in itself.'[138] Again, as Innis did, he urged Canadians not only to evade the perils of the American connection, but also to steer a course between Communism and American imperialism, avoiding the shoals of either revolutionary system. Autonomy in foreign policy meant for Creighton that Canada should accept and seek accommodation with Communist regimes, while at the same time working with NATO, the Commonwealth, and the United Nations.[139] Canada, in brief, had to counterbalance its continentalist orientation with an external policy that both recognized the destructive character of the power blocs and worked towards the unification of cultures and ideologies.

To overcome a short-sighted external policy Creighton urged Canadians to look to the past for guidance. Only through a better understanding of Canadian history and a renewal of the principles that had guided former leaders could continentalism be identified and defeated. Specifically, Creighton saw the nation-building and foreign policies of Sir John A. Macdonald as having a resounding relevance, especially for Canadians of the 1950s.[140]

For Creighton, Macdonald had realized the threats of continentalism to Canadian sovereignty, which were manifested once again in the post-war period. His basic objective was to establish a transcontinental nation that would have an autonomous existence in North America. 'His fundamental aim,' Creighton continued, 'was to protect Canada from the dangers of continentalism; and it is the dangers of continentalism, economic, political, military, which now seem to be pressing in upon us steadily and from every side.'[141] Creighton hoped for the resurrection of the spirit, if not the substance, of Macdonald's approach to Canadian-American relations. He hoped that Canadians would understand that Canadian autonomy implied not merely a separation from Great Britain, but, most important, independence in North America. Above all, Macdonald's approach would demonstrate the 'essential character' of Canada, a country that had gained independence from the British peacefully and that continued to derive strength from its traditional affiliations with Britain and the Empire-Commonwealth.

Ultimately, Macdonald's work had shown that 'for a whole generation Canada had been fighting the wrong kind of imperialism.'[142] As Innis had argued previously, Creighton felt that Canada's struggle for distinctiveness was, in reality, a struggle for survival on the North American continent.

Reflecting the travails of the Cold War and concerns about continentalism and American imperialism, Creighton's musings on post-war Canada also revealed a deeper desire to contribute to a still-evolving sense of nationality. Even as late as the mid-1950s Canada, for Creighton as for others, was in a state of becoming. Canadians stood in the mid-twentieth century where they had been a half-century earlier. Materially, the post-war boom in minerals, petroleum, and other natural resources paralleled the prosperity of the Laurier wheat boom. Creighton queried how these resources should best be used. 'Upon what national plan should [Canada] try to develop this second huge bounty of good fortune?,' he asked.[143] More fundamentally, Creighton realized that Canada was at a crossroads not only because of burgeoning continentalism but also because it was struggling to find its own identity. Unsure of itself, its character, and the principles that should underpin its future development, Canada to Creighton, was a nation in danger of drift. Recently emergent into nationhood, yet threatened by continentalist colonialism, it was indeed a 'young country' 'clamouring for interpretation.'[144]

Recognizing the nation's plight, Creighton set about explaining the Canadian psyche. Characteristically, he turned to history for answers. Canada, Creighton taught, had developed in contradistinction to its geographical proximity to the United States. Historically, the dominion had been different from the United States. It lacked a revolutionary tradition and had tried to remain entirely separate from America culturally as well as politically. 'British North America had sought to achieve a distinct and separate political existence in the Western hemisphere,' Creighton declared in 1957; 'she had tried to preserve her identity against the levelling, standardizing impact of American continentalism. Moreover, the British connection was key to Canada's struggles. Only through 'the maintenance of her vital connection with Europe,' Creighton averred, could Canada succeed in this effort. Initially, after 1867 Canada relied on Britain for military and diplomatic support. By the late nineteenth century, it depended on intangible cultural and spiritual connections to the Empire. The Anglo-Canadian alliance served Canadians just as well after Confederation as it had before 1867.

It enabled Canada to develop on an autonomous course; for it fore-stalled the omnipresent influence of American continentalism. It had helped the country to achieve its singular great goal: the maintenance of a separate political and cultural existence in North America. 'For Canada,' Creighton concluded, 'the imperial connection was not a parent-child relationship which ended in an appalling row, but an adult partnership which was prolonged more at the instance of the junior than of the senior partner.'[145]

Creighton wanted to show Canadians the enduring pertinence of the Canadian identity which was far from being a historical process remote in time and contemporary relevance. For him, the post-war age was not only a period of growing American influence, but also an era in which policy-makers, intellectuals, and many Canadians at large had lost an understanding of the true nature of Canada. This trend was encapsulated in the 'authorized version' or 'Liberal Interpretation' of Canadian history, terms of derision Creighton used to refer to what he saw as Liberal apologists and Grit historians and their writings. According to the authorized version, Canadian history was not a struggle for autonomy on the continent, but instead an effort to gain independence from Great Britain. For historian Arthur Lower and others, Canada, as a nation, was defined in terms of the abandonment of British ties. As Creighton lamented, there was no recognition of the critical role that the Empire played in curbing American influence; what was most pernicious, there was no appreciation of the dangers of creeping continentalism. The necessary corollary of severing ties with Britain, moreover, was a growing affinity with the United States. The Liberal historians had simply replaced one brand of imperialism with another. Indeed, for Creighton, the authorized version had got it all wrong: it completely misconstrued the nature of the Canadian nationality; it denied Canada's fundamental links to the British Crown and misunderstood Canada's evolution towards autonomy. As such, Creighton suggested, the Liberal view misrepresented Canada's relationships among the English-speaking peoples of the North Atlantic, denied Canada's traditions and heritage, and, ultimately, wilfully misled an entire generation of Canadians.[146]

Despite the discouraging vicissitudes of Canadian-American relations, Creighton and others remained sanguine about opportunities to interpret and define the Canadian identity. Creighton believed that a good many Canadians had begun to realize what he and Innis had recognized: the deleterious effects of American economic and military preponderance in North America. Amid the climate of political change of 1957–8,[147] a few had even begun to realize that Canadian 'misconception[s] had [their] origin[s] in a totally mistaken historical theory, the Liberal Interpretation, which misrepresented Canada's essential character, ignored her basic necessities, and altered the direction of her principal trend.'[148] Indeed, Creighton took solace in the fact that the influence of the pernicious doctrine of Canadian history was coming to an end. Although Canada's 'tribulations' were not over, the 'delusions which created them [were] gone, and ... the authors of the delusions [were] no longer unquestioned oracles.' 'A definite epoch in the history of Canadian history [had] come to an end,' he continued. 'A new generation of professional historians [had] arisen,' one that would have 'more respect for the manifold facts of the Canadian experience.'[149] Freed from the fetters of Liberal myth-making, the work of defining the Canadian character and making the nation could proceed.

William Lewis Morton was one of the new generation of historians to whom Creighton referred. By the late 1950s, Morton's conception of the Canadian character reflected many of Creighton's biases. Morton agreed with Creighton that the Liberals, especially Mackenzie King and O.D. Skelton, had destroyed Canada's relationship with the Empire-Commonwealth. Canada's position in the North Atlantic triangle had been 'so irradiated by the American presence,' Morton wrote, employing graphic imagery, 'that it sickens and threatens to dissolve into a cancerous slime.'[150] In response to this deplorable state of affairs, Morton urged the resurrection of the imperial connection. As Creighton and Innis had done some time before, Morton considered the association with Great Britain vital to Canada's effort not only to define a national identity, but also to defend Canadian autonomy. He emphasized that ties to Britain allowed Canada to be distinct from America and, therefore, to maintain a separate national existence in North America. Politically, Canada derived its distinctiveness from its monarchist inheritance. To Morton, the monarchy provided the checks and balances necessary to avoid the inadequacies of Jacksonian democracy and to afford a more advanced conception of political freedom. Whereas republicanism tended to level citizens, to individualize and free them, Morton argued, it bound them nonetheless through 'social conformity' and 'an inherent social intolerance.' In ensuring that legal sovereignty rested on foundations independent of the results of the last election,' the monarchy ensured that 'however political sovereignty might be diffused through the electorate,' 'the last essential of government, the maintenance of peace and order, would be independent of popular impulse.'[151] Morton believed that there were higher principles to which the monarchical system aspired – namely, peace, order, and good government – which were not necessarily guaranteed by the republican system. From these political precepts Canada ultimately derived its political liberty.[152] For Morton, as for Creighton, Canada's freedom emerged because of, not in spite of, colonial ties.

Owing to Canada's political traditions – 'freedom through evolution in allegiance,' not 'revolutionary compact' – the nation was in a state of evolution. Canada, Morton explained, sprang forth from harsh geographical and climatical conditions, in accordance to French traditions, 'nourished by British freedom,' and 'fortified by American experience.' Yet unlike the republic, its destiny was still to be worked out. The Canadian experience was different from the American in that it was a 'Burkean partnership of the generations.' Instead of a revolutionary compact on which a sense of liberty could be built, Canadian society depended on 'the historical and objective reality of law personified by the monarchy and modified as need arises by the Crown in Parliament.' Based on these few important political principles, Morton observed, Canada was ever developing, ever in search of fulfilling its destiny. This basic fact was true even in the post-war age, an era during which globalization threatened Canada's future. Indeed, in response to continentalism, Morton implored Canadians to rediscover their political traditions and to extend them to current relations with the United States. Canadians, he argued, 'must bring to the working out of the American alliance the same persistence in freedom and the same stubborn ingenuity' that had generated the nation's free institutions and characterized the free association of Canadian culture. Ultimately, he advised Canadians to build on the sense of identity and purpose established through the long association with Great Britain. Although the national destiny was as yet undetermined, Canadians could help to ensure the future of their nation by remaining true to their traditions and inheritances. Like Creighton, Morton looked to the past not only as a source of national identity,[153] but also as a beacon to guide Canada past the numerous perils of the second half of the twentieth century.

Thus, for Creighton, Morton, and others of the new breed of historians,[154] conserving traditions and learning the lessons of history were critical both to defining Canada's cultural identity and to contributing to the future of the nation. Contextually, the work of these intellectuals developed in relation to a changed political milieu; the reaction against

American imperialism (in all forms) was certainly strengthened by the development of post-war political conservatism. Morton and the others also extended the work of the Massey commissioners. Their historical writings and nationalist myth-making not only responded to the menace of Americanization, but also constituted, as the Massey *Report* did, a corpus of writings that provided insight into Canada's nature as a nation and civilization. Equally important, their writings were concerned with building 'spiritual' (cultural) structures that seemed to be losing ground to materialism. Canada, by the late 1950s, was rapidly modernizing. The country's gross national product had grown from almost $25 billion in 1954 to over $31 billion just three years later.[155] With the tremendous surge in new wealth arose once more the issue of the country's cultural progress. Would Canadians parlay their increased prosperity and leisure time into cultural activities and 'cultural nation-building' as the culture critics had hoped, or would they ignore cultural issues and focus instead on material advancement? The attitudes of the Massey commissioners, the historians, and other culture critics had been abundantly clear on this point. Of course, they believed that the development of cultural forms – structural, intellectual, or otherwise – was vital to the progress of the nation. This objective underpinned the Massey Commission and was the implicit purpose of the writings of Morton, Creighton, and other conservative cultural nationalists. The federal government's position, by contrast, was uncertain. Despite the positive initial reaction to the Massey *Report*, the Liberal government delayed the implementation of almost all of the commission's recommendations. Pipelines, highways, seaways, and economic nation-building took precedence over cultural developments. The government's attitude towards culture seemed ambivalent at best.

Only by late 1956 did government policy on culture seem to leap forward. In an address to the National Conference on Higher Education entitled 'Cultural Progress in Canada,' Prime Minister Louis St Laurent announced his decision to recommend to Parliament the creation of the Canada Council. The council would help to administer grants and scholarships in the fields of the arts, humanities, and social sciences; foster Canada's cultural relations abroad; and establish a national commission in conjunction with UNESCO. Just as significant, however, St Laurent discussed his government's new-found commitment to cultural advancement in reference to the broader scheme of nation-building. 'In the cultural field,' he noted, Canadian development was 'much slower than in the economic field.' Like other modern nations, Canada had become preoccupied with material and technological growth. It had subordinated spiritual development to economic advancement. Echoing the deeply held sentiments of the culture critics, St Laurent advised Canadians to redress the balance. The time had arrived, he declared, for national development 'to parallel what has taken place in the economic field.'[156] In achieving this important goal, Canadians must foster the development of cultural institutions both at home and abroad. Canada, St Laurent proclaimed, ought to become a source of culture, of spirit, and a haven for a world that was in need of cultural regeneration. 'With that purpose in mind,' he concluded, '[Canadians] must further develop and enrich our national soul; [they] must achieve ... that broader outlook and that deeper insight into the things of mind which will enable them better to deal with problems of the present.'[157] Not only was spiritual growth as important to national development as material advancement, but cultural edification allowed the insight to identify and, ultimately, to come to terms with the problems of modern society. Culture, in the prime minister's view, was the very lifeblood of the modern Canadian nation.

Despite the prime minister's assurances to the contrary, doubts remained as to whether culture had really become a national priority.[158] St Laurent and the Liberals became enthused about the Canada Council only on the eve of a general election and only when a windfall of several million dollars became available to the federal government.[159] Without political pressures and financial resources, it is doubtful whether St Laurent would have made his pro-culture speech at all.

Whatever the motives of the Liberal government, the creation of the Canada Council nonetheless was highly significant both to the culture critics and in objective terms. Culturally, the council was of great symbolic as well as practical importance. Financially, it had been a 'revolutionary departure' in Canadian intellectual life; through the council, intellectuals and artists received the state support for which they had longed for decades.[160] The establishment of the council was important to critics, moreover, because it brought the issues raised by the Massey Commission into sharp focus. No longer was culture the concern of a few out-of-touch professors or longhaired artists. Through the Canada Council, it was to become a matter of national concern. Indeed, through the federal government, the culture critics believed that they had achieved a major triumph; they could now use the state to further the ends of culture and promote the development of Canada's spiritual life.[161] After a long wait, it seemed as though Canada's cultural progress might indeed keep pace with its material development.

The Canada Council therefore had achieved what the culture critics had wanted. It presided over a good percentage of viable projects, and there can be no doubt that it succeeded in its mandate – to 'foster and promote the study and enjoyment of, and the production of works in[,] the arts, humanities and social sciences.' Through the remainder of the decade and throughout the 1960s the council played a prominent role in the country's growth in the arts, academic developments, and the persistence of cultural institutions like the National Ballet.[162]

Despite these triumphs, however, the concerns of the culture critics were not allayed. By the late 1950s the second stage of the Cold War was under way. The period, initiated by the flight of Sputnik in 1957, emphasized global competition in which 'all the prizes went to the most prosperous country and the most sophisticated weapons system.'[163] Winning the arms race meant gaining the crucial advantage in the Cold War. Accomplishing this feat meant that North Americans had to place even greater emphasis on the advancement of science and technology. Education, as indicated in the last chapter, was essential to this objective. Indeed, the production of engineers, scientists, and technically educated workers – not the establishment of theatre companies or the endowment of scholars – was critical to the well-being of the nation. The Canada Council was certainly a significant accomplishment. In the rarefied atmosphere of the late 1950s and early 1960s, however, it could not compete with the exigencies of modern warfare and the rhetoric of Cold War politicians. Guns and technology, not culture, had captivated the public's imagination.

Sensitive to Cold War propaganda, culture critics denounced what they considered one of its most pernicious products: the acceleration of the technological imperative. George Parkin Grant, as we noted in chapter 2, was a vociferous critic of the 'technological society.' He acknowledged the impact of the nuclear arms race on the attitudes of North Americans towards technology. 'It is only necessary to see how rocked our society was when the Russians got that piece of metal up into the sky,' he declared in 1959. 'They had beaten us at our own game [the advancement of technique] – a game that we consider important.' In response to this deplorable set of circumstances, he continued, business and military leaders cried for tougher 'history makers.' Those individuals were charged with the responsibility of building more efficient weapons of mass destruction and developing the technology to defeat the Soviets: 'It is of supreme importance that we beat the Russians to the moon.'[164]

Grant realized, however, that the North American 'will to technique' was not a recent phenomenon, a mere product of the ideological and imperialist rivalries of the Cold War. Rather, for Grant, the technological imperative characterized the entire modern history of the west, and of North America in particular. The arms race simply gave emphasis to what had existed all along – the development of the scientific society. Although it seemed as if the Soviets had 'caught up with and in certain fields surpassed' North American society, Grant claimed, 'modern scientific civilization has been most extensively realized in North America.' What is more, this scientific culture entailed far more than the use of advanced machinery and the existence of a large corps of technically educated individuals. It implied, on the contrary, an entire culture entranced and indeed dominated by the will to technique. Above all, it led to the emergence of a conformist civilization, devoid of independent thought or individuality. 'Ours is a world of mass production and its techniques,' Grant explained, 'of standardized consumption and standardized education, of wholesale entertainment and almost wholesale medicine. We are formed by this new environment at all the moments of our work and leisure – that is, our total lives.'[165] As Grant would later remark, Canadian society in North America had evolved into the 'universal and homogeneous state.'[166]

Grant's message was thus not only that technology had come to predominate in the contemporary world, but also that technique had gravely affected western culture. Seduced by the glories of 'big department store civilization,' Grant argued, moderns had lost interest in important philosophical concerns. Instead of contemplating the true effect of science and technology on the modern world, they were content to live a life of material fulfilment and to increase their wealth and power through technique. Homogenization – the greatest effect of the will to technique – stymied cultural creativity and impaired the expression of individuality. So great was the 'power that society can exert against the individual,' Grant asserted, 'that it even subjects to dominance those very elites that seem to rule.'[167] Few escaped the conformity of mass culture; moderns, indeed, had little hope of comprehending what was happening to them because they were so bound up in the increasingly enervating milieu that was developing around them. Modern society, according to Grant, was beginning to

lose a sense of itself and, in consequence, was heading towards disintegration.

Nowhere was cultural homogenization more evident than in the
emergence of the American empire. And nowhere were the effects
more perilous for the Canadian culture. Grant interchanged 'Americanization' with modernization, homogenization, and the mass society.
He blamed Canada's demise as a 'local culture,' moreover, on the rise
of the American cultural monolith. Grant wrote that American culture
had penetrated Canada through the 'movies, the newspapers, and television, through commercialized recreation and popular advertising.'
The media 'described and exalted' American life, 'which is so perfectly
adjusted to the world of life insurance, teen-age dating, and the super-
market ... Here is the way all decent Americans live and here is the way
that all mankind should live.'[168] In this climate of mass communications, conformism, and consumer values, Canadians were losing their
sense of distinctiveness and were becoming a part of an all-encompassing American value system, all in an attempt to modernize. Modernization, Grant concluded, entailed the demise of the Canadian nation.
'Our culture floundered on the aspirations of the age of progress,' he
announced, explaining Canada's 'three-step' cultural decline: 'First,
men everywhere move ineluctably toward membership in a homogeneous state. Second, Canadians live next to a society that is the heart of
modernity. Third, nearly all Canadians think that modernity is good,
so nothing essentially distinguishes Canadians from Americans. When
they oblate themselves before "the American way of life," they offer
themselves on the alter of the reigning western goddess.'[169]

As did the Massey commissioners, Morton, Creighton, and the other
nationalist culture critics, then, Grant drew attention to the ruinous
effects of American culture. In contrast to these critics, however, Grant
saw little hope that Canadians would overcome Americanization. The
'technological society' was inimical to cultural development; it was an
inexorable process that destroyed the values on which the Canadian
nation had been built. Modernization had become a fait accompli by
the mid-1960s. Canadians, even if they tried, would have had difficulty
in resisting its lure. Thus, for Grant, the Canada of the post-war age
was to be lamented; by the mid-1960s it was, as a nation, already
dead.[170]

Although not as pessimistic as Grant, Northrop Frye echoed the philosopher's concerns about technological modernization. Frye, like
Grant, saw the technological imperative and the 'progress myth' as

central to the modern societal quagmire. Progress, for Frye, was a constant unveiling of the individual and communitarian identity. It was, in a word, the progressive uncovering of truth. In the technological age, however, progress had been misapprehended and had become increasingly bound up in the destruction of the human identity. A progress myth emerged, according to Frye, based on the notion that progress involved material and technical advancement. Spiritual and intellectual developments, in the modern system, were secondary to material growth. Ultimately crowding out the world of the intellect and the spirit, the myth of technological progress became all-pervasive.

Frye used the educational experience of modern students further to illustrate his points. Educational institutions, he claimed, performed a conflicting role in the social development of modern individuals. While enabling an understanding of where the student fit in society, they also were increasingly preoccupied with conditioning moderns to cope with the demands of modern society. On the one side of the student existed 'the ordinary social environment, the world of his television set, his movies, the family car, advertising, entertainment, news and gossip. On the other side [was] the school, and perhaps the church, trying to dislodge him from this lotus land and prod him into further voyages of discovery.' Frye went on, 'On the one side of him, [was] a difficult theoretical world of art and science, the principles of which he has not begun to understand; on the other side [was] a fascinating world of technology and rhetoric, which he can already handle with some competence, and in which he must live in any case ... As a rule, therefore, the world of technology and rhetoric [won] out.'[171]

The will to technique thus interfered with the capacity of individuals to think broadly. Instead, it seduced moderns into living in an intellectually impoverished environment of convenience and gadgetry. For Frye, the restrictive effects of the 'technological consciousness' on the modern mind were most disquieting. The technological imperative was at odds with the creative or 'educated' imagination, the very lifeblood of any culture; for it inhibited the expression of cultural creativity at both the individual and the societal levels. Nowhere was this distressing reality more apparent than in the world of the arts. The 'arts reflect the world that produces them,' Frye declared in 1961. Ironically, the modern arts represented a society that had become hostile to the spirit that underpinned the creative process. 'Painting, music and architecture,' Frye explained, 'not less than literature, reflect an anonymous and cold-blooded society, a society without much respect for personality and without much tolerance for difference in opinion, a society full of slickness, smugness and spiritual inanity.'[172] Thus, the modern arts reflected a society bent on the destruction of the western imagination.

In analysing Frye's view of the demise of the west, the decline of the 'educated imagination' is critical. Society's fundamental problem was that, increasingly, it failed to provide the conditions conducive to creative activity, the 'depowered site where "the poets can be heard."'[173] As Frye later explained, modern civilization suffered the ill effects of an imbalance between the 'myth of concern' – the 'conservative myth' on which the traditions and customs of society relied – and the 'myth of freedom.' A myth of concern, dealing with science and technology and a gradualist, progressive mythology that surrounded it, characterized the twentieth century. It was growing so unwieldy, according to Frye, that it threatened the existence of the myth of freedom. The technological myth so blunted perceptions of the world that moderns ignored the impact of the modern mythology. The perception of 'the world out there,' Frye wrote, became 'habitual,' and 'hence a pernicious mental habit develop[ed] of regarding the unchanging as the unchangeable, and of assimilating human life to a conception of a predictable order.' Inured to the technological society, moderns ignored the creative sides of their psyches. Most lamentably, they disregarded their creative abilities and hence lost their power to alter their environment; for the 'imagination is the source of power to change ... society.'[174] Of all the deleterious effects of the technological order the harshest, for Frye, was that the contemporary myth of concern had become so entrenched that it had become extremely difficult to supplant.

Although hopeful that the technological mythology might be defeated, Frye was greatly impressed by the pervasiveness of the modern myth of concern.[175] While expressing general concern about the sway of the technological imperative, he was especially preoccupied with the 'onslaught of the myth of concern' on the Canadian mindset. Here, Canadians' relationship with the natural environment is vital. Canadians, Frye claimed, had come to dominate nature; in Canada there had been 'little adaptation to nature: in both architecture and arrangement Canadian cities and villages express rather an arrogant abstraction, the conquest of nature by an intelligence that does not understand it.' Frye showed how the Canadian imagination, expressed through literature, had developed an awkward, even strained relationship with nature. The Canadian imagination, Frye wrote, had evolved in 'small and isolated communities surrounded with a physical and psychological "frontier," separated from one another and from their American and British cultural sources.' Strongholds of human values and laws, these communities were 'confronted with a huge, unthinking, menacing, and formidable physical setting.' Such communities, Frye concluded, employing his most famous phrase, were 'bound to develop ... a garrison mentality.'[176]

Canadians organized into 'closely knit' societies, Frye continued, to develop the moral and social values necessary to cope with their forbidding surroundings. Yet such communities were hostile to the development of the Canadian culture. In providing the safety of the group and security from individuality and distinctiveness, they were the embodiments of the 'herd mind,' which stifled toleration and dissent and therefore killed the intellectual environment that the creative imagination required to grow. Indeed, they furnished the solitude of mind in which 'nothing original can grow.'[177] With the spread of garrisons, the results of hostile relations with nature, 'something anti-cultural comes into Canadian life.' The alienation from nature reflected, for Frye, the separation from the imaginative process. Garrisons prevented the freedom inherent in individualism and hence the creativity of individual thought. The chief battle in North American society – the struggle between 'the domination of the individual by the technological materialism which has led to the conquering of space, and the attempt to order an inner space in the individual through the power of the imaginative vision' – was being won by materialist forces.[178] It seemed to Frye that the technological imperative had undermined the world of the poet and the artist, leaving little opportunity for the creative process to develop. Although culture was the ultimate authority in society, it was impotent, according to Frye, to assert its supremacy in a civilization that shunned it. In the battle against cultural philistinism the Canadian garrison proved unyielding indeed.

'The mood in which Canadians reached and passed the mid-point of the 1960s was troubled, disillusioned, and baffled,' Donald Creighton wrote in 1970, looking back on the latter stages of 'Canada's century.'[179] For Creighton, as for Frye and Grant, Canada had languished as a cultural entity, owing chiefly to the growth of the heretical notion of progress. Creighton agreed that the 'rapid growth of industrialism and urbanism in Canada and the increasing dependence of the Canadian people [would] gradually weaken and break down the native Canadian moral standards and cultural values, and undermine the inherited Canadian belief in an ordered and peaceful society and simple way of life.' Like Grant, he believed that American civilization had been responsible for the pervasive materialist ethos of modern times. The Americans had abandoned 'mythical and religious explanations for existence,' and had developed a religion of their own, founded on the belief that 'progress is the only good in life, and that progress means the liberation of man through the progressive conquest of nature by technology.' The decline of Canada involved, for the culture critics, much more than poor policies and a wrongheaded allegiance to American imperialism. Canada's demise stemmed from the adoption of a modernist mindset and the acceptance of American values. Canadians had accepted the American credo of 'continual economic growth.' 'To achieve economic growth,' Creighton concluded, 'they are prepared to sacrifice their independence, pillage their natural resources, contaminate their environment, and endure all the hideous evils of modern industrialization and urbanization. The American Empire is taking over the birthright of Canadians; and its imperial religion has taken over their minds.'[180]

Creighton's pessimistic musings about Canada's bleak future were perhaps extremist, but they nonetheless conveyed the mood, if not the substance, of the culture critics' views by the late 1960s. For most, Canadians had failed to meet the challenges of the post-war era. The 1960s were the critical years in which the drama of Canadian destiny was played out. 'The decade which began in 1961,' W.L. Morton wrote, 'tested every assumption of the Canadian identity and tried every fibre of the national body.' Of the three great challenges to the national identity, including the growth of Quebec nationalism and the 'end of Britain as the exemplar and inspiration of Canadian life,' continentalism was, for Morton, by far the most dangerous. 'American protection, investment, and friendship,' he asserted, 'carr[ied] with them a price, neither stated nor demanded but inevitable, of the complete Americanization of Canadian thought, government, and national purpose.' To survive, Canadians must 'reforge their unity' and repeat once again 'the his-toric Canadian rejection of external control, imperial and continental ... putting forth limits on a continentalism ... which bade all too easily to become unlimited.' If Canadians failed and hence if the 'frictions of the past decade continued and combined,' Morton concluded, 'they might well destroy Canada.'[181]

For Morton and the others, then, the cautious optimism of the 1950s had ended in Canada's centennial decade. The country had endured the discouraging vicissitudes of the nation-building process and had emerged in a dire state. As a cultural entity, it had yielded to the attractions of the mass media and lowbrow culture. Failing to realize the stultifying effects of consumerism and cultural Americanization, Canadians had allowed themselves to succumb to the lures of the technological society. The greatest objective of the Massey commissioners – to build the spiritual identity of the nation on the basis of the Arnoldian ideal – had disintegrated in a milieu increasingly hostile to order, stability, and beauty. A new age of anarchy was prevailing, in which the battle against the philistines had been lost. For the cultural nationalists, Canada had suffered the supreme indignity of losing a sense of its history, its tradition, and its destiny. The Canadian identity had been challenged on all fronts. As an autonomous nation-state and as a distinct cultural entity, Canada was a country in decline. For the culture critics, the bitterest reality was that, while Canada showed enormous promise, the forces of modernity had proved too strong to resist. In the realm of culture, Canada had left behind its conservative inclinations and had been transformed into a modernist state.

The quest to formulate a Canadian cultural identity had thus ended in failure. Critics identified Canadian cultural poverty and, through instruments such as the Massey Commission, presented their findings to the Canadian public. Embroiled in other concerns, however, Canadians seemed largely to ignore the efforts of the high culturalists. With the triumph of the mass society and the will to technique, statements on the importance of high culture seemed quaintly anachronistic. And although the cultural nationalists succeeded in raising awareness concerning the inherently 'tory' and anti-American identity of the dominion, their efforts were largely limited to the cloistered environment of the Canadian intelligentsia. As we will discover in greater depth in the next chapter, the Canada of the '1960s had little sympathy for the tory interpretation of Canada. Rooted in the past, the strictures of tory scholars were anathema to a populace embroiled in intense social and political change. Conservative cultural nationalism simply did not accord with the increasingly plural outlooks of Canadian politics and Canadians at large. Confronted by a modernized world-view, antimodernists became more acutely aware of their own marginality. As Davies's character lamented, Canada was indeed turning out to be a 'hard country to live in.'

6

The World We Have Lost: Conservatism and the Revolutionary World

What I am going to say is the result of prolonged exposure to the continuing crisis of our western society – to the crisis of the democratic governments and free institutions during the wars and revolutions of the twentieth century. Now it does not come easily to anyone who, like me, has breathed the soft air of the world before the wars that began in 1914 – who has known a world that was not divided and frightened and full of hate – it does not come easily to such a man to see clearly and to measure coolly the times we live in. The scale and scope and complexity of our needs are without precedent in our experience, and indeed, we may fairly say, in all human experience.

Walter Lippmann, 1954

To social critics like Walter Lippmann[1] the period after 1914 was a time of revolution unparalleled in the history of the west. The Second World War and the post-war years were the culmination of decades of unprecedented social chaos and strife. Juxtaposed to the old order, the modern age was characterized by human tragedy and moral malaise. The world that had emerged from the Great War constituted a sharp break with the traditions and outlooks of the old order. For Lippmann and others, the social order of the pre-1914 period seemed lost for all time.

Facing the extraordinary exigencies of the twentieth century, social critics and like-minded intellectuals looked to themselves as those most capable of addressing the problems of modernity. Their self-appointed task was to assess reasons for cultural decline. It was also to aid a society that had been besieged by revolutionary forces. To achieve this most important objective, the social critics endeavoured to conserve the old order, whose remnants were rapidly disintegrating. Not reactionaries who disdained change and all that supplanted the ancient, they nonetheless wanted to preserve the values and traditions that they believed formed the core of western civilization. They wished, furthermore, to counterbalance the current world-view that was firmly ensconced in the modern age with views of universal and enduring significance. Above all, they desired to stabilize the social order by adhering to the Burkean precept that progress is achievable only in reference to past successes; advancement relied on the slow, but inexorable building on past accomplishments, physical, moral, philo-sophical, and intellectual. Their ideal social conception, in short, looked as much to the past as it did to present and the future.

Fundamentally, the critics of modernity were conservatives. Their social criticism, their view of the prospects of culture, and their con-ception of the ideal social order, in which the scholar-cum-social philosopher played an integral role, were informed by an inherent conservatism. Their perception of the mid-twentieth century as a revo-lutionary period and a time of ceaseless change, moreover, demon-strates their respect for the cultural and intellectual characteristics of the past as much as it displays their anti-modernist predispositions. The criticism of modernity, in other words, implied also the reassertion of the attributes of the old order in place of the new. It entailed, at bottom, an attempt to forestall the demise of the established structures in favour of novel ones. The focus here, therefore, is not only on the critique of the various aspects of modernism, but also on the societal critics' intrinsic conservatism. The effort to preserve the 'good society' unified the critics of modernity as much as did pessimistic attitudes towards science and technology or views on cultural and academic modernization. Repeated references to the 'living past,' though often mythologized, constituted the main response to the question of modernity.

Equally important to the social order was the role of the intellectual. Through the capacity to take the long view of cultural problems, the scholar gained insight into the riddle of modernity. Implicit to the conservative response to modernism was the critic's effort to exalt the intellectual and himself as enlightened citizens. Societal critics endowed themselves with the quasi-Platonic responsibility of acting as prophets of the new age. They wanted to reassert the relevance of the social philosopher and show how, as intellectuals, they occupied soci-etal positions of crucial significance. Above all, theirs was an attempt to restore intellectuals to a rightful place within the social hierarchy. The conception of the intellectual's role in society was vital to the conservative response to the modern world.

Ultimately, however, the modern age marginalized and eventually displaced the enlightened intellectual. For the anti-modernists, the greatest irony was that the individuals most capable of allaying the effects of modernity were those whom moderns disdained and eventually rendered irrelevant. The triumph of modernity was embodied not merely in the arrival of the mass society or the predominance of the will to technique. It was also encapsulated in society's disregard for truth and conservative values. Most of all, it was symbolized in the displacement of the enlightened intellectual. Although characterized by objective developments and historical realities, modernity was linked inextricably to anti-modernists' perceptions of their own social demise.

For many critics of modernity, the mid-twentieth century was paradoxical. There had been extraordinary advances in science and technique, abundant material wealth, and standards of living that were higher than ever before. Yet at the same time the period after the war was one of great distress. It was not surprising, British political economist Harold Laski wrote in 1952, that 'in a period like ours of insecurity, of violence, and of deep distrust, the prevalent mood everywhere should be one of somber pessimism and bitterness ... There is a fear of communism, fear of war, fear of depression, fear of a growth of doubt about the values inherent in [our] way of life.' For Laski, there was a growing chasm between the 'traditional values' of the former social order and the way in which moderns currently lived.[2] This rift was the cause of the tensions and insecurities of the modern world.

Vincent Massey also identified the stunning incongruities of the modern period. 'On the one hand,' Massey declared in a 1953 address, 'we seem to have at our disposal power and wealth, knowledge and freedom hitherto undreamed of; on the other hand we see, if not among ourselves, among other peoples ... mass ignorance, mass slavery, mass poverty, misery and cruelty on which even in imagination we cannot bear to look.'[3] In the midst of the confusion and anxiety of the modern era, one thing for critics such as Massey and Laski had been abundantly clear: something had gone terribly amiss in the so-called 'age of progress.'

Several factors accounted for the rise to prominence of a mistaken notion of progress, that is, the concept that advancement was reducible to material and technological growth. Perhaps the most fundamental of these elements, according to the critics of modernity, was the demise of freedoms intrinsic to the advent of mass or 'false' democracy. In chapter 4 we discussed the role of democracy in educational reform, and in the last chapter we explained critics' views on the deleterious effects on Canadian culture of 'mass democracy.' It remains for us to understand the role of modern democracy, in the minds of critics, to function as an illiberal and destabilizing force.

From the early 1940s on, there grew a debate as to the nature and impact of democracy and, even more important, the essence of true democratic freedom. For many social observers, democracy had devolved into unrepentant egalitarianism. As such, it undermined the aristocratic conception of democracy: not only that freedoms were unfettered by a hierarchical social order, but also that they were fostered by an inegalitarian social framework. Social observers, moreover, agreed that mass democracy cultivated a close-minded, uncritical stance on fundamental social problems. It produced another potent societal paradox: purporting to be a crucial source of freedom, modern democracy actually stifled human creativity and hindered individuality of thought and character. Democracy, it seemed, was contributing to a period already rife with propaganda, rhetoric, and dangerous totalitarian ideologies. Only through educating the masses about the inveterate character of democracy, the critics argued, could the freedom-destroying affinities of modern ideologies be curbed. The common man had to be guided from the folly of his own socio-political beliefs, and it was the duty of the enlightened individual to perform this vital task. Indeed, true freedom relied both on the intellectual and on the application of intelligence to the social process.

Although by the interwar period debate over mass democracy had already begun, the crisis atmosphere of the 1940s stimulated discussion on the basic socio-political features of western societies. From the middle phase of the war on, a spate of publications appeared in Canadian learned journals and elsewhere, all concerned with the fate of 'democracy.'[4] Although the writers were responding to the growing political-ideological crisis, they wished to do more than simply criticize totalitarianism and point out the inestimable merits of democratic societies. The Second World War and subsequently the Cold War were not merely conflicts for territory or efforts to 'make the world safe for democracy.' Instead, the major conflagrations were more important, authors argued, in terms of their effects on western civilization. They marked an end-point in the centuries-old development of what Hilda Neatby called the 'democratic cycle.' The student of western history, Neatby commented in 1942, 'finds himself faced with a strange and startling contrast. The eighteenth century was an Age of Reason, or the Age of Enlightenment. We do not yet know what title posterity will bestow on our age, [but] it can hardly be flattering. We seemed to have passed from the age of reason to the age of madness, barbarism, and anarchy.'[5]

What Neatby meant by this 'unflattering' epithet was that the fundamental principles of democracy – individualism, freedom from governmental arbitrariness, and a rational world-view – had been threatened in the age of world wars. By the 1940s the scientific, economic, and political developments that contributed to a free and peaceful order in the eighteenth and nineteenth centuries seemed to be irrevocably imperiled. Supposedly gone forever, the worst abuses of the ancient régime had reappeared, for Neatby, by the middle of the twentieth century. The western world's most enlightened men had ceased their search for a resolution of the greatest philosophical malaise of the century. Instead, 'the mind of the age' had evolved into mere technical knowledge, engaged in the 'production of instruments of death and destruction.' Even more worrisome was the fact that the fundamental precepts of democracy had been undermined. By the close of the nineteenth century, Neatby argued, the democratic 'ideal of reason' was 'rapidly giving way to the ideal of force.'[6]

The demise of democracy continued, according to Neatby, in spite of the western democracies' triumph in the Great War. The war, in fact, accelerated the process; it was the 'first round' that pitted 'the new doctrine of force and race and the old one of reason and humanity.' Subsequently, the victors attempted and failed to 'organize society on the principles in which they professed to believe.' They were unsuccessful, Neatby hastened to add, owing to an overarching complacency. Leaders of western nations watched in apathy the rise of totalitarian states, the growth of the masses, the sundering of the individual, and the 'degeneration of eighteenth century idealism.'[7] In a time of renewed conflict, it seemed that they were now active participants in the decline of democracy. The democratic cycle had passed from a faith in human reason to a form of organized mob rule.

Not content merely to chronicle the decline of democracy, Neatby ended her by article proffering insight on the decay of democratic principles. The reasons for decline were quite simple. The introduction of democratic precepts had not happened gradually, allowing the integration of older ideas into the new society. It had arisen, on the contrary, in 'revolutionary fashion.' The old regime had been violently overturned. Through the revolution, Neatby stressed, not only tyranny but also discipline, religion, and respect for order and hierarchy had been destroyed. The democratic upheaval thus was not entirely 'progressive.' Although Neatby did not dispute the fundamental soundness of democratic theory – she deeply appreciated the merits of individualism, especially in the 'mass age' (see chapter 4) – she objected to the revolutionary penchant for discarding, in the name of progress, all that had passed before. Only through a combination of the best of the old and new orders, she insisted, could humanity hope to extricate itself from the perils of the democratic cycle. At its best, she explained, the 'old régime stood ... for absolutism along with common moral standards accepted and enforced; the nineteenth century antithesis was liberty, with the assertion of the dignity of the free individual. The danger of one is tyranny, and of the other, anarchy. If twentieth century democracy cannot produce a synthesis in the form of freedom and individual worth translated in terms of common moral standards accepted and enforced, it will suffer annihilation, and justly.'[8]

In spite of Neatby's admonitions, however, it appeared as though modern democracy had failed in this quest for balance. For many, it seemed as though the true democratic spirit that Neatby sought had been lost. Force and power and humanity's penchant for dominating seemed to have prevailed over idealism. These realities became especially apparent during the Second World War. In 1941 historian Arthur Lower argued that there was a great increase in political control made manifest in restrictions of individual freedom, organization, assembly, and due process. A new type of control-oriented state, Lower averred, was coming into existence in Canada.[9] As Harold Innis phrased it, 'centralization and force' had come to 'dominate the Anglo-Saxon world.'[10] As noted in chapter 2, Lower, Innis, and others deplored the rise of wartime controls and the sundering of free institutions. Even more disquieting, however, was the modern state's inclination to use democracy as a means of hiding the illiberalities of the age. Modern governments endorsed propaganda, censorship, and a more general restriction of free thought and belief all in the name of 'winning the war.' For Lower, the greatest irony of the war, a confrontation designed to guard freedom, was that it led to the denial of freedom. Echoing Neatby, Lower argued that the war threatened the emergence of a new state with little concern for the liberties on which Canadian society had been built. War is the 'most awesome' of humanity's 'mass actions,' Lower declared. It 'overwhelms us by the magnitude of the experience it threatens to impose upon us and prevents objective thinking.'[11]

H.W. Wright put the plight of modern democracy even more cogently than did Lower. In a 1940 article entitled 'The Values of Democracy,' Wright showed how many moderns claimed that, given the 'present emergency,' 'democracy' 'would be justified' in employing unusual means to protect itself from the perils of the wartime world. It could resort to 'every device of early education and adult propaganda supplemented by drastic censorship,' he continued, 'which would implant in the minds of its citizens that form of religious belief, of social philosophy and of nationalistic sentiment allied to, or consistent with, its aims.' Wright also identified a critical inconsistency with the wartime purposes of democracy. In establishing an ideology, modern democracy not only abandoned its fundamental values of free thinking, but also threatened its citizens with the rigidities and conformities of the totalitarian régimes. 'If the purpose of democracy is to establish freedom of individual thought and utterance, of individual initiative and enterprise in the practical sphere, and of individual taste in aesthetic enjoyment and recreation,' Wright reasoned, 'it is impossible to see how democracy could impose, or even undertake to teach any specific religious belief, cosmic philosophy, historic or economic theory, standards of artistic excellence or social propriety, without stultifying its own aims and betraying its own values.'[12]

A restrictive yet nominally 'democratic' socio-political order thus was anathema to observers such as Lower and Wright. This criticism of wartime democracy also resonated throughout the work of Harold Innis. As indicated in chapter two, Innis's concepts of the 'monopoly of knowledge' and media bias as much referred to current governmental trends and the suppressive climate in Canadian universities as they were central aspects of his new communication theories. Like Lower and Wright, Innis was concerned to the point of obsession with the maintenance of the indispensable elements of democratic societies: free thought and critical enquiry. The concept of bias and, more accurately, the identification of the limitations of thought, was vital to his social critique. Understanding bias and maintaining free thought were the means by which individuals and societies could help to preserve liberal values. They were key, most of all, to avoiding the transgressions of 'wartime democracy.' 'Oral and written words,' Innis wrote in 1946, 'have been harnessed to the demands of modern industrialism.' '[W]ords [i.e., propaganda] have carried a heavy additional load in the prosecution of war and have been subject to unusual strains.' 'The first essential task' of moderns, Innis resolved, responding to the extraordinary exigencies of the mid-1940s, was 'to see and to break through the chains of modern civilization.'[13]

Doubtless the effects of the war greatly influenced critics' perceptions of liberal democracy. The end of the war, however, did not mean a cessation of scepticism about and, indeed, outright hostility to modern democracy. In the post-war period, in fact, there was a heightened anxiety about the plight of democratic principles. The power and force inherent to totalitarian regimes abroad and control-oriented democracies closer to home continued to plague the post-war world. As Lower indicated, humanity's 'desire for power' did not die out with the end of hostilities; people could fight each other through 'advertising campaigns rather than bullets.' The satisfaction of their 'primitive urges, whether [they] win or lose, is just as great.'[14] For Lower and others, modern humanity seemed predisposed towards the expression of force.

Post-war society was marked by an even greater threat to liberal democracy. In addition to the political-ideological organization of force, the advent of 'mass democracy' posed, for the anti-modernists, a daunting challenge to traditional democratic ideals. For many critics, democratic societies degenerated not merely because of the rise of authoritarianism and other external forces; rather, civilization was uprooted from within. The rise of the philosophy of 'mass man' contributed greatly to this upheaval. As Walter Lippmann argued, problems arose with the new, 'democratic' image of humankind. The modern 'conception of human nature – one in which desire is sovereign and reason is the instrument for serving and satisfying desire,' Lippmann wrote, 'has become increasingly the accepted image of man in the modern world. It is upon this image of man,' he added, 'that our secular education had been based, and our social philosophy and our personal codes. Our world today is in the hands of masses of people who are formed in this image and regard it as indubitably the true and scientifically correct conception of human nature.' The 'fashionable image' of humankind, Lippmann announced, was 'the image of an uncivilized barbarian.'[15]

While seemingly benign, barbarism actually posed a grave menace to society. This threat arose, Lippmann argued, precisely because moderns wished to see themselves only in terms of their new-found acquisitive image. They rejected the spiritual and contemplative side of the human psyche and instead reduced human happiness to a Hobbesian quest for the satisfaction of an endless list of wants and needs. The 'secular man,' Lippmann declared, is the individual who 'obeys his impulses and knows no reason that transcends his wishes.' Disquieting in and of itself, this monolithic and indeed distorted view of humanity implied further problems. Most troubling, according to Lippmann, was the penchant for avoiding the deeper issues of human existence and instead seeking solace en masse in the acquisitive ethos. The repression of individualism and the ascendance of a herd mentality were basic to the destruction of the west. Entrapped by a narrow definition of material progress and lacking a refuge in individual contemplation, moderns sought sanctuary in 'the masses of their fellow beings, becoming anonymous, faceless, and no longer persons.' 'They are a horde,' Lippmann concluded, discussing the contribution of mass men to societal decay, 'arising within our civilization rather than invading it from without. They are a horde of beings without autonomy, of individuals uprooted and so isolated and disordered that they surrender their judgment and their freedom to the master of the horde ... The dissolution of Western society – as we have seen it demonstrated in the lands where it is totally advanced – in an organized barbarism which makes the lives of all who fall within its power "poor, nasty, brutish, and short."'[16]

Lippmann's strictures presaged a post-war onslaught against mass man.[17] Writing soon after the end of the war, for example, H.W. McCready contended that a lack of regard for the values of individualism marked the current 'crisis of tradition.' The tradition of individualism, McCready asserted, that 'had built our western civilization certainly appears to be moving fast towards extinction.' He went on, 'The fundamental value of the individual person and his welfare, rights and liberty ... are increasingly surrendered to the new gods of the mass age – Community, Nation, Efficiency, Power and Plan.'[18]

Malcolm Muggeridge, the editor of *Punch*, echoed Lippmann's and McCready's concerns on the demise of individualism. In a piece entitled 'Farewell to Freedom? The State, the Person, the Faith,' Muggeridge claimed that the individual, in both totalitarian and democratic communities, had 'withered away.' He argued that in the 'Free Societies,' of which politicians and common folk were so proud, 'the same drift of servitude is apparent as in the Slave Societies across the Curtain.' Indeed, the 'great Leviathan' was 'waxing ever fatter' all over the globe.[19]

Muggeridge identified a more fundamental source of the attack on the individual and personal liberties: the press. Reflecting the criticisms of Innis, Marshall McLuhan, and others, Muggeridge stated that the press had 'increasingly become more a purveyor of orthodoxy than an expression of individual views.' It was 'in the process of succumbing to the collective zeitgeist.'[20] Accounting for the emergence of the mass society in Canada, W.B. Munro blamed the rise of American mass culture. '"American" influences on Canadian ways of life have been expanded by the vogues of the automobile, the motion picture, and the radio,' Munro wrote to Donald Creighton in 1948. 'These influences are not usually apparent in the laws of the land or in the formally-announced procedures; they creep in from below and affect the tastes of the people without their knowing it ... And the strength of these influences, for good or evil, is not surprising when you remember that such a substantial fraction of Canada's population lives within fifty miles of the border.'[21] Whatever the causes, the culture of the common man, in the words of Muggeridge, 'incorporate[d] [moderns] in a herd,' made them follow 'the herd destiny,' and, ultimately, 'destroy[ed] the purpose of [their] being.'[22]

The critique of the 'culture of the masses' reflected the ideological battle of the 1940s and 1950s. Nazi Germany and the Stalinist Soviet Union demonstrated to the critics of modernity, among others, just how fragile modern democracy was. As noted in chapter five, critics were preoccupied not only with the effects of ideologies of mass persuasion, but also with the rise of new doctrines of 'false' democracy. These dogmas pervaded the post-war period; Canadians became caught, for instance, in the traps of material improvement and consumer enjoyment. As George Grant observed in 1955, the act of consuming had become an 'end in itself.' Canadians of the post-war age identified themselves as 'consuming animals.' As such, they became enslaved by a materialist society for which spiritual goods had little meaning. Materialism, Grant declared, 'so sets the tone and pattern of our society that the standards it imposes close people off from knowing what life is for ... The boom world creates like an aura its own standard of success – of what really matters in life – and that aura lies over everything, choking people with the fear of failure in terms of those standards, and cuts us off from any truer vision of life.'[23]

The standardizing effects of consumerism were matched by the democratic ideal in education. With Hilda Neatby, Vincent Massey, and others, Grant argued that mass education was integral to 'mass democratic society.' Parents and 'progressivists' alike were not interested in the education of children, but rather, they felt that students 'should be fitted for success and adjustment.' Most of all, they 'accepted the philosophy of worldly success and adjustment as a true account of what the schools are for.'[24] Thus, for Grant, modern education adapted the masses to the exigencies of the post-war world. Ultimately, it was a means of making 'democratic' citizens.

For many Canadians, the democratic ethos extended even to the family. Post-war authorities warned that Canadians must practise the values of democracy if Canada were to ward off the errors of totalitarianism and build a strong and free society. They emphasized that, as a pioneer society, Canada was different from its European predecessors. Indeed, the Canadian family derived strength from the fact that it lacked the patriarchal structures of its European counterparts. Canadians must capitalize on their advantages, the experts reasoned, by further democratizing family life: budgeting and activity planning should be open to all family members, and family councils should be encouraged to promote a cooperative familial environment.[25] The family, in other words, must mirror the egalitarianism and toleration of society at large. That hierarchy and overt control had little place in the democratic family reflected the post-war predisposition against authoritarianism. Like education, to Canadians after the war the democratic family became essential to a post-war world order beset by totalitarian heresies.

Many Canadians thus emphasized the merits of democratic levelling. This democratic ethos, however, was not simply a response to authoritarianism. For Canadians, post-war society was surrounded by a multitude of lurking threats: inflation, unemployment, juvenile delinquency, Soviet expansionism, and, most lamentably, nuclear annihilation. The 'cult of domesticity,' suburbanization, materialism, and mass consumption – all assertions of modern democratic values – were ways of assuaging the uncertainties of the post-war age. The democratic, progressive life was a means to achieve the control and stability that the modern age lacked. Indeed, it provided Canadians with an escape from a manipulative and unstable world. Far from merely being a liberty-engendering political doctrine, democracy touched every aspect of modern Canadian life. Ultimately, in offering the means of liberating moderns from uncertainty and instability, it seemed to hold the key to broader societal freedom.

As we have seen, the critics of modernity vociferously denounced modern democracy. They believed that moderns were led astray by false notions of progress and erroneous doctrines of freedom and that the obsession with 'democracy' in its many forms prevented moderns from seeing the world as it truly was. If moderns were consumed with buying cars, moving to the suburbs, and denouncing the unredeemable evils of Communism, then how could they transcend the narrow limits of the modern value system and thus see the true problem of modernity? Indeed, a main reason that critics despised mass democracy was that it was inimical to a measured, humanistic critique of modernity. In other words, it precluded the sage advice of humanists and therefore marginalized some of society's most important individuals. Under these conditions, it is not surprising that the critics perceived themselves as increasingly insignificant, even irrelevant, in the 'democratic' society.

Critics also reviled mass democracy because it upset the balance of modern societies. In considering all humans equal, modern democracy failed to account for the different roles of the various strata of society. Above all, it ignored the value of the intelligentsia to the social process. Showing their tory affinities, the anti-modernists were convinced of the enduring social benefits of privilege. Hence, it was their self-appointed duty to reassert the social relevance of the intellectual to society, even if that meant inflating the importance of the intellectual class. Indeed, critics advanced an alternative view of the free and democratic society, based in part on historical precedent and in part on an idealized conception of the intellectual as citizen. Their purpose was both to overcome the unmitigated levelling of the modern world and thus to restore intellectuals to their appropriate social standing. Countenancing the creation of a hierarchical, quasi-Platonic social structure to which the social philosopher would make key contributions, they hoped to secure for themselves a place in a hostile democratic world.

There were several uses for the intellectual in the social process. In an era of unprecedented socio-political strife, the most pressing of these was the role of intelligence in achieving peace, liberty, and social stability. According to many social observers, the world must be re-educated for peace. In an article written for the *Canadian Forum*, Nora McCullough argued that there was much more to the reconstructionist phase of post-war development than a balanced economy and full employment. She argued that moderns lacked a 'real knowledge of our own society' and, indeed, of the entire world. This dearth of information combined with a growing apathy towards the exigencies of the post-war world. Both drawbacks had to be remedied before moderns could be prepared for the challenges of peace. Educators, McCullough indicated, had an important role to play in effecting these changes and also in laying the groundwork for peace.[26]

Other observers envisioned a more integral purpose than did McCullough for educators and the educational process. In 'Education for an Enduring Peace,' for instance, philosopher John A. Irving claimed that 'educators should lead in creating the intellectual atmosphere conducive to social change.' He advocated the creation of 'a new educational outlook,' which would help to develop not only 'facility in the investigation of social facts, but also the capacity to formulate rational value-judgments based ... on sound philosophical analysis.'[27] The social sciences, which were central to understanding the post-war age, must be tempered with an emphasis on social ethics and social philosophy. As such, social scientists might foster the awareness and responsibility necessary to deal with the tumultuous changes of the post-1945 epoch. Thus, in Irving's view educators had a responsibility both to students, and, most important, to the society in which they worked and thought. The achievement of peace and stability was perhaps their most important obligation to the social order.

Writing about the place of education in a democratic society, Robert Wallace agreed with much of the substance of Irving's strictures. He argued that a democratic and peaceful society was realizable only through the attainment of common societal values and ideals. Education and the achievement of an intellectual life were, in turn, indispensable to the fulfilment of these objectives. Wallace touted the benefits of liberal education to present 'knowledge as a unity,' and to develop 'intellectual interests which may persist though life.' For these elements not only contributed to the intellectual existence of western man, but also strengthened 'common experience' and with it the 'forces that make for freedom.' The 'real life' of democracies, Wallace concluded, 'consist not in things with which we are surrounded, but in our efforts ... to reach out to the highest truths we know,' and to realize 'the great end which mankind may serve.'[28] Liberation, on both a personal and a societal level, was the ultimate result of this quest for truth.

For Wallace and others, the search for values clearly had implications that resounded through the ages. Although always related to this quest, a liberal education had a more direct role to play in the lives of individual citizens. In *Twilight of Liberty,* for example, classicist Watson Kirkconnell discussed the role of educational institutions in developing a responsible citizenry. He derided modern education because it debased standards and endeavoured to fit society's youth into the industrial-democratic order. This system of education, Kirkconnell remonstrated, provided students with 'a minimum of knowledge, skill, and manners.' Students received 'some rudimentary training in the use of tools and baking-dishes. They are also taught to cooperate with the laws of the state.' Contemporary education, Kirkconnell concluded, was merely a means of adapting 'young barbarians' for life in the social order 'of which they form a part.'[29]

More than simply denouncing mass education, however, Kirkconnell provided insight into the higher functions of education. True education, he argued, attempted to develop 'in the minds of young men and women ... that the true end of existence lies ... in personal self-realization, partly through the social services of their employment, partly through the happy cultivation of their [intellectual] powers, and partly through a devotion to domestic and social relationships.' In other words, it enabled students to transcend the minimalist goals of democratic education and to see instead the 'greater significance of life in its intellectual, aesthetic, and moral aspects.' In developing the whole individual, it followed that education and the intellectual life more generally facilitated the creation of a knowledgeable and dutiful citizenry. Quoting Julius Caesar, Kirkconnell stated that it is '"a nobler thing to remove the barriers of intellectual life than to extend the boundaries of an empire."'[30]

Other observers agreed with the spirit of Kirkconnell's pronouncements. Hilda Neatby, for instance, argued that education was central to the creation of a true democracy. Like Kirkconnell, she attempted to expose the fallaciousness of 'democratic equalitarianism' in education. Foreshadowing what she was to write a few years later, Neatby denounced democratic education's 'stress on group activity' and its commendation of 'team work and cooperation.' These fallacies ignored the truth that 'democracies live by the achievements of solitary original thinkers.' 'Without these,' she added, democratic societies were 'bound to collapse into the mass hysteria that throws up a Hitler.' Indeed, Neatby argued for a reassertion of the 'essentials of a liberal education,' and a 'new interpretation' of these attributes 'in relation to democratic life.' Above all, she advocated a comprehension of democracy as a reflection of the 'development of all human faculties not excepting the highest of all – the power of creative thought.'[31] In enabling creativity and critical thought and, by implication, in creating a responsible and intelligent citizenry, education helped to create a truly free democracy.

Even more forthright on the role of a liberal education in establishing a democratic citizenry was Northrop Frye. Like Kirkconnell and Neatby, Frye castigated 'progressive education' primarily because of its stifling effect on moderns. For Frye, the Deweyite ideals of 'invulnerable wisdom and backslaphappy sociability' prepared individuals simply for complacency and mediocrity. Most of all, 'progressivism,' whether it be embodied in education theory or in the materialist ideal of modern society, ignored the greater objective of establishing '[high] standards of human mentality.'[32] In other words, it disregarded the fact that social improvement came not from adjusting humankind to its social surroundings but rather from the liberation of human thought and creativity. A liberal education, Frye argued, as Kirkconnell and Neatby had done before him, was instead 'designed to produce the democratic gentleman.' Rightfully conceived, education exposed individuals to 'the great works of culture,' and created the realization that in these great works resides the 'mainspring of all liberal thought.'[33] Through liberal education, then, individuals gained access to the modes of critical and creative thought. As such, they became, for Frye, endowed with the capacity to identify and avoid progressivist and other fallacies of the modern age. Those with a liberal education were the true democratic citizens of modern society. The 'purpose of liberal education today,' Frye claimed, 'is to achieve a neurotic maladjustment in the student, to twist him into a critical and carping intellectual, very dissatisfied with the world, very finicky about accepting what it offers him.' 'The man with a liberal education will not have an integrated personality or be educated for the living: he will be a chronically irritated man.'[34]

Harold Innis echoed Frye's view of the liberal education and its relationship to the democratic social order. Modern society, Innis asserted, ought to be 'concerned with strengthening intellectual capacity, and not with the weakening of that capacity by the expenditure of subsidies for the multiplication of facts.' Educators should be 'concerned like the Greeks with making men, not with overwhelming them with facts ... Education is the basis of the state and its ultimate aim and essence is the training of character.' To Innis, the purpose of education was to cultivate integrity and dedication and to encourage moderns to serve society. Education was not intended merely to prepare the learned for scholarship in specialized fields of knowledge; rather, it encouraged personal qualities of wisdom and judgment, balance and perspective. It therefore allowed moderns to contribute to the culture of which they formed a part. Instead of merely moulding individuals for acceptance among the masses, liberal education, for Innis, recognized the value of personal character and thus enabled humankind to resist the drudgery and standardization of everyday industrial-democratic life.[35] For Innis, Frye, and the others, liberal education was vital to the preservation and perseverance of free civilization.

Liberal learning thus was key to creating an 'anti-environment' to the modern industrial-democratic order. Critics also advanced a vision of the rightful social order, one that stressed the critical importance of intelligence and an 'intellectual class.' In this conception, the intellectual played the role of sage patriarch to the unwashed masses. The intellectual had become the saviour of post-war society. Through his understanding and benevolence western culture had the opportunity to progress and overcome its current travails. Through his wisdom, society would save itself from itself, and regain the values, ideals, and freedom that had gone absent. For critics, the intellectual held the answers to the problems of social instability that mass democracy and other mistaken ideologies had tried to address. The enlightened individual, in consequence, must occupy a place of importance in modern society. More than the aristocrat, the businessman, or even the scientist, for the critics he was society's most capable leader. He took on quasi-mythic proportions. As such, his social significance, and indeed that of his entire class, ought to be guaranteed.

In an article entitled 'Are Men Equal?' Robert M. Ogden captured the essence of this idealized vision. Ogden argued here that humans were simply not equal in terms of their 'potentialities of service.' Some were more apt than others to lead. In the past, those who 'fortuitously achieved rank, wealth, or intellect' were society's leaders. In the modern era, by contrast, the 'true aristocrats' were those 'whose service [had] earned for them the right to be so called.' 'The true aristocrat,' Ogden continued, 'is a catalyst, and his service is a meliorating influence among those with whom he works.' The modern age, he declared, must be one in which emerged an 'Aristodemocracy,' a society in which prevailed 'a few persons whose intelligence has brought them rank and wealth to catalyze the ways of common men into friendly channels of behaviour.' While the 'masses' must be 'adequately fed and housed,' and have 'the freedom to move about,' society must be led by those individuals capable of '"correct" leadership' – those who are motivated by a 'bid for perfection' and therefore in working for the best interest of their fellows.[36]

Poet T.S. Eliot concurred with this notion of a hierarchical social order. Writing in 1948, Eliot discussed the 'doctrine of élites' and how it constituted a 'radical transformation of society.' He advocated the establishment of a society in which 'all positions ... should be occupied by those who are best fitted to exercise the functions of the positions.' Indeed, Eliot defended aristocracies and argued against the creation of a classless society. Echoing Plato, he claimed that the truly progressive society was one in which 'an aristocracy should have a peculiar and essential function.' Like Ogden, he believed that an elitist society was the precondition of a free society. 'What is important,' he reasoned,[37]

> is a structure of society in which there shall be from top to bottom a continuous gradation of cultural levels; it is important to remember that we should not consider the upper levels as possessing *more* culture than the lower, but as representing a more conscious culture and a greater specialization of culture [italics in original]. I incline to believe that no true democracy can maintain itself unless it contains these different levels of culture ... [I]n such a society as I envisage, each individual would inherit greater or lesser responsibility towards the commonwealth, according to the position in society which he inherited – each class would have somewhat different responsibilities. A democracy in which everybody had an equal responsibility would be oppressive for the conscientious and licentious for the rest.

Abhorring the idea of social levelling, Eliot believed instead in the fundamental importance of a hierarchical society, particularly one in which the intellectual élite played a vital role.

The notion of a quasi-Platonic society had adherents among many of the critics of modernity. Donald Creighton, for example, illustrated the relationship between humanistic education and the leadership role in western societies. In Britain, at the beginning of the nineteenth century, he wrote, the 'humanities remained subjects of central importance,' and 'were now accepted as the appropriate training grounds for statesmen ... A first class in "literae humaniores," in "greats" was a clinching demonstration of talent which opened all careers in politics and administration, as well as in the church, the law, literature and the press.' '[I]t is not too much to say,' he added, 'that the Modern Commonwealth, east and west, and [Canada] as one of its greatest realms, are the creations of men who were trained in language and literature, in history and philosophy.' Indeed, some of the great governors of the dominion – Bond Head, the Marquis of Lansdowne, Baldwin, Draper, Howe, Brown, Macdonald, and Laurier – were 'university men' brought up on the classics.[38]

Watson Kirkconnell agreed with Creighton on the importance of liberal arts learning to leadership. 'If the civilized values of the race are to survive,' he asserted in 1952, 'we shall need to have a fair number of men in our communities who have a strong grasp of moral principles and whose minds ... can rise above those details to a sense of their broad human significance.' 'Much of the greatness of Britain's political life,' Kirkconnell stated, 'lies in the fact that so many of the nation's leaders – men like Burke, Fox, Peel, Gladstone, Asquith, Grey and Balfour – have been classical scholars or philosophers, or have, like Bright and Churchill, steeped themselves in the finest of English literature.'[39]

The liberal arts did not simply prepare individuals for political leadership. Instead, the intellectual played an even more important role, according to critics, as a cultural beacon. Harold Innis argued, as we have noted, that western cultures ought to value humanist intellectuals because they were the individuals capable of leading society out of its sociocultural malaise. Humanists were able to discriminate between timeless values and values that were bound to specific 'empires' or cultural-historical contexts. In Innisian parlance, they were able to expose and perhaps correct the effects of bias and monopolies of knowledge. Through the acknowledgment of cultural biases, Innis believed that intellectuals could transcend their limiting effects and attempt to resolve the pressing philosophical problems that their society faced. Humanists, society's 'creative individuals,' were, in consequence, vital contributors to the social order.

Innis cited classicist and mentor C.N. Cochrane to illustrate this point. 'Men will fail,' he wrote, '"unless they prove themselves capable of energy and initiative, of intelligence and moral daring, comparable with that displayed by [intellectuals] of the past."'[40] For Innis, the intellectual was the inheritor and, indeed, the purveyor of the two great forces of European civilization: the Christian religion, for the development of the individual, and the Greek tradition, 'for the mind and intellect.' Society must remain vigilant, he concluded, in 'emphasizing the importance of the individual and [in] attempting to effectively maintain the spark of civilization ...'[41]

American political philosopher Peter Viereck also discussed the wider import of the intellectual. In *The Unadjusted Man: A New Hero for Americans*, Viereck ennobled the 'unadjusted man' – 'the humanist, the artist, the scholar.' Unlike the 'well-adjusted' or the so-called common man, the unadjusted individual was distinct in that he did not conform to the modern industrial-democratic order. Rather, he was the 'final irreducible pebble' that 'sabotages the omnipotence of even the smoothest-running machine.' His values were not determined by 'democratic plebiscite' but rather were the product of his classical education, his wisdom, and his philosophical understanding of the world. The unadjusted man was indeed the 'new American hero' precisely because he was 'the prophet and seer, the unriddler of the outer universe.'[42] Thus, the intellectual was for Viereck, as for Innis, indispensable to comprehending and rectifying the defects of the modern world.

In a letter to Hilda Neatby, Massey commissioner and president of the University of British Columbia, N.A.M. MacKenzie, best summarized the chief 'worth' of this unadjusted individual. 'I believe very strongly,' he wrote in 1950, 'that if the humanities are to count for anything in this day and generation they will have to be associated directly with the lives that we lead and with the lives of our citizens in all walks of life. The ancients whom we now study and admire lived in and made their contribution to contemporary society ... I would like to think that our humanists, including those in our universities, were doing the same for their society.' Through these contributions, Mac-Kenzie stressed in concluding his letter, intellectuals derived their fundamental social import. Humanists, he urged, must be encouraged 'to keep in touch with their society and with the forces of a cultural kind, even though these be vulgar that are shaping it and influencing it.' For through this effort, 'the rest of the community will realize that they exist and will attach some importance to them, even though they disagree violently with some of the things they say and do.'[43] For MacKenzie, Viereck, and the other intellectuals, humanists by virtue of their training and cultural outlook, had an undeniable and enduring social relevance.

The heightened awareness of the role of intelligence appeared against the backdrops of academic modernization and the quest for the revitalization of Canadian culture (see chapters 3 and 4). It was also the product of the disdain that intellectuals felt for the masses and mass society more generally. Intellectuals reviled 'mass men' because commoners formed a social constituency very different from that of the intelligentsia. They feared the masses because of their tendency to disturb social equilibria and to disrupt the orderly unfolding of history. Critics viewed mass society as a force with profound revolutionary implications. Their effort to reassert the social importance of the intellectual was in part an attempt to allay the effects of mass culture and thus to stabilize civilization. More fundamentally, their conservative predispositions reflected a greater desire to reassert the aristocratic significance of the intelligentsia. The post-war years presented to critics a grave threat to the social positions of the intellectual elite: the all-pervasive doctrine of democracy and material process threatened their social status. Thus, in the period after the war critics endeavoured to subdue the masses and to re-establish themselves as vital components of the modern order. As Neatby argued, there was a need 'to lay down a programme for the elite and the many,' and to issue 'a blue print for a platonic society with gold, silver and brass carefully distinguished from each other.'[44] The dire need for stability was to be met through reaffirming the foundational hierarchical basis of western societies and, most significant, through placing the intellectual at the top of a new social order.

Socio-cultural paternalism was just one aspect of the conservative impulse. The Canadian critics of modernity responded to the exigencies of the post-war age also by proposing cultural-intellectual constructs that challenged those of the modern period. The re-emphasis of the Crown, the Commonwealth, and the Anglo-Canadian constitutional inheritance, along with other elements of the British cultural nexus, characterized their efforts to contest Americanization, the Liberal interpretation of Canada's past, and other aspects of modernity. Critics endowed Canada with conservative qualities to strengthen the nation as a cultural entity and also to allay the pervasive influence of modernization. Their underlying purpose was to contribute to a national culture resistant to revolutionary transformations and capable, at the same time, of sustaining conservative values and outlooks. Not simply a means of creating a national identity, Canadian conservatism was a powerful ideological tool used to stabilize a national culture in a time of profound change.

The war sparked considerable debate on Canada's relations with Great Britain and, specifically, with the Empire-Commonwealth. Many questioned the endurance of the Commonwealth as an important international organization. Given the weakened condition of post-war

Britain and the dubious prospects of the Commonwealth in an era of declining imperialism, there seemed little hope that Britain, the dominions, and the colonies could recapture past glories. Yet, for the anti-modernists, much rested on the continuing significance of the Commonwealth. They believed that the Commonwealth was critical to the development of Canada and a national identity. The connection to Britain and its dominions also served the time-honoured function of combating the American influence on Canada; in the end, it was the key to the dominion's autonomous development on the North American continent.

George Grant's 1945 pamphlet *The Empire, Yes or No?* typified this pro-imperialist bent. In it Grant assessed Canada's prospects in a world dominated by a burgeoning American imperialism. Canada, he reasoned, could survive as an autonomous country only within the Commonwealth. Otherwise it would 'soon cease to be a nation and become absorbed into the U.S.A.'[45] Canadians had succeeded in establishing an independent state only by balancing their 'geographic North Americanism' with their 'political Britishness.' In the post-war age, Grant counselled, Canada would maintain its independence by retaining its links to the Commonwealth, thereby avoiding integration into the two great continental empires. As Innis remarked three years later, Canada must encourage a political-cultural association separate from American or Soviet imperialism. This 'third bloc' would be based on Canada's European cultural inheritance and was embodied in the concept of the Commonwealth.[46] For Grant, Innis, and others, the Commonwealth was central to evading American imperialism in all forms. Britain, in short, must function as it always had: as a crucial counterweight to inexorable continentalism.

The Anglo-Canadian nexus was a complex phenomenon. Its preservation implied, for critics, more than simply avoiding American political, cultural, and economic influences. Rather, it was inextricably linked to the growth of the Canadian national identity. As Grant claimed in an article entitled 'Have We a Canadian Nation?' there were positive reasons why Canada ought to cultivate relations with Britain. Canada, after all, was historically a 'British nation,' and it ought to remain so. However, Canadians could no longer defend the British heritage by appealing to tradition alone. Instead, Grant urged that they discover the foundations on which Canada's British heritage rested. The nation's identity was based 'on certain conscious ideas,' one of the most important of which was that, unlike the United States, Canada had never severed its ties with western Europe. It was a conservative country, in other words, whose connections to Europe were vital to its identity. In addition to its anti-revolutionary tradition, Canadian conservatism implied a notion of responsible freedom in which personal liberties ought not to conflict with the freedom of others or disturb the social order. Regard for law and order, Grant noted, was firmly rooted in Canadian political culture; it was a natural element of the Canadian concept of liberty. These 'values and traditions of decency, stability and order,' Grant declared, 'have been the best basis of our national life.' They must be preserved if Canada was to continue as a nation.[47]

For Grant, Canadians had qualities that made them special because of their British heritage. Perhaps most representative of Canada's distinct tradition was the British monarchy. The Anglo-Canadian Crown was a powerful symbol for conservatives. Against the backdrop of the coronation of Queen Elizabeth II in 1953, Governor General Vincent Massey explained the importance of the Crown to Canadians. In his coronation day broadcast, Massey demonstrated the unifying purpose of the monarchy. 'A Coronation,' he announced to his audience, 'is the greatest and most moving historical pageant of our time.' But to Canadians 'it is something more even than that.' 'It was part of ourselves,' and 'represents in a very special way our national life. It stands for qualities and institutions which mean Canada to every Canadian,' he went on, echoing his nephew Grant's observations of a few years earlier,[48]

> which for all our differences and all our variety have kept Canada Canadian. How much the Crown has done to give us our individual character as a nation in the Americas. It shapes our contribution to Western democracy. The Crown itself, as a golden object, may repose in London, but as a cherished symbol it plays and has played a unique role in our national life long before our Sovereign became officially the Queen of Canada. Great truths have been brought home by what we have seen and heard today – the sense of continuity, of oneness with the past derived from our ancient monarchy; the unifying force which comes from that something in our Constitution which stands above all our differences and dissensions, and which everyone of us can respect. The Queen wears 'the Sign which unites us all.'

According to the conservative critics, the Crown was a potent, unifying symbol for Canadians. Aside from its symbolic function, however, the monarchy also characterized the greater British tradition in North

America. As Massey remarked, the Crown was central to the emergence of a free and tolerant society. Since the Glorious Revolution of 1688 it had been associated with parliamentary government, and had 'achieved its greatest dignity and power through Parliament.' Canadians retained this link. They had embraced the principles of constitutional monarchy, and with these, the notion that the rule of law was the means of gaining freedom. Canada therefore had a very different conception of freedom from that of the United States. Canadians, Massey added, did not oppose the American conception of liberty that was bound up in 'the ideals of human dignity, human equality, and human well-being in a material sense.' Yet their political values revolved around toleration, peace, order, and good government, and other principles of the constitutional monarchy. For Massey, this political inheritance was the chief contribution of the English to western civilization.[49]

Elaborating on the importance of the Crown to the dominion, economist John Farthing concurred with many of the governor general's contentions. In a book provocatively entitled *Freedom Wears a Crown*, Farthing showed how the monarchy was 'not merely a far-off institution ... but [rather] holds a place of primary significance in our own established order of democratic government.' That Canada had a royal as opposed to a republican democracy was 'no idle distinction.' Being loyal to the throne was more than a 'mere matter of sentiment.' Instead, 'it had to do with a basic ideal of social life, and with a fully enlightened attachment to the highest ideal of democracy that the life of man has ever known.' In the 'British monarchical order,' Farthing concluded, this 'universal ideal has been preserved and most highly developed.'[50]

Friend and erstwhile scholarly collaborator Eugene Forsey enthusiastically agreed with Farthing's assertions.[51] Forsey, a former politician and party ideologue, scholar, and political activist, declared that the Crown was the 'centre and symbol' of the 'real heritage of all Canadians': parliamentary responsible government. The monarchy was indispensable to the British democratic order and was the guardian of the constitution. As such, it represented the sole protection of the people. The Queen, Forsey wrote, encapsulating his view of the Anglo-Canadian monarchical tradition, 'is the guardian of our democratic constitution against subversion by a Prime Minister or Cabinet who might be tempted to violate that Constitution and deprive us of the right to self-government.' At the same time, the Crown ensured that people 'are not prevented from governing' themselves.[52] It acted as a key counterweight to executive power, thus enabling the proper and free functioning of the constitution. For Forsey, as for Massey and Farthing, liberty did indeed emanate from authority.[53]

Along with the monarchy, conservatives stressed the significance of the British Commonwealth of Nations. Despite long-term decline and partial dissolution,[54] the Commonwealth nonetheless had much to offer the dominion and indeed the entire post-war world; it was a template for a new and peaceful world order. As Donald Creighton remarked in a letter to the president of the Ford Foundation, it afforded 'a unique example of the working of democracy through cooperation.' Creighton went on, 'Internally and externally, the Commonwealth has developed democratic institutions and advanced international peace. Studies of the cultural, social, economic, military and political relations within the Commonwealth are studies of democracy in the strategy of peace.' There was a need, therefore, to 'make known' throughout the world 'the genius for co-operation' and the other freedom-engendering attributes of the Commonwealth.[55] The socio-political and cultural organization of the Commonwealth was thus, for Creighton, truly sublime.

Vincent Massey also praised Canada's membership in the Commonwealth, calling it 'our greatest achievement.' Massey emphasized its role as a 'countervailing force against the erosion of our sense of identity.' Association with the Commonwealth, he argued, was a way to maintain the already strong attachment most English-speaking Canadians had to the ideals of the mother country. It fostered unity, moreover, in countering the arguments of those 'suspicious of the imperial connection – ardent Canadian nationalists of the 1930s active on the western prairies, and some of the intellectuals of French Canada.'[56]

More than functioning merely as an agent of true Canadianism, however, the Commonwealth had a wider purpose. Following Creighton, Massey demonstrated how it had become an exemplar to the international order. It was a diverse, yet tolerant and cooperative organization that provided important policy alternatives in an era of growing power blocs. '[A]s a grouping of friendly nations making widely differing responses to the Cold War,' Massey explained, Commonwealth nations have 'cut across the frozen configuration of international politics.' Member nations, he added, have to consult each other and have 'regard for the interests of the whole.' This sense of internationalism was indispensable to a post-war world in which bridges between nations had been destroyed. The Commonwealth was emblematic of international toleration and entente. Against a background of international, even racial strife, Massey declared that 'the ideal of a multiracial Commonwealth offers ... an object lesson in tolerance and understanding between white and non-white peoples. Canadians in all walks of life are attracted to this aspect of the Commonwealth, even if they know (or should know) that in practice the ideal has been sadly tarnished.'[57]

Massey, Creighton, and the others were thus very concerned over the fate of the Anglo-Canadian alliance. While informed by the economic and political circumstances of the post-1945 period, their preoccupations must be seen first as outgrowths of the pro-British, pro-Empire sentiments that characterized the history of Canadian 'toryism' (see chapter 1). Specifically, the nationalist views of the post-war conservatives closely paralleled those of the Canadian imperialists of the late nineteenth and early twentieth centuries. George Parkin, George Munro Grant (G.P. Grant's grandfathers), George Denison, and Stephen Leacock, among other imperialists, realized that as a national entity, the dominion had languished since Confederation. It was one of their main purposes to revitalize Canadian nationalism by explaining and establishing their own conception of Canada. Central to their view was that Canada derived its strength, its cultural identity, and its entire 'sense of power'[58] from its association with Great Britain. More than that, Canadian imperialists believed that owing to its northern climate and vast resources Canada was to become in the near future the seat of the Empire. The last Anglo-Saxons to toil in a harsh northern climate, from which always emerged superior civilizations, English-speaking Canadians were prepared to lead the Empire into the next century. By assisting the Empire and strengthening, not diminishing, ties to Great Britain, in essence the dominion would be helping itself. Indeed, the imperialists thought that imperial unity would be a cure-all for the problems of economic downturn, ethnic tensions, provincialism, and, most worrisome of all, American continentalism.

As Carl Berger has shown, ideas on imperial federation and Canadian imperialism more generally died out after 1914. The anti-materialism and jingoistic pro-British ideas of the imperialists simply became irrelevant in the industrial age. However, the imperialist idea took much longer to fade. Specifically, while the agrarianism, Social Darwinism, and intense British nationalism were eliminated, there remained a core of toryism that persisted well into the twentieth century. The imperialists' toryism – 'a total acceptance of assumptions which underlay their admiration for the British constitution and the agricultural economy, their belief that in national and individual affairs the acceptance of duties was more important than requesting privileges, and their insistence on abiding by tradition and precedent'[59] – continued to be the guiding principles of the latter-day conservative nationalists. Indeed, the reverence of Massey, Creighton, Farthing, and the others for the Commonwealth and the British political tradition bore a close resemblance to the Anglophilia of the Canadian imperialists. The notion that Canada was, and should remain, a 'British nation' was fundamental to both groups of ideologues. The imperialists' contempt for democracy and their respect for the role of privilege was also passed on to later tory critics. George Grant's *Lament for a Nation*, in the words of Berger, was merely a 'depressing footnote' to imperialist thought. Thus, while much time had passed and the historical circumstances were different, there was considerable continuity in the core ideas and key outlooks of both groups. The British nexus remained central to the conservative vision of the nation.

Contemporary historical conditions also influenced the view of the conservative nationalists. By the 1950s Canada had modernized both economically and politically. Since the early twentieth century, the dominion had become increasingly dependent on the United States as a trade partner and foreign investor. During the interwar period this long-term trend was amplified, as American investment in Canadian industries reached unprecedented levels. Canada's 'branch plant' economy continued to be Americanized throughout the Second World War and post-war periods. In 1940 trade with Britain exceeded trade with the United States.[60] By 1948, however, exchange with the United States had increased to $1.5 billion, almost 50 per cent of the dominion's annual trade. Two years later Canadian-American commerce accounted for 64 per cent of all Canadian trade. Trade with Britain, by contrast, decreased to 22 and 20 per cent of the nation's total trade for 1948 and 1950, respectively. In 1957, furthermore, the United States invested $8.4 billion of $10 billion foreign direct investment into Canada. As economic activity with Britain waned, the dominion increased its reliance on the United States. Economically and financially, Canada had fallen into the American orbit.[61]

Perhaps more important than the nation's economic dependence, in the eyes of critics the Canadian government also gravitated towards an 'Americanized' external policy. During the war, Mackenzie King's administration, partly from necessity, had become closely tied to the United States in the defence of North America.[62] This close military relationship continued under Prime Minister Louis St Laurent. The North Atlantic Treaty Organization (NATO) established in April 1949, exemplified this persistent tendency. Originally conceived as a means of reducing military dependence on the United States,[63] NATO expanded the military predominance of the United States in the North Atlantic and much of Europe. Instead of allowing Canadians freedom to pursue foreign policy alternatives, however, it bound Canada to an American-led anti-Communist bloc.[64] As historian Kenneth McNaught asserted, NATO meant for Canada 'acquiescence [to] Washington's ideological anti-communism.'[65] Moreover, a year after the signing of the NATO agreement Canada became embroiled in the Korean War. Ostensibly under the auspices of the United Nations, Canada's participation in Korea was, in reality, a response to the American presence in East Asia. As Creighton remarked, 'the action of the United Nations in Korea [was] a very imperfect disguise for American military intervention in the Far East.'[66] The formation of the North American Air Defense plan (NORAD) and the Distant Early Warning (DEW) Line later in the decade simply continued the Americanization of Canadian defence policy.[67] As the decade wore on, the prospects of an autonomous defensive and foreign policy seemed improbable. The Canadian government appeared to have abdicated control to its American counterpart.

Conservative critics implored Canadians to look beyond American imperialism as the sole explanation of Canadian dependence. They themselves blamed Liberal leaders for Canada's pro-American policies. George Grant, for example, chided the Liberals for failing to understand the importance of the British nexus. The Liberals denied Canada's British character and wanted to sever ties with the Commonwealth, he remonstrated, and therefore were 'bad Canadians.' They had contravened the work of Macdonald, Laurier, and Borden, all of whom had fought hard to make Canada a separate entity. Furthermore, they had allowed Canada to become 'a mere satellite like Bulgaria on the borders of a great Empire.' Yet, they still deceived the Canadian public in saying 'sovereign, independent nationalist Canada is playing its fine and noble role in the U.N.'[68] Grant best summarized the anti-Liberal position in a letter to his mother. '[O]n the level of Canadian foreign policy,' Grant declared, hardly concealing his vitriol, 'I have nothing but contempt for the successors of Mackenzie King. Pearson now gets up and says that we must guard against Canadian dependence after years of the party he serves selling out this country to the Americans by weakening the only alliance that we could possibly have that would give us even a modicum of independence [i.e., an alliance with Britain]. The Liberal Party has gained votes in this country by appeals to nationalism for two generations first by a refusal to be close to the power that once could have maintained peace and now by attacking the Empire that has taken its place. Oh how I find democratic nationalism contemptible.'[69]

Grant was not alone in his contempt for 'democratic nationalism.' Harold Innis distrusted the motives behind the American involvement in Korea. He also scorned the whole idea of the NATO alliance. He wrote: 'Pearson seems to be as active as possible in selling us down the river to the United States.'[70] Donald Creighton was just as vociferous as Grant and Innis in his denunciation of the Liberal party's pro-Americanism and the Grits' distrust of the British nexus. More than any other Liberal, William Lyon Mackenzie King was the subject of Creighton's vituperation. Writing in 1954, shortly after the former prime minister's death, Creighton attacked King and his external policies. On a personal level, Creighton charged that King was without passion of any kind: '[King] united a grey colournessness of style, a grey ambiguity of thought, and a grey neutrality of action. He became an acknowledged expert in the difficult business of qualifying, toning down, smoothing out, and explaining away ... With his squat, solid, unremarkable presence, and his earnest rather whining voice he became the veritable embodiment of the uncertainties, the mental conflicts, the parochial terrors of the Canadian people between the wars.'[71]

In addition to his penchant for obfuscation, Creighton went on, King had drawn up damaging external policies. Specifically, he had presided over the dismantling of the Anglo-Canadian connection. Until 1919, Creighton explained, Canada and the other dominions and colonies had worked hard to maintain the diplomatic unity of the Empire. After King's accession to power, however, Canada had set about formulating and implementing 'her own foreign policy separately from the United Kingdom.' King and the Liberals were bent on achieving complete autonomy within the Empire, a pursuit that had resulted in the 'resounding declaration of the Balfour Report of 1926, and the Statute of Westminster of 1931.'[72] Under King's direction, in short, Canada had gained full autonomy within the Empire.

Despite the seeming triumph, Creighton urged caution. Achieving independence within the Empire was, in fact, King's most egregious contribution to the Canadian nation. Instead of developing new initiatives, King's Liberals had established an external policy that was 'derivative, imitative, and lacking in conviction.' The PJBD, NATO and other defence agreements of the 1940s exemplified, for Creighton, King's penchant for uniting Canadian interests with those of the United States. Under King's guidance, Canada had become a de facto colony of the United States, 'accepting a position not very different from that of Panama or Cuba.' Creighton also vilified the Liberals for enabling the British connection to lapse. Without Britain's guidance, Creighton asserted, 'Canada instinctively fell back on the old habits of colonialism.' Without the British counterweight, it fell prey to the 'continental imperialism of the United States.'[73] By severing imperial ties with the United Kingdom, King had ensured that Canada failed to establish itself as a 'separate and distinct' identity on the North American continent. Ultimately, the Liberals had contributed to the disintegration of the Canadian nation and had done a grave disservice to all Canadians.

For Creighton, Liberal complicity in the destruction of the Canadian nationhood was not confined merely to external policy. Rather, it extended to the so-called Liberal interpretation of the Canadian character. As noted in the preceding chapter, what Creighton derisively termed the 'authorized version' of Canadian history was deceptive because it portrayed Canada's struggle for nationhood simply as the gaining of autonomy from Great Britain. It therefore obscured the very real 'British' origins of the Canadian nation. More than that, it concealed the enduring relevance of the British connection for Canada in the post-war world. The Liberal nationalist ideology of historians such as Lower and Underhill and pseudo-academics such as Skelton and Dafoe was for Creighton and the others stultifying, monolithic, and false. It presented a fallacious picture of the emergence of the Canadian nation and created a mythology that did not befit the needs and circumstances of Canadians. Most of all, it destroyed a true understanding of the Canadian nationality, to which Creighton, Grant, Massey, and the others made fundamental contributions. For this reason it was despised. John Farthing captured the essence of the impact of Liberal nationalism. 'A very real distinction exists between our present pure-Canada nationalism and a true Canadian nationhood,' Farthing wrote. 'At the root of the distinction,' he continued, 'lies our attitude to what had been known in Canada as the British tradition. According to our new nationalists this tradition is something that belongs only to the British Isles and is therefore an alien influence in the life of the people who should have their own traditions and should admit nothing in their national life that is not wholly and purely of Canada.'[74]

Along with identifying the perfidy of the Liberal nationalists, critics also wanted to express the righteousness of a conservative-nationalist mythology. The conservative strictures of the post-war period were designed in large measure to counterbalance wrong-headed Liberal ideologies.[75] They were meant to disseminate truths about Canada's historic relations and therefore to provide insight for a nation mired in an identity crisis. Ultimately, Canadian conservatism was a means of counteracting disturbing modernizing trends like American imperialism by articulating and recording the 'true' nature of the Canadian experience. Just as significant, conservative doctrines intended to contribute to a 'true' social order built on truth, freedom, and social justice. As Farthing declared, affiliation with the British monarchy gained for Canadians access to the 'highest ideals' of democracy ever known.[76] British democracy was not merely a means of deflecting the influence of American political dogmas; it was a means to a positive definition of political freedom. Indeed, for Farthing and others, the expression of Canada's conservative nature was essential to the achievement of the good life.

Whatever their motivations and aspirations, conservative intellectuals did precisely what their detested Liberal counterparts had done before them: they established a mythology that was congruent with the perceived needs and circumstances of the present age. Like the Liberals, they set about defining the Canadian experience both in historic terms and, more significant, in reference to the needs of the dominion in the post-war era. Both mythologies, in short, purported to offer the truth about Canada's historic experience and the nation's real character. The main difference was that the conservative myth-makers endeavoured to undermine the reigning Liberal mythology and replace it with their own version of the Canadian reality. In this objective, they achieved a degree of success. As the 1950s progressed and as the conservatives themselves gained confidence through the triumph of Diefenbaker conservatism, their mythology grew in stature. By the end of the decade, Canadian conservatism appeared to have come of age.

Probably the most articulate myth-maker, W.L. Morton, made it his purpose to define and apply the idea of Canadian conservatism. As explained in the previous chapter, in works like *The Canadian Identity* Morton elaborated on Canada's British character and its conception of freedom and on other aspects of the Canadian experience. Integral to his view of Canadianism, however, was political conservatism. The dominion, Morton stressed, was 'not founded on a compact.' As such, 'the final governing force in Canada is tradition and convention. Self-government came to Canada,' he continued, 'by administrative change gradually worked out rather than by the proclamation of principles ... [N]o one could declare what the Canadian destiny was to be.' Rather, Canadians wished to develop their country in relation to past triumphs. For Morton, Canada was not a revolutionary nation, but rather was one that maintained a deep, quasi-Burkean respect for the successes of prior generations. '[I]f among the spiritual forefathers of America were John Calvin, Robert Browne, and John Locke,' he ended, 'those of Canada were Bishop Bossuet, Edmund Burke, and Jeremy Bentham.'[77]

In the spring of 1959 Morton encapsulated his thought on Canadian conservatism. In 'Canadian Conservatism Now,' he set out the first principles of the conservative phenomenon. First, he emphasized the need for 'law and order' and 'civil decency, without which society dissolves in anarchy.' Next was a respect for tradition. Morton urged deference for the 'experience of the race' or 'the wisdom of our ancestors.' He countenanced not 'ancestor worship,' but instead 'the realization that, important as the individual is, he is what he is largely in virtue of what he is in blood and breeding, and of what he has absorbed, consciously or unconsciously, formally or informally, from home, church, school and neighbourhood. He subscribes to Burke's definition of the social contract as a partnership in all virtue, a partnership between the generations, a contract not made once for all time, but perennially renewed in the organic processes of society, the birth, growth and death of successive generations.' Loyalty and the 'need for continuity in human affairs' were the next first principles. Echoing Edmund Burke, Morton showed that conservatives appreciate elements of permanence in their lives. Although they did not dismiss change outright, transformation 'should come by way of organic growth, not deliberate revolution or skillful manipulation'; for 'Such change leads to the continuity that makes permanence possible.' Last, conservatism implied for Morton a communitarian spirit – an appreciation of family, kinships, neighbourhood life – that was vital to the 'organic' nature of the society.[78]

Moving from the generalized descriptions, Morton next expounded upon the origins and, most important, the relevance of Canadian conservatism. He first stressed the significance of French-Canadian conservatism. He showed how many observers had failed to recognize the continuing impact of the Roman Catholic tradition in both Quebec and the whole of Canada. Nevertheless, Morton placed greater emphasis on the 'Loyalist strain of Canadian conservatism,' chiefly because of its 'extraordinary [relevance] to the circumstances of our ... day.' The Loyalists had brought to Canada a tradition of constitutionalism. Their political heritage, he claimed, accepted the role of the monarch as well as that of the people; it involved 'three divided powers of king, courts, and parliament each checking and balancing each other so that the authority of the government was maintained while the liberty of the subject was assured, the greatest miracle wrought by English political genius.' Not only were Loyalists champions of the balanced constitution, Morton stressed, but they also stood against the greatest abuse of the emerging American political order: mass democracy. Herein lay the historic and indeed the contemporary pertinence of loyalism. Loyalists, Morton asserted, had 'refused to see the king struck from the constitution, to be replaced by an elected democrat'; 'they refused,' he went on, citing Chief William Smith, 'to see "all America abandoned to democracy."' 'How right they were,' he concluded simply.[79]

The loyalist inheritance was certainly important in combating the misapprehensions of American political dogma. Yet for Morton, Canadian conservatism had an even greater contribution to make to mid-century society. The utility of conservatism, he explained, its contribution to the good society, was predicated upon the conditions of modernity. Society at mid-century was in a state of flux. Urban-industrialization, the rise of 'scientific research,' the 'enormous acceleration of the pace of social change,' and the demise of 'philosophic individualism' characterized this period of transformation. Conservatism and, specifically, 'a conservative philosophy for our times and circumstances,' Morton argued, would allay the effects of modernization. It was to provide a remedy for the impermanence, confusion, and instability that infected western societies. A purveyor of 'absolute values' and 'the established norms of our western tradition,' Morton explained, it was to work against the 'relativism of liberal thinkers' for the 'infection it is.' Based on humanist ideals, he went on, referring to the inhumanity of the machine age, conservatism would never forget that 'people are themselves of absolute value,' and that 'they are ... the test of justice, of the good life, and of all social and economic values.' Following Hilda Neatby and the other 'restorers of learning,' it insisted that 'among men as endowed by nature, there is no equality,' and that 'there is liberty in men to realize what is in them.' It restored, in other words, the primacy of the individual, the personality, and the intellectual as the core of the collectivity. Conservatism, Morton suggested, would champion the individual – particularly the intelligent individual – to combat an age of standardization and anti-intellectualism. It was, in short, the invaluable alternative to the ever-growing scourge of modernity. To lose the 'contest' for conservatism, he ended dramatically, 'would be not only a tragedy ... [i]t would be a betrayal, of past, of future, of the soul of man.'[80]

Other conservative intellectuals did not advance such a detailed conception of Canadian toryism. Nonetheless, Morton must be seen as part of a small group of thinkers who denounced liberalism and put forth instead a 'tory' vision of the nation. Although the views of Morton and Creighton sometimes deviated on issues of national unity and the Canadian identity,[81] Creighton was a prominent member of this coterie. He was a key contributor to the burgeoning conservative movement of the 1950s. Creighton's toryism came out in his historical writings, specifically, in his work on Sir John A. Macdonald.

In the late 1940s and early 1950s Creighton was consumed with a biographical reassessment of Canada's pre-eminent statesman. As he later admitted, works such as *The Young Politician* (1952) and *The Old Chieftain* (1955) were efforts to rehabilitate Macdonald, whom 'Liberal' historians, in Creighton's words, had denigrated as 'easy-going, convivial, bibulous, none too scrupulous ... [a] master of the dubious arts of political expediency.' For Creighton, however, Macdonald was little like the Liberal caricature. Instead, he was a master politician, statesman, and, most important, a paragon of Canadian toryism. Macdonald's conservatism, Creighton explained in 1957, was a 'moderate or liberal Conservatism'; 'He believed firmly in the monarchy, the British connection, the parliamentary system, [and] responsible government.'[82] Indeed, Macdonald was the political embodiment of the loyalist principles of which Morton spoke so highly.

More than a theoretical conservative, Macdonald's toryism was embodied in a vision of Canada's nationhood. It was most fundamentally expressed, for Creighton, in one supreme political purpose: the creation of a transcontinental union in North America. Macdonald's initiatives – the protectionist tariff, the construction of the Canadian Pacific Railway, and the National Policy – extended the historical geo-economic realities of Canada: the St Lawrence and Saskatchewan river systems. Canadian federation in 1867 constituted the logical conclusion to this process of development. Most significant, it involved the preservation and expansion of the Canadian fact in North America. Historically, Creighton contended, Canadians had 'persistently followed policies devised to strengthen our unity from ocean to ocean and to maintain our separateness in North America. Our defences against the "continentalism," which has so often threatened us from the South, have been based on the east-west axis provided by nature ... Confederation gives us our transcontinental political union.' Creighton stressed, 'Sir John A. Macdonald's national policy provided the framework for an integrated transcontinental economy.'[83] Through union and the national policy, Canadians could realize their common traditions and inheritances; they could work to 'expand, develop, preserve, and defend' their distinctiveness in North America.[84] Macdonald's programs indeed had been much more than notable political accomplishments; they were enduring national triumphs – core elements, according to Creighton, in achieving the Canadian destiny.

Creighton believed that Macdonald had been a great leader, a man to appreciate and emulate, not only for his contemporaries but also for subsequent generations. He had possessed the rare quality of greatness, Creighton suggested, because he had understood the essential conditions of the Canadian nationality. Through his actions, he had taught Canadians to be true to their character and their past. He had shown that Canada's destiny was achievable only by realizing Canada's defining qualities. Indeed, Macdonald had been, for Creighton, a paragon of Canadian conservatism. He had subscribed to Burkean precepts in agreeing that progress could be attained only in reference to the past and in relation to those characteristics, such as Canada's British heritage and its geo-economic characteristics, which made the nation distinct. He had seen the St Lawrence River system[85] and the British nexus as the ancestors of modern Canada, and, what was important, he had made it his main purpose to put forth policies that would preserve the Canadian character. Macdonald's nation-building policies, Creighton asserted, and his conservative approach to the future, were his enduring legacies. It was left to future Canadians to understand their nationality in the way that Macdonald had done. It was their chief duty, Creighton claimed, to build on the work of Canada's great first prime minister.

Although rooted in mid-Victorian Canada, Macdonald's conservatism indeed had a transcendent quality. Macdonald was, in Creighton's words, 'as vividly contemporary as any Canadian politician now living.'[87] His vision of the nation transcended time and therefore applied as much to the historical conditions of the late nineteenth century as to those of the late 1950s. Creighton expressed the relevance of Macdonald in an address to Prime Minister John Diefenbaker on the importance to Canada of a national broadcasting system. 'Canadian strength and Canadian unity,' Creighton began, citing Macdonald's great purpose, 'ultimately depend upon Canada's maintenance of her autonomy and spiritual independence on the North American continent ... A national broadcasting system can do for us in the realm of mind and the spirit, precisely what ... old and tested national policies [of Macdonald] have done in the political and economic sphere. A steady flow of live programmes along the east-west life line will express Canadian ideas and ideals, employ Canadian talent, and help unite our people from sea to sea and from the river unto the ends of the earth.'[88] In 1957 Creighton commented on the nation-building qualities of the CBC: 'The cultural and intellectual advancement of our people is surely just as essential to the national well-being as are our political sovereignty or our economic prosperity. The Canadian Broadcasting Corporation not only gives scope to the talents of our musicians, actors, playwrights, authors, commentators, and scholars: it also enables Canadians to maintain their intellectual freedom and to express their own interests and their own points of view in the realms of politics, economics, and society ... Canada should surely hold fast to every means of maintaining its intellectual independence and promoting its cultural maturity. Surely these things are essential to the populous, prosperous, and successful Canada of which Sir John A. Macdonald dreamed nearly a hundred years ago.'[89]

In addition, Creighton emphasized the necessity of a Macdonald-like approach to defence and external affairs at mid-century. As noted in the last chapter, Creighton was preoccupied with the menace of continentalism. In particular, he loathed the continuing subjugation of Canadian foreign policy to that of the United States. He urged Canadian decision-makers to relinquish the country's reliance on American policies and develop instead an independent approach to foreign relations. 'Canada's first duty is to remember that she is a separate and autonomous nation in North America,' Creighton announced at the Couchiching Conference of 1954. 'Her most important contribution' in international politics 'will be to speak her own mind politely but firmly on all occasions.' 'North America is not the world,' he added resolutely, 'and the world will not willingly accept North American domination.'[90] Although the nation-building and the Cold War eras were worlds apart, continentalism was still a threat to be identified and overcome. The lessons of Sir John A., for Creighton, never lapsed. Whether in broadcasting, defence, or foreign policy, Creighton measured Canada's success in relation to the inestimable achievements of Canada's greatest statesman. Although dead for nearly three-quarters of a century, in the second half of the twentieth century Macdonald continued to embody the essence of the Canadian identity.

Creighton's view of Macdonald's vision inspired the historian and influenced his own view of the nation. In a word, it inspired Creighton's conservatism. Although distinct, Creighton's toryism was part of a greater whole. Creighton must be considered with fellow historians W.L. Morton and John Farthing, journalist Judith Robinson, constitutional expert Eugene Forsey, and philosopher George Grant, as intellectuals who criticized the Liberals for their contribution to the sterile political milieu of the early 1950s. The crux of the complaints of these critics was that the Liberals under Mackenzie King had undermined traditional Canadian institutions and had abandoned traditional orientations. As Forsey took pains to point out, for instance, King had little regard for parliamentary responsible government. Through his use of plebiscites and his 'presidential' practices of governance he had subverted the Anglo-Canadian parliamentary tradition. Further, in attacking the monarchy in Canada, as Morton, Farthing, Creighton, and others emphasized, the Liberals had undermined the British connection and threatened potent national symbols and identities. As Forsey noted, Canadians debated the retention of affectations such as 'Royal Mail' and 'dominion.' The British tradition was 'attacked venomously,' he declared, 'by people who thought it was dying and wanted it dead.' Prompted by the Liberal government, '[they] demanded a clean break from the past.'[91] More than simply initiators of ill-conceived policies or corrupt governmental practices, then, King and his colleagues had committed a much graver set of transgressions: the Liberals, in the eyes of their conservative critics, had done the unthinkable – they had destroyed the conservative heritage of the country.

Ensconced within the tradition of tory thought (as we have seen the imperialists were), the conservatism of Creighton and the others was also firmly rooted in the political history of the 1950s and early 1960s. Politically, the Liberal party dominated the 1950s just as it had presided over the 1940s. When it came time to call another election, the St Laurent Liberals seemed the likely choice for another term in office. Yet, the 1957 election did not provide the expected result. The Canadian electorate turned out the Liberals and voted in a Progressive Conservative government under a new leader, John G. Diefenbaker. After twenty-two uninterrupted years of Liberal rule, Canada's political landscape had at once been drastically altered.

For the conservative critics, the 1957 election interrupted the grievous reign of the Liberals. Just as significant, it ushered in what Morton, Creighton, and others hoped was a new age of conservatism. At least at the beginning, leading tory thinkers expected Diefenbaker's Conservatives to correct the wrongs of the Liberals.[92] They hoped furthermore that the Tories would re-establish and strengthen Canadian traditions and reaffirm the Canadian identity. The 1957 election was a significant phase in the development of the post-war tory mythology. It was a flashpoint in the history of the country for the conservative critics, because it marked the triumph of the tory vision of the nation. Canadians, finally, had chosen correctly. For one brilliant moment in post-war Canadian history, it seemed that the forces of good had prevailed.

John Diefenbaker was so important to conservatives because he embodied several of the key principles of Canadian toryism. The first of these was Canada's British orientation.[93] An ardent monarchist, Diefenbaker made it the responsibility of his government to reinvigorate the imperial connection. One of his first acts was to attempt to increase trade with the British. On 7 July 1957 he announced his government's intention to divert 15 per cent of Canada's imports from the United States to the United Kingdom. Although the plan was ill conceived,[94] it indicated Diefenbaker's desire not only to increase interactions with the British and the Commonwealth more generally, but also to use the imperial nexus as a way to counterbalance Canada's increasing dependence on American goods and markets. True to the tory credo of Macdonald, Creighton, and the other modern conservatives, Diefenbaker employed Britain and the Commonwealth as a means to deflect the ever-present threat of continentalism.

Just as significant as Diefenbaker's Anglo-affinities was his notion of northern development. The new prime minister was enthused about developing the Canadian north, because he saw Canada's northern reaches as the source of the country's future economic and national growth. Echoing the tory nationalism of turn-of-the-century Canadian imperialists and, more recently, of historians Creighton and Morton,[95] he presented a view of the country that was intended to transcend the narrow-minded national policies of the Liberals – prosperity through economic continentalism. Diefenbaker, in his own words, 'advocated a twentieth-century equivalent to Sir John A. Macdonald's national policy a uniquely Canadian economic dream.' The Liberals offered policies that stated that 'what was good for General Motors was not only good for the United States but good for Canada.' 'In contrast,' Diefenbaker continued, 'we offered a policy of positive government' that had its 'historical origins' 'in the first Conservative ministry in Confederation.' Indeed, the Diefenbaker government intended to emulate the positive state action and nation-building that were intrinsic to the political programmes of Macdonald. It 'offered a new national policy of regional and northern development.' Its main 'objective,' ultimately, was 'to continue Macdonald's historic task of nation-building within the context of modern requirements and circumstances.' Of all the governments after 1918 one had finally emerged, in the minds of the tory critics, that recognized the significance of Macdonald's approach to building the nation.[96]

Despite the Tories' best efforts, however, Diefenbaker's governments failed, by and large, to implement conservative principles. Diefenbaker's British trade scheme was a non-starter, and his attempt at revivifying Canadian participation in the Commonwealth likewise achieved little success. Trade between the United Kingdom and other Commonwealth members was threatened as Britain increasingly looked to Europe for its economic future. Without Britain as its focal point, the Commonwealth was doomed as an influential economic unit. In addition, Diefenbaker's efforts to establish a more independent defensive stance also failed. Intended to give Canadians equal voice in the air defence of the continent, the North American Air Defense agreement (NORAD) proved inadequate to guarantee Canadian interests during the Cuban missile crisis in 1962.[97] Endeavouring to be resolute, even defiant, Diefenbaker appeared weak and indecisive on the issue of nuclear weapons. Instead of engendering widespread support, his tough stand on atomic weapons not only decreased his popularity, but proved to be his undoing. Lester Pearson, the leader of the Opposition, capitalized on the issue of nuclear armaments on Canadian soil and defeated the Conservatives in the election of 1963. Diefenbaker's tenure as the leading advocate of toryism had come to an end.

Prominent conservative thinkers acknowledged that Diefenbaker had erred during his time in office. As early as October 1959 Morton, a long-time Conservative and supporter of John Diefenbaker, had bemoaned the ineffectuality of the new Tory government. 'The country seems to be prospering while its political life goes to the dogs,' he wrote to Murray S. Donnelly, provost of United College at the University of Manitoba. 'I think Diefenbaker is proving most inadequate as a prime minister, if only because he cannot shake the fear of defeat. We are going to pay long and bitterly,' Morton closed his letter, 'for the 22 years of Liberal rule.'[98]

Donald Creighton described as 'ill-fated' Diefenbaker's efforts 'to escape from the domination of American defence and foreign policy, and to make an independent Canadian decision in the controversial issue of nuclear disarmament.' On the overall achievement of the Tories Creighton declared: 'The Progressive-Conservatives had fought Howe's Pipeline Bill to the last; but though much was expected of the Diefenbaker government, it failed to adopt a positive policy of economic nationalism.'[99]

George Grant also criticized the Tories. He believed that Diefenbaker offered muddled approaches to Canadian-American relations. Further, the prime minister was unsure of what Canada ought to be. Hence, his vision of the nation foundered. More than proving deficient in economic and defensive policies, Diefenbaker confounded rhetoric and policy. Most problematic, he continued to use rhetoric even when it failed to produce favourable results.[100] Like Morton and Creighton, Grant understood that Diefenbaker the politician and the policy-maker proved incapable of meeting the exigencies of the modern dominion.

Although critical of Tory failures, conservative intellectuals nonetheless applauded Diefenbaker's unswerving advocacy of Canadian interests. Creighton, for instance, celebrated Diefenbaker's guile. He called him 'The only Canadian in power who dared seriously to question the wisdom of American leadership in defense and foreign policy.' He lauded Diefenbaker's defiance amid the crisis environment of October 1962. The prime minister 'declined to make the automatic response to American initiative in the Cuban crisis ... he dared to postpone the adoption of nuclear weapons against the wishes of the Kennedy administration.'[101] Unlike Pearson and the Liberals, he was no lackey of the Americans. Creighton thus acknowledged the enduring message of the Diefenbaker régime.[102]

Perhaps even more than Creighton, George Grant also emphasized Diefenbaker's resolve. Grant was firmly behind the Progressive Conservatives during the nuclear arms controversy. He wrote to Tommy Douglas, imploring the New Democratic party (NDP) leader not to join forces with the Liberals, defeat the government, and vote 'Diefenbaker out in the name of a servant of the United States like Lester Pearson.'[103] Whatever the inadequacies of John Diefenbaker, Grant had 'never felt such political loyalty [as he did] for [External Affairs Minister Howard] Green and Dief.' He praised the nationalism of these Tory statesmen. Green and Diefenbaker, in Grant's words, took the position of 'neutralism, a simple refusal to accept any demand from the present imperialism.' Indeed, Grant looked beyond Diefenbaker's political style and his ill-considered decisions. Instead, Diefenbaker's conservatism was to be commended; it was essential, after all, to Canada's struggle against the onslaught of 'imperialism.' The Tory leader's inadequacies notwithstanding, Diefenbaker was the 'apotheosis of straight loyalty.'[104] Ultimately, he remained the best hope for Canadian independence in the universal and homogeneous state.

The 1950s were a period of conservative myth-making. Impassioned statements on the relevance of the Crown and the British connection and on the nation's conservative heritage combined to produce a modern tory firmament. Post-war conservatism culminated, late in the decade, in the defeat of the Liberals and the rise to power of Diefenbaker nationalism. For the movement's intellectual leaders, Canadian toryism seemed at last to have arrived.

The tory triumph was all too brief. Whereas the late 1950s were a period of promise and stability, the 1960s proved to be just the opposite: a time of socio-political unruliness and disarray during which Canadian and western societies underwent profound transformation. The decade was reminiscent of the tumultuous 1940s. For many it was revolutionary, full of agitation, excitement, challenges to authority, and quests for ideological renewal. It was a time of social re-evaluation: student protests, burgeoning feminist and environmentalist movements, and profound social upheaval, embodied by the development of the 'counterculture.' Student demonstrations, Vietnam and nuclear weapons protests, and, in Canada, the arrival of the Front de Libération du Québec (FLQ) were particularly violent manifestations.

A crisis of authority in western social and political institutions was the root cause of the tumult of the 1960s.[105] The quest for stability, embodied in the cult of domesticity, materialism, and democracy, had provided a period of calm in the 1950s. Politically, the Cold War climate marginalized the radical movements of the interwar era, and the St Laurent Liberals provided a businesslike government. Socially, Canadians were still reacting against the disquietude of almost forty years of war, depression, and then war again. For the most part, they were too caught up in raising families and improving their material conditions to embroil themselves in larger political and ideological issues. Most bought into the rhetoric of democracy and anti-Communism, although this visceral and largely unreflective participation in world politics was as far as they went.

The 1960s disrupted the stolid calm of the 1950s. In foreign policy, greater numbers of citizens across the continent questioned the policy directions of the cold warriors. In America, nuclear strategies and east Asian policies came under increasingly close public scrutiny. In Canada, many joined the small circle (including Creighton and the other conservatives) who criticized monolithic approaches to international politics. Established in November 1959, the Combined Universities Campaign for Nuclear Disarmament (CUCND) represented new attitudes towards the Cold War. Although small in membership, the CUCND (along with the Voice of Women) managed to get 142,000 signatures on an anti-nuclear petition.[106] The newly formed NDP, moreover, took as its foreign policy stance a basically anti-nuclear position.

Added to growing political dissent was the reaction against the social authority of the 1950s. As Doug Owram indicates, the civil rights movement of the United States was vital in shaping the 1960s. It made an 'indelible mark on the post-war generation' because it demonstrated that 'a belief in racial inequality was so unacceptable as to not be a subject for serious intellectual discussion.' In the context of socio-ideological upheaval of the 1960s, the impact of the civil rights movement was twofold. First, it showed that the old political order, embodied in the fascistic tactics and segregationist politicians of southern governments, was simply out of touch with current movements towards racial harmony and equality. As such, it legitimized resistance to civil authority.[107] Second, it greatly reinforced the post-war ethic of democracy. It affirmed that all citizens, regardless of colour, creed, or ethnicity, ought to be treated the same. In pointing out glaring socio-economic and racial disparities, the movement made it clear that much work needed to be done to safeguard the democratic society. Indeed, the democratic spirit of the civil rights movement combined with later movements, such as Women's Liberation, urban poverty, native rights, and, of particular note to Canada, Quebec's Quiet Revolution, to reinforce the democratic-egalitarian tenor of the decade.

Although lacking the same explosive and violent tensions, the Quiet Revolution comes closest to the civil rights movement in its idealist grandeur and high moralism. At its base, the Quiet Revolution was about modernization and reform. On the one hand, it involved over-turning the highly conservative and sometimes repressive Union Nationale government of Maurice Duplessis. The Duplessis regime represented all that was corrupt and anti-progressive about Quebec. Replacing it and the prevalent church-dominated social and educational institutions meant that Quebec had rejected a highly conservative socio-political structure and could therefore completely modernize. The Quiet Revolution was as much about forsaking old institutions and an entire conservative era as it was about becoming 'maîtres chez nous.'

More than social and political modernization, the Quiet Revolution was bound up in the ideological rhetoric of reform and oppression and implied the need for social equality and economic parity. As the civil rights movement had done for the United States, a modernizing Quebec gave Canadians a cause. As separatist Pierre Vallières claimed, the Québécois were the 'white niggers of America.' Vallières was trying to claim the moral high ground for French-speaking Quebeckers, as had been done for Blacks in the south. That he succeeded among the many Canadians who were sympathetic to the modernizing plight of Quebec indicates the importance of the 'Quebec issue.' Indeed, led by Prime Minister Lester Pearson, most English-speaking Canadians wanted to understand the Québécois in the hope of resolving the Quebec problem. Their end goal was to address the needs of an important minority and thus to achieve the objective of national unity. In the spirit of the democratic age, they believed that the Québécois deserved to gain the equality that had been denied them for generations.

With the Quiet Revolution and other social-political movements, the 1960s had become a democratic-reformist age. Even more than the 1940s, the 1960s engendered bitter disillusionment for conservative intellectuals. Rather than expanding on the tory mythology or offering advice on how to apply conservative principles, academics such as Creighton and Grant renewed their critique of the country's development. If not utter despair, then alienation and disappointment characterized the mood of conservatives. The tory ideologues considered themselves marginalized in an increasingly egalitarian society (one that applauded 'democratic nationalism' in all its forms, especially the accommodation of Quebec). If the late 1950s were conducive to the development of the tory mythos, in brief, then events in the following decade contributed greatly to the demise of Canadian conservatism.

Extant before the Diefenbaker years, the critique of modernity and the attendant dirge for Canadian conservatism erupted after 1963.

George Grant's *Lament for a Nation* was perhaps the most devastating commentary on these baneful developments. Significantly subtitled *The Defeat of Canadian Nationalism*, the book was a political mourning for 'the end of Canada as a sovereign state.' Writing in the months after the 1963 Tory defeat, Grant demonstrated the symbolic value of the Diefenbaker administration. He admitted that inconsistencies and confusion bedevilled Diefenbaker's government, and his long essay indicted the policies and approaches to governing of the Diefenbaker Conservatives. Nevertheless, he stressed the nobility of Diefenbaker's political objectives: the winning of Canadian independence and the strengthening of Canadian nationalism. In spite of Diefenbaker's defects, the Tories were Canada's last hope. 'The 1957 election,' Grant explained, 'was the Canadian people's last gasp of nationalism.' The defeat of the Tories meant the end of Canadian sovereignty in North America. Most perniciously, Diefenbaker's downfall signalled the death of the Canadian idea, which was 'grounded in the wisdom of Sir John A. Macdonald ... that the only threat to nationalism was from the south' and was embodied in the notion that 'to be a Canadian was to build, along with the French, a more ordered and stable society' than the United States.[108] This reality had passed; Canada, Grant claimed, was at a new stage of its existence.

Grant lamented more, however, than the advent of continentalism and the decline of the British nexus – the nationalist-political components of the Canadian conservatism. *Lament* was also a commentary on Canada's fate: the inexorable and irrevocable integration into the American empire. This integration meant more than the union of economic, defensive, or foreign policies; it implied Canada's merger into what Grant termed the 'universal and homogeneous state.' Grant showed that it was absurd to expect that Canada, a nation existing next to an empire that was the core of modernity, could avoid absorbing American attitudes and ideological trappings. Canada's assimilation into the American empire was represented not merely in the triumph of continentalism, but also in the acceptance of the doctrine of liberalism. As evidenced in chapters 2 and 5 of his book, the liberalism that had engulfed all of North America was the crux of modernity. North American liberalism entailed, above all, the pursuit and augmentation of individual freedom. As Grant wrote, it allowed no 'appeal to the human good' 'to limit [individuals'] freedom to make the world as they choose.' 'Social order,' he continued, 'is a man-made convenience, and its only purpose is to increase freedom. What matters is that men shall be able to do what they want when they want ... "Value judg-ments" are subjective ... the human good is what we choose for our good.'[109] Liberalism thus was completely subjectivist and relativist except for one overriding good – the unremitting struggle to safeguard individual liberty against the combined tyrannies of revealed truth, philosophical constants, and enduring moral verities. It offered a tightly circumscribed, and indeed erroneous, view of the 'good life.' As such, it characterized, for Grant, the turpitude of modernity.

Bereft of moral standards and objective judgments, liberalism was not simply a depraved ideology. It was also a profoundly deleterious aspect of modernization; for it interfered with moderns' understand-ing of themselves, their worldly objectives, and their place in the universe. In a word, liberalism undermined an independent, philo-sophical understanding of the world. With no conception of the good life, nor any preconceived system of values, modern liberalism implied the 'end of ideology' for Grant. The quest for progress alone – material and technological progress – characterized the dogma, making irrele-vant all other approaches that did not include a similar vision of real-ity. Liberalism marginalized and subsumed other appeals to human freedom. It taught that no freedom could exist outside its bounds. Its only 'good,' Grant claimed, was to increase individual liberty as it saw fit.[110] Modern liberalism stultified moderns' perceptions of society because it crowded out competing views, denied the existence of abso-lute values, and presented itself as the only viable approach to individ-ual and collective freedom. Along with mass culture and modern technique, it contributed the ideological core of Grant's universal and homogeneous state.

A profoundly influential and burgeoning ideology, liberalism also impinged upon conservatism. For Grant, the growing predominance of liberalism meant the demise of the doctrine of conservatism. The 'impossibility of conservatism as a viable political ideology,' Grant wrote, marked the modern era. Modern conservatives, he explained further, faced a dilemma: 'if they are not committed to a dynamic tech-nology [i.e., to the concept of technological freedom], they cannot hope to make any popular appeal. If they are so committed, they cannot be conservatives.' Thus, beset by the inexorable forces of modernity, 'con-servatives' cannot conserve; they can be no more than 'defenders of whatever structure of power is at any moment necessary to technolog-ical change.' Indeed, there was no longer any such thing as an integral conservative. Contemporary conservatives, Grant noted, 'are not con-

servative in the sense of being custodians of something that is not subject to change. They are conservatives, generally, in the sense of
advocating a sufficient amount of order so that the demands of technology do not carry society into chaos.'[111]

Thus, no longer true to its original purposes and objectives,
traditional conservatism had disintegrated. Its demise, Grant added,
was particularly lamentable for Canada. Although Diefenbaker had
attempted to realize Canadian tory traditions and orientations, for
instance, he ultimately succumbed to the ineluctable allure of mid-
twentieth-century liberalism. Like so many other conservatives, he was
fated to perform the emasculated role of the modern conservative. The
Diefenbaker debacle, moreover, was simply a microcosm of the defeat
of Canadian conservatism at large. Like Diefenbaker, Canada could not
meet the expectations of its tory heritage. The vast majority of Canadians were destined to live entirely within the forms and assumptions of
liberalism. Canada as a corporate entity was destined to be a second-
rate member of the liberal-industrial order centred in the United States.
Technological liberalism had destroyed the Canadian nation just as it
had moral philosophy. With the disintegration of nationalism, ultimately, came also the demise of Canada's distinctiveness, its outlooks,
and perspectives. For Grant, Canadian toryism was dead.[112]

Less given to philosophical observations, Donald Creighton concurred nonetheless, with the general tenure of Grant's arguments. As
the 1960s wore on, Creighton devoted more of his energies to analysing bitterly the defeat of Canadian conservatism. The dismantling of
the Canada's tory identity was understandable, for Creighton, in the
decline of the 'Empire of the St Lawrence' and the concurrent rise of
continentalism. In contrast to Grant, who highlighted 1963 as a year of
tremendous symbolic significance, Creighton claimed that the decline
of the 'Empire' – the apotheosis of Canadian economic and political
integration – dated from 1940. Since that momentous year, 'Canada has
been exposed to the irresistible penetrative power of American military and economic imperialism.' Beginning with the Ogdensburg
Agreement of 1940, Canada's 'subordination to American foreign policy and American capital had continued progressively with scarcely a
serious interruption.' Its participation in NATO, its acceptance of
American leadership in the Korean War, and its willingness to permit
its defensive policy to be determined by American anti-Communist
mania all indicated the tendency towards a more complete continentalism. By the post-Diefenbaker era, Creighton claimed, Canada's conti-

nentalist orientation was fully realized. The real leader of the Liberals during the party's re-ascent to power was not Lester Pearson but John F. Kennedy. American press agents and presidential advisers worked closely with the Liberals, according to Creighton, to defeat the Progressive Conservatives and to claim Canada as the northernmost extension of the American realm. 'About the only manifestation of American power that was spared Canada in the [Bomarc] crisis [of 1963],' he remarked acerbically, 'was the sight of tanks rolling up Parliament Hill in Ottawa.'[113] Canadians, in short, had surrendered to the American eagle.

What was worse about Canada's growing subservience was that it appeared irreversible. In large measure because of Canadian neglect, the British Empire had dissolved after 1945. Not only was its military power gone forever, but its 'moral influence' in international affairs and its considerable potential economic clout had also ended. The Korean War and the Suez crisis, Creighton proclaimed, had 'dealt it blows from which it could not recover.'[114] The upshot was that Canada now stood alone. Shorn of its historic partnerships, the dominion was unable to provide a counterweight to the growing influence of the American empire.

Perhaps even more irksome than the decline of the Empire-Commonwealth was Canada's integration into the American ideological realm. Echoing Grant, Creighton explained the American penchant for conquering nature and harnessing natural resources for unending human consumption. Creighton agreed that North Americans had come to subscribe to what Grant called technological liberalism. 'The United States,' he wrote in 1971, 'has become the most advanced technological society of modern times. The American people subscribe, with fewer reservations and qualifications than any other people on earth, to the belief that progress means the liberation of man through the progressive conquest of nature by technology. The possibilities of the future, it has always been confidently assumed, are infinite; there must be no limitations on the satisfaction of whatever human wants industry decides to create by modern advertising.' This line of thinking proved particularly problematic, according to Creighton, because it had now become the credo of Canadians. Not only had the Americans 'stripped what the most richly endowed half-continent in the world can provide,' but they also had influenced Canadians' view of progress and imbued them with a stridently modern vision of freedom. 'Canadians, like Americans,' he explained, 'have been brought up to believe, as a cardinal article of national faith, that their natural resources were unbounded and inexhaustible.' Although this 'dictum' had proved false, many Canadians still believed it; they adjusted their values, their very identity to the American way of life. 'If Canada had decided to reserve its inheritance for its own people,' it might have had an almost limitless supply of resources, Creighton lamented. 'But we have now denied ourselves this choice; it will never be open to us again. We have come close to admitting that Canada is expendable in the service of the American technological empire.'[115]

Continentalism was a formidable, perhaps even an insurmountable, foe in Canada's history. Creighton felt that there was also an internal threat to the Canadian tory character. By the mid-1960s he had begun to rail against an increasingly prominent, and what he considered erroneous, view of the nation. He denounced as sheer fantasy the notion that Canada was a bicultural country and that the dominion's fathers had created the nation out of a bicultural compact. In an article tellingly entitled 'The Myth Of Biculturalism' (1966), Creighton took pains to undermine the position of those Canadians who put forth this fallacious understanding of the nation's heritage. The Confederation conferences, he explained, 'were not organized on ethnic or cultural lines, and their purpose was not a bilateral cultural agreement. On the contrary, their purpose was a political agreement between Canadians, both English-speaking and French-speaking on the one hand, and Maritimers on the other. It must always be remembered that the great aim of Confederation was a strong federal union of all the British provinces' in North America. '[T]he discussion of ethnic and cultural questions occupied a very minor part of the proceedings ... There was nothing that remotely approached a general declaration of principle,' he declared emphatically, 'that Canada was to be a bilingual or bicultural nation.'[116] The implications of Creighton's statements were clear. While Canada had always been linguistically and ethnically diverse, that diversity did not detract from its singular purpose and its common destiny. For Creighton, far from being a legal recognition of Canadian diversity, Confederation was, in fact, an acknowledgment of the new country's Laurentian heritage and its British traditions. It was a highly significant precondition, in short, in the realization of Macdonald's vision of the nation.

Creighton's pronouncements on Confederation were efforts to clarify history from a conservative perspective. They were also vividly contemporary. He believed that Confederation gave force to his own vision of

Canada. His interpretations were also designed to discredit a movement gaining prominence in the 1960s. Creighton castigated French-Canadian nationalism precisely because nationalists reinterpreted Canada's past for their own political purposes. To the nationalists, Creighton argued, Confederation was not a matter of good government or of economic growth; it was, instead, an instrument to satisfy French-Canadian cultural needs and to fulfil French-Canadian cultural aspirations. They 'grotesquely exaggerated the importance of language and culture' in Canadian history. They emphasized that, owing to the nation's new-found bicultural and bilingual heritage, Canada's 'real essence' 'must henceforth lie in the formal recognition of Canadian cultural duality.' Predicating their arguments on a skewed vision of Canadian history, Creighton declaimed, they attempted to redefine the essential components of the Canadian nationality. The recent obsession with reforming Canada according to its bicultural and bilingual pedigree was nothing more than a slick propaganda campaign to mislead a gullible public.[117] The Royal Commission on Bilingualism and Biculturalism, moreover, reflected the widespread sympathy, especially from the ruling Liberals, that the promotional campaign had garnered. According to Creighton, French-Canadian nationalists thus had misrepresented history and used the past to hoodwink a growing number of Canadians in the present. Above all, they had distorted Canada's origins and destinies and thus had betrayed the Canadian identity.

Canada had evolved by the late 1960s and early 1970s into what Creighton termed 'A Divided and Vulnerable Nation.'[118] The incessant continentalization of Canada's economy and culture and the growth of liberalism combined with internal strife to engender a country unsure of its beginnings and of its future direction. Creighton, like Grant, saw the 1960s as a decade of decline for the Canadian nation. What was more, there was little hope for the resurrection of a true and honest Canadianism. For both commentators, Canada's prospects were bleak.

Perhaps not as pessimistic, W.L. Morton nevertheless agreed with the substance of Grant's and Creighton's message: Canada had experienced enormous strains in the 1960s. 'Canada,' Morton wrote in 1964, 'is at a crossroads. Either we go forward in the community that has come into being over three and a half centuries ... or we disappear as Canada and as Canadians.'[119] As the decade continued, however, he became less sanguine about Canada's future. Echoing Creighton's arguments, Morton saw Canada emerging into the 1970s as a weakened, insecure nation.

Morton claimed that there were three great challenges to the Canadian identity in the 1960s: the Quiet Revolution and the growth of Quebec nationalism; the decline of Great Britain as a Great Power and the 'end of Britain as the exemplar and inspiration of Canadian life'; and 'the realization of Canadians that American protection, investment, and friendship, carry with them a price, neither stated nor demanded but inevitable, of the complete Americanization of Canadian thought, government, and national purpose.'[120] First, concerning French-Canadian nationalism, Morton put forth a critique similar to that of his colleague Creighton. Morton disdained Quebec nationalists' misuse and distortion of Canadian history. Like Creighton, he argued that Quebec nationalists ignored or wilfully distorted historical fact. As a consequence, they advanced a misleading notion of cultural duality. 'They are asking us to resume the dualism,' he explained, 'the duality of political sovereignty that ... was deliberately and emphatically discarded by both English and French in the confederation scheme of 1867.' While Morton was more willing than Creighton to recognize minority rights, the two historians concurred on the 'cultural' implications of Confederation. The fathers of Confederation had 'liquidated' dualism, Morton declared, in favour of 'a vast new combination of the Canadas and the Maritimes.'[121] Any claim to the contrary was clearly a distortion of the past.

Although he believed it to be a historic fallacy, Morton condemned dualism not just for historic reasons. Like Creighton, he feared that the assertion of the myth of Canada's cultural duality would poison the contemporary climate and undermine the Canadian identity. Cultural and linguistic duality, he wrote in 1964, 'destroy the civil and economic significance of the Canadian unity. [They] blight the significance of the Canadian experiment.' Intended to strengthen the Canadian nation, dualism instead obscured historical realities and hindered the development of a strong, centralized nation with common goals and purposes. For Morton, to include dualism as a tenet of modern Canadianism was 'folly.'[122]

Morton's and Creighton's comments on Quebec and national unity were voiced within the context of the Quiet Revolution and the federal government's response to the Quebec issue. Sensing a great danger to national unity, the Liberal government of Lester B. Pearson reacted quickly to the Quiet Revolution. Upon taking office in 1963, Pearson called a royal commission to investigate the status of bilingualism in the federal government bureaucracy as well as in the provinces and in the minds of Canadians at large. The preliminary report of the Royal Commission on Bilingualism and Biculturalism was not promising. Canada, in the words of Davidson Dunton, chairman of the commission, was passing through the greatest crisis of its history without being fully conscious of the fact. The commissioners found, furthermore, that for the first time Quebeckers had seriously rejected the agreement of 1867. They made two important preliminary recommendations: they advised that English-speaking Canada abandon its attitude of superiority towards Quebec; and they advocated instead an 'equal partnership' between the two majorities of Canada.

Despite these dire realizations, there was some optimism. The commission reported that unlike the situation in the recent past, Canadians outside Quebec were no longer oblivious to Quebec issues. As the Quiet Revolution gained momentum in Quebec, Canadians throughout the country seemed concerned about what Quebec wanted and about what it would take to accommodate Quebec and make the Québécois feel at home within Canada. There were additional reasons for optimism. Reaction to the report was generally favourable. There was certainly denunciation of the report – some newspapers and citizens complained that French Canada had yet again taken over the national agenda. It seemed also that the farther one got from Quebec, criticism for the report grew. Most Canadians, however, seemed to understand Quebec's plight and accepted that change was needed. They realized that Quebec was the key to national unity; if Quebec was not brought in as a full partner in Confederation, then national unity would suffer, and ultimately the country might be torn asunder.[123]

Morton and Creighton numbered among the royal commission report's chief detractors. As we have noted, they chided the commission for presenting a bastardized view of Canada's past and current constitutional status but most of all, because it placed Quebec at the top of the national agenda. Indeed, the conservative-nationalists objected to the commission not simply because of its inaccurate views and tainted recommendations; they despised it because it took precious attention away from the imperial nexus, Macdonald's nation-building, Canada's tory heritage, and other aspects integral to the conservative vision of the country. The Quebec issue had derailed the momentum of the tory freight train of the late 1950s. Through the liberal nationalists, Quebec was holding the nation hostage, something that ultimately would have grave consequences, namely, the demise of tory Canada. Against the backdrop of the Quiet Revolution and the liberal nationalism of the 1960s, feelings of frustration and alienation grew among the conservative nationalists. In a few short years Quebec had not only radically altered the issue of national unity, but also stifled the prospects of tory nationalism.[124]

The Quebec problem troubled the conservative nationalists, in large measure because it deflected attention from vital issues like the weakening of the British connection. The decline of 'British' Canada was, indeed, as important as the Quiet Revolution. As noted, Morton was an unabashed supporter of the imperial tie. The British nexus, he argued, 'had always added to the momentum of [the] Canadian nationality.' Britain had been 'the brightest of Canada's windows on the world. It was a prime Canadian interest to keep that tie strong, the window clear,' Morton continued, extending the metaphor. Yet after a brief period of regeneration during the war, 'the tie had weakened, the window darkened.'[125] The British Empire had become, for Canadian nationalists like Morton, 'little more than an academic concern' and 'a vague racial sentiment.'[126]

For Morton, the ending of the British Empire affected Canada in an 'ultimate [and] fundamental way.'[127] It meant, above all, that Canada was alone in North America. Uncontested Americanization was indeed the chief impediment to the development of the Canadian nation. As Morton pointed out, continentalism was a constant feature of Canada's national existence. The pressures of Americanization continued to build into the post-war era. 'After 1961,' Morton explained, Canada experienced 'ever-growing dependence on American investment, accompanied more and more by direction of the Canadian economy by Americans and the steady vitiation of American technology and its inevitable running dog, American advertising.' The unabated continentalism of the 1960s, Morton went on to argue, manifested itself in 'a crescendo of apprehension about the fate of Canada.' Through James E. Coyne, governor of the Bank of Canada, Walter Gordon, and economist Melville Watkins, Morton claimed, Canada's plight was realized. Gordon and Watkins, for instance, had exposed 'the extraordinary degree to which American capital had ... come to dominate Canadian life.'[128] George Grant's *Lament for a Nation* (1965) and Donald Creighton's *Canada's First Hundred Years* (1970), moreover, were well-rounded commentaries on the plight of modern Canada.

Morton's own essay, 'Canada under Stress in the Sixties' (1971), among others, can also be added to this list. Less pessimistic than Grant or Creighton, Morton emerged from the 1960s hopeful that Canada's tory destiny was realizable. He hoped that continentalism, separatism, and other modern 'frictions' might be controlled.[129] Yet Morton was a realist. Like that of Grant and Creighton, his work in the 1960s was also a sombre warning that continentalism and other forces threatened the Canadian identity. As it was for other Canadian nationalists, Canada, for Morton, was at a crossroads. To survive, Canadians must realize their corporate identity and understand the threats to that nationality. 'Either we go forward in the community that has come into being over three and a half centuries,' he remarked, 'or we disappear as Canada and as Canadians.'[130] Morton, in short, understood the realities of the last third of the century. If the impediments to Canadian nationalism persisted unchecked, Canada would suffer grave consequences. If the discord of the 1960s 'continued and combined,' he warned, 'they might well destroy Canada.'[131]

Events of the 1960s were indeed inimical to the development of the Canadian identity. They did more, however, than undermine Canadian traditions; during the decade conservative critics saw the emergence of the fully modernist consciousness, a new world-view that embraced change as a defining characteristic. As such, the age was hostile to the values of permanence and stability. For those critics, the 1960s were a time of revolutionary transformation, a profound rejection of values, traditions, and continuities. They represented not only a break with the past, but more important, the destruction of preservationist tendencies and traditional orientations. They demonstrated that the transition between the Victorian order and the new world had finally come to a close. In a word, the 1960s represented the triumph of modernism.

That the events of the decade particularly distressed the critics of modernity is clear. Although engrossed in the task of nation-building, W.L. Morton had an opportunity to reflect on the greater implications of modernity. In 1964 he discussed a 'time of great depression' that was as much a part of his growing disenchantment with the modern era as it represented his concern over the plight of the nation. Referring to the despair that overcame him after the symbolic defeat of 1963, Morton revealed, '[S]uddenly I realized with the rush of an avalanche, and with all the clarity of loss that the world in which we live, the world I had bothered with and had tried to keep in modest repair, that world no longer existed. It was no longer there, it had vanished. I was like a man alone in the Arctic waste, in the twilight and with no landmark.' A 'collapse of assumptions,' a 'desiccation of values' characterized this dolorous period. Indeed, the 1960s signalled the end of the Victorian world of

Morton's upbringing. Most significant, they symbolized the rupture of outlooks and sociocultural values centuries in the making.[132]

Even more direct than Morton on the tumultuous nature of the 1960s was Northrop Frye. For Frye, the 'sixties' were years of unmitigated change, 'an age of undirected revolution.'[133] 'All kinds' of revolutionary movements distinguished it; Blacks, women, students, unions, or any group distinct from the 'establishment,' Frye claimed, developed movements. Yet the revolutionary age penetrated deeper; it also impinged on the intellect, and, specifically, on one's perception of reality. The 1960s were 'the McLuhan age'; they were a period of 'becoming adjusted to new techniques of communication, more particularly the electronic ones.' The 'news media' were particularly important to Frye in this new technological period. They exemplified the turbulence of the age. Whereas life consists generally of routine and continuity, Frye explained, 'news' is that which breaks the routine. Through the fabrication of 'issues,' the news media polarizes debate and forces people to come down on one side or the other. 'Thus,' Frye explained further, 'the new media have, already built into them, as a necessity of their existence, the quality of undirected revolution.'[134] Along with the myriad socio-political reactions against the established order, they contributed to the anarchy of the age.

Frye went even further, however, claiming that the revolutions of the 1960s had become a defining feature of the period. To illustrate his point, he likened the tumult of the decade to a war. The penchant for pitting the 'counterculture' against the 'establishment,' he explained, resembled a battle between two nations or two fighting factions. For previous generations the First or Second World War defined their formative periods; the generation growing up during the 1960s had its own defining event: the 'revolutionary' struggle against the oppressive establishment. This 'war,' he added, also took on 'warlike manic depressive qualities.' 'As in war, where carnage and exhilaration can stand side by side, in the 1960s it [was] permissible to tout the moon landing as the greatest event since creation, and yet still have the depressive side of self-destructive activities of the youth.'[135] The 1960s, for Frye, thus made manifest the incongruities of war. For the 'combatants,' however, the age afforded no such clarity of vision. Instead, it demonstrated only the virtue of the fight and the importance of revolution. The period had indeed a powerful hold on the minds of those who lived through it.

Perhaps not as reflective as Frye or even Morton, others commented, nonetheless, on the distinct, volatile nature of the 1960s. Hilda Neatby, for example, saw the decade as a culmination of several long-term trends. By the late 1960, she believed, civilization was in grave danger. Western civilization, which Nazism and later Communism had imperiled from without and scientism and false ideas of democracy had endangered from within, now faced its greatest challenge because of 'a failure to teach the young to love religion, learning and books.' As her biographer writes, Neatby 'had been warning of the possibility of collapse of civilization for thirty years. The rise of student power now seemed to be a clear sign of the coming end – the rising up of the unlearned against those who were failing to teach.'[136]

Like Neatby, Creighton considered the 1960s the culmination of an epoch, the epitome of modernity. During the decade modern materialist tendencies accelerated: industrialization and urbanization 'moved forward with increasing speed'; 'the building of houses, "high rise" apartments, hotels, shopping plazas, and city-centres never seemed to catch up with the demand'; technology 'lightened the business of living to an extent which would have seemed miraculous only thirty years before.' 'The average Canadian of the 1960s,' Creighton concluded, 'had the benefit of services which, in ancient times, could have been provided only by about four hundred slaves.'[137]

Expressed in a different manner, Claude Bissell concurred with Neatby's and Creighton's views on the changeability of the 1960s. For Bissell, president of the University of Toronto, change at his institution and Canadian universities generally reflected greater social transformation. The Canadian university, he asserted, continued to be 'feudalistic' in structure into the early part of the decade. Despite intrusions of the state and private business, the university's hierarchical structure had been maintained so that 'initiatives could be strongly exercised at the top,' while the faculty could retreat to the 'safety, security, and the illusion of freedom in a separate, protected kingdom.' After 1968, however, the edifice collapsed: 'the hierarchical separation was challenged, first by the staff and then by the students; the alliance of the university with business and government was attacked, on the left from staff and students, who saw it as corrupting, and on the right by government, who rejected an alliance of partners and called for a master-servant relationship; the sanctity of knowledge was questioned and new qualities were exalted – sensitivity, involvement, a feeling of community solidarity. University education was thought of not as something to be earned by the sweat of the brow or by superior performance in examinations; it was a natural right, and, therefore, should be subsidized.'[138] Sit-ins, student disorder, and occasional violence on campuses, furthermore, reflected the demands of an increasingly vocal youth and the increasingly politicized environment of the decade. The venerable academy had become a sounding board for the stresses of life in the late 1960s.

Whether manifested in student unrest, material and technological advancement, or in national-cultural change, the 1960s were a period of transformation. As such, they provided a backdrop for the decline of Canadian conservatism. Conservatives themselves suggested that the age contributed to the demise of conservatism in its many guises. They were right. Conservatism simply could not withstand the centrifugal forces of the decade. During the 1960s the critics saw the development of trends inimical to the concept of 'aristodemocracy,' indeed, the fruition of a democratic culture that had little association with intellectual democracy. Concern for the American civil rights movement, a growing interest in gender parity, and, specifically in the Canadian context, sympathy for goals of linguistic and cultural equality all characterized the modernist concept of democracy and freedom. Dissent movements of many kinds added to the burgeoning democratic culture. Protests such as those over the Vietnam War, nuclear armaments, student power, and the role of women engendered discord. Yet they also showed the willingness of Canadians to voice concern over pressing issues. Perhaps most indicative of this tendency towards democratization was the development of the democratic universities. As explained in chapter 4, the university moved from being an institution for the education of the elite to a community-oriented facility designed to provide a training that most young Canadians had now come to expect, even demand. With growing numbers of Canadians attending universities, the prospect of establishing a Platonic hierarchy was becoming remote indeed. The fight for educational democracy, which had been initiated with Deweyite educational concepts, had now penetrated all levels of the system. From the perspective of conservatives, the universities had been lost to the masses.

The notion of intellectual democracy thus could not survive the hostile 1960s. It languished in the hothouse environment of modern democracy, egalitarianism, and most of all, the 'revolutionary' movements of protest, student discontent, and separatist nationalism. The tory-nationalist mythology suffered a similar fate. As we will see next, in the later 1960s there was a resurgence of nationalist sentiment. The New Left and other nationalist groups embraced the conservative nationalism of Harold Innis, Donald Creighton, George Grant, and others. Thus, they seemed to resurrect a dying tradition. Yet the new nationalism stressed primarily the anti-American features of tory nationalism. As such, it largely ignored Canada's tory heritage, its enduring conservative character, or its inherent 'Britishness.' As a result, there was very little sense of a positive Canadian identity based on the traditions of Canadian toryism. The remnants of tory nationalism had been co-opted to service the needs of a class-based ideological movement. Nonetheless, the death of the new nationalism by the 1970s was the final blow for the conservatives. Although different from the tory vision of Creighton and the others, it had represented an opportunity for conservative nationalists to influence Canadians and to show them the importance of a conservative-nationalist vision. As national fervour faded, however, the last chance of the intellectual elite to gain real relevance in the eyes of the new generation also diminished.

The 1960s were, in sum, markedly different from the decades that had preceded them. The post-war period was, to be sure, a tumultuous time. Yet it seemed to have connections with past values and orientations that made possible the rise of mythologies such as intellectual democracy and the tory identity. In the 1960s these links seemed to be disappearing for good; Canada was in a stage of cultural and intellectual redefinition and re-formation. Amid the chaos and intellectual ferment of the age, Canadians became inured to values rooted in history and tradition. By the 1970s, as we will see in the next chapter, intellectuals rarely criticized society or offered conservatism as a means to counteract the abuses of the modern age. When they did so, they could be sure that their voices were marginalized and, worse still, that their thoughts were not taken seriously. The ascendancy of modernity was thus complete.

7

Epilogue: The Demise of the Conservative-Nationalist Vision and the Triumph of Modernity

When in 1965 Dalton Camp became president of the Progressive Conservatives, the end of the old-style conservatism of the party was near. Camp was elected on the strength of his desire to review the leadership of John Diefenbaker. At the subsequent leadership convention, held in Toronto in September 1967, Diefenbaker went down to an ungracious defeat. After ranting at his detractors and vigorously defending his policies and political visions, he finished a humiliating fifth on the first ballot. Diefenbaker continued to sit in the House of Commons as a bitter critic of Liberalism and in defiance of his own party and its new leader, Robert Stanfield.

In spite of this political tenacity, however, Diefenbaker's ouster was fraught with significance. Camp's triumph resulted in a deeply divided party. More than that, it ushered in a new era for the Progressive Conservatives, one in which the party embarked on a new direction, a firm departure from the policies of the past. Stanfield endeavoured to develop policies to move the party away from Diefenbaker's curious amalgam of prairie populism and traditional conservatism. In doing so, he tried to court the young and the urban-dweller.[1] What was more fundamental, Stanfield initiated important changes in party doctrine. He moved the party away from Diefenbaker's 'unhyphenated Canadianism' and instead tried to ensure that his party would reflect current political realities and address the concerns of a wider sweep of the Canadian populace. Within a few short years he extricated the party from the policies and outlooks of Macdonald, Borden, Meighen, Diefenbaker, and their like.

In a much larger sense, Stanfield's emergence symbolized the demise of the Canadian tory tradition that had been decades in the making. It also mirrored the fundamental changes that were occurring in Canadian society. The transformation of the tory national-political vision – in part, the belief in the dominion's inherent British character and in an unified, pan-Canadian culture – showed how issues of pluralism and Quebec's place in the federation had come to overshadow conservative-nationalism. More distressing, it indicated how the Conservative party, the historic bastion of tory values,[2] had succumbed to the pressures of modern social and political realities. To the tory critics, the Conservatives were becoming like their despised Liberal rivals. The early Diefenbaker period had seemed full of promise; the period that followed was characterized by despair and further marginalization of the voices of the spokesmen of Canadian toryism.

The death of the old Conservative party dealt a severe blow to traditional conservative nationalism. After the party's demise, this form of nationalism continued only in fragmented form in the theory and rhetoric of the New Left. Despite certain affinities, the new nationalism of radical youth was not compatible with the values of the old movement. Whatever the similarities between the two types of nationalism, by the mid-1970s the nationalism of the New Left also was waning. When it failed, the remnants of traditional nationalism failed along with it. Ultimately, the tory vision of Canada was vanquished, while the Liberal service state prevailed.

Vital to the new direction of the Conservative party was an acceptance of Canada's bicultural nature. Under Diefenbaker the question of French-Canadian nationalism had been largely ignored, but Stanfield's Conservatives made Quebec an important issue. As the 1968 party platform indicated, while 'Canada is, and should be, one nation,' it was nevertheless foundationally a bicultural entity. The country was composed of 'two founding peoples with historic rights to maintain their language and culture.' Party platforms and electoral strategies were supplemented with political action. Stanfield's selection of Marcel Faribault as his Quebec lieutenant in 1968 was an acknowledgment of the electoral importance of the province. It also demonstrated the Tories' rejection of the pan-Canadian cultural nationalism of Diefenbaker and that of the party's forebears. For, as Faribault himself stated, the 'deux nations' idea was a historical reality and 'should always be remembered, the more for being so often ignored in the past.' In an April 1972 speech delivered in Toronto, the heart of old 'British' Ontario but now a symbol of the ethnic diversity of the new Canada,

Stanfield reaffirmed his rejection of a monolithic national vision. Canada, he claimed, was not a nation that 'believed in the philosophy of the melting pot.' Nor was it a country 'where it is necessary to submerge your national origins, or forget the language of the country of your birth in order to function as a good citizen.'[3] Unhyphenated Canadianism and an overarching Britishness were dead as first principles of Canadian Conservatism.

The marginalization of old policies and party attitudes reflected the country's prevailing mood. The Conservatives' new Quebec policy pointed to the country's generally accommodating attitude towards French Canada. The Royal Commission on Bilingualism and Biculturalism, as we noted in the last chapter, had made English-speaking Canadians aware of the issues of the Quiet Revolution. As the centennial approached, the political mood favoured a resolution of the increasingly troublesome Quebec question. The year 1967 was particularly significant. Under the leadership of Ontario Premier John Robarts, for instance, representatives of provincial governments were summoned to Toronto to try to resolve the Quebec question. The meeting, more of a think-tank, was called the Confederation for Tomorrow Conference. At the conference, which took place in November 1967, the premiers were able to convince Quebec Premier Daniel Johnson that the Canadian house could indeed be refurbished and modernized so as to accommodate a wayward son. Pearson's government followed Robarts's example. It called a constitutional conference for February 1968 to gather information on how to change the British North America (BNA) Act. This meeting was tacit acknowledgment that the structures of the country required fundamental change if Canada was to survive into its next century. The election of a new prime minister in June was perhaps most significant of all. As historian Ramsay Cook has argued, the election of Pierre Elliott Trudeau was the culmination of a growing, though very fragile, national consensus. Trudeau's promise to reform the federal system to allow for a truly equal partnership between French and English Canada was palatable to most segments of Canadian society. With Trudeau's electoral triumph, the federal government had, for the first time in a long while, legitimate claim to the broad support of Canadian opinion.[4]

Through the beginning of the new decade, additional constitutional dialogues, such as the Victoria conference in 1971, provided further testimony to the willingness of Canadian politicians to resolve the Quebec question. The English-speaking provinces continued to be

open to a pluralistic view of the nation. The Québécois were also pressing for change. Much had been altered in the province in last decade
and a half. As late as the Tremblay Commission (which had reported to
the Quebec government in 1956), the hoary pre-modernist, pre-industrial character of the Quebec people was emphasized. Specifically, the
commissioners railed against industrialization. 'If the Conquest put
French Canadians out of tune with the political institutions,' they reasoned, 'the industrial revolution put them out of harmony with social
institutions.' Here the commissioners echoed the arguments of the old
French-Canadian nationalists: modernism, in the forms of the materialism, born of industrialization, they contended, detracted from the
fundamental spiritual virtues of the French-Canadian people. The
industrial process was 'in complete disaccord with the Catholic French
Canadian culture.' It fostered materialism and individualism over spiritualism and communalism; it was technical and scientific rather than
humanist. Quebeckers, the commissioners concluded, had to choose
between 'the Christian concept and materialism, either in its pragmatic
or philosophic form.'[5] The options were clear: to choose the modern
world was to ensure the demise of the race; to opt for traditional
French-Canadian values would help to safeguard 'la survivance.'
    In the years following the Tremblay Commission, however, the prov-
ince was transformed. The urban-industrial process, which had begun
decades earlier, intensified throughout the late 1950s and the 1960s.
More important, French-speaking Quebeckers experienced a revolution in outlooks and attitudes. According to historian Michael Behiels,
they underwent a 'revolution of mentalities.'[6] Led by the intelligentsia,
the Québécois (as they were now calling themselves) began to de-
emphasize the all-encompassing role of the church and spirituality in
their lives. Instead, they began to emphasize the material conditions of
French-speaking Quebeckers and agitated in favour of becoming the
financial 'masters of their own house.' In addition to material betterment, they sought liberal and modern reforms such as the separation
of church and state and increased democratization. Thus, new values
and outlooks combined with the nationalization programs of the
Lesage government to ensure that by the late 1960s Quebec had
become fully modern.
    This Quiet Revolution was, as we have seen, indicative of the change
of the 1960s. More fundamentally, it proved to be a microcosm of modernization for the country at large. Within a decade Quebeckers had
undergone the ideological (if not the scientific and industrial) transfor-

mations that English Canada had been experiencing for decades. Events in Quebec were, in consequence, fraught with meaning, especially for the critics of modernity.

At best, critics considered pre-modern Quebec a bulwark against the intrusion of modernity. George P. Grant, for instance, considered Roman Catholicism and the social structures of French Canada to be barriers to the development of the universal and homogeneous state. Through the conservatism of Catholicism, Grant explained, French Canadians could find their salvation.[7] Adding her voice to Grant's, Hilda Neatby stressed the cultural values inherent to the French-Canadian civilization. 'Looking at each culture [French and English speaking],' Neatby asserted, 'the English have much to learn from Quebec on appreciation of intellectual and artistic values, of general culture as distinguished from specialization, of the value of family ties, of a community as well as an individual expression of religious belief.'[8] At worst, critics saw Quebec as a quaint, pre-modern society that had withdrawn into itself and therefore posed little threat to the development of a wider, pan-Canadian nationalism. Indeed, Donald Creighton intimated throughout his writings in the post-war period the subservience of French Canada and the French-Canadian identity to the greater goal of national unity.[9] Even as his colleagues were becoming sensitized to the issue of the Quiet Revolution, Creighton's position remained unchanged: Canadians must avoid bilingualism and biculturalism and remain true to the great nineteenth-century nation-state. The establishment of a pan-Canadian identity was, for Creighton and the other conservatives, central to the development of an enduring Canadianism.[10]

Given these views of Quebec, the disruptions of the 1960s were highly significant. First, they represented, to the anti-modernists, the end of an alliance to past traditions and values. The advent of a modern, technocratic state exemplified the triumph of political modernization. Second, the Quiet Revolution challenged the conservative vision of the nation. The new Quebec nationalism simply could not be reconciled with the older strain of Anglo-Canadian nationalism. A modernized Quebec detracted from one of the most fundamental objectives of the conservative nationalists: the development of 'one Canada,' a vision based on historical formulations and steeped in traditional national outlooks. Thus, along with continentalism and an accommodating national mood towards Quebec, Quebec modernization erected a massive, perhaps even insurmountable, barrier to conservative nationalism.

Aside from the problems posed by Quebec and the Quiet Revolution, developments in English-Canadian nationalism also contributed to the demise of Canadian toryism. Whereas in the 1950s and early 1960s conservative-nationalist history had been vibrant under the guidance of Creighton, Morton, and Grant, by the mid-1960s this approach was disappearing. The reorientation of the Progressive Conservative party accelerated this trend. Once the domain of conservatives, nationalism and nationalist history were co-opted by the New Left.

Composed chiefly of students and young professors, the New Left was an amorphous movement preoccupied with students' issues, the Vietnam War, civil rights, and the bureaucracy of the multiversity. Among the intellectual leadership of the movement, however, foreign investment, specifically, increased American involvement in the Canadian economy, became key issues. At the end of the 1960s corporate America had penetrated deeply into the Canadian economy. The peak year for foreign ownership in Canada was 1972, with the petroleum industry (99 per cent foreign ownership) and the manufacturing industry (72 per cent foreign ownership) leading the way. Furthermore, 'foreign,' predominantly American, investment continued to flood into Canada. Even Canadian universities, which had grown so much in the previous few years, were home to many American scholars.[11]

The New Leftists responded to these distressing developments. Using Marx, they argued that Canada had historically developed as a 'continentalist' and 'liberal' entity, dependent on American capital. More significant, they employed the theories of the conservative nationalists to explicate the plight of modern Canada. Through the latter half of the 1960s New Left theorists carefully studied the strictures of the tory nationalists. Extrapolating from Harold Innis, who had laid bare Canada's character as a marginal economy, they showed how Canada lived in a subservient, peripheral arrangement vis-à-vis the United States;[12] from George Grant, they stressed that Canada was developing, under the influence of its technologically advanced southern neighbour, into a universal and homogeneous state.[13] Using Innis, Grant, Morton and Creighton, they provided a devastating critique of the historical liberal hegemony in Canada.[14] Like their intellectual antecedents, they railed against the pro-Americanism of the Liberal party; and, as the critics of academic modernization had done, they even denounced the increasingly technocratic, Americanized, and antihumanist bent of the multiversity.[15]

Gad Horowitz went further than merely co-opting the ideas of the conservative nationalists. He endeavoured not only to define Canada's 'un-American' political culture, but also to make a theoretical link between Canadian toryism and socialism. In *Canadian Labour in Politics* (1968), Horowitz argued that unlike the political culture of another new society, the United States, that of anglophone Canada did not develop a monolithic liberal mythology that was exclusive of other ideologies; instead, toryism and socialism were very much aspects of Canada's political traditions. He contended that English-speaking Canada was characterized by non-liberal elements – that is, tory and socialist 'touches.' One of the most important un-American character-istics of English Canada, he wrote, was the 'failure of English-Cana-dian liberalism to develop the one true myth, the nationalist cult, and the parallel failure to exclude toryism and socialism as "un-Canadian"; in others words [it did not exclude] the legitimacy of ideological diver-sity in Canada.'[16]

Having established Canada's tory and socialist elements, and hence Canada's political distinctiveness in North America, Horowitz went on to demonstrate the interrelationship between the two ideologies. He argued that the 'corporate-organic-collectivist ideas' inherent to tory-ism were vital to the development in Canada of socialism; they joined with the 'radical rationalist-egalitarian' component of liberalism to establish the preconditions for socialism. In short, Horowitz claimed that in toryism, itself a remnant of pre-Enlightenment political culture, were contained the very seeds of the modern ideology of socialism.[17]

Claiming that it was more than a theoretical relationship, however, Horowitz demonstrated the socialist precursors of Canadian conserva-tism. As one example, he cited the willingness of the Conservative party – a principal repository of Canadian toryism – to 'use the power of the state for the purpose of developing and controlling the econ-omy.' Unlike American conservatives, who had no tradition of using public power in aid of national purposes, Canadian conservatives were willing to restrain individual rights to serve the common good. The best example of the interplay of the tory and socialist ideologies, however, was the phenomenon of 'red toryism.' Horowitz defined the red tory as an individual who has affinities to both conservative and socialist ideas, whether in a vague or casual sense or as a 'conscious ideological Conservative with some "odd" socialist notions (W.L. Mor-ton) or a conscious ideological socialist with some odd tory notions (Eugene Forsey).' More than this, red toryism implied the sharing between 'tory and socialist minds' of '*some* crucial assumptions, orientations, and values' to such an extent that the two ideologies seem 'not as enemies but as two different expressions of the same ideological outlook' (italics in original).[18] It entailed a world-view that shared tory and socialist elements so thoroughly that it was impossible to say that its proponents preferred one ideology over the other. For Gad Horowitz, George Grant epitomized this highest conception of red toryism. Indeed, Grant's political ideas, his associations with both the Conservatives and the NDP, his defence of Diefenbaker and the British tradition, and his attack on liberal individualism and Americanization all were proof, in Horowitz's mind, of the interconnectivity of toryism and socialism.

As Gad Horowitz and others attempted to show, there seemed to be considerable intellectual affinities between the old conservative nationalists and the New Leftists, between toryism and socialism. Both groups were drawn together not only as a result of a shared world-view, but also because of a common reaction to certain historical realities. Both profoundly distrusted Liberal foreign policy and the technocratic state. In the minds of the members of both groups, the Liberal technocrats were the real enemies of Canada. Further, old and new nationalists alike shared an aversion to the values and ultimate objectives of the American empire. They despised the fact that the United States had become Canada's national ideal. What is more, they both wanted much more than simply to explain the historical conditions of Canada or to theorize about current predicaments. They desired, on the contrary, to counter the unprecedented influence of the United States in Canada. Above all else, like the tory critics, the New Left wanted to extricate Canada from the clutches of American cultural and economic imperialism. As it was for Creighton, Morton, and the others, nationalism was the way to resolve this most pressing problem. Thus, despite the differences of the intellectual movements, many of the key tenets and objectives of traditional nationalism lived on in the new variant. The New Left provided consolation for a failing tradition; it provided a glimmer of hope in a desperate age.

Traditional nationalism, especially in its anti-continentalist, anti-liberal aspects, was popular among members of the New Left for a variety of reasons. American foreign policy seemed increasingly disquieting, especially in the light of U.S. involvement in Vietnam. On the domestic front, urban riots, campus violence, and a spate of political assassinations showed that the American concept of democracy was not one to imitate. More important, members of the New Left were attracted to nationalism because the expression of a national identity was a means of allaying the intrusion of American capital as well as pernicious American political and philosophical doctrines. As one proponent of the New Left put it in 1970, the purpose of Canadian nationalism must not be doctrinal, but must oppose the liberal individualism and the 'democratic capitalism' of the United States. '[I]ts purpose,' the author continued, 'must be to preserve on the northern half of this continent, a society which does not share the liberal conformitarianism, the isolationism and the messianism of the United States.'[19]

As it did for the conservative nationalists, nationalism for the New Leftists had a very specific role to perform. It functioned as the main means by which Canada had staved off the continentalizing United States. Thus, it was vital to maintaining the integrity and indeed the very independence of the Canadian nation. Even a cursory reading of any one of a variety of issues of the *Canadian Dimension*, the New Left's main forum, revealed this basic utilitarian purpose. While dubious of the outcome, George Grant, the old tory nationalist, urged advocates of nationalism to 'preserve ... what is left of Canadian sovereignty.'[20] For Grant, as for the New Leftists, economic and ideological continentalism was a blight on modern Canada, a condition for which nationalism seemed to be the only cure.

Despite considerable similarities and some common purposes, however, there were fundamental differences between conservative and New Left nationalism, the most important of which was in their definitions of the character of Canadian nationalism. Whereas the Canadian tory identity was crucial to conservative-nationalism, socialism was the sine qua non of the New Left nationalists.[21] While humanist traditions, a British heritage, and tory values differentiated Canadians from Americans for the conservative nationalists, the New Leftists quantified Canada's distinctiveness chiefly in terms of its socialist affinities. For the New Leftists, Canadian nationalism had little to do with Canada's tory orientations and its colonial outlooks; instead, Canada was set off from its American neighbour by a history of state involvement in directing the economy and in building the nation more generally.[22] State interventionism must persist, they advised, into the 1970s and beyond; for through a 'new National policy not of cultural tariffs but of cultural bounties and subsidies,' Canada might defend itself against cultural imperialism. Likewise, through the restriction of American investment and the 'Canadianization' of industries and businesses,

Canada could evade continental assimilation. In a word, for the New Left, socialism was co-extensive with nationalism and Canadian socialists were, by definition, Canadian nationalists. As Gad Horowitz remarked, 'We are nationalists because, as socialists, we do not want our country to be absorbed by the citadel of world capitalism.'[23]

There were further differences. Radical social activism and civil disorder were anathema to traditional toryism. The revolutionary climate in which the New Left was ensconced was the very environment against which the conservative critics reacted. Conservatives simply could not countenance the social utopia that was central to the New Left. Similarly, the New Left's sympathetic attitudes towards Quebec were repugnant to the old nationalists, especially hardliners like Creighton. Last, the New Left's 'socialist egalitarianism' did not accord with the anti-modernists' indictments of democracy or the idea of an aristodemocracy. The youth-academic movement of the late 1960s was never truly representative of the values of traditional nationalism. Thus, in spite of commonalties, the movements' incompatibilities proved to be too formidable to overcome; and despite New Leftists' ongoing reliance on traditional nationalism as the intellectual core of the movement, the New Left offered a fundamentally different national vision from that of the tory nationalists.

By the late 1960s this new vision, shorn of its colonial orientation yet preserving an anti-American, anti-Liberal perspective, was beginning to build momentum. New nationalism became increasingly important, outside the New Left, among students, academics, and urban, middle class supporters of the New Democratic Party (NDP). For these groups, socialism, radicalism, and left-wing nationalism merged as a means of forestalling the inexorable American advance and thus safeguarding Canadian independence. The Waffle movement epitomized burgeoning anti-American nationalism.

A Marxist-nationalist movement, the Waffle developed as a subgroup of the NDP. Growing in support, it almost overwhelmed the forces of moderate social democracy in the party. The Waffle owed its widespread appeal to its basic socialist and anti-American position: Canada could not develop unless it promoted government control over its economy and thus avoided the allure of American bourgeois capitalism. In addition to youth and university radicals, Canadians at large seemed receptive to the Waffle's message. In a poll taken in 1967, for example, 60 per cent of Canadians indicated that foreign ownership endangered political autonomy. Almost half of those polled thought that foreign control of Canadian industry was an issue of major concern.[24]

Although Waffle leader, James Laxer, failed in a bid to become leader of the NDP, and although in June 1972 Waffle members were expelled outright from the party, the movement's eventful history reflects the popularity of a virulent strain of anti-American nationalism. Also indicative of the Waffle's most popular cause was the spate of Marxist-nationalist publications that appeared in the period. John Porter's *The Vertical Mosaic* (1965), Kari Levitt's *Silent Surrender* (1970), and Malcolm Reid's *The Shouting Signpainters* (1972) were some of the more prominent examples of this trend.[25] In the writing of Canadian history, to take another instance, some historians and many graduate students discovered the merits of neo-Marxian analysis and the applicability of Marx to the Canadian condition.[26] Socialism and nation-building seemed a natural fit for this generation of students and academics, just as the maintenance of colonial ties had been for the previous generation of tory nationalists.

Despite the Waffle's rapid rise and a widespread recognition of the merits of anti-American nationalism, the new nationalism failed to endure as a central, Canadian mythology. The rhetoric of anti-American nationalism and the rhetoric of the New Left more generally certainly persisted into the mid-1970s. As a former president of the University of Toronto acerbically put it, these years continued to be 'drenched in the jargon of the New Left.'[27] Nevertheless, by mid-decade the advocates of the new nationalism had failed to hold their supporters. Just as Creighton, Morton, and the others had done before, they had failed to make nationalism a widespread doctrine to which all Canadians could subscribe and that would guide national policies.

The reasons for the failure of the new nationalism are manifold. Part of the demise was associated with the decline of youth culture and youth issues. Socially and culturally, the Canada of the period 1968–73 experienced rapid change. Causes such as the war in Vietnam, minority oppression, and student radicalism, around which the youth of the late 1960s had coalesced, were waning. In addition, issues such as environmentalism, women's equality, and minority rights had become increasingly mainstream and therefore were championed not only by radical youth. Moreover, by 1975 the leading edge of the baby boom generation was approaching the critical age of thirty. With demographic change and through the mainstreaming of social issues, the 'youth revolution' of the 1960s was in eclipse.[28]

Even more fundamental was the political decline of youth movements, specifically, of the New Left. The period 1968–73 was a tumultuous time for youth organizations such as the Company of Young Canadians (CYC) and the Canadian Union of Students (CUS). Whereas both organizations were garnering considerable media coverage in the late 1960s, by the mid-1970s they had become mere remnants of a youth radicalism that was well past its prime. The demise of the New Left best illustrates the decline of youth politics. Through increasingly radical tactics, even an advocacy of violent protest, the New Left was becoming discredited among Canadians at large. Most significant, it was losing the sympathy of the generation of youth from whom it had drawn most of its support. The decline of the Waffle movement simply added to the waning fortunes of the New Left. While the rise of the Waffle had indicated a greater concern over nationalist issues, the demise of the movement also represented contemporary trends and meant the triumph of old-style, mainstream socialism and therefore the end of radical socialist-nationalism. The old guard of the NDP was able to cleanse the party of radical, youth-oriented socialism. Indeed, the Waffle's failure dealt a 'dose of reality' to youth interested in reform.[29] Most of all, it signalled the effective end of the New Left and new nationalism in Canada. Although the rhetoric persists, academic pieces on neo-nationalism continue to be written, and elements of the New Left continue in the NDP, the 1972 demise of the Waffle meant the end of a widespread acceptance of the doctrine of new nationalism.

The rise and functional death of new nationalism are significant for two reasons. First, the neo-nationalists took away from conservatives control over the nationalist movement. Indebted to some of the interpretations of traditional nationalism but never enslaved by them, the new nationalists presented a notion of Canada that was socialist and anti-continentalist. Yet they made little room for the 'tory' vision of the nation. Thus, the new nationalists did much to supplant older doctrines and orientations that they deemed immaterial or irrelevant to Canadian circumstances. The incompatibilities between the two movements ultimately overcame any of their commonalties and resulted in the eclipse of the older tradition.

Second, and paradoxically, new nationalism constituted the last chance for a unifying Canadian mythology that was linked, however tenuously, to traditional nationalism. While the conservative nationalists may not have agreed with the socialist underpinnings of new nationalism or with the latter's failure to rest on conservative-historical foundations, it was, for the conservative-nationalists, the last remaining opportunity for Canada to avert continentalism and preserve its independent position. George Grant's dabbling in the movement exemplified the faint hopes of a generation of tory nationalists.[30] With the waning of new nationalism, however, even this less-than-satisfactory option had been closed off. When Pierre Trudeau was elected, Canadians seemed to be concerned with less rather than more nationalism.[31] Even Canadian historians, moreover, who traditionally had been responsible for defining the nation, its myths, and identities, had moved from writing national histories to publishing material that stressed Canada's 'limited identities': regionalism; and a concern for ethnic, labour, and women's history.[32] In the last analysis, the marginalization of the New Left sounded the death knell of traditional nationalism. Even in a corrupted form, old-style nationalism had failed to create a niche among Canadians. The New Left's decay thus marked the terminus of a nationalist tradition that traced its origins from the Loyalists, through the imperialists, and Tory leaders such Macdonald, Borden, Meighen, and Diefenbaker.

In 1966 Charles Hanly queried, 'Will America replace Great Britain as our national ideal?' The fact that he asked the question at all indicated that there was at least a residue of tory nationalist sentiment among academics and Canadians at large. In responding to his own query, however, Hanly was less than hopeful. He knew that Canada was gravitating towards a new empire and that the nation was about to reassert its colonial tendencies. The failure of traditional nationalism only a few years later seemed to confirm Hanly's prophecies and Canada's new directions. The battle for Britain had been lost. Canada had become a fully North American nation. Traditional Canadian nationalism was dead.

Like the rise of Quebec nationalism, the death of traditional nationalism constituted a severe blow to the cause of the anti-modernists. It implied the end of the last opportunity to appeal to any widespread popular mood that favoured the development of an enduring Canadianism. Once vigorous critics of the national-social order and always seeking a greater social significance, by the mid-1970s the anti-modernists had become marginalized and largely irrelevant. With Innis and Massey long dead and Grant, Neatby, Morton, and Frye turning to other concerns, Donald Creighton was the sole remaining voice of conservative dissent. In his last book, *The Forked Road: Canada,*

1939–1957 (1976), he continued his bitter denunciation of liberal Canada and those who had sold out the nation to American interests. Creighton expressed the hopelessness of Canada's plight, finally admitting that there was no possibility of returning to the Anglo-Canadian virtues of former times. The title was also as misleading as it was pessimistic; for Creighton, who died of cancer a few years after writing the book, never really explained the other option for Canada. Rather, he simply focused on the last formative stage of a triumphant liberal Canada. Like the branch of criticism he represented, he was devoid of solutions for the problems that beset modern Canada. His work thus highlighted the ultimate inconsequence of the tory vision, and as such, it was a fitting epitaph for a group of scholars whose criticism simply did not accord with modern realities and whose complete marginalization had left them bereft of all hope. Canadian toryism, established so long before, died with those who, like Creighton, had guided it through the modern age.

Notes

1: Introduction

1 A.B. McKillop, *A Disciplined Intelligence: Critical Enquiry into Canadian Thought in the Victorian Era* (Montreal, 1979), 230

2 Note that McLuhan's critique of modernity is limited to the early part of his academic career. Later, while still sceptical about the changes intrinsic to modernization, he came to accept change and to leave behind his critical views of the modern world.

3 As indicated, Frye and McLuhan, while they agreed with the most fundamental general principles of toryism, were not articulate spokesmen of the tory tradition. Note that 'tory' with a lower-case 't' refers throughout this work to the conservative intellectuals, the 'anti-modernists,' or the 'critics of modernity' (see chapter 1), who are the subjects of this book. 'Tory' with a capital 'T' refers to a member of the Conservative or, as of 1942, the Progressive Conservative party.

4 Donald Creighton, 'Education for Government,' *Queen's Quarterly*, 62 (Winter 1955), 532

5 Carl Berger, *The Sense of Power: Studies in the Ideas of Canadian Imperialism, 1867–1914* (Toronto, 1970)

6 Ibid., 31–2

7 Ibid., 196. These are Berger's words.

8 See Berger, *Sense of Power*.

9 J.M.S. Careless, 'Frontierism, Metropolitanism and Canadian History,' *Careless at Work: Selected Canadian Studies* (Toronto, 1990), 107

10 Ibid.

11 See Frank O'Gorman, *The Emergence of the British Two-Party System, 1760–1832* (London, 1982), chapter 2.

12 See W.L. Morton, 'Canadian Conservatism Now,' in H.D. Forbes ed., *Canadian Political Thought* (Toronto, 1985).

13 See Donald Creighton, *John A. Macdonald*, vol. I: *The Young Politician* (Toronto, 1952) and Creighton, *John A. Macdonald*, vol. II: *The Old Chieftain* (Toronto, 1955).

14 The vigorous, almost shrill, defence of institutions like as the university and 'true' notions of democracy become comprehensible against the backdrop of the totalitarianism of the war and post-war periods.

15 Quoted in A.B. McKillop, *Matters of Mind: The University in Ontario, 1791–1951*, 219 (Toronto, 1994)

16 In this way, the anti-modernists were as utilitarian in their application of functional values as were the proponents of the modern technological-scientific society.

17 The penetration of American culture into Canada dates from an earlier time, at least from the period after the First World War. The culture critics argue, with some historical justification (although these things are hard to measure), that the American influence in Canada intensified after the second war.

18 William L. Marr and Donald G. Patterson, *Canada: An Economic History* (Toronto, 1980), 389, 396

19 See Richard Allen, *The Social Passion: Religion and Social Reform in Canada, 1914–28* (Toronto, 1971), and Ramsay Cook, *The Regenerators: Social Criticism in Late Victorian English Canada* (Toronto, 1985).

20 Massey's biographer, Claude Bissell, highlights Massey's Anglophilia in the second of two volumes tellingly entitled *The Imperial Canadian*. Claude Bissell, *The Imperial Canadian: Vincent Massey in Office* (Toronto, 1986).

21 W.L. Morton, 'Towards a New Conception of Confederation?' An address to the Seventh Annual Seminar of the Canadian Union of Students, 'The Dualism of Culture and the Federalism of Power'; unpublished draft copy (4 September 1964), W.L. Morton Papers, William Ready Division of Archives and Research Collections, McMaster University Library, Hamilton, Canada, Box 6, Canadian Union of Students, 3–4

22 Creighton spent his final two decades in a red brick farmhouse in Brooklin, Ontario, while Massey passed his time at his country estate, Batterwood.

23 Martin J. Wiener, *English Culture and the Decline of the Industrial Spirit: 1850–1980* (Cambridge, 1981)

24 Innis, Neatby, Morton, and McLuhan, as noted, grew up on small farms. Frye was the son of a struggling hardware salesman; Creighton and Grant also had few pretenses to high-class status.

25 Despite assertions to the contrary, the Massey commissioners abhorred all trappings of lowbrow culture. Although they attempted to hide their contempt, their disdain for the goals of modern democracy and the culture of 'mass man' was made abundantly clear.

26 Engineers, professionals, technicians, and applied scientists generally.

27 There were a large number of Methodists among the anti-modernists. Creighton, Frye, and Massey were Methodists; Innis was a Baptist, Neatby a Presbyterian, and Morton an Anglican. Grant dabbled in several Protestant religions, while McLuhan, who was born a Protestant, converted to Roman Catholicism in the late 1930s.

28 Professors between ages twenty-five and forty-nine made, on average, $3,078 annually, compared with teachers and engineers, who made $2,119 and $2,206 respectively.

29 McKillop, *Matters of Mind*, 551; Paul Axelrod, *Scholars and Dollars: Politics, Economics, and the Universities of Ontario, 1945–1980* (Toronto, 1982), appendix, table 1. See also chapter 4.

30 H. Blair Neatby, unpublished, untitled lecture given at the University of Alberta (on the development of the professoriate in Ontario, 1950–1970), Fall 1993

31 John Bartlet Brebner, *Scholarship for Canada. The Function of Graduate Studies* (Ottawa, 1945), 13–19

32 Chicago offered Innis more money, a greatly reduced teaching load, and therefore freedom to pursue his new researches in the field of communication.

33 'In June 1950,' Creighton wrote, 'when the Korean War broke out, we discovered how nearly identical our ideas had become.' Both Creighton and Innis were in Ottawa, Innis was busy with his work on the Royal Commission on Transportation, and Creighton occupied himself with the first volume of his Macdonald biography. They met for long talks on the Korean situation. In Creighton's words: 'We both regarded the action of the United Nations in Korea as a very imperfect disguise for American military intervention in the Far East; but we were quickly made to understand that in Ottawa it was better to keep these reprehensible opinions to ourselves. The members of the Department of External Affairs were united in the exalted belief that the Korean War was a holy crusade in support of the collective system; and one of them informed me curtly that he wanted to hear no more of my sacrilegious aspersions on a noble cause.' See Donald Creighton, 'Introduction,' in *Towards the Discovery of Canada: Selected Essays* (Toronto, 1972), 8. Also, Innis dedicated his book *The Strategy of Culture* (Toronto, 1952) to Creighton and his wife Luella.

34 For example, Creighton and Morton differed on the issues of Quebec nationalism and bilingualism and biculturalism. See chapter 6.

35 However, an inordinate number of anti-modernists – Innis, Creighton, Neatby, and Morton – were historians, and Massey also studied history.

36 Some notable works on the question of modernity are Judith Stamps, *Unthinking Modernity: Innis, McLuhan, and the Frankfurt School* (Montreal, 1995); David B. Marshall, *Secularizing the Faith: Canadian Protestant Clergy and the Crisis of Belief, 1850–1940* (Toronto, 1992); Cook, *The Regenerators*; and McKillop, *Disciplined Intelligence*.

2: Science and Technique

1 Bryan D. Palmer, *Working-Class Experience: The Rise and Reconstitution of Canadian Labour, 1800–1980* (Toronto, 1983), 97

2 Douglas Owram, *The Government Generation: Canadian Intellectuals and the State 1900–1945* (Toronto, 1986), 17

3 W.E. Houghton, *The Victorian Frame of Mind, 1830–1870* (London, 1957), 33–6

4 Quoted in A.B. McKillop. *Matters of Mind: The University in Ontario, 1791–1951* (Toronto, 1994), 167

5 Ibid., 167, 168

6 Lobbying went on, in spite of the fact that education came under provincial jurisdiction (section 93 of the BNA Act). The advocates of applied sciences programs argued that technical education fell under section 91 and that the federal government was responsible for the economic requirements (such as technical education) of nation-building. See ibid.

7 Quoted in McKillop, *Matters of Mind*, 169

8 Ibid., 154

9 Ibid., 155, 156. McKillop thinks Loudon's address was of 'major importance for the history of science in Canada, for it was a manifesto declaring Loudon's complete commitment to the German research ideal as found in its universities.'

10 James Loudon, 'The Universities in Relation to Research,' *Proceedings of the Royal Society of Canada* (Ottawa, 1902), appendix A, XLIX; cited in Trevor H. Levere and Richard A. Jarrell, eds, *A Curious Field-Book: Science and Society in Canadian History* (Toronto, 1974), 215–16, 216, 218.

11 McKillop, *Matters of Mind*, 155, 158

12 Dr A. Stanley Mackenzie, 'The War and Science,' *Proceedings and Transactions of the Royal Society of Canada*, section 3, 12 (1918); cited in Levere and Jarrell, *Curious Field-Book*, 184.

13 Ibid., 185, 186

14 McKillop, *Matters of Mind*, 175

15 Philip C. Enros, 'The University of Toronto and Industrial Research in the Early Twentieth Century,' in Richard A. Jarrell and Arnold E. Roos, eds, *Critical Issues in the History of Canadian Science* (Thornhill, Ontario, 1983), 159, 164

16 Wilfred Eggleston, *National Research in Canada: The NRC 1916–1966* (Toronto, 1978), 1, 5

17 The council was mired by adverse timing; for by the time government officials received the proposal, the war had ended. To complicate matters, the council's chief advocate in governmental halls, the minister of commerce and trade, Sir George Foster, had left with Prime Minister Borden for the Paris Peace Conferences. What little headway could be made materialized in terms of the creation in April 1919 of a special committee of Parliament to study the proposal. A bill was introduced in Parliament on scientific research on 8 April 1921, but it was eventually defeated in the Senate. Only later was the cause of scientific research taken up again, this time by new NRC president H.M. Tory. The institute was finally realized when construction of the new 'temple of science' was begun on the banks of the Ottawa River. For the origins of the council, see Eggleston, *National Research in Canada*, and Mel Thistle, *The Inner Ring: The Early History of the National Research Council* (Toronto, 1966).

18 Eggleston, *National Research in Canada*, 24, 25, 34

19 Thistle, *Inner Ring*, 14

20 Although by the 1880s British and American social scientists had already begun studying the socio-economic effects of urban-industrialization, social science in Canada had to await further industrial development. Clearly, the belated development of the social sciences in Canada compared with other nations, such as Britain and the United States, demonstrates how the emergence of Canadian social sciences was inextricably tied to Canada's delayed industrial development. See Owram, *Government Generation*, 13.

21 Ibid., 19

22 See, for instance, Adam Shortt, 'The Influence of Daily Occupations and Surroundings on the Life of the People,' Sunday Afternoon Addresses, Third Series (Kingston, 1893); Shortt, 'The Social and Economic Significance of the Movement from the Country to the City,' *Addresses Delivered before the Canadian Club of Montreal* (Montreal, 1912–13), 62–71.

23 Barry Ferguson, *Remaking Liberalism: The Intellectual Legacy of Adam Shortt, O.D. Skelton, W.C. Clark and W.A. Mackintosh* (Montreal and Kingston, 1993), 46, 49

24 S.E.D. Shortt, *The Search for an Ideal: Six Canadian Intellectuals and Their Convictions in an Age of Transition* (Toronto, 1976), 134

25 Ferguson, *Remaking Liberalism*, 110

26 Ibid.

27 Owram, *Government Generation*, 62

28 Ibid., 66

29 At the core of King's Industrial Disputes Investigation Act (1907), in which strikes and lockouts were prohibited pending investigation by a government board, was the philosophy that the social anarchy that can result from labour strife must be avoided at all costs. The philosophical justification was that 'there is no right greater to that of the Community as a whole.' See Paul Craven, *'An Impartial Umpire': Industrial Relations and the Canadian State, 1900–1911* (Toronto, 1980), 71–3, 86–7, 31.

30 See Owram, *Government Generation*, 69, 73.

31 Ferguson, *Remaking Liberalism*, 240

32 Donald Creighton, *Harold Adams Innis: Portrait of a Scholar* (Toronto, 1957), 81–2

33 McKillop, *Matters of Mind*, 133

34 Carl Berger, *The Writing of Canadian History: Aspects of English-Canadian Historical Writing since 1900*, 2nd ed. (Toronto, 1986), 89, 88

35 Harold Innis, 'A Bibliography of T. Veblen,' *Southwestern Political and Social Science Quarterly*, 10 (June 1929), 25, 24

36 Robert F. Neill, 'The Work of Harold Adams Innis: Content and Context,' PhD thesis, Duke University, 1966, 88

37 Harold Innis, *Problems of Staples Production in Canada* (Toronto, 1933), 30; 94–7

38 Technological improvements lower costs, extend the market, and restructure the time horizons of the system. See Neill, *Work of Harold Adams Innis*, 129, 88.

39 Berger, *Writing of Canadian History*, 101

40 For a country the size of Canada, with its vast distances and its difficult terrain but small population, transportation costs remained high until the 1930s. It was no wonder that debt levels rose and further investment ceased.

41 Neill, *Work of Harold Adams Innis*, 132

42 See Innis, 'The Role of Intelligence: Some Further Notes,' *Canadian Journal of Economics and Political Science*, 1 (1935), 280–6.

43 Owram, *Government Generation*, 132

44 Creighton, *Harold Adams Innis*, 82, 83

45 An address to the members of the Liberal-Conservative Summer School in Newmarket, Ontario, September 1933. Quoted in ibid., 83

46 Quoted in ibid., 83. In critiquing scholars' move away from academia into political life, Innis was referring especially to colleagues such as Frank Underhill and other members of the League for Social Reconstruction. The LSR represented for Innis exactly what he deplored: a group of intellectuals who had shunned university life and decided that the scholar's most appropriate role in society was active political participation in government.

47 Innis, 'Role of Intelligence,' 280–7

48 See F.H. Knight, 'Social Science and the Political Trend,' *University of Toronto Quarterly* (July 1934), 407–27, and E.J. Urwick, 'The Role of Intelligence in the Social Process,' *Canadian Journal of Economics and Political Science*, 1 (1935).

49 Innis, 'Role of Intelligence,' 280–1

50 Ibid., 284. The paradox was that bias changed the nature of the social sciences almost to the point of making the true role of the social scientist unrecognizable; yet the proliferation of bias would make the social scientist aware of its existence and its effects on the social sciences and thus would restore her to her rightful role of seeking truth and eliminating bias.

51 Ibid., 284, 283

52 Unlike Urwick, who advocated a highly relativistic approach to social scientific study, Innis still suggested that objectivity in scholarship was tenable, assuming the proper functioning of the university and the scholar within it. Ibid., 283; see also L.A. Pal, 'Scholarship and the Later Innis,' *Journal of Canadian Studies*, 12 (Winter 1977), 34.

53 Berger, *The Writing of Canadian History*, 102

54 Harold Innis, 'The Penetrative Powers of the Price System,' in Innis, *Political Economy in the Modern State* (Toronto, 1946), 160–1. See also Walter Lippmann, *Public Opinion* (New York, 1922; reprinted 1965).

55 Innis, 'Penetrative Powers,' 161

56 He showed how, with the development of linotype, the telegraph, and other improvements in the way that news could be collected, newspaper editors and journalists were enabled to gather and distribute more and more news.

57 Innis, 'Penetrative Powers,' 22.

58 The organization of news agencies was important; for it was through the structuring and packaging of the news in accordance with the perceived needs of the readership on the whole that larger circulations were achieved. 'The application of steam power to the production of paper, and in turn of the newspaper,' Innis concluded, 'followed by the telegraph and the exploitation of human curiosity and its interest in news, created effective channels for the spread of information.' See Harold Innis, 'On the Economic

Significance of Culture,' *Journal of Economic History,* Supplement 4, *The Tasks of Economic History* (December 1944), 86.

59 Innis writes, 'The significance of the newspaper to the social sciences has been evident in the deterioration, since Adam Smith, shown in the increasing obsession with facts and figures in relation to the short run immediate problems of bureaucracies, in the increasing specialization and departmentalization of the social sciences, and in their consequent divisiveness and sterility. Economic history has suffered either as a handmaiden of bureaucracy or a sink of antiquarianism.' See Harold Innis, 'The Newspaper in Economic Development,' in Innis, *Political Economy,* 31, n.48.

60 Lippmann, *Public Opinion,* 8, 8–9, 10

61 Ibid., 257

62 Innis cited Lippmann directly but sparingly. See Innis, 'Penetrative Powers,' 160–1. Nevertheless, he had considerable intellectual affinity with Lippmann. Lippmann's *Public Opinion* was inspired by Graham Wallas and the latter's work on the intrusion into the life of moderns of false truths. Innis also relied on Wallas's ideas. He admitted dependence on the work of Wallas in his 1948 piece entitled 'A Critical Review.' As Wallas and, indeed, Lippmann did, Innis also points 'to the danger that knowledge was growing too fast for successful use in social judgment.' See Harold Innis, 'A Critical Review,' in Innis, *The Bias of Communication* (Toronto, 1951; reprinted 1973), 191.

63 Innis, *Bias of Communication,* 33–4

64 See Harold Innis, *Empire and Communication* (Toronto, 1950; reprinted 1972).

65 Harold Innis, 'A Plea for Time,' Sesquicentennial Lectures (Fredericton 1950), 11

66 Harold Innis, *The Strategy of Culture* (Toronto 1952), 14

67 Innis, *Empire and Communication,* 9

68 Innis, *Bias of Communication,* 132, 139

69 E.J. Urwick to Innis (18 November 1940), Harold Innis Papers, University of Toronto Archives (UTA), Box 011, file 15, B72-0025, and Urwick to Innis (30 December 1942), Box 011, file 15, B72-0025

70 Innis 'This Has Killed That,' *Journal of Canadian Studies,* 12 (Winter 1977), 3

71 Ibid., 4

72 There can be no doubt that the Second World War repulsed Innis. A veteran of the Great War, he was a converted pacifist who, in much of his correspondence or addresses of the 1940s, made unfavourable references to the current conflict. He called war a tragedy in terms of the loss of human life, the tolls of which were 'never repaid' (Innis, 'This Has Killed That,' 4). Elsewhere, he referred to battles fought during the war as 'massacres' or

'atrocities' and the use of the atom bomb as an event so profoundly 'disturbing to the moral sense of Anglo-Saxons that Churchill [had] to say it was necessary' ('Values' Discussion Group, 5 April 1949, Harold Innis Papers, University of Toronto Archives (UTA), Box 030, file 06, B72-0003, 3–4). Indeed, the massive slaughtering of the war resulted, in Innis's mind, in the breakdown of an international moral code (ibid.). While many of his contemporaries championed the economic benefits of the war and the need to combat Fascism, Innis was convinced that the war was an event of no redeeming value whatsoever and contributed instead to the depletion of human resources and the dulling of moral sensibilities. See Innis, 'This Has Killed That.'

73 Harold Innis, 'A Plea for The University Tradition,' *Dalhousie Review*, 24 (1944), 299–300. Much more will be said on Innis and the university in chapters 3 and 4.

74 Harold Innis, 'The University in the Modern Crisis,' in *Political Economy in the Modern State* (Toronto, 1946), 74

75 See James W. Carey, *Communication as Culture: Essays on Media and Society* (London, 1989; reprinted 1992), 147.

76 Lewis Mumford wrote about the relationship between technology and culture. In *Technics and Civilization*, he showed how at present (1934) machine advancement outstripped social development. He was convinced, however, that machine development would slow down with respect to social development and that an equilibrium between technological advancement and social organization would be achieved. He implicitly agreed with Innis that modern society needed to 'reorient technic' and that this 'consists in bringing it more completely in harmony with the new cultural and regional and societal and personal patterns we have coordinately begun to develop' (434). His view is alien to that of Innis, however, because he sees technology being controllable and hence not dictating the structure of social organization. Mumford's view on the relation between society and technology is generally a positive one, while Innis's view most definitely is not. See Mumford, *Technics and Civilization* (1934), 417–35.

77 Arthur Lower, 'The Social Sciences in the Post-War World,' *Canadian Historical Review*, 22 (March 1941); quoted in Welf H. Heick, ed., *History and Myth: Arthur Lower and the Making of Canadian Nationalism* (Vancouver, 1975), 108. Note that, unlike Innis, Lower had confidence in the traditional role of social scientists to take an active part in public life and, in consequence, to provide a check against the new state and protect against its abuse of social freedoms. In the end, the war represented both a period of great change and also an opportunity for Canada and its intellectuals; it was an opportu-

nity for Canadian social scientists to impress their understandings and out-looks of the future of a young, emerging nation. Lower writes: 'A new order is struggling to be born among us, but in genetics as in other things we cling to *laissez-faire* ideas; none of us knows much about [the new age]. *The great problem [is] trying to divine the nature of the future, and as social scientists, perhaps even essaying to act as midwives'* (106; my italics).

78 Donald Creighton, 'Memorandum for the Conference on American Thought' (no date, 1944?), Donald Creighton Papers, National Archives of Canada (NAC), MG 31 D77, v. 1, General correspondence, 1944, #2, 2

79 Creighton to John Marshall, associate director of the humanities, the Rockefeller Foundation), 21 February 1944, v. 1, Donald Creighton Papers, NAC, MG 31 D77, General correspondence, 1944, #2, 1

80 Grant to Mother, Easter [n.d., 1939?], George Parkin Grant Papers, NAC, MG 30 D59, v. 38; Mrs W.L. Grant Correspondence; file: Queen's University, 1

81 In chapter 3 much more will be said on issues of free enquiry, the conflict between the humanities and the sciences, and the roles of government and war.

82 The War Measures Act (WMA) was the operative instrument of the federal government's emergency power. The dominion government enacted 6,414 orders under the WMA. These orders had the force of law and circumvented parliamentary debate. See Robert Bothwell, Ian Drummond, and John English, *Canada since 1945: Power, Politics, and Provincialism*, rev. ed. (Toronto, 1989), 53.

83 The government brought war-related industries directly under its control. By the end of the war, 85 per cent of all non-agricultural labour fell under its control. Ibid., 55, 53.

84 In return, the provinces were to receive grants, based on complex formulae, designed to provide per capita grants and statutory subsidies. This is the genesis of transfer payments. Note that the provinces of Ontario and Quebec established autonomous taxation systems.

85 McKillop, *Matters of Mind*, 529, 557, 558, 531. McKillop outlines the views of educators who appreciated the 'training school role' of the university, such as C.R. Young (dean of University of Toronto's faculty of applied science and engineering). Between 1931 and 1945 graduates in applied science and engineering, he noted, increased by 81 per cent. In the same period, graduates in arts increased only 23 per cent.

86 See ibid., chapter 13 and 557. Much more will be said on change and the university in this period in chapters 3 and 4.

87 Canadian Social Science Research Council (November 1942), *Brief to the*

Canadian Government, Donald Creighton Papers, NAC, v. 15, H.A. Innis, 1924–54, MG 31 D77

88 Vincent Massey (1948, April 23), 'Address by the Right Honourable Vincent Massey before the Graduate Organization of the University of Toronto for Kingston and District, Kingston, Ontario.' Vincent Massey Papers, UTA, 421(08), B87–0082, 5–6

89 George P. Grant, 'The Teaching of Philosophy in English-Speaking Canada,' draft copy (24 October 1950), Hilda Neatby Papers, Saskatchewan Archives Board (SAB), II. 93; file: Grant, Professor G.P., 'The Teaching of Philosophy in English-Speaking Canada,' 3. See also George Grant, '"Philosophy" in Canada,' *Royal Commission Studies: A Selection of Essays Prepared for the Royal Commission on National Development in the Arts, Letters and Sciences* (Ottawa, 1948).

90 Donald Creighton (n.d.), 'Education for Government: What Can the Humanities Do for Government?' Unpublished manuscript, Donald Creighton Papers, NAC, v. 15; Education for government, MG 31 D77, 1

91 Hutchins, along with Mortimer J. Adler, edited the fifty-four-volume series entitled *Great Books of the Western World*.

92 Hutchins's views here are reminiscent of those of Innis on the role of the scholar. See Innis, 'The Role of Intelligence.'

93 See Bruce O. Watkins and Roy Meador, *Technology and Human Values: Collision and Solution* (Ann Arbor, 1977), 87.

94 Claude Bissell, 'Herbert Marshall McLuhan,' in George Sanderson and Frank Macdonald, eds, *Marshall McLuhan: The Man and His Message* (Golden, Colorado, 1989), 6

95 Marshall McLuhan, *The Mechanical Bride: The Folklore of Industrial Man* Boston, 1951), 43

96 'McLuhan to Clement McNaspy, S.J., 15 December, 1945 [15 January 1946?],' in Matie Molinaro et al., eds, *Letters of Marshall McLuhan* (Toronto, 1987), 180. McLuhan was not opposed to the study of the classics in literature; rather, he welcomed it.

97 This is something the 'mediaevalism' of Hutchins and Adler failed to provide. McLuhan, *Mechanical Bride*, 44.

98 This rejection of the 'greats' approach and propensity to study the salient features of modern culture characterized McLuhan's shift from literary studies to his early work on the effects of technique. His first important book in this new field, *The Mechanical Bride* (1950), was an effort to analyse the impact of the so-called unofficial education.

99 Although scholars have acknowledged McLuhan's contributions as a media theorist during the height of his scholarly career in the late 1950s and

the 1960s, there has been little study of his social critique of the 1940s and early 1950s and, hence, little sense of how McLuhan's pre-Innisian views emerged. An effort is made here to trace the early development of McLuhan's views of the technological society.

100 Marshall McLuhan, 'American Advertising,' *Horizon* (October 1947), quoted in Eric McLuhan and Frank Zingrone, eds, *Essential McLuhan* (Concord, Ontario, 1995), 13, 14.

101 Marshall McLuhan, 'Education of Free Men in Democracy: The Liberal Arts,' *St Louis Studies in Honor of St Thomas Aquinas* (St Louis, 1943), 49, 50

102 McLuhan, *Mechanical Bride*, quoted in McLuhan and Zingrone, eds, *Essential McLuhan*, 21

103 McLuhan, 'Education of Free Men in Democracy,' 49

104 McLuhan, *Mechanical Bride*, 21, 33

105 Ibid., 40, 7, 87

106 Kenneth Norrie and Douglas Owram, *A History of the Canadian Economy* (Toronto, 1991), 414

107 Vincent Massey, 'Address to the Canadian Club of London, England, 1 July 1953,' draft copy, Hilda Neatby Papers, SAB, I.12 (Massey, Vincent, 1951–69, (1), A139, 2. See also 'Canada: Her Status and Stature,' in Vincent Massey, *Speaking of Canada: Addresses by the Right Honourable Vincent Massey* (Toronto, 1959), 6, 5.

108 Vincent Massey, 'Useful Knowledge,' Convocation of the University of Manitoba, draft copy, Hilda Neatby Papers, SAB, I.12 (Massey, Vincent, 1951–69), (2), A139, 4. See also 'Useful Knowledge,' in Massey, *Speaking of Canada*.

109 Harold Innis, 'Implications of the Interactions between Values and Resources,' unpublished address, 2 October 1949, Harold Innis Papers, UTA, B72-0003, Box 20, file 33, 1, 9

110 Innis to Cole, 20 January 1950, B72-0025; 011, 01. Innis's 'plea for time' and Massey's concern for the demise of spiritual values were reflected in many other post-war social critics. Historian Hilda Neatby railed against 'the age of scientific materialism' because it overemphasized presentist concerns as opposed to the concern with tradition and the historical, cultural, and religious inheritance of western humanity. See Neatby, 'Special Study on Canadian History,' draft copy, Hilda Neatby Papers, SAB, II. 103, Special Studies: Neatby, Hilda, 'Special Study on Canadian History,' A139, 21–2. This crisis of values was reflected in the work of the Massey Commission and the concern over the fate of higher learning after the war. See chapters 3 through 5.

111 Quoted in Owram, *Government Generation*, 15, 15–16

112 George Grant, 'The Uses of Freedom,' *Queen's Quarterly,* 62 (Winter 1955), 518

113 Ibid., 520–1

114 Ibid., 521

115 George Grant, *Technology and Empire: Perspectives on North America* (Toronto, 1969), 137, 28

116 Arthur Kroker, *Technology and the Canadian Mind: Innis, Grant, and McLuhan* (Montreal, 1984), 18–19

117 Quoted in William Christian, *George Grant: A Biography* (Toronto, 1993), 143

118 Grant, 'The Teaching of Philosophy in English-Speaking Canada,' 7, 5–6

119 Grant does admit that there are scholars in Canada who, like him, identified a problem of philosophic values. The Massey Commission and scholarly efforts, such as those of C.N. Cochrane and Harold Innis, were efforts to pursue a 'philosophical approach' to modern humanity's problems. Hence, they comprise a reaction against the advent of the technological imperative. See chapter 4.

120 Grant, 'The Teaching of Philosophy in English-Speaking Canada,' 8

121 Ibid.

122 George Grant, *Philosophy in the Mass Age* (Toronto, 1959), 7–8

123 Grant, *Technology and Empire,* 88–9

124 Malcolm M. Wallace, 'The Present Status of the Humanities in Canada,' Study submitted to the Massey Commission. Hilda Neatby Papers, SAB, II. 110, Special Studies: Wallace, 'The Present Status of the Humanities in Canada,' A139, 1. See also Malcolm M. Wallace, 'The Present Status of the Humanities in Canada,' *Royal Commission Studies: A Selection of Essays Prepared for the Royal Commission on National Development in the Arts, Letters and Sciences* (Ottawa, 1948).

3: The Modernization of Higher Learning in Canada I

1 A.B. McKillop. *Matters of Mind: The University in Ontario, 1791–1951* (Toronto, 1994), 101

2 Quoted in Robin S. Harris, *A History of Higher Education in Canada, 1663–1960* (Toronto, 1976), 259

3 McKillop, *Matters of Mind,* 200, 203

4 Quoted in Marlene Shore, *The Science of Social Redemption: McGill, the Chicago School, and the Origins of Social Research in Canada* (Toronto, 1987), 31

5 Ibid., 31–2, 31

6 Mel Thistle, *The Inner Ring: The Early History of the National Research Council* (Toronto, 1966), 53–4, 54–5

7 Quoted in McKillop, *Matters of Mind*, 322, 322–3

8 Ibid., 323

9 At the core of this concept is the idea that the university's chief function is to serve the pressing needs of society. Hence, higher learning is consumed not with producing thinkers or philosophers, but with students trained to perform specific tasks that ultimately further the ends of industrial society. See Michael R. Harris, *Five Counterrevolutionists in Higher Education: Irving Babbitt, Albert Jay Nock, Abraham Flexner, Robert Maynard Hutchins, Alexander Meiklejohn* (Corvallis, Oregon, 1970), 30–5.

10 See McKillop, *Matters of Mind*, 322–61, 329.

11 Harris, *History of Higher Education*, 383

12 McKillop, *Matters of Mind*, 326

13 Ibid., 327, 332–3

14 Paul Axelrod, *Making a Middle Class: Student Life in English Canada during the Thirties* (Montreal, 1990), 59

15 See McKillop, *Matters of Mind*, 331, and Doug Owram, 'Economic Thought in the 1930s: The Prelude to Keynesianism,' in Raymond B. Blake and Jeff Keshen, eds, *Social Welfare Policy in Canada: Historical Readings* (Toronto, 1995), 179.

16 Axelrod, *Making a Middle Class*, 58, 59

17 McKillop, *Matters of Mind*, 335, 338. See also J. Rodney Millard, *The Master Spirit of the Age: Canadian Engineers and the Politics of Professionalism, 1887– 1922* (Toronto, 1988).

18 Figures from Harris, *History of Higher Education*, 403

19 There was a concern that engineering schools produced too many graduates for the economy to absorb throughout the 1920s and 1930s. Many, indeed, had to go to the United States to find work. See McKillop, *Matters of Mind*, 341.

20 Axelrod, *Making a Middle Class*, 68

21 See Michael Bliss, *The Discovery of Insulin* (Toronto, 1982)

22 Axelrod, *Making a Middle Class*, 68–9

23 Pediatrics, neurology, internal medicine, and surgery were refined into areas such as psychiatry, orthopedics, plastic surgery, and proctology. See Axelrod, 69.

24 These were anatomy, gynecology and obstetrics, medicine, pathology, physiology, surgery, pharmacology, and biochemistry. See McKillop, *Matters of Mind*, 356, 351–2.

25 Axelrod, *Making a Middle Class*, 69. Unlike engineering, medical faculties stagnated throughout the interwar period, with few full-time faculty appointments and few new research facilities. Enrolment numbers did not

increase as readily as they did for engineering and commerce and political economy. The Department of Psychiatry, however, experienced a substantial increase in enrolment in the interwar period. See Harris, *History of Higher Education*, 401.

26 See Thorstein Veblen, *The Higher Learning in America: A Memorandum on the Conduct of Universities by Business Men* (New York, 1918; reprinted 1994), and James G. Greenlee, *Sir Robert Falconer: A Biography* (Toronto, 1988), 138–9.

27 McKillop, *Matters of Mind*, 304

28 A Cody Commission recommendation, quoted in ibid., 375

29 This was to be achieved through enlarging the powers of the president and creating a board of governors that was, in McKillop's words, 'to act as a buffer between the presidency and the Ministry of Education.' Ibid.

30 By 1920 the universities of western Canada had similar financial relationships with their provincial governments. The Norris government of Manitoba adopted the 1906 University of Toronto Act, which had given financial stability to the university, among other things, while it also had served as the paradigm for the three provincial universities created after 1906. See W.L. Morton, *One University: A History of the University of Manitoba* (Toronto, 1957), 108.

31 Veblen, *Higher Learning in America*, 63–4, and McKillop, *Matters of Mind*, 364

32 See McKillop, *Matters of Mind*, 364–5. The issue of academic freedom became prominent in the face of increased governmental involvement and the 'corporatization' of the academy. Yet it must be noted, as stated above, academic freedom was often an unrealized ideal of Canadian academics. Overtures had been made to the concept, medieval in its origins, from the Victorian age, but the reality was that academic freedom was never a cornerstone of the Canadian university. Thus, the critics of the modern university often refer to idealized notions of academic liberty rather than to historical situations. See Falconer's remarks on the nature of academic freedom, below. Also see the idealized conception of the university of critics in chapter 4. Academic freedom is but one aspect of the mythologized university.

33 The Leonard incident was protracted and convoluted. See Greenlee, *Sir Robert Falconer*, 275–84.

34 See McKillop, *Matters of Mind*, 369, 371.

35 Ibid., 372, 365–73

36 In the wider, American idea, professorial utterances were afforded protection from censure both outside and within the walls of the academy. In barring academics at Toronto from participating in politics (and therefore forcing them to behave like judges or senior civil servants), Falconer

eschewed the wider American conception. That he had to make these deter-
minations and that he decided against wider academic liberty are indicative
of the nascent state of academic freedom in Canada. See Ibid., 371.

37 See Greenlee, *Sir Robert Falconer*, 284
38 Quoted in ibid., 285
39 Quoted in McKillop, *Matters of Mind*, 376
40 Greenlee, *Sir Robert Falconer*, 286
41 See McKillop, *Matters of Mind*, 380.
42 Ibid., 381, 382
43 Ibid., 383
44 Carl Berger, *The Writing of Canadian History: Aspects of English-Canadian
Historical Writing since 1900*, 2nd ed. (Toronto, 1986), 79
45 Quoted in McKillop, *Matters of Mind*, 384
46 Berger, *Writing of Canadian History*, 79
47 Ibid., 79
48 Ontario Premier Mitch Hepburn and Opposition leader George Drew
denounced the foreign policy views of George Grube of the *Canadian
Forum*. While vilified for asserting that funds directed towards a British-
centred foreign policy was money wasted, Grube was not subject to disci-
plinary action. He worked for independent Trinity College, and therefore
the province could not officially reprimand him. Underhill's situation was
different. See below.
49 Quoted in Berger, *Writing of Canadian History*, 78
50 Quoted in McKillop, *Matters of Mind*, 397. Note also that several senior
colleagues defended Underhill and threatened Cody with insubordination
should the incident be unfavourably resolved. Once he had shown regret at
the offending nature of the phrases and promised to be more careful in his
rhetoric, however, Underhill again escaped without official censure. See
Berger, *Writing of Canadian History*, 82.
51 The Toronto daily press did not defend Underhill. In fact, Underhill found
his only support, aside from his own journal, the *Canadian Forum*, in B.K.
Sandwell, editor of *Saturday Night*.
52 Several outraged citizens called for Underhill's ouster and indeed the muz-
zling of other disloyal professors. See McKillop, *Matters of Mind*, 396–7, 398.
53 The concept implies that universities' basic raison d'être was to provide for
the immediate needs of society and to prepare students to fulfil practical
and technical duties within industrial society. See Harris, *Five Counterrevolutionists*, 30–41.
54 Veblen, *Higher Learning in America*, 76, 49, 47, 49, 42, 44
55 Quoted in Harris, *Five Counterrevolutionists*, 181. Meiklejohn defined a

liberal education, in the words of Harris, as 'the cultivation of powers enabling citizens to order their relations with themselves, their fellows, and the world' (170).

56 Ibid., 52, 58. Babbitt was a disciple of Matthew Arnold, who argued that there was a cultural elite in society – the 'saving remnant' in Arnold's words – responsible to preserve standards and provide guidance for society's lesser members. Babbitt very much shared Arnold's cultural elitism.

57 Quoted in ibid., 65

58 The critics of American higher learning presented one resilient theme: that the university had become more of a reflection of a largely materialistic society and less of a beacon to the emerging social order. From Veblen through Meiklejohn and Babbitt, the theme was clear. In the drive to settle, industrialize, and gain prosperity, issues concerning scientific or technical matters had begun to outstrip the objective of preserving cultural values and the search for wisdom. Most of all, the university had failed to take a leadership role in terms of cultural development. The social function of the university was certainly not to provide the human resources to advance humanity's material conditions; rather, it was to enhance humans, spiritually, culturally, even morally.

59 Nichols Murray Butler, 'Academic Freedom in a Changing World,' *The Obligation of Universities to the Social Order: Addresses and Discussion at a Conference of Universities under the Auspices of New York University November 15–17, 1932* (New York, 1933), xiv–xv

60 P.E. Corbett. 'The Function of the University,' *Queen's Quarterly*, 40 (February 1933), 14–15. Corbett's comments must be seen in the light of the material, utilitarian culture that emerged after the war. Society treated scholars and scientists according to what they produced, not for their intrinsic worth. In the words of R.O. Earl, 'people are [nowadays] becoming increasingly impatient. They want results which they can see and feel, and they are not disposed to continue feeding and clothing professors if they do not get their money's worth in return. The pressure of life is coming home to the universities.' 'The Universities at Bay,' *Queen's Quarterly*, 43 [Autumn 1936), 291)

61 Corbett, 'Function of the University,' 14, 18

62 Ibid., 19, 22

63 Ibid., 14

64 Harold Innis, 'The Role of Intelligence: Some Further Notes,' *Canadian Journal of Economics and Political Science*, 1 (1935), 280–7. See also chapter 2.

65 Harold Innis, 'A Note on the Universities and the Social Sciences,' *Canadian Journal of Economics and Political Science*, 1 (1935), 286

304 Notes to pages 91–9

66 Innis, 'The Role of Intelligence,' 284, 285

67 Innis, 'A Note on the Universities,' 286–7

68 Harold Innis, 'Discussion in the Social Sciences,' *Dalhousie Review*, 15 (January 1936), 401–13; quoted in Daniel Drache, ed., *Staples, Markets, and Cultural Change: Selected Essays, Harold A. Innis* (Montreal, 1995), 446. Innis thought that university authorities had been concerned solely with the appearance of free thought within the university. They cared nothing about the problems of how to achieve free discussion and the wider, social function of academic discovery. See also Innis, 'A Note on the Universities,' 286.

69 Drache, *Staples, Markets, and Cultural Change*, 455–8, 450, 451

70 Harold Innis, 'The Passing of Political Economy,' *Commerce Journal* (1938), 3–6, quoted in Drache, *Staples, Markets, and Cultural Change*, 440–1

71 McKillop, *Matters of Mind*, 509–10; Innis, 'Passing of Political Economy,' quoted in Drache, *Staples, Markets, and Cultural Change*, 438–40

72 Quoted in McKillop, *Matters of Mind*, 520

73 Sir Edward Beatty, 'Freedom and the Universities,' *Queen's Quarterly*, 44 (Winter 1937), 471, 466

74 Arthur Lower, 'The Social Sciences in the Post-War World,' *Canadian Historical Review*, 22 (March 1941), quoted in Welf H. Heick, ed., *History and Myth: Arthur Lower and the Making of Canadian Nationalism* (Vancouver, 1975), 105–6, 106, 110

75 Ibid., 112, 111, 114

76 Ibid., 112

77 James S. Thomson. 'The Universities and the War,' *Queen's Quarterly*, 47 (Spring 1940), 4

78 McKillop, *Matters of Mind*, 522

79 The NRMA required fit single men and widowers between the ages of twenty-one and forty-five to register for service in home defence.

80 McKillop, *Matters of Mind*, 524

81 Ibid., 529–30

82 Ibid., 528

83 Thomson, 'Universities and the War,' 6

84 Ibid., 7

85 Watson Kirkconnell, *Twilight of Liberty* (London, 1941), xi

86 Thomson, 'Universities and the War,' 7

87 Ibid, 7, 9

88 In spite of the arguments of political scientist Daniel Drache, who titles an entire section of his edited collection of Innis essays 'The Intellectual as Citizen,' the scholar's active participation in government and private interests repulsed Innis. See Drache, *Staples, Markets, and Cultural Change*.

89 See Harold Innis, untitled memorandum ['rough draft'] (n.d.), Harold Innis Papers, University of Toronto Archives (UTA), Box 23, file 10, B72-0003; and Innis 'Economics and Business,' unpublished manuscript (n.d.), Harold Innis Papers, UTA, Box 012, file 47, B72-0003.

90 Innis, 'Economics and Business,' 1

91 Innis, untitled memorandum, 1

92 Innis, 'Economics and Business,' 2

93 Lower, quoted in Heick, *History and Myth*, 108

94 Donald Creighton, *Harold Adams Innis: Portrait of a Scholar* (Toronto, 1957), 109

95 Harold Innis, 'Address to the President' (n.d., 1941?) Harold Innis Papers, UTA, Box 005, file 18, B72-0003, 1, 2. Innis was fundamentally opposed to Underhill's view that the scholar should take up positions outside academia, and he urged the scholar to remain in the ivory tower. See note 88.

96 Innis to Donald Creighton (15 February 1941), Donald Creighton Papers, National Archives of Canada (NAC), v. 1; General Correspondence, 1941, 31 D77

97 Innis, 'Address to the President,' 2

98 Ibid.

99 Harold Innis, 'A Plea for the University Tradition,' *Dalhousie Review*, 24 (1944), 298, 299–300

100 Innis to H.J. Cody (3 December 1943), Harold Innis Papers, UTA, Box 005, file 18, B72-0003

101 Innis to G.M. Weir (8 March 1943), Harold Innis Papers, UTA, Box 005, file 18, B72-0003. See also an untitled memorandum concerning the Social Science Research Council (SSRC) and the post-war problem of the University (no date, 1948?), Harold Innis Papers, UTA, B72-0003.

102 Harold Innis, 'Adult Education and Universities,' in Innis, *The Bias of Communication* (Toronto, 1951; reprinted 1973), 204

103 *Scholarship for Canada* was a report commissioned by the Canadian SSRC. Council officials chose Brebner to write the report because he was a scholar working in America (though Canadian born) and therefore had 'no ax to grind.' See John Bartlet Brebner, *Scholarship for Canada. The Function of Graduate Studies* (Ottawa, 1945), 3, 13, 13–14, 14.

104 Principals Wallace and James, of Queen's and McGill universities, respectively, were rumoured to have been poised to ask the NCCU for permission to close faculties of arts in Canadian universities, along with certain programs in other faculties. It was also rumoured that Prime Minister Mackenzie King would put the plan immediately into effect. See McKillop, *Matters of Mind*, 533.

105 Although several members of the council signed the memorandum, it is evident from the style that Innis himself drafted all or most of the text.

106 Canadian Social Science Research Council *Brief to the Canadian Government* (November 1942), Donald Creighton Papers, NAC, v. 15, H.A. Innis, 1924–54, MG 31 D77, 2, 3

107 Ibid., 3

108 Humanists rallied under the threat of curtailment of instruction and resolved, owing to the initiative of Innis and R.H. Coats (dominion statistician), to create an association of humanists similar to the CSSRC. Accordingly, the HRCC was created by the end of 1943 at the instigation of Innis and under the initial leadership of Watson Kirkconnell and A.S.P. Woodhouse.

109 McKillop, *Matters of Mind*, 539

110 Innis, 'A Plea for the University Tradition,' 299

111 Harold Innis, 'The Church in Canada,' in *Time for Healing*, Twenty-Second Annual Report of the Board of Evangelism and Social Service (Toronto, 1947), 2

112 Watson Kirkconnell and A.S.P. Woodhouse, *The Humanities in Canada* (Ottawa, 1947), 6, 7, 6–7, 7

113 Ibid., 8, 11

114 Kirkconnell, *Twilight of Liberty*, 176, 184, 185, 185–6, 187. Note that Kirkconnell did not advocate the return of formal religion or the promotion of religious dogma of any kind. Instead, he wished to emphasize the need to evoke the spiritual part of the human psyche; for he believed that that aspect of humanity had been under siege in the recent past.

115 Harold Innis, 'The University in the Modern Crisis,' in Innis, *Political Economy in the Modern State* (Toronto, 1946), 80–1

116 See Harold Innis, *The Idea File*, ed., William Christian (Toronto, 1980) section 2/19, 9. Here, Innis writes: 'Ivory tower is essential if [a] universal point of view [is] to be attained.'

117 Innis, 'Plea for the University Tradition,' 65, 71

118 Donald Creighton to John Marshall (10 May 1943), Donald Creighton Papers, NAC, v. 1, General Correspondence: 1943, 31 D77, 1, 1–2

119 'Values' Discussion Group, 22 March 1947, Harold Innis Papers, UTA, Box 030, file 06, B72-0003, 2. This group of Toronto scholars met at the university in the second half of the 1940s. The main goal of the meetings, which were led, in turn, by one of the group's members, was to assess the role of values in modern life. Most important, the scholars wished to understand the part played by the university in influencing societal values.

120 Ibid., 8 March 1949, 1, 2

121 Ibid., 22 March 1947

4: The Modernization of Higher Learning in Canada II

1 *Report of National Conference of Canadian Universities on Post-War Problems* (Toronto, 1944), 7. The executive of the NCCU appointed this committee in 1942 to study post-war problems of Canadian universities. Four meetings of the committee were held in total and the report of the 13 June 1944 meeting was published along with several appendixes on 'special issues.'

2 R.C. Wallace, 'The Arts Faculty and Humane Studies,' in ibid., 54–7, 57, 58–9

3 Harold Innis, 'The Problem of Graduate Work in Canada,' in *Report of the National Conference of Canadian Universities on Post-War Problems*, 59

4 W.R. Taylor, 'The University and Education,' in Richard M. Saunders, ed., *Education for Tomorrow: A Series of Lectures Organized by the Teaching Staff of the University of Toronto* (Toronto, 1946), 62. See also Hardolph Wasteneys, 'Education for the Professions,' in ibid., 81–93 for a discussion of how humane studies should pervade professional education.

5 Quoted in A.B. McKillop, *Matters of Mind: The University in Ontario, 1791–1951* (Toronto, 1994), 557

6 Paul Axelrod, *Scholars and Dollars: Politics Economics, and the Universities of Ontario, 1945–1980* (Toronto, 1982), 22

7 Robin S. Harris, *A History of Higher Education in Canada, 1663–1960* (Toronto, 1976), 528

8 Ibid., 468; see also McKillop, *Matters of Mind*, 548.

9 See McKillop, *Matters of Mind*, 559–60.

10 E.A. Corbett, 'Adult Education,' in Saunders, ed., *Education for Tomorrow*, 64–80

11 McKillop, *Matters of Mind*, 560

12 Ibid.

13 Note that Gilmour later spoke on the need for McMaster to remain small and to retain its 'community of spirit': that is, Christianity should still remain an integral part of arts and science programs. He recommended that if new faculties 'should be set up, their students should not be out of proportion' with the numbers of arts and science students. In response to profound change of his institution, Gilmour thus paid lip service to old values and ideals. See G.P. Gilmour, *Higher Education in the Canadian Democracy* (Hamilton, 1948), 18–19.

14 Only a few academies, such as the University of Ottawa, were entirely privately funded by the early 1950s.

15 The so-called veterans boom will be discussed below.

16 Ontario Treasurer Leslie Frost's budget speech of 16 March 1944; quoted in Axelrod, *Scholars and Dollars*, 80

17 Hepburn actually decreased grants to Ontario universities during the 1930s and was hesitant to increase funding during the war. The Drew administration, by contrast, greatly superseded the funding levels of its predecessor.
18 See Axelrod, *Scholars and Dollars*, 80.
19 McKillop, *Matters of Mind*, 559
20 Harris, 564, 565
21 Steacie made existing alliances between the council and the universities stronger. He thus solidified the importance of Canadian institutions of higher learning as the focal points of fundamental and applied research.
22 See Axelrod, *Scholars and Dollars*, chapters 2 and 3.
23 Harris, *History of Higher Education*, 567, 571. The vast majority of CSSRC funding for the period 1940–57 came from private American foundations such as the Carnegie Foundation (which provided over $100,000) and the Ford Foundation (which provided nearly a half a million dollars). Governments and private organizations, by contrast, provided only $82,525. The Rockefeller Foundation contributed $150,648 to the HRC, while the Carnegie Foundation paid out $137,130.
24 Watson Kirkconnell and A.S.P. Woodhouse, *The Humanities in Canada* (Ottawa, 1947), 206, 207
25 John Bartlet Brebner, *Scholarship for Canada: The Function of Graduate Studies* (Ottawa, 1945), 45
26 Kirkconnell and Woodhouse, *Humanities in Canada*, 205, 206
27 B.S. Keirstead and S.D. Clark, 'The State of the Social Sciences in English-Speaking Canada,' Special Study to the Royal Commission on the Arts, Letters, and Sciences, draft copy, Hilda Neatby Papers, Saskatchewan Archives Board (SAB), II. 94, Special Studies: Keirstead, Professor B.S., and Clark, S.D. 'The State of Social Sciences in English-Speaking Canada,' 1; see also Keirstead and Clark, 'The State of Social Sciences in English-Speaking Canada,' *Royal Commission Studies: A Selection of Essays Prepared for the Royal Commission on National Development in the Arts, Letters and Sciences* (Ottawa, 1948). The deterioration of graduate and undergraduate teaching was the necessary concomitant of the exodus of scholars from Canadian universities. See also Harold Innis, 'Memorandum for the sub-committee on social sciences' (n.d.), Harold Innis Papers, University of Toronto Archives (UTA), Box 012, file 47, B72-0025, 2.
28 Brebner, *Scholarship for Canada*, 34, 34–5
29 Quoted in Axelrod, *Scholars and Dollars*, 81
30 Harold Innis, 'The University in the Modern Crisis,' in Innis, *Political Economy in the Modern State* (Toronto, 1946), 75
31 Brebner, *Scholarship for Canada*, 73

32 Keirstead and Clark, 'State of Social Sciences,' SAB, 15; see also Keirstead and Clark, 'State of Social Sciences,' *Royal Commission Studies*, 166.
33 Innis, *Political Economy in the Modern State*, xvii
34 Harold Innis, 'A Plea for the University Tradition,' in Innis, *Political Economy in the Modern State*, 299, 73
35 See Malcolm M. Wallace, 'The Present Status of the Humanities in Canada,' Special Study to the Royal Commission on the Arts, Letters, and Sciences, draft copy, Hilda Neatby Papers, SAB, II. 110, Special Studies: Wallace, 'The Present Status of the Humanities in Canada,' A139, 4; Malcolm M. Wallace, 'The Present Status of the Humanities in Canada,' *Royal Commission Studies: A Selection of Essays Prepared for the Royal Commission on National Development in the Arts, Letters and Sciences* (Ottawa, 1948).
36 Vincent Massey, 'The Modern University: Progress and Digression,' *Address to the 75th Anniversary Convocation of the University of Western Ontario, London*, in Massey, *Speaking of Canada: Addresses by the Right Honourable Vincent Massey* (Toronto, 1959), 83
37 James S. Thomson, 'Canadian Universities Face the Future,' *Queen's Quarterly*, 52 (Autumn 1945), 264
38 Donald Creighton, 'Canada in the World,' draft copy, [1953?], Donald Creighton Papers, National Archives of Canada (NAC) v. 11; 'Canada in the World,' MG 31 D77, 8. See also Donald Grant Creighton, 'Canada in the World,' in G.P. Gilmour, ed., *Canada's Tomorrow: Papers and Discussion Canada's Tomorrow Conference, Quebec City, November 1953* (Toronto, 1954).
39 Thomson, 'Canadian Universities,' 262, 262–3
40 Kirkconnell and Woodhouse, *Humanities in Canada*, 10, 11
41 The mechanism by which humanists could fulfil this goal was by accessing intellectual, esthetic, and moral systems of other cultures, past and present, and applying them to strengthen the current moral order. See Kirkconnell and Woodhouse, 11–12 and Thomson, 'Canadian Universities,' 263–4.
42 Innis, 'University in the Modern Crisis,' 73
43 Richard M. Saunders, ed., 'Introduction,' *Education for Tomorrow*, xi, x
44 Vincent Massey, 'Address by the Right Honourable V. Massey, C.H. to the Convocating Class, Convocation Hall, University of Toronto,' draft copy (21 November 1947), Vincent Massey Papers, UTA, 421(08), B87–0082, 8, 8–9
45 George P. Grant, 'The Teaching of Philosophy in English-Speaking Canada,' draft copy, (24 October 1950), Hilda Neatby Papers, SAB, II. 93; file: Grant, Professor G.P., 'The Teaching of Philosophy in English-Speaking Canada,' 2, 2–3, 19. See also George P. Grant, '"Philosophy" in Canada,' *Royal Commission Studies: A Selection of Essays Prepared for the Royal Commission on National Development in the Arts, Letters and Sciences* (Ottawa, 1948)

46 Ibid. (draft copy), 19
47 H.A. Innis, 'Charles Norris Cochrane, 1889–1946,' *Canadian Journal of Economics and Political Science*, 12 (February 1946), 96
48 Harold Innis, 'A Plea for Time,' Sesquicentennial Lectures (Fredericton, 1950), 1
49 Harold Innis, *The Bias of Communication* (Toronto, 1951, reprinted 1964), 33–4
50 Hilda Neatby, 'Special Study on Canadian History,' Special Study to the Royal Commission on the Arts, Letters, and Sciences, draft copy, Hilda Neatby Papers, SAB, II. 103, Special Studies: Neatby, Hilda, 'Special Study on Canadian History,' A139, 167. See also Neatby, 'National History,' *Royal Commission Studies: A Selection of Essays Prepared for the Royal Commission on National Development in the Arts, Letters and Sciences* (Ottawa, 1948).
51 Massey, 'Modern University,' 87
52 W.L. Morton, 'Clio in Canada: The Interpretation of Canadian History,' *University of Toronto Quarterly*, 15 (April 1946), quoted in A.B. McKillop, ed., *Contexts of Canada's Past: Selected Essays of W.L. Morton* (Toronto, 1980), 104
53 Desmond Pacey, 'The American Scholar To-Day,' *Queen's Quarterly*, 50 (Winter 1943–4), 357
54 N.A.M. MacKenzie, 'Presidential Address,' National Conference of Canadian Universities Twenty-Third Meeting Held at McGill University, 22–24 May 1947, unpublished report (n.d. 10, 11)
55 Pacey, 'American Scholar To-Day,' 354
56 Kirkconnell and Woodhouse, *Humanities in Canada*, 11
57 J.S. Thomson, 'The Conflict of Values in Education,' Address by President J.S. Thomson, National Conference of Canadian Universities Twenty-Second Meeting Held at the University of Toronto, 27–29 May 1946, unpublished report (n.d.), 43, 45
58 See Donald Creighton, 'Education for Government: What can the humanities do for government?, unpublished manuscript (n.d.), Donald Creighton Papers, NAC, v. 15; Education for government, MG 31 D77, 8. Here, Creighton writes that the humanities enabled humans 'to evaluate, [and] to make judgments, in a realm where judgment can only be made by a nice discrimination born of experience and wisdom.'
59 Thomson, 'Conflict of Values,' 45
60 MacKenzie, 'Presidential Address,' 10, 9, 11
61 Wallace, 'Present Status of the Humanities,' 5. Wallace makes an interesting about-face here. It was he, along with Cyril James of McGill, who in 1942 wanted to halt instruction in the humanities for the duration of war. See chapter 3, n.104.

62 Vincent Massey, 'Address by the Right Honourable Massey before the Graduate Organization of the University of Toronto for Kingston and District, Kingston, Ont., 23 April 1948,' unpublished address, draft copy, Vincent Massey Papers, UTA, 421(08) B87-0082, 10–14

63 Canada, Royal Commission on National Development in the Arts, Letters and Sciences, *Report* (Ottawa, 1951), 143, 563. Neatby wrote most of the report in 1949–50. She consulted many of the special studies and other written submissions, of course, and was influenced to a degree by the commission's cross-Canada hearings. Ultimately, however, she wrote the *Report*, and thus it reflects her biases.

64 Watson Kirkconnell, *Liberal Education in the Canadian Democracy* (Hamilton, 1948), 5

65 See chapter 3 and Arthur Lower, 'The Social Sciences in the Post-War World,' *Canadian Historical Review*, 22 (March 1941); quoted in Welf H. Heick, ed., *History and Myth: Arthur Lower and the Making of Canadian Nationalism* (Vancouver, 1975), 106.

66 Thomson, 'Address,' 260

67 Innis referred to the importance of Oswald Spengler's thought on the rise and decline of civilization in *Empire and Communications* (Toronto, 1950), 3; in Innis, *The Idea File*, ed. William Christian (Toronto, 1980) section 29/49, 264; and in Innis, *Bias of Communication*, 90, 132. In each case, Innis refers to the Spengler's concern for modern civilization and, in general terms, the latter's reasons for the decline of the west.

68 Harold Innis, *The Strategy of Culture* (Toronto, 1952), 14

69 Paul Litt, *The Muses, the Masses, and the Massey Commission* (Toronto, 1992), 170

70 Doug Owram, *Born at the Right Time: A History of the Baby Boom Generation* (Toronto, 1996), 167. See also Angus McLaren, *Our Own Master Race: Eugenics in Canada, 1885–1945* (Toronto, 1990).

71 J.A. Corry, *Farewell the Ivory Tower: Universities in Transition* (Montreal, 1970), 54

72 Hilda Neatby, *So Little for the Mind* (Toronto, 1953), 3

73 Harold Innis, 'Industrialism and Cultural Values,' *Papers and Proceedings of the American Economic Association, American Economic Review*, 41 (1951), 208

74 MacKenzie, 'Presidential Address,' 12

75 Owram, *Born at the Right Time*, chapters 1–3

76 An excerpt from 1878 federal budget speech; quoted in Wallace Gagne ed., *Nationalism, Technology and the Future of Canada* (Toronto, 1976), 19

77 Kenneth Norrie and Douglas Owram, *A History of the Canadian Economy*, 2nd ed. (Toronto, 1991), 411

312   Notes to pages 133–8

78 Quoted in Owram, *Born at the Right Time*, 17
79 Ibid., chapter 3
80 Ibid., chapter 2
81 Quoted in Michael Hayden, ed., *So Much to Do, So Little Time: The Writings of Hilda Neatby* (Vancouver, 1983), 289
82 George P. Grant, 'Teaching of Philosophy,' 5
83 Vincent Massey, 'Useful Knowledge,' Address at the Convocation of the University of Manitoba, draft copy, Hilda Neatby Papers, SAB, I. 12 (Massey, Vincent, 1951–69) (2), A139, 4
84 Wallace, 'Present Status of the Humanities,' 5
85 Quoted in Robert Bothwell, Ian Drummond, and John English, *Canada since 1945: Power, Politics, and Provincialism* (Toronto 1981; rev. ed. 1989), 89
86 Watson Kirkconnell, *Seven Pillars of Freedom: An Exposure of the Soviet World Conspiracy and Its Fifth Column in Canada* (Toronto, 1944; revised 1952), ix
87 See also Kirkconnell, *Liberal Education*, 15–18.
88 Donald Creighton, for example, showed how individuals characterized the ideological natures of the 'Free World' and of the East. People, Creighton explained, considered the former to be free, democratic, Christian, capitalist, and righteous in almost every regard and Communist countries to be almost the direct opposite. See Creighton, 'Canada in the World.'
89 Litt, *The Muses, the Masses, and the Massey Commission*, 85. Much more will be said on the impact of democracy on modern culture in the next chapter.
90 Taylor, 'University and Education,' 56
91 Vincent Massey, 'Address by the Right Honourable Vincent Massey before the Chamber of Commerce, Hamilton Ontario, April 21st, 1948,' draft copy, Vincent Massey Papers, UTA, 421(08), B87-0082, 10, 5
92 Harris, *History of Higher Education*, 451, 457. The twofold increase of full-time enrolments put a heavy strain on university resources. It is beyond the scope of this chapter, however, to outline the implications of the vast influx of new university students on the staffs and infrastructures of the institutions. See McKillop, *Matters of Mind*, 550–4.
93 Owram, *Born at the Right Time*, 113, 117
94 The educational systems in most Canadian provinces shunned married women teachers and resorted instead to young, unmarried instructors or 'spinster teachers.' By the mid-1950s, however, married women became very significant contributors to the overall number of educators. For example, they comprised up to 30 per cent of the teaching population in Manitoba, and schools in Ontario would have had to close had it not been for the return of married teachers.
95 Owram, *Born at the Right Time*, 118

96 Neatby, *So Little for the Mind*, 15, 12, 43, 42

97 Hilda Neatby, *A Temperate Dispute* (Toronto, 1954), 25, 21, 85–6

98 Ibid., 18

99 Neatby charges that while Dewey eulogizes 'the scientific, democratic, [and] materialist society,' he forgets that this society was the production of '"passive" listeners, readers and thinkers,' who are, for him, beneath contempt. Dewey is thus anti-intellectual and his anti-intellectualism leads him to an erroneous understanding of his world. See Neatby, *So Little for the Mind*, 25.

100 See also John K. McCreary, 'Canada and Progressive Education,' *Queen's Quarterly*, 56 (Spring 1949), 56–67.

101 See, among others, Russell Kirk, 'Academic Servility: An Issue beyond Politics,' *Queen's Quarterly*, 62 (Spring 1955), 1–11; J. Bartlett Brebner, 'The Faith of a Scholar: Against the Sins of Pride,' *Queen's Quarterly*, 62 (Summer 1955), 184–7.

102 As early as 1951, Hilda Neatby remarked in a letter to Vincent Massey: 'Canada seems singularly indifferent to her university question; the Americans, on the contrary, have produced two ten-column pages of lists of article titles (in periodical index or some such) in two years 1949–51.' Neatby to Massey, 9 November 1951, 451(05) B87-0082

103 This was the title given to the conference proceedings. See C.T. Bissell, ed., *Canada's Crisis in Higher Education. Proceedings of the Conference Held by the National Conference of Canadian Universities at Ottawa, November 12–14* (Toronto, 1957), v.

104 McKillop, *Matters of Mind*, 565

105 Bissell claimed that the 130,000 figure that Sheffield cited was remarkably accurate, since the universities independently calculated a similar rate of expansion by the middle of the 1960s. See Bissell, *Canada's Crisis*, 5.

106 McKillop, *Matters of Mind*, 566

107 Bissell, *Canada's Crisis*, v, vi, 244–6. The committee decided that the use of students and staff resources and the 'securing of sufficient staff to meet the needs of the new student population' as well as the subsidiary problem of staff funding were the main difficulties with which modern universities would have to deal. Large enrolment increases required not only expanded university infrastructures – residences, cafeterias, meeting halls, recreational and classroom facilities – but also extended teaching staffs. The University of Alberta, for example, expected its staff to grow by 100 per cent in its faculties of Arts and Engineering by 1965, while McGill anticipated an increase of 125 per cent in the Faculty of Arts and Science and of 185 per cent in the Faculty of Engineering (Bissell, *Canada's Crisis*,

5). Other universities, especially in western and central Canada, anticipated similar expansions in staff. Since about 60 per cent of university
operating expenses pay staff salaries, more staff meant that operating
costs would at least double by the mid-1960s. Through capital and staffing
costs, the rise in enrolments entailed a great expenditure for Canadian
universities.

108 Sidney E. Smith, 'Educational Structure: The English-Canadian Universities,' in ibid., 8, 11

109 Ibid., 11–12

110 Ibid., 8–12

111 Steacie himself was a scientist and head of the NRC, the largest research
organization in Canada. He was also, in Claude Bissell's words, an
'instinctive humanist,' very much attuned to the needs and goals of liberal
arts learning. See Claude Bissell, *Halfway up Parnassus: A Personal Account
of the University of Toronto, 1932–1971* (Toronto, 1974), 34.

112 E.W.R. Steacie, 'The Responsibility of the University in the Training of
Scientists and Technologists,' in Bissell, *Canada's Crisis*, 41, 43

113 John Ely Burchard, 'The Role of the Humanities and Social Sciences: The
Training of Scientists and Technologists,' in ibid., 55, 57

114 See Davidson Dunton and Dorothy Patterson, eds, *Canada's Universities in
a New Age. Proceedings of a Conference of Canadian Universities and Colleges at
Ottawa, November 13–15, 1961* (Ottawa, 1961). The NCCU was renamed
National Conference of Canadian Universities and Colleges (the NCCUC).

115 The CIA reported that the Soviet Union would graduate 1.2 million students in pure science during the 1950s while the United States would
graduate only 990,000. See Axelrod, *Scholars and Dollars*, 24, 25.

116 Owram, *Born at the Right Time*, 179

117 H.F. Légaré, Introduction to the Conference,' in Dunton and Patterson,
eds, *Canada's Universities*, vi

118 Quoted in Harris, *History of Higher Education*, 587–88. Throughout the
1960s, moreover, the federal government was preoccupied with the search
for a means of establishing and maintaining a national policy on research.
Among other things, it succeeded in establishing the Science Council of
Canada (1966).

119 Quoted in Bissell, *Halfway up Parnassus*, 49

120 Claude Bissell, 'The Problems and Opportunities of Canada's Universities,' in Dunton and Patterson, eds, *Canada's Universities*, 6

121 Owram, *Born at the Right Time*, 179–80

122 Quoted in Axelrod, *Scholars and Dollars*, 28.

123 Bissell, 'Problems and Opportunities,' 10

124 J.E. Hodgetts, 'Introduction: Higher Education in a Changing Canada,' in Hodgetts, ed., *Higher Education in a Changing Canada: Symposium Presented to the Royal Society of Canada in 1965* (Toronto, 1966), xi

125 Owram, *Born at the Right Time*, 180

126 H.J. Somers, 'Summation of Conference,' in Dunton and Patterson, eds, *Canada's Universities*, 150

127 Hodgetts, 'Introduction,' xviii

128 Quoted in Owram, *Born at the Right Time*, 180

129 Quoted in William Christian, *George Grant: A Biography* (Toronto, 1993), 328

130 Northrop Frye, 'The Critical Discipline,' Address to the Royal Society of Canada's Symposium, Canadian Universities Today, draft copy (1960?), Northrop Frye Papers, Victoria University Library (VUL), 88 Box 1, P, 5–6 See also Frye, 'The Critical Discipline,' in George Stanley and Guy Sylvestre, eds, *Canadian Universities Today: Symposium Presented to the Royal Society of Canada in 1960* (Toronto, 1961).

131 Northrop Frye, 'By Liberal Things,' Installation Address by Northrop Frye, Principal, Victoria College, 21 October 1959, draft copy, Northrop Frye Papers, VUL, 88 Box 1, L, 6

132 Ibid., 110, 8, 11, 8–9

133 Northrop Frye, 'Preserving Human Values,' An Address by Dr. H. Northrop Frye, Principal of Victoria College, for the Annual Meeting of the Social Planning Council of Toronto, draft copy (27 April 1961), Northrop Frye Papers, VUL, 88 Box 47, File #1, 2

134 Frye, 'The Critical Discipline,' 11

135 Northrop Frye, 'Academy without Walls,' unpublished draft copy, Northrop Frye Papers, VUL, 88 Box 1, N, 10

136 Northrop Frye, 'The Changing Pace in Canadian Education,' unpublished paper, draft copy (24 January 1963), Northrop Frye Papers, VUL, 88 Box 1, Q, 5, 8

137 Corry, *Farewell the Ivory Tower*, 19–21, 21

138 Ibid., 54

139 A.R.M. Lower, 'The Canadian University: Time for a New Deal,' *Queen's Quarterly*, v. 62 (Summer 1955), 256, 249

140 Bissell, 'Problems and Opportunities,' 5 ·

141 Marshall McLuhan to John Bassett, 13 January 1964, H. Marshall McLuhan Papers, NAC, v. 18; reel 2055, MG 31 D156

142 Richard Schlatter, 'The Ford Humanities Project at Princeton: The Job of the Humanist Scholar' (1961), W.L. Morton Papers, William Ready Division of Archives and Research Collections, McMaster University Library, Hamilton, Canada (MUL), Box 1, File A (misc.), 3, 2

143 E.W.R. Steacie, 'The Task of the University Today,' in Stanley and Sylvestre, eds, *Canadian Universities Today*, 4

5: Battling the Philistines

1 W.H. Alexander, 'The End of an Age,' *University of Toronto Quarterly*, 5 (January 1946), 109, 111, 110–11, 112
2 Harold Innis, Marshall McLuhan, and George Grant also discussed the emergence of a technological imperative that characterized modern cultures in the west. See chapter 2.
3 James S. Thomson, 'The Unbinding of Prometheus,' *University of Toronto Quarterly*, 15 (October 1945), 1, 2, 1–2. See also George Grant, 'The Minds of Men in the Atomic Age,' in H.D. Forbes, ed., *Canadian Political Thought* (Toronto, 1985), 284–9.
4 S. Basterfield, 'The Influence of Science on the Cultural Outlook,' *University of Toronto Quarterly*, 23 (January 1954), 179, 180, 181–3
5 Ibid., 184
6 K. Rayski-Kietlitcz, 'The Canadian Cultural Pattern,' *Dalhousie Review*, 30 (1950–1), 173
7 Peter Viereck, 'Two Aspects of Freedom,' *Dalhousie Review*, 32 (Spring 1952), 4, 12–14
8 John A. Irving, 'Moral Standards in a Changing World,' *Dalhousie Review*, 24 (1949–50), 121, 124, 122–3, 124
9 Canadian Social Science Research Council, *Brief to the Canadian Government* (November 1942) Donald Creighton Papers, National Archives of Canada (NAC), v. 15, H.A. Innis, 1924–54, MG 31 D77. See also Harold Innis, 'A Plea for The University Tradition,' *Dalhousie Review*, 24 (1944), 303, for a discussion on the infiltration of government into politics. Innis wrote: 'Nothing has been more indicative of the decline in cultural life in Canada since the last war than the infiltration of politics in the Universities.'
10 See Harold Innis, 'Implications of the Interactions between Values and Resources,' unpublished paper (2 October 1949), Harold Innis Papers, University of Toronto Archives (UTA) B72-0003, Box 20, file 33.
11 Harold Innis, 'Minerva's Owl,' in Innis, *The Bias of Communication* (Toronto, 1951; reprinted 1973), 5
12 Ibid., 30–1, 31
13 Ibid., 33
14 See chapter 4, n. 67.
15 Innis, *Bias of Communication*, 34
16 Frank Underhill called Toynbee 'the most fashionable historian of our day.'

Yet he went on to denounce Toynbee and the latter's approach to history. See F.H. Underhill, 'Arnold Toynbee, Metahistorian,' *Canadian Historical Review*, 32 (September 1951), 201, 207, 202.

17 Matthew Arnold, *Culture and Anarchy*, ed. Samuel Lipman (New Haven, Connecticut, 1994), 166

18 Arthur Lower, 'I Came Back and I Am Content,' *Maclean's* (1 July 1951); quoted in Welf H. Heick, ed., *History and Myth: Arthur Lower and the Making of Canadian Nationalism* (Vancouver, 1975), 101–2

19 Susan Stone-Blackburn. *Robertson Davies, Playwright: A Search for the Self on the Canadian Stage* (Vancouver, 1985), 12. Note that Davies made little attempt to ensure the historical veracity of his play. Sainte-Vaillier, not Laval, was actually the bishop of New France during the period in question. Davies substituted Laval for Sainte-Vaillier because he was a better-known historical figure and was a more effective foil to Governor Frontenac. Chemène is a Huron waif whom Frontenac had sent to Paris to be educated and trained as an actress. Purely the creation of Davies's imagination, she, along with Frontenac, are the chief proponents of cultural development.

20 Ibid.

21 Robertson Davies, *Overlaid*, in Davies, *Two Plays: At My Heart's Core and Overlaid* (Toronto, 1991), 106–7, 113–14

22 Stone-Blackburn, *Robertson Davies, Playwright*, 18

23 Ibid., 52

24 Rowlands, in Stone-Blackburn's words, 'speaks despairingly of the twenty- five years he has spent trying to share with Canadian students "the trea- sures of a great literature," when only three among them all could recog- nize the wealth he offered, and these three have all left Canada for the US. "God, how I have tried to love this country! ... How I have tried to forget the paradise of Wales and the quick wits of Oxford! I have given I all have to Canada – my love, then my hate, and now my bitter indifference. This raw, frost-bitten country has me wrung out, and its raw, frost-bitten people have numbed my heart."' Quoted in ibid., 55–6; see also below.

25 See Robertson Davies, *Four Favourite Plays* (Toronto, 1949), 20–2. Note that Nicholas endeavours to defend his contemplated move to the United States by describing the relative merits of the United States and Canada as cul- tural entities. He says (with considerable passion) to Rowlands in defence of his prospective homeland: the United States is a place where a 'high standard of living means something more than merely a high standard of eating.' '[B]ehind all the commercialism and vulgarity, there is a promise, and there is a promise here, as yet, for men like me. I am not patient! But I am not unreasonable! I can live on a promise, but in a country where the

questions that I ask meet only with blank incomprehension, and the yearnings that I feel find no understanding, I know that I must go mad, or I must strangle my soul with my hands, or I must get out and try my luck in a country which has some use for me.'

26 Ibid., 95. Heartened by Szabo's bravado, Nicholas also resolves to remain in Canada: 'If you can stay in Canada, I can, too' (98).

27 Ibid.

28 It is beyond the scope of this chapter to outline the genesis of the Massey Commission. See Paul Litt, *The Muses, the Masses, and the Massey Commission* (Toronto, 1992) for a discussion of the commission's origins.

29 Vincent Massey, N.A.M. MacKenzie, Arthur Surveyor, Henri-Georges Lévesque, and Hilda Neatby were the commissioners in question. Neatby prepared most of the *Report*.

30 Brooke Claxton, the chief initiator of the commission, experienced this indifference first hand when his proposal for a commission on culture was rejected at the Liberal Convention of 1948. Later, he drew up a memorandum to Prime Minister Mackenzie King, dated 29 September 1948, outlining the terms of reference of such an inquest and suggesting that Massey should be its head. King, who cared little for matters cultural, rejected Claxton's overtures; and although Claxton finally succeeded in having the commission called under the new Liberal government of Louis St Laurent, St Laurent told Pickersgill, a key adviser to King during the 1940s, that he was sceptical about 'subsidizing "ballet dancing."' See Bernard Ostry. *The Cultural Connection: An Essay on Culture and Government Policy in Canada* (Toronto, 1978), 56–7; Robert Bothwell, Ian Drummond, and John English, *Canada since 1945: Power, Politics, and Provincialism* (Toronto 1981; rev. ed. 1989), 154.

31 Canada's retarded cultural development was no doubt real. As stated in chapter 4, however, the Massey commissioners and others forming cultural 'pressure groups' wanted to exaggerate Canada's cultural deprivation so as to develop a popular opinion favourable to their goals of cultural advancement. Above all, they wanted to show that Canadian culture was at a critical juncture and that it could be advanced only through the aid of the government purse.

32 Canada, Royal Commission on National Development in the Arts, Letters and Sciences, *Report* (Ottawa, 1951), 12, 12–13

33 Edward McCourt, 'Canadian Letters,' in *Royal Commission Studies: A Selection of Essays Prepared for the Royal Commission on National Development in the Arts, Letters and Sciences* (Ottawa, 1948), 67

34 Ibid., 68, 70, 73, 74

35 Canada, *Report*, 10
36 Robertson Davies, 'The Theatre,' in *Royal Commission Studies*, 371, 373
37 Malcolm Wallace, 'The Humanities,' in *Royal Commission Studies*, 114
38 George Grant, '"Philosophy" in Canada,' in *Royal Commission Studies*, 5. Chapter 2 contains a discussion of G.P. Grant's 'Philosophy.' The main thrust is Grant's juxtaposition of the contemplative and the active, the philosophical and the scientific, and how, ultimately, Canadian society had come to favour the latter, 'technological' values over their philosophic counterparts. See chapters 2 and 4.
39 Note that Grant 'loathed' the term 'culture' and the appellation 'cultural' courses. He did acknowledge the contemplative approach to life as the focal point of any civilization. 'Culture,' for Grant, was therefore inextricably linked to continuous pursuit of a philosophical understanding of one's environment. Philosophy was not merely a subject of theoretical enquiry, a topic to be forgotten once it had been taken out of the academic world. It was, rather, 'a way of life that all must strive for' (2). See Grant to Mother (n.d.), George Grant Papers, NAC, v. 39; Mrs W.L. Grant Correspondence; file: Dalhousie University, MG 30 D59.
40 Hilda Neatby, 'National History,' *Royal Commission Studies*, 216, 215–16, 216
41 See Litt, *The Muses, the Masses, and the Massey Commission*, 53, 70–1, 76–7.
42 Canada, *Report*, 19, 20
43 Ibid., 22, 20
44 Ibid., 40–1
45 Arthur Surveyor disagreed with the other commissioners on the CBC and broadcast policy generally. Accordingly, he wrote a dissenting report on the issue. See Litt, *The Muses, the Masses, and the Massey Commission*, 216–20.
46 Canada, *Report*, 35, 39
47 Ibid., 42. George Grant lauded Neatby's analyses. He wrote: 'Your proposals about television and broadcasting seemed to this layman particularly intelligent and courageous.' George Grant to Hilda Neatby (17 June 1951), Hilda Neatby Papers, Saskatchewan Archives Board (SAB), II. 36, General Correspondence, 1949–51, A139. See also Hilda Neatby, 'Memorandum to Chairman on an Informal Investigation of T.V. Programmes Made in New York' (May 1949), Hilda Neatby Papers, SAB, II. 37, Memoranda to Chairman, 1949–51, A139.
48 Canada, *Report*, 47. On this point, Harold Innis added: 'The mass media of the twentieth century have entrenched materialism.' The 'subjection of individual minds to unification and standardization by mass media cannot lead to the reflection of other values than those that the people already have; materialism can only be a more general belief as a result of the actions of the

press, motion pictures, radio and television. These media are interested in following public opinion because they must appeal to the largest common mass of the people in order to make their advertising effective ... Mass media and advertising have grown out of materialism and support the further existence of materialism ... [They] are not conscious intelligences any more than are the values judgments of a society, and it is equally difficult in each case to imagine a way out of the dilemma which our demand for non-existing resources is creating.' Innis, 'Implications of the Interactions,' 8–9.

Neatby suggested, however, that Canada need not succumb to 'the television tyrants [private commercial broadcasters] of the United States.' Aided by 'public support,' its stations did not have to be 'on the air thirteen hours a day,' showing a succession of soap operas and other commercial broadcasts. Rather, Canadian television broadcasters could 'follow the example of the BBC with fewer shows, more carefully chosen, rehearsed and produced.' For Neatby, in brief, the 'great problem' of television was how to curtail commercialism and 'to make television what it might be at its best – a remarkable means of instruction and entertainment for the whole family together at home.' See Neatby, 'Memorandum to Chairman,' 11.

49 Canada, *Report*, 39, 38, 296
50 The commissioners were extremely careful not to tout culture during their country-wide tour (in 1949). They worried that they would alienate the people they encountered by introducing foreign elements into their lives. During the promotional tour, they were quick to play up the 'nation-coming-of-age' notion as a means to explain the need to expand cultural activities. All the while, they maintained a sort of 'low-brow pretense.' See Litt, *The Muses, the Masses, and the Massey Commission*, 65. Elsewhere, Vincent Massey demonstrated his willingness to achieve a middle ground between the highbrow and the lowbrow. In a 1948 address to business leaders on the ties of education to business, he characterized a 'highbrow' as a 'man whose education has outstripped his intelligence,' and one who 'does education no good.' '[He seems] to have forgotten the very simple purpose which education should serve.' Massey continued, arguing that this is 'where the layman comes in.' Indeed, the layman believes that education would benefit from 'the closer attention of the average citizen to this all-important activity.' Clearly, Massey was playing to a non-academic audience. Again, he played up the importance of the 'common man,' although it is doubtful he truly believed what he was saying. See Vincent Massey, 'Address by the Right Honourable Vincent Massey before the Chamber of Commerce, Hamilton Ontario, 21 April 1948, Vincent Massey Papers, University of Toronto Archives (UTA), 421(08), B87–0082, 2, 3.

51 Canada, *Report*, 24

52 See Litt, *The Muses, the Masses, and the Massey Commission*, chapter 6,
    'The Battle for the Airwaves,' for more. Litt asserts that the commissioners
    recommendations on media rested on their 'perceptions of the electronic
    media as the primary means of informing and educating Canadian citi-
    zens.' They wanted to make the CBC the single greatest agency for national
    unity, understanding and enlightenment.' (214). The commissioners sup-
    ported their desire by arguing that there was a 'demand ... that national
    radio be used as an instrument of education and culture came from every
    section of the country.' Canada, *Report*, 36.

53 Litt, *The Muses, the Masses, and the Massey Commission*, 85, 88

54 Ibid., 86

55 Donald Creighton, 'Education for Government: What Can the Humanities
    Do for Government?' unpublished paper (n.d.), Donald Creighton Papers,
    NAC, v. 15; Education for government, MG 31 D77, 9

56 Hilda Neatby to T.J. Allard (12 October 1954), Hilda Neatby Papers, SAB,
    VI. 175, 'So Little for the Mind': General Correspondence, 1953–71 (5),
    A139, 2

57 Marshall McLuhan, *The Mechanical Bride: The Folklore of Industrial Man*
    (Boston, 1951), 58, 58–9

58 Ibid., 94–7

59 Vincent Massey, 'Christian Social Order in a Changing World,' Address to
    the Montreal Council on Christian Social Order, 5 November 1953, draft
    copy, Hilda Neatby Papers, SAB, I. 12 (Massey, Vincent, 1951–69) (4), A139,
    4. See also Vincent Massey, 'Christian Social Order in a Changing World,' in
    Massey, *Speaking of Canada: Addresses by the Right Honourable Vincent Massey*
    (Toronto, 1959).

60 In a letter dated 18 March 1954 to Neatby, Massey asked Neatby's advice on
    the 'Montreal Address.' Massey wondered whether 'the neglect of the indi-
    vidual and the preoccupation with the mass' would be irrelevant to his
    main arguments on the 'new barbarism.' Massey to Hilda Neatby (18
    March 1953), Hilda Neatby Papers, SAB, I. 12 (Massey, Vincent, 1951–69)
    (3), A139. See Neatby's response, below.

61 Hilda Neatby to Vincent Massey (23 March 1953), Vincent Massey Papers,
    UTA, 585(07), B87-0082

62 Hilda Neatby, *A Temperate Dispute* (Toronto, 1954), 30, 34

63 Vincent Massey, 'Some Lions in the Path,' Address to the Alumni of the
    Collège de Montréal, Wednesday 27 October 1954, draft copy, Hilda Neatby
    Papers, SAB, I. 12 (Massey, Vincent, 1951–69) (5), A139, 4. See also Vincent
    Massey, 'Some Lions in the Path,' in Massey, *Speaking of Canada*.

64 Neatby, *A Temperate Dispute*, 34
65 Massey, 'Some Lions in the Path,' 4
66 Harold Innis. 'The Church in Canada,' in Daniel Drache, ed., *Staples, Markets, and Cultural Change: Selected Essays, Harold A. Innis* (Montreal, 1995), 459
67 Quoted in Campbell A. Ross, 'The Neatby Debate and Conservative Thought in Canada,' PhD thesis, University of Alberta, 1989, 147–8
68 Hilda Neatby to Vincent Massey (23 March 1953), Hilda Neatby Papers, SAB, I. 12 (Massey, Vincent, 1951–69) (3), A139, 2–2a
69 Quoted in William Christian, *George Grant: A Biography* (Toronto, 1993), 45–6
70 Brief of the Fiddlehead Poetry Society to the Royal Commission on National Development in the Arts, Letters and Sciences; quoted in Litt, *The Muses, the Masses, and the Massey Commission*, 89–90
71 As Marshall McLuhan queried in 1951: 'Does "freedom" mean the right to be and do exactly as everybody else? How much does this kind of uniformity depend on obeying the "orders" of commercial suggestion? If it takes a lot of money to conform in this way, does conformity become an ideal to strive for?' McLuhan, *Mechanical Bride*, 117
72 Neatby, *A Temperate Dispute*, 25. Malcolm Wallace agreed implicitly with Neatby about the origins of democratic freedom. He also concurred that 'group thinking' not only engendered the common conception of 'true liberty,' but it also hindered the pursuit of real democracy. '[H]ating and fearing Communism,' he wrote in 1951, was 'a sterile creed and [hence] inadequate to live by.' Canadians should instead 'decide to make [their] practice of Democracy correspond more closely to the noble [humanist] principles on which it was founded. [They] may then recover the initiative in the cold war ... and find [themselves] committed to a constructive programme which will absorb all our energies.' Wallace, 'The Present Status of the Humanities in Canada,' *Royal Commission Studies*, 118
73 Massey, 'Christian Social Order in a Changing World,' 4
74 Neatby, *A Temperate Dispute*, 25
75 Creighton, 'Education for Government,' 5
76 Vincent Massey, 'Address by the Right Honourable V. Massey, C.H. to the Convocating Class, Convocation Hall, University of Toronto, draft copy of an unpublished address (21 November 1947), Vincent Massey Papers, UTA, 421(08) B87-0082, 5
77 N.A.M. MacKenzie, Neatby's and Massey's colleague, also warned Canadians about the menace of mass society to liberal democracy. While Canadians appeared free from totalitarianism in the political sense, they were not

free 'from many of the challenges posed by the new techniques devised to influence and control the great masses of people.' Thus, they were like their counterparts elsewhere in the world in that they were prone to the 'development of standardization in all its phases' and hence subject to a different, more insidious variety of totalitarian control. See Norman A. MacKenzie, 'The Challenge to Education,' in G.P. Gilmour, ed., *Canada's Tomorrow: Papers and Discussion, Canada's Tomorrow Conference, Quebec City, November 1953* (Toronto, 1954), 161. Adjustment to the group, MacKenzie added, could not be equated to 'democratic living.' For, he continued, 'one can have the most satisfactory adjustment to groups within the framework of the most deadly totalitarian systems. To be well adjusted to a maladjusted society is therefore not a democratic virtue but the road to democratic ruin' (176).

78 B.K. Sandwell, 'Present Day Influences in Canadian Society,' *Royal Commission Studies*, 6–7
79 Canada, *Report*, 18
80 Sandwell, 'Present Day Influences,' 5, 6, 5–8
81 Quoted in Litt, *The Muses, the Masses, and the Massey Commission*, 171
82 Claude Bissell, *The Imperial Canadian: Vincent Massey in Office*, vol. 2 (Toronto, 1986), 218
83 Vincent Massey, 'Broadcast by the Right Honourable Vincent Massey for the Home Service of the BBC, 1 July 1951,' draft copy, Vincent Massey Papers, UTA, 424 (04) B87-0082, 4
84 As Bissell claims, Massey and the other commissioners did not deserve the charge of being 'anti-American.' Yet, although the commissioners attempted to be as objective as possible in their strictures on American influence, there can be no doubt of their opposition to the penetration into Canada of American culture. See Bissell, *Imperial Canadian*, 218.
85 George P. Grant, 'The Teaching of Philosophy in English-Speaking Canada,' draft copy (24 October 1950), Hilda Neatby Papers, SAB, II. 93; file: Grant, Professor G.P., 'The Teaching of Philosophy in English-Speaking Canada,' 28–9. Note that in the draft copy, Neatby highlighted this passage, indicating that it should be quoted in the *Report*. Grant's words were indeed cited.
86 Ibid., 19–20a
87 Ibid., 7. Note, again, that Neatby marked 'Quote' on this passage.
88 Norman A. MacKenzie, 'The Challenge to Education,' in G.P. Gilmour, ed., *Canada's Tomorrow*, 171–2
89 Canada, *Report*, 271
90 Neatby, *Temperate Dispute*, 25. Submission to 'providence and [the] love of God,' for Neatby, enabled the individual to partake in the freedom inherent

324 Notes to pages 188–90

to the transcendent and therefore to escape the narrowness of modern society. See also Neatby to Massey (23 March 1953), Hilda Neatby Papers, SAB, 585(07) B87-0082.

91 Grant, 'The Teaching of Philosophy in Canada,' 7. Like Neatby, Grant advocated rationale contemplation combined with religious faith. Indeed, faith in the transcendent was, for Grant, the precondition on which the philosophic approach rested.

92 Massey, 'Convocation Hall Address,' 6

93 Wallace, 'Present Status of the Humanities,' 6

94 Watson Kirkconnell and A.S.P. Woodhouse, *The Humanities in Canada* (Ottawa, 1947), 7

95 Neatby, *Temperate Dispute*, vii, 25

96 Wallace, 'Present Status of the Humanities,' 4

97 Kirkconnell and Woodhouse, *Humanities in Canada*, 7

98 Neatby, *Temperate Dispute*, 38

99 Hilda Neatby, *So Little for the Mind* (Toronto, 1953), 13

100 Neatby, *Temperate Dispute*, 38

101 Vincent Massey, 'The Crisis in Higher Education,' Address by Vincent Massey, C.H., at a meeting held under the auspices of the Synod of the Ecclesiastical Province of Canada, draft copy (18 May 1949), Vincent Massey Papers, UTA, 392(05), B87-0082, 5, 6

102 Harold Innis, unpublished address [title unknown] (n.d.): Harold Innis Papers, UTA, Box 22, file 11, B72-0025, 7–8

103 Innis, 'Church in Canada,' 461

104 Quoted in Michael Hayden, ed., *So Much to Do, So Little Time: The Writings of Hilda Neatby* (Vancouver, 1983), 295

105 Hilda Neatby, 'The Pragmatic Paradox: A Traditionalist Looks at Canadian Education,' unpublished paper, draft copy, n.d. [1951?] Vincent Massey Papers, UTA, 409(16), B87-0082, 2, 9

106 Hilda Neatby, 'Cultural Evolution,' in G.P. Gilmour, ed., *Canada's Tomorrow*, 222, 223. In the discussion that followed, Jean-C. Faladreau, chairman of the Department of Sociology of Laval University, provided a powerful statement in support of Neatby's views. He declared: 'The artist of the age of the atomic bomb, of the age of imperial totalitarianism ... cannot feed on the fatness of "material encouragement," nor on the idealized memories of a Victorian childhood ... He must wrestle *alone* with Fate, through Hell and Purgatory. If he can, he must also remember that Paradise can be conquered by spiritual violence' (italics in original) (316–17).

107 Vincent Massey, Address by the Right Honourable Vincent Massey before the Graduate Organization of the University of Toronto for Kingston and

District, unpublished address, draft copy (23 April 1948), Vincent Massey
Papers, UTA, 421(08), B87-0082, 5–6, 13
108 Massey, Convocation Hall Address, 8
109 Canada, *Report*, 167
110 See Vincent Massey, 'Useful Knowledge,' Address at the Convocation of
the University of Manitoba, draft copy, Hilda Neatby Papers, SAB, I. 12
(Massey, Vincent, 1951–69) (2).
111 Arnold's name and famous phrase resound in the writings of the culture
critics. Arnoldian thought was especially prominent in the Commission
Report and in the work of Massey and Neatby.
112 Arnold, *Culture and Anarchy,* 47, 48–9, 48, 48–9, 47
113 See Litt, *The Muses, and the Masses, and the Massey Commission,* 104
114 Canada, *Report,* 273, 293–5, 355. The CBC needed $3 million over and
above its $7.5 million annual income. The commissioners argued that the
federal government should make up for shortfalls arising from production
increases and other factors.
115 Ibid., 381, 272, 382. Vincent Massey outlined the desperate need for government funding of the arts, letters and sciences in his prior work, *On Being
Canadian* (Toronto, 1948). The chapter 'Threads of National Unity' served as
a precursor to many of the recommendations on federal funding for culture
(45–66). Also note the way that the commissioners attempted to shame the
federal government into sympathizing with its proposals. Referring to the
quasi-obsessive preoccupation of governments in military concerns and
enlarging defence budgets, they asked: 'Are not tanks more needed than
Titian, bombs more important than Bach?' (274). The reposte to the rhetorical question by now had become blatantly obvious to the observant reader.
While 'military defences must be made secure,' the commissioners argued,
'cultural defences equally demand national attention' (275). Indeed, cultural concerns constituted 'spiritual weapons' and only on 'spiritual
strength' could lasting peace be secured. Canadians, for these reasons,
'must strengthen those permanent institution[s] which give meaning to our
unity and make [them] conscious of the best in [their] life' (274).
116 Litt, *The Muses, the Masses, and the Massey Commission,* 104
117 Massey, *On Being Canadian,* 128. Canada could preserve its cultural traditions '[o]nly by reason of constant and unremitting effort, and back of this
effort must be the awareness of [cultural] differences.' Vincent Massey,
'Foreign Policy Begins at Home,' Address by the Right Hon. Massey at
MacDonald College, draft copy (26 February 1947), Vincent Massey
Papers, UTA, 421(09), B87-0082, 29
118 By culture, Massey meant not only 'those concrete institutions, parliamen-

tary and judicial which we have inherited, which are lasting things, but to those more intangible ways of thinking which we also have from Great Britain which will evaporate if we do not remain aware of them.' Massey, 'Foreign Policy Begins at Home,' 29. He added that institutions of higher learning 'should help keep Canada Canadian.' This did not mean that they should promote jingoism, but rather that the university should 'interpret and represent the spirit of our country in its highest sense and help us withstand those subtle forces which would lead to the erosion of our Canadianism.' Massey, Kingston Address, 8

119 Vincent Massey to Evelyn Wrench (21 May 1929), Vincent Massey Papers, UTA, 032(06), B87-0082

120 Vincent Massey, 'Canadian Club Speech,' at Niagara, draft copy (13 March 1953), Hilda Neatby Papers, SAB, I. 12 (Massey, Vincent, 1951–69) (3), A139, 4, 3. Massey added, on the importance of British political values to the cultural life of the nation: 'And it is true to say of all our leaders that the more profound their belief in Canada as a nation, the more insistent have they been in supporting the Crown and in developing its Canadian character' (2).

121 Quoted in Massey, Kingston Address, 4

122 Massey, Convocation Hall Address, 2

123 Hugh MacLennan, *Two Solitudes* (Toronto, 1945)

124 B.K. Sandwell, 'Present Day Influences,' 2

125 Massey, On Being Canadian, 20, 21

126 Ibid., 20

127 Hilda Neatby to Reverend Georges-H. Lévesque (13 August 1953), Hilda Neatby Papers, SAB, I. 3, General Correspondence, 1914–75 (4), A139, 2

128 See Litt, *The Muses, the Masses, and the Massey Commission*, 112

129 Canada, *Report*, 271

130 Harold Innis, 'Great Britain, the United States, and Canada,' 281; Innis, *The Idea File*, line 43, 16. See also A.R.M. Lower, *Colony to Nation* (Toronto, 1946)

131 Innis, 'Great Britain, the United States, and Canada,' 287–8. Innis was ultimately pessimistic about the outcome; he thought it unlikely that Canada would be able to effect this third bloc.

132 Harold Innis, *The Strategy of Culture* (Toronto 1952), 1, 19

133 Donald Creighton, *Harold Adams Innis: Portrait of a Scholar* (Toronto, 1957), 19

134 Innis, *Strategy of Culture*, 20

135 Donald Creighton, 'Doctrine and Interpretation of History,' in Creighton, *Towards the Discovery of Canada: Selected Essays* (Toronto, 1972), 40.

136 Donald Creighton, 'Canada in the World' in Gilmour, *Canada's Tomorrow,*
248
137 Quoted in Carl Berger, *The Writing of Canadian History: Aspects of English-
Canadian Historical Writing Since 1900,* 2nd ed. (Toronto, 1986), 226–7
138 Creighton, 'Canada in the World,' 248, 249
139 Berger, *Writing of Canadian History,* 226. Note that Creighton stressed the
importance of maintaining the British connection as a means of surviving
amid the main power blocs of the Cold War era. While France might join
Italy, divested of its great power status, he claimed that Great Britain
would persist and 'recover a good deal of its old authority'; and while
Great Britain and other potential leader-nations in Asia might be second-
rate powers compared with the superpowers, especially the United States,
they still exerted 'a secondary leadership of great importance.' 'It is in
their company that Canada might aspire. She is not of their stature yet. But
in fifty years time, how far away will she be from it? Power may become
multiple again, and this would encourage the rise of new states to emi-
nence. Power is at present dual – the prerogative of the United States and
this duality is prolonged and strengthened by the fact of the Cold War.'
See Donald Creighton, 'Canada in the World,' draft copy [1953?], Donald
Creighton Papers, PAC, v. 11; 'Canada in the World,' MG 31 D77, 6.
140 Berger, *Writing of Canadian History,* 221–2
141 Quoted in ibid., 227
142 Donald Creighton, 'Introduction,' in Creighton, *Towards the Discovery of
Canada,* 10. For Creighton, few Canadians had realized what Macdonald,
Innis, and Creighton himself had understood: the inestimable dangers of
American imperialism to Canada's national development.
143 Donald Creighton, 'Macdonald and the Anglo-Canadian Alliance,' in
Creighton, *Towards the Discovery of Canada,* 222
144 Donald Creighton, 'Towards the Discovery of Canada,' in ibid., 48
145 Donald Creighton, 'Doctrine and the Interpretation of History,' in ibid., 43,
44
146 See Creighton, *Towards the Discovery of Canada.*
147 The Progressive Conservative party, under the leadership of John G.
Diefenbaker, made a resurgence in this period. See chapter 6.
148 Creighton, 'Introduction,' in Creighton, *Towards the Discovery of Canada*
149 Creighton, 'Doctrine and the Interpretation of History,' 45
150 Quoted in Berger, *Writing of Canadian History,* 252
151 W.L. Morton, *The Canadian Identity,* 2nd ed. (Toronto, 1972), 106. According
to Morton, Canada rejected both popular sovereignty and majoritarian
democracy. Political loyalty, in consequence, rested with the Crown, not

with the state as an expression of the popular will. Canadians were loyal to the monarch and hence did not have to conform politically. Because they did not foster conformist impulses, monarchical institutions were central to a pluralist and, ultimately, a free society.

152 See W.L. Morton, 'Canadian Conservatism Now,' in Forbes, *Canadian Political Thought*, 303–5.

153 Morton, *Canadian Identity*, 86, 113. Those monarchical principles already express along with the 'moral precept' that 'societies may in free association, by careful definition and great patience, make mutual accommodations of sovereignty without loss of independence' (87). Morton here was referring to Canada's bicultural circumstances and the accommodation of French- and English-speaking Canadians. For Morton, the Canadian experience was sort of an analogue of the Commonwealth experience in that there is a free association in self-government among both founding peoples of Canada and the members of the Commonwealth. '[The Commonwealth spirit] was the work of Canadians of both the major stocks, it is the outward expression of our domestic institutions, and its spirit informs Canadians of all other origins with an equal pride in free institutions elaborated by the Canadian political genius' (112–13).

Morton singled out other elements that both differentiated Canada from the United States and were important to the Canadian identity. Canada's northern character, for instance, formed a significant part of the Canadian identity. Neither a 'a second-rate United States' nor 'a United States that has failed,' Canada was 'separate and distinct in America' because its history was marked by 'a distinct and even a unique human endeavour, the civilization of the northern and arctic lands' (93). Its 'separate origin in the northern frontier,' Morton went on, meant that 'Canadian life to this day is marked by a northern quality, the strong seasonal rhythm which still governs even academic sessions ... The line which marks off the frontier from the farmstead, the wilderness from the baseland, the hinterland from the metropolis, runs through every Canadian psyche' (ibid.).

154 See Roger Graham, *Arthur Meighen: A Biography* (Toronto, 1960) and John Farthing, *Freedom Wears a Crown*, ed. Judith Robinson (Toronto, 1957) as other examples of conservative historians. Much more is said on conservative views of the nation and Canadian history in chapter 6.

155 Bernard Ostry, *The Cultural Connection: An Essay on Culture and Government Policy in Canada* (Toronto, 1978)

156 Louis St Laurent, Address by the Prime Minister the Right Honourable Louis St Laurent to the National Conference on Higher Learning (12 November 1956), Vincent Massey Papers, UTA, 370(14), B87-0082, 2. See

also C.T. Bissell, ed., *Canada's Crisis in Higher Education. Proceedings of the Conference Held by the National Conference of Canadian Universities at Ottawa, November 12–14* (Toronto, 1957).

157 St Laurent, Address to National Conference, 17

158 Clearly, St Laurent fashioned his address for his audience of humanists and humanist sympathizers. Furthermore, the Canada Council had been given only grudging assent by Parliament, and Canadian artists and intellectuals still were suspicious of the idea of state support for theatre, music, films, and literature.

159 Owing to the Killam and Dunn endowments – a $100 million bonanza.

160 Berger, *Writing of Canadian History*, 179

161 See Litt, *The Muses, the Masses, and the Massey Commission*. Litt writes that the process of lobbying 'hastened the arrival of a new era in which culture was recognized as a legitimate concern of government, and as such, one that required serious attention, coordinated management, and a comprehensive strategy. Through its public hearings, the Massey Commission expedited an incipient change of attitude within Canadian political culture [Remember the lukewarmness and occasional hostility of King's government-to-government policy on culture.]' According to Litt, this was hardly revolutionary, and he criticizes historians of the commission who say it was, but it was highly significant nevertheless (248). Litt ends with the idea that the arts council was the bureaucratic embodiment of the cultural elite because, first, the council was to be a well-connected organization of those in the elite, but still well insulated from popular criticism; second, the elite saw it as a base for the improvement of the masses and Canadian liberal democracy. The culture critics did not think of the council as a way to aggrandize their own power (though this was the charge of its opponents), but rather, as a way to encourage rather than direct cultural development. 'This stipulation was rooted in the liberal conviction that a centrally directed culture would be both politically dangerous and culturally artificial, but it also reflected the nationalist imperative to create an indigenous culture with popular appeal. Suspended somewhere between government and the people and belonging wholly to neither, the arts council proposal was the bureaucratic embodiment of the cultural elite and its liberal humanist nationalism' (185). Frye argued in *Culture and the National Will* (Ottawa, 1957): 'With the Canada Council Act, federal aid for universities is linked with federal aid for culture. The principles involved for culture are precisely the same ... It is logical to link the university and culture: in fact it could almost be said that the university today is to culture what the church is to religion: the social institution that makes

it possible. It teaches the culture of the past, and it tries to build up an educated public for the culture of the present' (4).

162 J.L. Granatstein, 'Culture and Scholarship: The First Ten Years of the Canada Council,' *Canadian Historical Review*, 55 (1984), 474

163 Claude Bissell, *Halfway up Parnassus: A Personal Account of the University of Toronto 1932–1971* (Toronto, 1974), 48

164 George P. Grant, *Philosophy in the Mass Age* (Toronto, 1959), 37

165 Ibid., 15

166 George Grant, *Lament for a Nation: The Defeat of Canadian Nationalism* (Toronto, 1965), 53

167 Grant, *Philosophy in the Mass Age*, 16

168 Ibid., 20

169 Grant, *Lament for a Nation*, 54

170 This is the broadest theme of Grant's *Lament for a Nation*.

171 Northrop Frye, 'The Critical Discipline,' Address to the Royal Society of Canada's Symposium, Canadian Universities Today, draft copy [1960?], Northrop Frye Papers, Victoria University Library (VUL), 88, Box 1, P, 3–4

172 Northrop Frye, 'Academy without Walls,' unpublished paper, draft copy, Northrop Frye Papers, VUL, 88, Box 1, N, 9

173 David Cook, *Northrop Frye: A Vision of the New World* (Montreal, 1985), 18

174 Northrop Frye, *The Critical Path: An Essay on the Social Context of Literary Criticism* (Bloomington, Indiana, 1971), 49, 97

175 Frye argues first that the myth of freedom is hard to sustain, given the 'narcotic attraction' of a closed mythology of concern. The study of literature is the first step to counter the suffocating effects of the myth of concern (ibid., 157). What Frye advocates to prevent the destruction of western imagination is to re-educate society about its mythological heritage. He believes that poetry exists, in part, to take on and create a new mythology: '[T]here are two cultures in society, one in the main area of sciences, the other an area covered by something that we are calling mythology. They co-exist, but are not essentially interconnected' (ibid., 96).

176 Northrop Frye, 'Conclusion to *A Literary History of Canada*,' in Northrop Frye, *The Bush Garden: Essays on the Canadian Imagination* (Toronto, 1974), 224, 225

177 Ibid., 226

178 Cook, 12

179 Donald Creighton, *Canada's First Century, 1867–1967* (Toronto, 1970), 344

180 Donald Creighton, 'Canadian Nationalism and its Opponents,' in Creighton, *Discovery*, 280, 281

181 Morton, *Canadian Identity*, 115, 116, 150

6: The World We Have Lost

1 Walter Lippmann, 'The Shortage of Education,' *Atlantic Monthly*, 193 (May 1954); quoted in Clinton Rossiter and James Lare, eds, *The Essential Lippmann: A Political Philosophy for Liberal Democracy* (New York, 1963), 29
2 Harold J. Laski, *The Dilemma of Our Times: An Historical Essay* (London, 1952), 53, 53–4
3 Vincent Massey, 'Christian Social Order in a Changing World,' Address to the Montreal Council on Christian Social Order, draft copy (5 November 1953), Hilda Neatby Papers, Saskatchewan Archives Board (SAB), I. 12 (Massey, Vincent, 1951–69) (4), A139, 2. See also Vincent Massey, 'Christian Social Order in a Changing World,' in Vincent Massey, *Speaking of Canada: Addresses by the Right Honourable Vincent Massey* (Toronto, 1959).
4 Among others, see H.W. Wright, 'The Values of Democracy,' *University of Toronto Quarterly*, 10 (1940–1), 68–88; Hilda Neatby, 'The Democratic Cycle,' *Dalhousie Review*, 22 (1942–3), 470–5; Harold Innis, 'Democracy and the Free City,' in Citizen's Research Institute, *Bulletin: The Importance of Local Government in a Democracy*, 84 (May 1945); J.A. Corry and J.E. Hodgetts, *Democratic Government and Politics* (Toronto, 1946); Robert C. Wallace, 'Education in a Democratic Society,' *Queen's Quarterly*, 53 (1946–7), 430–6; A.R.M. Lower, 'Why Men Fight,' *Queen's Quarterly*, 54 (1947–8), 187–200; H.L. Stewart, 'The Superseding of Democracy,' *Dalhousie Review*, 30 (1950–1), 145–58; Rodney Grey, 'Korea and "Western Values,"' *Queen's Quarterly*, 57 (1950–1), 281–91; John A. Irving, 'The Manifesto of Democracy,' *Queen's Quarterly*, 58 (1951), 312–26.
5 Neatby, 'Democratic Cycle,' 470
6 Ibid., 472–3, 474
7 Ibid.
8 Ibid., 474, 475
9 Arthur Lower, 'The Social Sciences in the Post-War World,' *Canadian Historical Review* 22 (March 1941); quoted in Welf H. Heick, ed., *History and Myth: Arthur Lower and the Making of Canadian Nationalism* (Vancouver, 1975), 108
10 Harold Innis, 'Preface,' *Political Economy in the Modern State* (Toronto, 1946), xv
11 Lower, 'Why Men Fight,' 190
12 H.W. Wright, 'The Values of Democracy,' 84
13 Innis, 'Preface,' *Political Economy*, vii, viii, vii
14 Lower, 'Why Men Fight,' 191
15 Walter Lippmann, 'Man's Image of Man,' *Commonweal* 35 (1942); quoted in Rossiter and Lare, eds, *The Essential Lippmann*, 163

16 Ibid., 165, 167, 167–8
17 In addition to the works cited in nn. 18, 19, and 23 below, see Stewart, 'Superseding of Democracy'; Irving, 'Manifesto of Democracy'; Wallace, 'Education in a Democratic Society.'
18 H.W. McCready, 'The Defence of Individualism,' *Queen's Quarterly*, 52 (1945–6), 71
19 Malcolm Muggeridge, 'Farewell to Freedom? The State, the Person, the Faith,' *Queen's Quarterly*, 61 (1954), 305, 306
20 Ibid., 307
21 William B. Munro to Donald Creighton (15 June 1948) Donald Creighton Papers, National Archives of Canada (NAC), v. 2, General correspondence, 1948, 31 D77
22 Muggeridge, 'Farewell to Freedom?', 311
23 George Grant, 'The Minds of Men in the Atomic Age,' in H.D. Forbes ed., *Canadian Political Thought* (Toronto, 1985), 286
24 Ibid., 287
25 Douglas Owram, *Born at the Right Time: A History of the Baby Boom Generation* (Toronto, 1996), 45, 46
26 Nora McCullough, 'Education for Peace,' *Canadian Forum*, 26 (September 1946), 133
27 John A. Irving, 'Education for an Enduring Peace,' *Queen's Quarterly* 52 (1945–6), 401, 403
28 Wallace, 'Education in a Democratic Society,' 435, 436
29 Watson Kirkconnell, *Twilight of Liberty* (London, 1941), 175
30 Ibid., 176
31 Hilda Neatby, 'Education for Democracy,' *Dalhousie Review*, 24 (1944–5), 47, 50. See also chapter 4.
32 Northrop Frye, 'A Liberal Education,' part II, *Canadian Forum*, 25 (October 1945), 163
33 Frye, 'A Liberal Education,' part I, *Canadian Forum*, 25 (September 1945), 135
34 Frye, 'Liberal Education,' part II, 164
35 Harold Innis, 'Adult Education and the Universities,' *Report of the Manitoba Commission on Adult Education* (Winnipeg 1947); quoted in Harold Innis, *The Bias of Communication* (Toronto, 1951; reprinted 1973), 203, 203–7
36 Robert M. Ogden, 'Are Men Equal?' *Queen's Quarterly*, 55 (1948–9), 431, 432
37 T.S. Eliot, *Notes towards the Definition of a Culture*, in Eliot, *Christianity and Culture* (New York, 1940; reprinted 1949), 109, 121
38 Donald Creighton, 'Education for Government: What Can the Humanities Do for Government?' unpublished manuscript (n.d.), Donald Creighton Papers NAC, v. 15; Education for Government, MG 31 D77, 4, 4–5

39 Watson Kirkconnell, *Seven Pillars of Freedom* (Toronto, 1944; rev. ed. 1952), 102

40 Harold Innis, 'Charles Norris Cochrane, 1889–1945,' *Canadian Journal of Economics and Political Science*, 12 (February 1946), 97

41 Harold Innis, Memorandum to President H.J. Cody [1943?]; quoted in Robert F. Neill, 'The Work of Harold Adams Innis: Content and Context,' PhD thesis, Duke University, 1966

42 Peter Viereck, *The Unadjusted Man: A New Hero for Americans. Reflections on the Distinction between Conforming and Conserving* (New York, 1956; reprinted 1962), 5

43 N.A.M. MacKenzie to Hilda Neatby (20 February 1950), Hilda Neatby Papers, Saskatchewan Archives Board (SAB), II. 36, General Correspondence, 1949–51, A139, 1

44 Hilda Neatby to W.W. Robinson [editor, Clarke, Irwin] (31 August 1953), Hilda Neatby Papers, SAB, I. 6, Clarke, Irwin 1952–69, A139, 1

45 Quoted in William Christian, *George Grant: A Biography* (Toronto, 1993), 109

46 See Harold Innis, 'Great Britain, Canada, and the United States' (1948), in Daniel Drache, ed., *Staples, Markets, and Cultural Change: Selected Essays, Harold A. Innis* (Montreal, 1995); see also chapter 5.

47 Quoted in Christian, *George Grant*, 108; see also 108–9.

48 Vincent Massey, 'Coronation Day Broadcast,' draft copy (2 June 1953), Hilda Neatby Papers, SAB, I. 12, (Massey, Vincent, 1951–69) (3), A139, 2. See also Vincent Massey, 'The Meaning of the Coronation,' Coronation Day Broadcast, 2 June 1953, in Vincent Massey, *Speaking of Canada: Addresses by the Right Honourable Vincent Massey* (Toronto, 1959).

49 Vincent Massey, 'Canadian Club Speech,' Niagara, Ontario (13 March 1953), SAB, I. 12 (Massey, Vincent, 1951–69) (3), A139, 2, 3

50 John Farthing, *Freedom Wears a Crown*, Judith Robinson, ed. (Toronto, 1957), 27, 27–8, 28

51 Forsey had been working with Farthing and mutual friend Judith Robinson (who went on to edit *Freedom Wears a Crown* after Farthing's death in 1954) on a book whose title was to be *The British Tradition in Canada*. The project faltered, however, and each went on to complete other projects. Note, also, that Forsey referred to Farthing's work as that 'precious little book.' See Frank Milligan, 'Eugene A. Forsey: An Intellectual Biography,' PhD thesis, University of Alberta, 1987, 394 n.3.

52 Eugene Forsey, 'Crown, Parliament and Canadian Freedom,' unpublished article (1952); quoted in ibid., 402, 412–13

53 Other conservatives, like W.L. Morton, were staunch monarchists. Along with Eugene Forsey ('Monarchy in Government'), Gad and Jean Horowitz

('Charles Bonenfant'), Morton was to write 'The Monarchy as a Symbol' as his contribution to a collection of essays on the monarchy in Canada. However, no compilation was ever produced. See W.L. Morton Papers, William Ready Division of Archives and Research Collections, McMaster University Library, Hamilton, Canada (MUL), Box 56; 'Monarchy in Canada.' Morton's affections for the Crown and the British tradition were well known. See below and see Morton, *The Canadian Identity* and *The Kingdom of Canada: A General History from Earliest Times* (Toronto, 1963).

54 Pakistan, India, Ceylon, Burma, and Israel seceded from the Commonwealth in 1947.

55 Donald Creighton to Paul G. Hoffman [president, Ford Foundation] (24 January 1951), D.G. Creighton Papers, NAC, v. 10, HRCC, 1949–52, 31, D77, 1

56 Vincent Massey, 'Canadians and Their Commonwealth,' 68th Romanes Lecture Delivered at Oxford, draft copy (1 June 1961), Hilda Neatby Papers, SAB, I. 12 (Massey, Vincent, 1951–69) (8), A139, 91, 93. See also Vincent Massey, 'Canadians and Their Commonwealth,' in Massey, *Confederation on the March: Views on Major Canadian Issues during the Sixties* (Toronto, 1965), 85–101.

57 Massey, *Canadians and Their Commonwealth*. Canadians at large prided themselves on the fact that the Commonwealth was transformed from a purely white organization into a multi-racial body. They regarded Canada's participation in it as a noble contribution to international harmony. See Robert Bothwell, Ian Drummond, and John English, *Canada since 1945: Power, Politics, and Provincialism* (Toronto, 1981; Revised 1989), 125.

58 See Carl Berger, *The Sense of Power: Studies in the Ideas of Canadian Imperialism, 1867–1914* (Toronto, 1970).

59 Ibid., 263–4, 261

60 Trade was $508 million, 43 per cent of all Canadian exports to Great Britain, compared with $443 million in trade with the United States.

61 See J.L. Granatstein et al., *Nation: Canada since Confederation*, 3rd ed. (Toronto, 1990), 406–9; Kenneth Norrie and Douglas Owram, *A History of the Canadian Economy*, 2nd ed. (Toronto, 1991), 411; Bothwell, Drummond, and English, *Canada Since 1945*, 189.

62 The establishment at Ogdensburg, New York of the Permanent Joint Board on Defence (PJDB) coordinated the defence strategies of Canada and the United States. J.L. Granatstein, *How Britain's Weakness Forced Canada into the Arms of the Americans* (Toronto, 1989), shows how Canada had no choice but to abandon Britain and rely more heavily on the Americans for defence.

63 By preserving a democratic and friendly Europe, Canadian NATO negotia-

tors thought that Canada could avoid becoming reliant on the United States.

64 Canada, moreover, had hoped that NATO would be a means of extending cultural and economic relations between member nations. The Americans, by contrast, viewed the agreement simply as a military alliance. As the Cold War threatened to erupt into open hostilities by 1950, it became apparent that the American conception had triumphed.

65 Quoted in Bothwell, Drummond, and English, *Canada since 1945*, 263

66 Donald Creighton, 'Introduction,' *Towards the Discovery of Canada: Selected Essays* (Toronto, 1972), 8

67 NORAD was a North American air defence plan, under which Canadian and American officers would jointly administer an integrated defence force under supreme American command. The DEW Line was chain of more than forty stations built across the Canadian and American Arctic from 1954–7 to warn North Americans of an impending Soviet air attack. The significance of both is the integration of defensive strategy under American initiative and leadership.

68 Christian, *George Grant*, 110, 138

69 G.P. Grant to Mother [late 1940?], George Grant Papers, NAC, v. 39; Mrs W.L. Grant Correspondence; file: Dalhousie University, MG 30 D59, 1

70 Quoted in Bothwell, Drummond, and English, *Canada since 1945*, 90

71 Donald Creighton, 'Canada in the World,' in G.P. Gilmour, ed., *Canada's Tomorrow: Papers and Discussion Canada's Tomorrow Conference, Quebec City, November 1953* (Toronto, 1954), 228

72 Ibid., 229

73 Ibid., 231, 248, 230, 229

74 Farthing, *Freedom Wears a Crown*, 13, 14

75 Harold Innis summarized the meaning of Creighton's first volume of his biography of Macdonald to both the writing of Canadian history and the expression of the national psyche when he declared: 'I need hardly say that judging from these chapters alone [of the biography which Creighton gave him to read], it is clear to me that this will be the most significant work we have had in biography and the most important work in the field of history within the last half century. The book will compel a rewriting of Canadian history. It makes one realize the extent to which Canadian history has been dominated by the liberals and raises suddenly the question as to why another approach has been completely neglected until the second half of this century ... All I can say is that it will be the most significant work in Canadian historical writing for a long period.' Harold Innis to Donald Creighton (6 June 1952), Donald Creighton Papers, NAC, v. 2; General Cor-

respondence, 1952, file 1, MG 31 D77. In a similar vein, historian G.F.G.
Stanley congratulated Creighton on the latter's CBC addresses June 1959.
He remarked to Creighton: 'much of my enthusiasm for your remarks
stems from the fact that I am so wholeheartedly in sympathy with them.
You have advanced points of view which I think should be given wider
publicity among historians and students of Canadian History. Too long
have we been exposed to the "Whig" interpretation of Canadian History.'
G.F.G. Stanley [Head of the History Department at the Royal Military
College] to Donald Creighton (5 October 1959), Donald Creighton Papers,
NAC, v. 9; Television Broadcasts, 1959, MG 31 D77. Vincent Massey, for
his part, denounced as fallacious, and indeed more myth than reality, the
notion that Canadian national development was that of a struggle for
autonomy against the 'forces of darkness in 10 Downing Street.' He
objected to the interpretation of the development of 'dominion status' as a
sort of liberation. See Massey, 'Canadians and Their Commonwealth,' 92.
76 Farthing, *Freedom Wears a Crown*, 27–8
77 W.L. Morton, *The Canadian Identity*, 2nd ed. (Toronto, 1972), 86
78 W.L. Morton, 'Canadian Conservatism Now,' in H.D. Forbes, ed., *Canadian Political Thought* (Toronto, 1985), 301, 302
79 Ibid., 302–3, 303. Morton outlined the other contributors to the tradition of Canadian conservatism. Through the Loyalists, the Earl of Shelbourne, 'the founder of British Canada,' and the Pitts, he argued, the main constituents of modern Canadian toryism had been put in place (304). It was left to John A. Macdonald, a conservative 'inspired through Elgin by the Peelites of the Pittite tradition,' to unify the diverse strands of toryism (306–7). The toryism of Macdonald constituted a historical conservatism on which all, even modern Canadians, could rely.
80 Ibid., 306, 307, 309
81 Creighton, for instance, implicitly disagreed with Morton's efforts to systematize and find the origins of conservative precepts. 'It is not necessary,' he wrote in 1957, 'to trace an idea back through Edmund Burke to Charles I in order to prove that it is a Conservative political principle.' See Donald Creighton, 'Macdonald and the Anglo-Canadian Alliance,' in Creighton, *Towards the Discovery of Canada*, 216. Rather, Canadian conservatism in the nineteenth century was 'not what Burke and his successors and commentators thought it ought to be in theory, but what Macdonald and his principal associates made it in practice' (Ibid.). Indeed, the political practice of John A. Macdonald was the focal point of Canadian conservatism for both the nineteenth and the mid-twentieth centuries. See below for further discussion.
82 Ibid., 211, 217

83 Donald Creighton, 'Address to the Prime Minister' [John G. Diefenbaker], unpublished address, draft copy [Spring 1958], Donald Creighton Papers, NAC, v. 8, Canadian Broadcast League, file 1

84 Creighton, 'Macdonald and the Anglo-Canadian Alliance,' 218

85 According to Creighton, the attributes of the Empire of the St Lawrence formed the basis of what emerged as the Canadian nation. These are the economic-financial aspect; the geographical east-west orientation of the system; an associated impulse towards westward expansion; and a political, Anglo-Canadian connection that evolved into Canadian Confederation. This system lasted for many years, fully sixty years after 1867, but it began to break down in the 1920s. From the 1920s, 'the familiar distinguishing characteristics of the Canadian nation began to weaken; and the historic themes of its history lost their old dominance. Up until the beginning of the Second World War the decline was gradual and slow; from that time on it has hurried forward, with steadily increasing rapidity, towards what now looks like its inevitable and final fall. What has happened to Canada? Why did it change direction so decisively? And where is it now bound?' Donald Creighton, 'The Decline and Fall of the Empire of the St Lawrence,' in Creighton, *Towards the Discovery of Canada*, 164

86 Macdonald, of course, is the main leader because of the vital decisions he made and the directions he set for national development. Creighton adds that Laurier and others picked up on the national policy style of Macdonald, and hence there is continuity in Canadian leadership. Of Macdonald, he writes that 'he developed policies which the country needed. I think he saw what the country needed and had a superb conception of the future of this country and what is necessary to achieve it.' Donald Creighton, 'A Long View of Canadian History' [the text of two half-hour programs originally presented on the CBC television network, 16 and 30 June 1959] (June 1959), Donald Creighton Papers, NAC, v. 9; Television Broadcasts, 1959 MG 31 D77

87 Creighton, 'Macdonald and the Anglo-Canadian Alliance,' 218

88 Creighton, Address to the Prime Minister

89 Donald Creighton to [?] Nowlan (25 November 1957), Donald Creighton Papers, NAC, v. 8; Canadian Broadcasting League, file 1, MG 31 D77, 1–2

90 Donald Creighton, 'Canada in World Affairs: Are We Pulling Our Weight?' unpublished address given at the Couchiching Conference (13 August 1954), Donald Creighton Papers, NAC, v. 11; 'Canada in World Affairs,' MG 31 D77, 4. Creighton added that Canadians' aim
    ought to be to enlarge the circle of nations which maintain ordinary diplomatic relations with each other, just as it is our natural human impulse

Notes to pages 251-2

to keep on speaking terms with those with whom we have to live and work. The Geneva Conference effectively dispelled the self-righteous fiction [of the Americans] that Chinese are diplomatic untouchables, and the acceptance of the government of the Chinese Republic as the effective government of China and its admission to the morally vacant seat in the Security Council of the United Nations are decisions which Canada and the rest of the world cannot afford to postpone much longer. Canadian opinion is something which the world now regards with a measure of interest and respect; and in the United Nations, in NATO, and in the Commonwealth, Canada occupies positions in which she can bring considerable influence. NATO links us with Europe: the Commonwealth brings us in touch with the East. And it is vitally important for Canadians to use and rely upon associations which unite contrasted cultures and bridge continents. (5)

91 Eugene Forsey, 'The British Tradition in Canada,' draft copy of an unpublished manuscript, Hilda Neatby Papers, SAB, I. 7 (Forsey, Eugene, 1953–70), A139, 1

92 In a letter to good friend and key Diefenbaker adviser Derek Bedson, George Grant heralded the 'wonderful news of the elections.' 'What a wonderful victory,' he went on. 'What a joy that the Canadian people were not so bemused that they could throw the rascals out.' 'Rarely in this life,' Grant concluded, 'do the loyal and the principled have their triumph in this world.' Indeed, he considered the 1957 Conservative victory as a 'triumph for loyalty, courage and principle.' See George Grant to Derek Bedson (13 June 1957), in William Christian, ed., *George Grant: Selected Letters* (Toronto, 1996), 192.

93 The prospects of renewing ties with the Empire-Commonwealth, for example, exhilarated Diefenbaker. At the 1957 Prime Ministers of the Commonwealth Conference (at Accra, Ghana), Diefenbaker made clear his affection for the British and the imperial connection. In the words of Graham Spry, who went to the conference, Diefenbaker made 'a very favourable impression by his energy and directness.' His comments were so ebullient that 'to read some of the cheaper newspapers one would think that Canada had not only rejoined the Commonwealth, but was almost going to amalgamate with the United Kingdom.' Quoted in J.L. Granatstein, *Canada, 1957–1967: The Years of Uncertainty and Innovation* (Toronto, 1986), 43–4

94 It would have meant that approximately 35 per cent of Canadian imports (provided by the Americans) now would be required to come from the United Kingdom. This expectation was wholly unrealistic; British exporters simply did not have the capacity to increase their exports to Canada at this rate. See ibid., 44.

95 See Donald Creighton, *Dominion of the North: A History of Canada* (Boston, 1944); Morton, *The Canadian Identity*, among others.

96 John G. Diefenbaker, *One Canada: Memoirs of the Right Honourable John G. Diefenbaker. The Years of Achievement, 1957–1962* (Toronto, 1976), 11, 15, 15–16, 16. Conservative intellectuals like Creighton openly encouraged Diefenbaker's Macdonald-like approach to state-building. In a letter to Mcdonnell, Creighton offered advice on the upcoming election strategy (1957) by giving a historical summary of Conservative and Liberal approaches to British import preference. He claimed: 'It would seem to me – if such a suggestion is not an impertinence – that the Conservative party might do better to continue along the course which it began last year by directly attacking the encroachments of the United States from a nationalist point of view rather than by seeking to appeal to the benefits, either economic or political, of the old Anglo-British alliance. The importance of British markets and of British diplomatic and military support has undeniably declined; but, on the other hand, Canada itself is definitely stronger than it used to be; and the defence of our boundary waters, our sources of fuel and power, our military and diplomatic autonomy, has become a matter of major concern to Canadians who are, unless I am greatly mistaken, full of worries and misgivings about our subordination in a continental' empire. Donald Creighton to [?] Mcdonnell (25 February 1957), Creighton Papers, PAC, v. 3; Gen. Correspondence 1957, file 3

97 See Granatstein, *Canada, 1957–1967*, chapter 5.

98 W.L. Morton to Murray S. Donnelly (6 October 1959), W.L. Morton Papers, MUL, Box 8; Donnelly, Murray, Provost of United College, University of Manitoba, 1

99 Creighton, 'Canada: A Divided and Vulnerable Nation,' 12

100 See George Grant, *Lament for a Nation: The Defeat of Canadian Nationalism* (Toronto, 1965), chapter 1.

101 Donald Creighton, 'Canadian Nationalism and Its Opponents,' in Creighton, *Towards the Discovery of Canada*, 274

102 Although critical of Diefenbaker a few years earlier, W.L. Morton was more sympathetic to the Tories in 1963. In a letter to Creighton, Morton argued that the Liberals might not win the upcoming election. The 'civil service mandarins,' he claimed, 'have failed to measure up to the expectation of victory. So the country is faced ... with the demonstrated inadequacy of both the conservatives and the Liberals.' In these conditions, he ventures further, the NDP thrives. Yet Morton blamed the political climate of the 1960s (not Diefenbaker specifically) for the degradation of Canadian political life. 'The mood of the country,' he continued, 'is becoming more and more grave and reflective. I think a realization is growing as to how

shallow, mediocre and ineffective Canadian politics have been. The country is not ready to entrust anyone with power.' W.L. Morton to Creighton (28 March 1963), W.L. Morton Papers, MUL, Box 6; Creighton, D.G., 1962–4; 2

103 Quoted in Christian, *George Grant*, 241. When the NDP proceeded to support the Opposition, however, Grant termed the party a 'kind of vacuous extension of the Liberals' and regretted his 'small association' with them. See George Grant to Derek Bedson (February 1963) in ibid., 215.

104 Ibid., 215, 245, 247

105 Owram, *Born at the Right Time*, 161

106 Ibid., 165

107 Ibid., 167

108 Grant, *Lament for a Nation*, 2, 5, 3–4. Grant claimed that 'American control [in Canada] grew at a quickening rate' during Diefenbaker's years in office (15). Until Diefenbaker decided to defy the Americans, first in the Cuban crisis and later over the nuclear arms issue, the Tory prime minister committed many acts that failed to allay the American influence in Canada. See ibid., chapters 1–3.

109 Ibid., 53, 54, 57

110 Ibid., 56

111 Ibid., 67

112 See ibid., chapter 5.

113 See Creighton, 'Decline and Fall of the Empire of the St Lawrence,' 169, 170–1, 171.

114 Ibid., 169

115 Donald Creighton, 'Continentalism and the Birthright of Canadians,' in Creighton, *Towards the Discovery of Canada*, 289

116 Donald Creighton, 'The Myth of Biculturalism,' in Creighton, *Towards the Discovery of Canada*, 261, 262

117 Ibid., 257, 256

118 See Creighton, 'Canada: A Divided and Vulnerable Nation.'

119 W.L. Morton, 'Towards a New Conception of Confederation?' An Address to the Seventh Annual Seminar of the Canadian Union of Students, unpublished address, draft copy (4 September 1964), W.L. Morton Papers, MUL, Box 6; Canadian Union of Students, The Dualism of Culture and The Federalism of Power, 2

120 Morton, *The Canadian Identity*, 116

121 Morton, 'Towards a New Conception of Confederation?' 10, 9. It is important to note, however, that unlike Creighton, Morton 'welcomed heartily' the Quiet Revolution, but only inasmuch as it enabled Quebec to release

itself from the medieval fetters of the past – the socio-political constraints of the Roman Catholic church and so forth. What he disliked about the Quiet Revolution was that it undermined Canadianism (8–9). Morton wrote: 'I repudiate the seeming belief on the part of many of my contemporaries, of the separatists in Quebec, like my friend Professor Michel Brunet, of the supporters of the new flag of the composition and spirit of the Royal Commission on Bilingualism as first conceived, that the past can be ignored. I deplore this frantic pretense that the past if it exists is regrettable and best forgotten, the frantic pretense that history can be swept aside and forgotten' (9). The new arrangement 'would be tolerable,' Morton explained, 'because it would not be a final majority or minority of French or English but a changing and varying, and therefore tolerable majority' (9). Confederation, according to Morton, involved 'the balancing of guaranteed provincial and minority rights with the creation of a new political majority' (9).

122 Ibid., 11. Morton also argued that Canada was a political nationality of 'no political duality, no associate, separate, or special political status for any province, or any cultural nationality. None can be tolerated because the Canadian community is made up of citizens equal in right and in status. Political duality in any form is denied and rejected in these remarks; cultural duality is urged both as a matter of doing justice to French Canada, and as needed for the maintenance of the political unity of the community.' See W.L. Morton, 'Brief to Royal Commission on Bilingualism and Biculturalism,' draft copy, W.L. Morton Papers, MUL, Box 1; Bilingualism and Biculturalism, 2.

In addition to denying the doctrine of cultural duality, Morton spoke against the divisiveness and the chauvinism of the Quiet Revolution. The propagandist tactics of the Quebec nationalists frustrated Morton as much as they had Creighton. Not only had the nationalists misapprehended their history, thereby misrepresenting the nature of Canada, they also made English-speaking Canadians scapegoats for the internal socio-political problems. Anglophones, the line of reasoning went, failed to honour their commitments and create a nation that safeguarded minority rights and that entrenched the principles of biculturalism and bilingualism. They also interfered with the social development of Quebec. They kept Quebeckers ignorant, denied French Canadians the opportunity to control their economic and cultural affairs, and, ultimately, made the francophones subservient to English Canada. Morton had little sympathy for this mythologized account of the development of modern Quebec. He denounced Quebec nationalists for blaming the ills of French-Canadian society on English-speaking Canadians. In a letter to Michel Brunet, a historian and leading Quebec nationalist, Morton urged French Canadians to take responsibility for their current plight. 'The circumstances of Quebec before 1960,' he wrote to Brunet in late 1964, 'were almost wholly the consequence of French Canadians wishing it so and keeping it so. French Canadians simply failed to use the weapons that were theirs at any time since Confederation.' He stated firmly, 'It is nonsense to suggest that a democratic majority with an unrestricted franchise is not master in its own house except by its own fault.' W.L. Morton to Michel Brunet (28 December 1964), Morton Papers, MUL, Box 2; Brunet, Michel (1956–73), 2. On the Québécois rejection of English Canada, Morton wrote: 'This rejection, as it seems, of what we value and to which we are committed, is what causes our reserve towards the Quebec revolution today. We have been ignorant of the realities of French Quebec, of course, and are at fault in being ignorant. But that at least is equalled by the French ignorance both of English Canada and of our common history. What does irritate us and cause us to lose patience now – a process that has gone very far, I am afraid – is the implication, sometimes made explicit, that English Canada [wilfully] perpetuated the pre-1960s régime in Quebec' (ibid.).

The implications of Morton's statements are clear. To deny the complicity of Quebeckers in the socio-political and economic development of their province was, at best, inaccurate. At worse, the indictment of English-speaking Canadians for the problems of modern Quebec fostered ill-will among Canadians. The Quiet Revolution was damaging and divisive. Instead of forging greater understanding, the Quiet revolutionaries succeeded in isolating Canadians. The Quiet Revolution was, for Morton, a marked tragedy for English-French relations.

123 See Bothwell, Drummond, and English, *Canada since 1945*, chapter 23.
124 As Creighton wrote in 1970: 'Susceptible to injury, open to attack; and, in my judgment, Canada was vulnerable in the 1960s in large measure because it was divided.' Creighton, 'Canada: A Divided and Vulnerable Nation,' 1. He felt that there were hopeful signs for a strengthening of unity (Quebec's recent election 1970), 'but for ten long years [Quebec] monopolized the attention and aroused the concern of a great many Canadians. It diverted them from the task of national defence and weakened their defensive powers at the very moment when external pressure from the United States was increasingly threatening the independence and integrity of Canada. When the decade of the 1960s opened, American influence on almost every phase of Canadian life, already great, was rapidly growing. In 1957, Canada had accepted a subordinate position in a

continental defence system. The progressive takeover of Canadian resources and industry by American capital has placed Canada very firmly in a continental economy dominated by the United States. The persistent, uninterrupted hammering of the American mass media – radio, television, motion pictures and periodicals – was gradually but surely transforming the nation into a cultural colony of the Republic' (1–2).

125 Morton, *The Canadian Identity*, 125

126 Morton, 'Towards a New Conception of Confederation?' 7

127 Ibid.

128 Morton, *The Canadian Identity*, 125–30, 130

129 Ibid., 150. Morton believed that increased American investment into, and control of, the Canadian economy awakened nationalist sentiment. Morton claimed that 'exercises in continentalism helped provoke the resurgence of national feeling [of Watkins, the Waffle movement, and others] and an analysis of continentalism for what it was, a betrayal of Canadian destiny and identity' (ibid., 133–4). See chapter 7.

130 Morton, 'Towards a New Conception of Confederation?' 2

131 Morton, *The Canadian Identity*, 150

132 Morton, 'Towards a New Conception of Confederation?' 2. Morton went on to explain the world that had been lost. 'It was, I suppose, a very narrow world. Narrow, that is, because it was, although lived in rural Manitoba, a very British world. Everything in daily talk, much in daily use, the whole reinforced and exaggerated by the illusion called prestige, was British – the point of reference in politics and business, the seat of fashion, the school of manners, the centre of scandal. The table dishes were British made, both the cheap and the dear, the jackknives, the tea caddies, the aperients, the best boots, the heaviest coats, the finest hats. The yearly calendars tended to picture a heroic lion or an intimidating battleship. And over the little white schoolhouse ... the Union Jack staunchly flew – a provincial statute had a few years before said it must, as it's done until this year' (3–4).

133 Northrop Frye, 'The Quality of Life in the 1970s,' Address to the University of Toronto Alumni, [?] 1971, draft copy, Northrop Frye Papers Victoria University Library (VUL), 88 Box 4, File e, 8

134 Ibid., 8, 10, 11–12. It also was 'the age of intense preoccupation with the effect of communication on society, and with the aspect of life that we call news' (8–9). Frye added: 'The emphasis on "confrontation" and similar words, the obsession with the discontinuous and uninstructed, the tendency to argue automatically that whatever one disagreed with was "out

of date," show how the anarchism and the preoccupation with media in the late sixties were aspects of the same thing' (10).

135 Ibid., 11–12

136 Quoted in Michael Hayden, ed., *So Much to Do, So Little Time: The Writings of Hilda Neatby* (Vancouver, 1983), 287

137 Donald Creighton, 'The Future in Canada,' in Creighton, *The Passionate Observer: Selected Writings* (Toronto, 1980), 21

138 Claude Bissell, *Halfway up Parnassus. A Personal Account of the University of Toronto, 1932–1971* (Toronto, 1974), 189–90, 91

7: Epilogue

1 William Christian and Colin Campbell, *Political Parties and Ideologies in Canada: Liberals, Conservatives, Socialists, Nationalists*, 2nd ed. (Toronto, 1983), 119

2 Gad Horowitz, *Canadian Labour in Politics* (Toronto, 1968), 19

3 Quoted in ibid., 119–20, 120. There was also recognition of Canada's growing multiculturalism. The platform document added that the founding peoples were 'joined and continue to be joined by people from many lands who have a right to play a full part in Canadian life' (120).

4 Ramsay Cook, *The Maple Leaf Forever: Essays on Nationalism and Politics in Canada* (Toronto, 1971), 20–2

5 Quoted in Ramsay Cook, *Canada, Quebec, and the Uses of Nationalism* (Toronto, 1986), 73.

6 Michael D. Behiels, *Prelude to Quebec's Quiet Revolution: Liberalism versus Neo-nationalism, 1945–1960* (Montreal, 1985), chapter 4

7 See William Christian, *George Grant: A Biography* (Toronto, 1993), 248–9, and George Grant to 'Mother' [Mrs W.L. Grant] (n.d.), George P. Grant Papers, National Archives of Canada (NAC), v. 39; Mrs W.L. Grant Correspondence; file: Dalhousie University, MG 30 D59.

8 Michael Hayden, ed., *So Much to Do, So Little Time: The Writings of Hilda Neatby* (Vancouver, 1983), 116–17. Neatby went on to say that '[I]t does us Canadians small credit as a "middle nation" defending the values of the western world if we do not consider it pure gain to be invited to take possession of the keys of a culture whose greatness will not be forgotten while western civilization remains. It is a pity that a country endowed with two such cultures should find bi-lingualism and biculturalism a problem rather than an opportunity' (117). Neatby's comments were, of course, written in response to the 'Bi & Bi' issue of the mid-1960s. Clearly, she was amenable to bilingualism and biculturalism.

9 Note that the tacit alliance between French and English Canada to which Creighton and others referred was more a idealized perception of French Canada than a historical reality. With the possible exception of Hilda Neatby, who studied French-Canadian history, few of the anti-modernists had much to do with French Canada.

10 See Donald Creighton, 'Introduction,' *Towards the Discovery of Canada* (Toronto, 1972), 14–15. On this point, there was much disagreement among the anti-modernists. Specifically, Creighton disagreed with the position of Morton that 'language is the one indispensable element in that identity and that biculturalism is therefore "the very essence of Canadian national aspirations"' (14). By contrast, Creighton remained firm. He stuck to his earlier position on bilingualism and biculturalism (see chapter 6). He showed that 'At a moment when national unity was more necessary than ever before to resist the weight of American continentalism, Canadians had permitted themselves to become involved in a divisive cultural problem; and the time and effort which might have gone into defence against the invader was likely to be sacrificed in a prolonged and vain effort to remake Canada and transform its constitution in the interest of cultural dualism ... These were the chief themes of the epilogue of *Canada's First Century* and of several talks given in 1970–1' (15).

11 Robert Chodos, Rae Murphy, and Eric Hamovitch *The Unmaking of Canada: The Hidden Theme in Canadian History since 1945* (Toronto, 1991), 53

12 See, for instance, M.H. Watkins, 'A Staple Theory of Economic Growth,' *Canadian Journal of Economics and Political Science*, 29 (May 1963), 80–100; Abraham Rotstein, 'Innis: The Alchemy of Fur and Wheat,' *Journal of Canadian Studies*, 12 (Winter 1977), 5; and, for a more recent example, Daniel Drache, 'Introduction,' *Staples, Markets, and Cultural Change: Selected Essays, Harold A. Innis* (Montreal, 1995).

13 See, for example, Melville Watkins, 'Technology and Nationalism,' in Peter Russell, ed., *Nationalism in Canada* (Toronto, 1966), and James Laxer, 'The Student Movement and Canadian Independence,' *Canadian Dimension. Kit No. 3: Canadian Nationalism* [Winnipeg, 1970?].

14 See, for instance, James Laxer, 'The Search for Canadian Nationalism,' in *Canadian Dimension. Kit No. 3: Canadian Nationalism*; reprinted from *Canadian Dimension*, 5. Laxer's historical analysis closely parallels those of Creighton, Morton, and Grant.

15 See, as examples, Robin Mathews, 'The Americanization of Canadian Universities,' and Melville H. Watkins, 'Education in the Branch Plant Economy,' both in *Canadian Dimension. Kit No. 3: Canadian Nationalism*.

16 Horowitz, *Canadian Labour in Politics*, 7, 9

17 Ibid., 5. Horowitz also suggested that as a purely liberal 'fragment,' the United States eliminated any remnants of toryism. This lack of tory ideas ultimately implied the incomplete development of American socialism.

18 Ibid., 10, 23

19 Gad Horowitz, 'On the Fear of Nationalism. Nationalism and Socialism: A Sermon to the Moderates,' in ibid., 2

20 George Grant, 'Canadian Fate and Imperialism,' in Horowitz, *Canadian Labour in Politics*, 26

21 For a discussion of the leftist nature of the new nationalism, see Horowitz, *Canadian Labour in Politics*.

22 Despite Horowitz's statements about the way in which Canadian toryism developed as a unique aspect of Canadian political culture, he was primarily interested in facilitating the development of Canadian socialism. He cared little for the advancement of the British connection or other traditional tory values. See also ibid.

23 Horowitz, 'On the Fear of Nationalism,' 2, 3

24 Owram, *Born at the Right Time: A History of the Baby Boom Generation* (Toronto, 1996), 300

25 There was also a bevy of articles on this topic, such as Daniel Drache, 'The Canadian Bourgeoisie and Its National Consciousness,' in Ian Lumsden, ed., *Close the 49th Parallel, Etc.* (Toronto, 1971), and edited collections, such as Lumsden's work, Gary Teeple, ed., *Capitalism and the National Question in Canada* (Toronto, 1972), and Abraham Rotstein and Gary Lax, *Getting It Back: A Program for Canadian Independence* (Toronto, 1974).

26 See Berger, *The Writing of Canadian History: Aspects of English-Canadian Historical Writing Since 1900*, 2nd ed. (Toronto, 1986), 264; Stanley Ryerson, *Unequal Union* (New York, 1968).

27 Quoted in Owram, 286

28 Ibid., 281

29 See ibid., chapter 11; also 289, 303.

30 See Grant, 'Canadian Fate and Imperialism.'

31 Cook, *Maple Leaf Forever*, 7; 20–2

32 J.M.S. Careless, '"Limited Identities," in Canada,' *Canadian Historical Review*, 50 (March 1969), 1–10. The term 'limited identities' actually originated in the mind of Ramsay Cook, to whom Careless gives credit for the idea. See J.M.S. Careless, *Careless at Work: Selected Canadian Historical Studies* (Toronto, 1990). See also G.R. Cook, 'Canadian Centennial Cerebrations,' *International Journal*, 22 (Autumn 1967), 663.

Index

War) role of the academic 95–6, 110

McCourt, Edward: on Canadian literary development 170–1
McCready, H.W.: and critique of modern values 224
McCullough, Nora: on importance of educators 227–8
Macdonald, Sir John A. 21, 248, 272, 284; and nation-building 248–9, 253, 258; toryism of 248–51, 258; view of continentalism and British connection 201–2
MacIver, R.M.: *Labour in a Changing World* 79–80
Mackenzie, A. Stanley 24
MacKenzie, N.A.M.: and critique of modern democracy 322–3 n.77; on high culture 187; on importance of cultured individual 234; on importance of humanistic values 127
McKillop, A.B. 21, 24, 72, 97
MacLennan, Hugh 163
McLuhan, Marshall 4, 16, 18, 65–6, 107; on consumerism 56–7, 179–80, 322 n.71; on education 56; effect of technology on culture 56–9; influence of Robert Maynard Hutchins on 55–6; *The Mechanical Bride* 57–9, 179; support of social role of modern university 153; on value of liberal arts 107–8
McMaster University: secularization of 115
McNaught, Kenneth 242
Mainland Branch of Canadian Authors Association: on cultural Americanization 185–6
Marshall, John 107

Mass culture 11, 136, 176–86, 192–4
Massey Commission. *See* Royal Commission on National Development in the Arts, Letters and Sciences
Massey, Vincent 4, 15, 16, 18, 173; on anti-Americanism 323 n.84; on biculturalism 196–7; on British connection 196, 237–8, 239–40, 288 n.20, 325–6 n.118, 326 n.120, 327 n.139; on Canadian identity 196, 237–8, 325 n.117; and critique of democratic values 183; and critique of mass culture 180, 218; and critique of materialism 60, 134; and critique of technical education 53, 192; on cultural Americanization 186; on democratic education 136–7; on government funding of the arts 325 n.115; on importance of cultured individual 190–1; on importance of history to analysis of cultural problems 124–5; on importance of humanistic values 12, 189; on material development 59–60, 218; on social role of academics 121; view of ideal role of higher education 121
Material development, 132–4, 202, 206, 207, 218
Materialism 156, 218–19
Mavor, James 69; on uses of social sciences 29
Medicine, study of 75–6
Meighen, Arthur 272, 284
Meiklejohn, Alexander: view of role of modern university 86–7
Modernization: definition of 3–4
Morton, W.L. 4, 5, 16, 18, 251, 278; on Americanization 214; on the British

Royal Commission on University of
Toronto 24
Ryerson Institute of Technology:
founding of 116

St Laurent, Louis 12, 242, 251, 255; on
Cold War 135; on cultural progress
206–7
Sandwell, B.K. 85; on Canadian identity 197; on cultural Americanization 184, 185
Saunders, Richard M.: on social role
of academics 123
Scott, Frank 163
Second World War: effect on democracy 219, 221, 222–3; effect on development of modern university
94–104, 109–10, 112
Sheffield, Edward 141
Shortt, Adam 33; on Canadian Political Science Association 31; on
industrial-capitalist system 28–9;
on involvement in government of
social scientists 32
Skelton, O.D. 69, 204, 244; view on
role of social scientists 29–30
Social Gospel Movement 15
Social sciences: and concept of efficiency 29–30; and concept of expertise 30–1; effect of Depression on
37; Mavor on 29; and problems of
industrial society 28; and relation
to government of 32–3, 33–4; role of
during Second World War 94–6,
109–10; Shortt on 28–9; Skelton on
29–30
Smith, Sydney: view of modern university 142–3
Spengler, Oswald 130, 162
Sputnik 145, 208

Stanley, G.F.G. 335–6 n.75
Stanfield, Robert 272–3: view of biculturalism 273–4
Steacie, E.W.R.: on compatibility of
arts and sciences 143–4, 314 n.111;
on strengthening ties between universities and National Research
Council 117, 308 n.21
Surveyor, Arthur 319 n.45

Taylor, R. Bruce 78
Taylor, W.R.: on reassertion of the arts
and humanities after Second World
War 113
Thomas, Lewis G.: and critique of
mass culture 181
Thomson, James 163; and critique of
technical education 97–8; and critique of technology 157–8; on contributions of university during Second
World War 96; on importance of
humanistic values 98–9, 127; on
post-war crisis of culture 130; view
of ideal role of university 121–2
Tory, Henry Marshall 114
Toryism 240–1; 'Aristodemocracy'
231–3, 234–5; and conservative
view of culture 217; decline of 255–
71, 272–85; explanation of 5–9, 287
n.3; Gad Horowitz on 278–9; of
John Diefenbaker 252–3, 254–5; of
New Left 277–80; of Sir John A.
Macdonald 248–51. *See also* Conservative-nationalist school of Canadian history
Toynbee, Arnold 130, 162
Tremblay Commission 275
Trudeau, Pierre Elliott 274

Underhill, Frank 27; on academic's